This book examines trends in inequality in the People's Republic of China. It contains new findings on inequality nationwide, as well as within the rural and urban sectors, with an emphasis on public policy considerations. Several chapters focus on inequality of income; others analyze poverty, inequality in wealth, and the distribution of wages. Attention is given to groups such as migrants, women, and the elderly, as well as the relationship between income and health care funding and the impact of the rural tax reform. A distinguishing feature of this book is its database. All contributors to this volume make use of a large, nationwide survey of Chinese households, the product of long-term cooperation between Chinese and international researchers that is unique in its scope and duration. Using these data, the contributors examine changes in inequality over nearly 15 years of the transitional era, from 1988 to 2002.

Björn A. Gustafsson is professor in the Department of Social Work at Göteborg University. His research covers empirical studies on poverty, social assistance, the distribution of economic well-being, and the welfare state, as well as the economics of immigration. Since the mid-1990s, one of his research interests has been poverty and the distribution of income in China. He has published articles in many academic journals. Professor Gustafsson coedited *Changing Patterns in the Distribution of Economic Welfare: An International Perspective* with Peter Gottschalk and Edward Palmer (Cambridge University Press, 1997) and *Poverty and Low Income in the Nordic Countries* with Peder J. Pedersen (2000).

Li Shi is professor of economics in the School of Economics and Business at Beijing Normal University. He is one of China's leading scholars on inequality and poverty. His past positions include director of the Center of Economic Transition and Development Studies at the Chinese Academy of Social Sciences. Professor Li's edited volumes include *China's Retreat from Equality* with Renwei Zhao and Carl Riskin (2001) and *Unemployment, Inequality and Poverty in Urban China* with Hiroshi Sato (2006). He has also served as a consultant to international donor organizations and has been a key contributor to China's *Human Development Report*.

Terry Sicular is professor in the Department of Economics at the University of Western Ontario. She has held posts at Stanford and Harvard universities and is one of North America's leading China economists. Her research has covered topics such as China's market reforms, rural labor and employment, capital flight, and inequality. She has published widely in scholarly journals and has served as a consultant to international donor organizations. Recent and forthcoming publications include "The Urban-Rural Income Gap and Inequality in China," *The Review of Income and Wealth* with Yue Ximing, Björn Gustafsson, and Li Shi (2007), and "Why Do Revolutions Succeed? The Role of Rational Choice in the Chinese Communist Revolution," *Homo Oeconomicus* (2004).

Inequality and Public Policy in China

Edited by

BJÖRN A. GUSTAFSSON
Göteborg University, Sweden

LI SHI
Beijing Normal University, China

TERRY SICULAR
University of Western Ontario, Canada

CAMBRIDGE
UNIVERSITY PRESS

CAMBRIDGE UNIVERSITY PRESS
Cambridge, New York, Melbourne, Madrid, Cape Town, Singapore,
São Paulo, Delhi, Dubai, Tokyo, Mexico City

Cambridge University Press
The Edinburgh Building, Cambridge CB2 8RU, UK

Published in the United States of America by Cambridge University Press, New York

www.cambridge.org
Information on this title: www.cambridge.org/9780521159050

First published 2008
Reprinted 2009
First paperback edition 2010

A catalogue record for this publication is available from the British Library

Library of Congress Cataloging in Publication Data

Inequality and public policy in China / Björn A. Gustafsson, Li Shi, Terry Sicular [editors].
p. cm.
Includes bibliographical references and index.
ISBN 978-0-521-87045-0 (hardback)
1. Income distribution – China.   2. China – Economic policy – 2000–   3. China – Social
policy – 21st century. 4. Equality – China.   I. Gustafsson, Björn.   II. Li, Shi.
III. Sicular, Terry, 1955– IV. Title.
HC430.I5I54 2007
330.951–dc22   2006101029

ISBN 978-0-521-87045-0 Hardback
ISBN 978-0-521-15905-0 Paperback

Contents

v

Tables and Figures

TABLES

FIGURES

Contributors

(*Note:* Chinese names of contributors are given in the Chinese order, i.e., the surname precedes the given name.)

Deng Quheng is assistant professor in the Institute of Economics of the Chinese Academy of Social Sciences, Beijing, China.

Ding Sai is assistant professor in the Institute of Ethnology and Anthropology of the Chinese Academy of Social Sciences, Beijing, China.

Björn Gustafsson is professor in the Department of Social Work at Göteborg University, Göteborg, Sweden, and research Fellow at the Institute of Labor (IZA), Bonn, Germany.

Azizur Rahman Khan is professor emeritus of economics at the University of California, Riverside, California, United States.

John Knight is professor of economics at the University of Oxford, Oxford, United Kingdom.

Li Shi is professor of economics in the School of Economics and Business, Beijing Normal University; professor in the Graduate School of the Chinese Academy of Social Sciences, Beijing, China; and research Fellow at the Institute of Labor (IZA), Bonn, Germany.

Luo Chuliang is associate professor in the Institute of Economics of the Chinese Academy of Social Sciences, Beijing, China.

Meng Xin is professor in the Division of Economics in the Research School of Pacific and Asian Studies, Australian National University, Canberra, Australia.

Edward Palmer is professor of social insurance economics in the Department of Economics, Uppsala University, Uppsala, Sweden, and head of the Department of Technical Modelling at the Swedish Social Insurance Agency.

Carl Riskin is Distinguished Professor of Economics at Queens College, the City University of New York, and senior research scholar at the Weatherhead East Asian Institute, Columbia University, New York, United States.

Hiroshi Sato is professor in the Graduate School of Economics at Hitotsubashi University, Tokyo, Japan.

Terry Sicular is professor of economics in the Department of Economics at the University of Western Ontario, London, Ontario, Canada, and senior Fellow at the Centre for International Governance Innovation (CIGI), Waterloo, Ontario, Canada.

Lina Song is professor of economic sociology and social policy, School of Sociology and Social Policy, University of Nottingham, Nottingham, United Kingdom.

Wei Zhong is professor in the Institute of Economics of the Chinese Academy of Social Sciences, Beijing, China.

Yue Ximing is professor in the School of Finance, Renmin University of China, Beijing, China.

Zhao Renwei is professor in and former director of the Institute of Economics, Chinese Academy of Social Sciences, Beijing, China.

Acknowledgments

This volume emerges from a long-term research effort supported by many individuals and organizations. In 1988 Keith Griffin and Zhao Renwei conceived the idea for a program of research on inequality in China with strong empirical foundations. They brought together a group of Chinese and international researchers who, with support from the Chinese Academy of Social Sciences and the Ford Foundation, organized the first in a series of nationwide household surveys that have since served as a major basis of knowledge about inequality and poverty in China. The research program has continued to the present, with a mix of new and old participants. In the mid-1990s Zhao Renwei and Carl Riskin took the lead in organizing a second survey project; the third round of the survey project, organized by the editors of this volume and serving as the basis of the research reported herein, took place in 2003. As we write, planning proceeds for a fourth round.

Over the years this research program has provided valuable training and research opportunities for successive generations of scholars, and it has generated timely analysis of trends in incomes and inequality in China through the transition époque. While our acknowledgments here focus on contributors to the current volume and the 2002 household survey project, we express our deep gratitude to those who initiated and have sustained this long-term body of work.

This volume and the 2002 survey project would not have been possible without substantial financial support from the Ford Foundation, the Swedish International Development Agency (SIDA), the Chinese Academy of Social Sciences, the National Foundation of Sciences of China, and the Japan Society for the Promotion of Science. Börje Ljunggren, at that time the Swedish Ambassador to China, and the Swedish Embassy to China helped secure last-minute funds for the survey of urban migrants. Additional funding was provided by the University of Western Ontario, the Centre for

International Governance Innovation (CIGI), and the Graduate School of Economics of Hitotsubashi University. We thank these organizations and individuals for their generous support.

The survey work was carried out by the National Bureau of Statistics (NBS) Urban and Rural Household Survey Teams. Individuals on the NBS survey teams not only conducted the survey, but they also provided invaluable advice and input regarding survey design. Huang Langhui, Xian Zude, Wang Youjuan, and Yang Junxiong at the NBS were especially helpful.

Along the way we received advice, suggestions, and ideas from many individuals, including Cai Fang, Sarah Cook, Martin Fournier, Lai Desheng, Scott Parris, Wan Guanghua, Wang Xiaolu, Andrew Watson, Yao Yang, Zhang Ping, Zhao Yaohui, and Zhu Ling. Several project participants went beyond the call of duty – Aziz Khan, John Knight, Carl Riskin, Hiroshi Sato, Lina Song, Wei Zhong, Yue Ximing, and Zhao Renwei. Deng Quheng, Ding Sai, Luo Chuliang, and Zhang Fan spent an enormous amount of time cleaning data. We thank these individuals, as well as the anonymous referees, for their invaluable contributions.

Two chapters in this volume have been published previously in somewhat different form, and we are grateful for permission to include them here. Chapter 3, "Growth and Distribution of Household Income in China between 1995 and 2002," by Azizur Rahman Khan and Carl Riskin, is a revised and shortened version of "China's Household Income and Its Distribution, 1995 and 2002," *China Quarterly*, no. 182, pp. 356–384. Copyright © 2005 by the School of Oriental and African Studies, published by Cambridge University Press, reproduced with permission. Chapter 6, "Growth, Inequality and Poverty: A Comparative Study of China's Experience in the Periods before and after the Asian Crisis," by Azizur Rahman Khan, is reprinted, with changes, from *Growth, Inequality and Poverty in China: A Comparative Study of the Experience in the Periods before and after the Asian Crisis*, International Labour Office (ILO), Discussion Paper 15, by permission of the ILO, Copyright © 2004 by the ILO.

We owe special thanks to Sharon Phillips who, with assistance from Paula Nopper, put the manuscript in publishable form and kept track of the many chapters as they were reviewed, revised, edited, and checked.

Finally, we thank the many thousands of respondents and their family members in rural and urban China for their participation in and cooperation with the survey project. They have made possible, and they provide the inspiration for, this volume.

Björn Gustafsson
Li Shi
Terry Sicular

ONE

Inequality and Public Policy in China

Issues and Trends

Björn Gustafsson, Li Shi, and Terry Sicular

I. Introduction

In recent decades China's economy has grown more rapidly and in a more sustained fashion than that of any other country worldwide. This growth has had many positive benefits, one of which is a substantial improvement in average standards of living. Most people in China have higher incomes, consume more and better goods, and live in better housing than ever before. Between 1988 and 2002, the time period covered in this volume, household income per capita on average nearly tripled in real terms (see Chapter 2). Also, life expectancy has increased, and education levels continue to rise.

With growth, however, has come a significant widening of income differences among households and individuals. Income inequality has risen from a relatively low level in the early 1980s to a level that is now considered high by international standards. Although increased inequality often goes hand in hand with economic growth and development, in China the speed with which the increase has occurred, and the level to which inequality has risen, is striking.

Inequality is not necessarily a problem. Most would agree that past policies in China had excessively compressed personal income differentials, so some increase was expected. Inequality reflecting differences in effort, experience, skills, investments, and risk can be justifiable from economic and social standpoints. Concerns arise, however, when incomes differ excessively in ways that reduce efficiency or violate accepted views of fairness and justice. In such situations inequality can erode social cohesion, generate social and political instability, and hinder economic growth. Concerns also arise if segments of the population are left behind with insufficient resources to meet basic needs or entitlements.

For much of the reform period China's economic policy has placed highest priority on growth and tolerated widening inequality. This approach was encapsulated in Deng Xiaoping's well-known statement that some people should be allowed to "get rich first." China's leaders have nevertheless been mindful of equity, and over time the government has adopted measures such as the rural poverty alleviation program, the Great Western Development Strategy, and a range of social insurance and welfare programs, mainly in urban areas, aimed at addressing particular distributional issues. These measures reflect concerns about the impact of income gaps on stability, as well as efforts by the Communist leadership to maintain political legitimacy.

Recently debate has reemerged in Chinese political circles about rising inequality, the direction of reform, and the priority placed on growth. In contrast to the beginning of the reform process when policy makers did not talk openly about inequality as a problem, political discourse and policy announcements have increasingly emphasized distribution and fairness. At the 16th Party Congress in 2002 the Chinese Communist Party (CCP) introduced the notion of a "*xiaokang* society." According to this concept, high growth should be kept as a goal, but it is not enough. Equity and social harmony, as well as sustainable development, are also important. More recently, the CCP has pledged to take steps to ensure that the benefits of growth are shared more fairly, with particular attention to the rural-urban income gap. This renewed commitment to equity is reflected in the agenda for China's 11th Five-Year Plan (2006–2010) and in the announcement in 2006 of measures to address lagging living standards in rural areas.

Interest in China's income distribution extends beyond its borders. China is the most populous country in the world, and so changes in the level and distribution of its income hold implications for global inequality and poverty. When trying to understand changes in inequality and poverty on a global scale, then, knowledge of trends in China is essential.[1]

China is also of general interest because its experience may provide evidence and insights relevant for understanding the relationship between inequality and development. The widely cited Kuznets curve suggests that rising inequality is a common phenomenon in early stages of development. This relationship has been critically examined in the literature and is subject to ongoing debate.[2] The experiences of formerly planned economies in

---

[1] See, e.g., Milanovic (2002), Bourguignon and Morrisson (2002), Deaton (2005), and Dollar (2005).

[2] See, e.g., Anand and Kanbur (1993).

Eastern Europe and Central Asia suggest that transition is also a major force at play. Some would argue that trade liberalization is also a contributing factor.[3]

The validity of concerns over inequality in China and the sorts of policies appropriate to addressing those concerns depend on the level and characteristics of that inequality. Knowledge about the level and characteristics of inequality requires systematic empirical analysis. Although the supply of knowledge about China's inequality has improved greatly over time, significant gaps remain. A large and growing literature exists on inequality among provinces and regions; less research has been done on inequality at the household and individual levels. In the literature on inequality among households and individuals, most studies examine inequality within urban areas or within rural areas. Studies on inequality nationwide are relatively scarce. Research on key facets of inequality, such as the distribution of wealth or the level of poverty, is spotty. Gaps also exist in knowledge about particular groups, such as migrants, women, minorities, and the elderly. Most studies rely on data more than a decade old. In a rapidly changing environment like China's, effective policy requires more up-to-date information. Data remain an underlying constraint, limiting the scope and timeliness of available studies.

The aim of this book is to contribute to knowledge on inequality in the People's Republic of China. It contains new findings on inequality nationwide, as well as in the rural and urban sectors, with an emphasis on public policy considerations. Although most chapters focus on inequality of income, the book also provides studies that analyze poverty, inequality of assets and wealth, and the distribution of wages. Some chapters examine particular subgroups such as migrants and the elderly; others investigate selected topics such as the relationship between income inequality and health funding or rural tax reform. In all cases the unit of analysis is the household or individual. Differences among provinces and regions receive attention here as a reflection of underlying inequality among households and individuals.

A distinguishing feature of this book is its database. All the contributors to this volume have made use of a large, nationwide survey of Chinese households. This survey is the product of long-term cooperation between Chinese and international researchers that is unique in its scope and duration. The survey project has been organized under the auspices of the Chinese

---

[3] See, e.g., Milanovic (2005).

Academy of Social Sciences and is known as the Chinese Household Income Project (CHIP). The CHIP survey was repeated at different points in time using similar methods and questionnaires. Past rounds of the survey were the basis for several important books and numerous scholarly articles and papers. In this volume we employ data from the most recent round, with comparisons over time using data from past rounds of the survey. The studies can thus examine changes that span nearly one and one-half decades of the transition epoch, from 1988 to 2002.

Unlike many datasets for China, the CHIP data cover large parts of the country. The sample's geographic span makes possible the analysis of inequality nationwide, as well as of spatial aspects of inequality. Several other features are noteworthy. The survey questionnaires were specifically designed for the purpose of analyzing Chinese household income. Consequently the database contains fuller information than is usually available on income and related variables. Also, the 2002 survey included a subsample of rural migrants living in urban areas. Most datasets exclude this increasingly important group. These and other features of the survey datasets are discussed in more detail below.

We begin in Section II with a discussion of the economic and policy environment that has shaped recent inequality trends in China. In Section III we describe the dataset that serves as the unifying basis for the studies in this book and explore some relevant empirical and measurement questions. Section IV outlines the main findings of the book, with attention to aspects that are new and different.

A major finding is that between 1995 and 2002 the level of income inequality in China remained relatively stable. This stability reflects the emergence of certain equalizing processes that have offset forces generating more inequality. Equalizing processes include the spread of off-farm wage employment in rural areas, catching up and convergence in household per capita income among provinces in eastern China, and the beneficial effects of widely shared macroeconomic growth. Yet, disequalizing forces continue. The large urban-rural income gap increased and became an even more dominant source of overall inequality. Education has emerged as an important factor underlying inequality.

Poverty, reversing past trends, declined between 1995 and 2002. This encouraging trend in poverty was accompanied by rising inequality in the distribution of wealth. The level of wealth inequality in 2002, however, was not overly high by international standards. Including rural-to-urban migrants in the calculations changes measured levels of inequality and poverty in China, but the impact is relatively modest.

These and other findings are discussed at more length below and in the individual chapters. Although this volume examines a wide range of facets of China's inequality, its coverage is far from exhaustive. We therefore conclude this introductory chapter by identifying key gaps in knowledge and suggesting directions for future research.

II. The Changing Context: Ongoing Policy Reform, Growth, and Inequality

Since the late 1970s China has embarked on a path of economic reform and transition. This period has been marked by the implementation of a wide range of significant reform measures, most aimed at promoting growth and development, and with consequences for the distribution of personal incomes. Here we focus on reforms since the late 1980s, the period covered by the studies in this volume.

A major theme of the reforms has been to expand the role of markets. In the early reform period markets were encouraged to emerge alongside planning in what was known as the "dual-track" system. At that time the reform policies focused on markets for goods. Planning continued for factors of production – land, labor, and capital – and markets for these factors remained undeveloped. The 1990s saw the continued dismantling of the system of administrative planning and pricing and the improved functioning of markets for goods and services. By the mid-1990s planned allocation had been eliminated for almost all consumer goods. In addition, at this time the government began to take steps to develop markets for factors of production.

With respect to labor markets, for example, the urban labor reforms have given enterprises more freedom to lay off and hire workers (see Chapter 9). This, together with the loosening of restrictions on rural-to-urban migration, has allowed labor markets to function more fully. Barriers to rural-urban migration were put in place during the planning period and embodied in the household registration or *hukou* system. The *hukou* system categorizes people as urban or rural residents and was an integral part of China's development strategy at that time, under which priority was given to urban industrialization. Urban workers were tied to their work units typically for their entire work life. In return, they received compensation consisting of wages, subsidies, reimbursements of medical and social services, an old age pension, and in-kind benefits, of which the most important was highly subsidized housing.

An urban *hukou*, received by those born to a mother having an urban *hukou*, has ever since served as an entry ticket to a better life, a life of first-class citizens. For many years it was impossible for people without an urban *hukou* to find a job or housing in urban China. During the reform period, formal and informal restrictions making it difficult for people without an urban *hukou* to earn income and find housing in urban areas have lessened. As a consequence, during the 1990s and continuing since 2000, a very large influx of migrants into urban areas has occurred.

During the 1990s factor market development was also furthered by ownership reforms. Small and medium-sized state-owned enterprises were privatized, converted into shareholding operations, or leased; for larger state-owned enterprises the government initiated a program of governance reform and corporatization. Such measures have made enterprises in both rural and urban areas more market-oriented, with implications for their employment and other behavior. The expansion of shareholding and private enterprise has provided an impetus for the expansion of financial and capital markets. The urban housing reforms are another aspect of factor market reforms in the 1990s. In a remarkably short time they have created from scratch markets for private real estate in urban areas.

In a market environment, earnings depend on households' endowments of factors such as labor, entrepreneurial ability, education or skills, experience, and physical or financial assets, as well as on the prices or returns of these endowments and stochastic factors. If markets function well, then prices for the same factor should be more or less equal among households, with differences in earnings reflecting differences in the households' endowments of productive factors. Thus the expansion of markets during the 1990s should have led to greater differentiation of incomes on the basis of household endowments and characteristics, and less differentiation on the basis of administrative criteria such as place of residence, type of work unit, and simple seniority. Also, with the expansion of markets for financial instruments and real estate, the importance of income from assets should increase, although not necessarily equally among households.

The process of factor price equalization, however, is as yet unfinished. Despite continued market reform in the 1990s and early 2000s, and while markets for most goods and many services are now well established, factor markets remain fragmented and incomplete. Thus, for example, worker mobility among urban residents in China is higher than before, but still much lower than in market economies. Unemployment and other forms of nonemployment have emerged, reflecting frictions and lack of market clearing in urban labor markets. Estimates of urban job separations and unemployment rates differ, but most observers agree that they have increased substantially since the late 1990s.[4] The expansion of unemployment and job separations has affected the urban income distribution, and poverty is now no longer solely a rural phenomenon.

Barriers to migration from rural to urban areas, while reduced, remain in place. Establishing a permanent foothold in the cities is still difficult, and much migration remains temporary. Obtaining an urban *hukou* and its associated benefits remains out of reach for most migrants. Migrants may earn more than those who remain in the countryside, but their economic and social status is still markedly lower than that of registered urban residents.

Markets for land and capital are also incomplete. Urban real estate markets have developed rapidly, but the same is not the case for farmland, which continues to be collectively owned and cannot be bought or sold through markets. Delay in fundamental reforms of the banking system and continued government interventions hinder fuller development of financial markets. Thus, even though markets may play an increasing role in determining household earnings and incomes, the returns to household endowments of land, labor, and capital undoubtedly still reflect the influences of market segmentation and administrative interventions.

A second major theme of the reforms has been the decentralization of economic decision making. Market reforms, of course, involve decentralization, as in a market system decisions regarding work, consumption, and investment are made in a decentralized fashion by households and firms. Decentralization has also occurred in the fiscal arena. Fiscal decentralization was initiated in the 1980s, but it continued thereafter, albeit with some recentralization in the mid-1990s. Following the tax reform of 1994, China has followed a system of tax assignment, under which revenues for certain taxes are retained locally, for others centrally, and for yet others shared according to set proportions between the center and local governments. Local governments fund much of their expenditures from retained or shared taxes, along with some local extrabudgetary funds.

---

[4] China's National Bureau of Statistics (NBS) publishes information on the number of registered unemployed persons, reporting a low percentage. Giles, Park, and Cai (2006) apply definitions of labor-force participation and unemployment in line with International Labour Organization recommendations and report the unemployment rate for urban China to have increased from 7.1 percent in January 1996 to 12.5 percent in November 2001. During the same period the labor-force participation rate decreased by as much as 8.9 percent, with its contribution to the employment rate going down by 12.2 percent. This is indeed a large decrease, but not uniquely large. For example, between 1990 and 1994 the Swedish labor-force participation rate decreased by 12.6 percent.

Under this system, public resources are closely related to the level of local economic development. Richer areas have more revenues and are better able to provide public services and to invest in local infrastructure. This has implications for the spatial distribution of incomes. For example, the returns to education are likely to be higher in a city that can afford to provide good telecommunications and transportation infrastructures than in a rural county. Differences in local government spending on education, health, and social services also affect opportunities for households to acquire endowments of human capital and other assets that generate income.

Public funds have also become increasingly important as the reforms have reduced the provision of social services by work units and collectives, leaving governments at different levels as important providers of social programs and insurance. Reformulation of social programs has taken place at different paces in different locations. In urban areas, for example, reforms have been adopted to make pensions portable among work units and to protect workers in the event that their employers go bankrupt. Also, systems of unemployment assistance have been put in place, and the central government has instituted a welfare program to provide a minimum guaranteed living standard to urban residents. Institutions have been established to collect social insurance fees and make payments to beneficiaries.

Much less progress has been made in rural areas. Despite some experiments with pension programs for rural residents, most rural households have no external source of old age support. Rural residents are largely responsible for their own health care expenses. Other types of public insurance are also generally unavailable, except in the most developed areas.

Spatial differences have been further reinforced by China's approach to trade liberalization. During the 1990s China carried out substantial trade reforms, which included the reduction of barriers to foreign trade and investment and culminated in China's entry into the World Trade Organization. Increased foreign demand for goods produced at low cost and growth in export processing industries have been important features of China's economic growth in recent years. Export processing has been fueled by large inflows of foreign direct investment.

A notable feature of China's trade reforms is that initial access was limited to a relatively small number of designated urban and coastal areas. During the 1990s access to foreign markets and investment greatly widened, yet areas favored early on had a head start. This gradual approach to trade reform, together with the fiscal decentralization, has contributed to ongoing spatial differences in living standards among provinces as well as among regions.

Living conditions differ widely across China's 31 provincial units, each having a population comparable in size to that of many countries. The degree of difference can be illustrated by considering each of China's provinces and provincial units as a country in the worldwide ranking of countries according to the United Nations Development Programme's Human Development Index, which captures differences not only in per capita real gross domestic product (GDP) but also in education and health. Most developed are Shanghai and Beijing in the prosperous East, which would rank 25 and 30, respectively, close to Greece and Hungary. In contrast, Guizhou and Tibet in the poorer West would rank much lower, at 122 and 129, comparable to Morocco and Namibia (see UNDP 2005).

III. Measuring Inequality: Data and Definitions

Measuring inequality is an empirical exercise that requires data and involves a range of issues with respect to survey strategy, data, and approach. Here we raise three main issues relevant to the study of China's inequality. First, what strategy is used to obtain the data? The way in which data are obtained can influence the suitability of the data to the task and the accuracy of the empirical findings. Second, what is the variable of interest, that is, over what variable do the researchers choose to measure inequality? Most studies of inequality in China analyze income inequality. We discuss some of the pros and cons of using income versus other variables. Third, where income is the major variable of interest, as it is here, how is it defined and measured? This question has received attention in the literature on income measurement; we focus on those aspects most relevant to China.

A. Strategies to Obtain Data

Where inequality among households and individuals is the focus of analysis as is the case here, researchers seek household-level data. Different strategies can be used to obtain household data. One is for the researchers to initiate and manage a survey from beginning to end. In this case the researchers formulate research questions; design and plan the data collection; monitor the fieldwork, coding, and cleaning; and finally analyze the data. Many studies of inequality in China follow this approach.[5] This strategy enables researchers to match the survey to their topic and theoretical framework. If the researcher is in control of the entire process and is skillful, the data can

---

[5] Gustafsson and Li (2006) provide a list of 25 articles published in English-language academic journals from 1998 to mid-2003 that have used this approach.

be of high quality. The major drawback of this approach is its cost, including both time and funds. Cost concerns mean that surveys of this type typically have limited temporal and geographic range, covering a single year and one or a few localities. Also, the data may be well suited only for investigation of a narrow set of topics closely related to the original research topic.

A second strategy is to employ data already collected by other researchers or by a government agency. This strategy has also been used successfully many times, most frequently with data collected by the Chinese National Bureau of Statistics (NBS), which carries out a large, annual household survey covering both rural and urban areas.[6] Collected in a harmonized way over large parts of China and over time, the NBS data can be used to study spatial differences and changes over time.

Several studies have discussed the sorts of information in the NBS household survey, how it is collected, and its availability to researchers.[7] One well-known problem with the NBS data is the definition of income, which is narrow in some respects (more on this below). Also, the quality and representativeness of the data are not easy to assess. Although researchers who have worked with NBS staff have found them to be highly knowledgeable and professional, the NBS has not published documents describing the details of the sampling, fieldwork, coding, and editing of the data. One aspect of sampling that is known is that the NBS sample frame has been based on China's household registration system, not on census data. Consequently, it has excluded the population of rural-to-urban migrants without formal status in cities. As this group likely has income higher than the rural population and lower than the urban population, its exclusion would cause understatement of urban inequality. Excluding migrants could also cause overstatement of nationwide inequality, although the precise effect would depend on the size of the migrant population and exactly where migrants fall in the income distribution.

Another problem with the NBS sample is that it probably underrepresents the poorest and richest households (Riskin, Zhao, and Li 2001). Many of the poorest households are located in remote areas and may be illiterate. The richest households rely heavily on income from private businesses,

---

[6] Gustafsson and Li (2006) provide a list of 14 articles in English-language academic journals that follow this approach.

[7] Gibson, Huang, and Rozelle (2003) discuss the design of the NBS urban household survey, and Park and Wang (2001) give details on how this information is used to obtain official numbers on poverty in urban China. Bramall (2001) assesses the quality of the NBS household surveys in both urban and rural areas. Chen and Ravallion (1996) and Ravallion and Chen (2007) summarize key features of the NBS household surveys.

income that is typically poorly documented and underreported. Also, the richest households are more likely to decline to participate in such surveys. Undersampling of the extremes in the distribution leads to understatement of inequality. This problem, however, plagues all income survey efforts in China and elsewhere. The NBS survey, given its size, is in this regard no worse and perhaps better than other available China surveys.

Finally, access to the NBS data is restricted. Most researchers have access only to aggregated or tabulated data in published sources. The few who have used the underlying household-level data have typically been limited to using relatively small subsamples covering one or a few provinces.

A third strategy for obtaining data, and the one used for this volume, combines elements of the first two approaches. Here the researchers developed a survey instrument appropriate for the topic of analysis and addressing relevant theoretical concerns. This instrument was then used to conduct interviews over a large sample of households drawn from the yet larger NBS household survey. The NBS carried out the fieldwork. To ensure data quality, members of the research team oversaw and participated in some of the survey work; the researchers also checked and cleaned the data. This approach allowed sufficient cost savings to make possible a large, geographically broad sample spanning several years. That said, the time and funds involved were still substantial, and the project required collaborative work from a team of scholars. Data collection on an annual basis was not feasible.

This approach was first employed in the late 1980s when a group of scholars at the Institute of Economics of the Chinese Academy of Social Sciences joined forces with researchers from other countries to collect data to understand inequality in China. In close cooperation with the staff at the NBS, they obtained a sample of rural households and a sample of urban households covering large parts of China. These samples were subsamples of the larger NBS household survey samples. They also developed a survey instrument that was consistent with the research framework. That initial project resulted in a dataset containing detailed information on income and related variables for 1988. To examine changes over time, the researchers repeated this effort seven years later and produced a comparable dataset for 1995. In the late 1990s the survey was again repeated, but only in urban areas, with the object of examining the distributional consequences of the urban reforms at that time.[8]

---

[8] The 1988 survey and analyses based on it are available in Griffin and Zhao (1993); for the 1995 survey see Riskin, Zhao, and Li (2001) and Khan and Riskin (2001). For the 1999 survey for urban China, see Li and Sato (2006). Data collected in the different projects have

Table 1.1. *The CHIP surveys – Basic features*

Sample	1988	1995	2002
Rural			
Provinces covered	28	19	22
Number of households	10,258	7,998	9,200
Number of persons	51,352	34,739	37,969
Urban			
Provinces covered	10	11	12
Number of households	9,009	6,931	6,835
Number of persons	31,827	21,694	20,632
Migrant			
Provinces covered			12
Number of households			2,005
Number of persons			5,318

Note: The provinces are named in the Appendix. In 1988 and 1995 Chongqing was included as part of Sichuan province in the rural as well as urban surveys; in 2002 Chongqing was again included in the urban and rural surveys, but as a separate province. This reclassification of Chongqing increased the number of provinces covered in both the rural and urban surveys by one between 1995 and 2002.

The most recent round of this survey project took place in 2003, producing the 2002 data used in this book. This survey covers a sample of 9,200 rural households in 120 counties and 6,835 registered urban households in 70 cities. New to this round is a sample of 2,005 rural-to-urban migrant households residing in cities, as well as a community-level survey for each of the 961 villages appearing in the rural sample. Table 1.1 provides basic information about the 2002 and prior CHIP surveys. The Appendix to this book gives more details on the 2002 and 1995 surveys.[9]

The resulting datasets have many attractive qualities. They cover a large geographic area and span multiple years; they are designed for the study of inequality and reflect the research topic and theoretical framework; and the involvement of the research team in the data collection and cleaning process addresses some quality concerns. The data nevertheless have certain drawbacks, one of which is that, as a subsample of the NBS survey sample, they have the same sampling biases. The addition of a migrant subsample

also been made available to other researchers, and many articles have been published in journals based on these datasets. Gustafsson and Li (2006) list 28 such articles published in English-language journals up to the beginning of 2004. Each of the surveys has also resulted in a Chinese-language book with content that overlaps with the English version.

[9] See Griffin and Zhao (1993) for details on the 1988 survey.

in 2002 goes part way toward addressing one of those biases, but even so the migrant subsample is imperfect. For example, it contains only households with fixed addresses and so excludes migrants living in transient lodgings or on work sites (see the Appendix).

The strategy used here, then, has produced a survey dataset with certain weaknesses. Some of the resulting biases cause exaggeration and others understatement of inequality in China. We are unable to determine the net effect. Despite these biases, the CHIP dataset has notable advantages over those used in other studies. Consequently, findings can be obtained that are relatively robust and that, with careful interpretation, provide a sound basis for understanding the level, structure, and changes in China's inequality.

B. Inequality of What?

The underlying objective of studies of inequality is to understand differences in welfare or living standards. Welfare is difficult to measure, as it depends on personal valuations and is a function of a wide range of social, economic, and physical factors. Researchers have used different variables as indicators of welfare, each with its advantages and disadvantages.[10] Choice among the various alternatives depends on which features of welfare are considered most important, on the question of interest, and on data availability.

Most studies of inequality in China, and many studies for other countries as well, use income as the variable of interest. Income is an attractive choice as it provides a homogeneous measure of households' ability to acquire goods and services. Also, it allows analysis of the contributions to inequality of different sources of income such as wages and earnings from self-employment. As it is widely used, comparison with other studies is possible.

From a theoretical perspective, one widely noted drawback of income as a measure of welfare is that it fluctuates from year to year and can vary systematically over the life cycle. Consequently, inequality of income measured at a point in time will overstate inequality in underlying lifetime or permanent income. Some researchers argue that for this reason consumption expenditures rather than income should be the variable of interest in analyses of inequality. If households can save and borrow, then in the face of income fluctuations they can maintain smooth consumption expenditures in line with their expected permanent income. In this case, consumption

---

[10] See Atkinson and Bourguignon (2000), Deaton (1997), Gradín, Cantó, and del Río (2004), and WIDER (2005) for discussions of the relative merits of different measures, especially income and consumption. Our discussion in this section draws on these sources.

provides a better indicator of permanent income and thus of underlying inequality in living standards.

The use of consumption also has drawbacks, however. Consumption, like income, can fluctuate over time, as needs can vary over the life cycle. Consumption also depends heavily on the habits and preferences of individuals, so that some measured inequality will be spurious. From a practical standpoint, using consumption raises difficulties in the treatment of infrequently purchased consumer durables and in the valuation of services. Given such problems, some argue that consumption is not necessarily a better measure of welfare than income.

We would argue further that certain features of China provide reasons to use income rather than consumption. In China financial markets are still undeveloped, and households have limited opportunities to borrow and save. The theoretical advantages of using consumption, then, are not so apparent. Problems also arise from a practical standpoint. Calculation of consumption expenditures involves multiplying prices times quantities over all the goods and services consumed. Due to China's transition from a planned to a market economy, price data are incomplete and imperfect, thus making calculation of consumption difficult. This issue is particularly relevant when researchers wish to use data from the 1980s and early to mid-1990s. Of course, prices are also needed to calculate the value of certain components of income, but the use of prices is less pervasive. Finally, data availability is a factor. Income data for China are more readily available than consumption data.[11]

In view of the above considerations, and so as to maintain continuity with past rounds of the CHIP survey and comparability with the large literature examining income inequality, the 2002 survey effort emphasized collection of income data. With a few exceptions, most of the chapters in this book analyze the distribution of income.[12] The exceptions are Chapter 5, which examines the distribution of assets and wealth, and Chapter 9, which analyzes the distribution of wages in urban areas. Wealth is of interest in its own right because wealth reflects household command over resources. Wages constitute a major component of urban income, and analysis of the changes in wage distribution can shed light on the impact of major urban

---

[11] Consumption data are used in studies by Wu and Perloff (2005) and Jalan and Ravallion (1998).

[12] The CHIP dataset used here, in fact, includes data on consumption expenditures as well as income. The consumption data were provided by the NBS, which collected them for its larger survey.

reform measures. These two chapters, then, provide information that is important in its own right and complementary to that in the other chapters.

C. The Definition and Measurement of Income

Having settled on income as the variable of interest, we must then consider the definition and measurement of income. Most analysts concur that income should include both cash and in-kind components. The major types of income are wages, net income from self-employment (including the value of farm products retained for own consumption), pension or retirement income, net interest payments, and net income from investments. An important form of in-kind income is imputed rents of owner-occupied housing. Since welfare depends on disposable income, taxes should be subtracted, and the value of government subsidies and transfers should be added in. Disposable income also includes some forms of interhousehold transfers, for example, migrant remittances. (See Smeeding and Weinberg 2001; WIDER 2005.)

In practice, household income survey questionnaires may not gather information on all of these components. For this reason, and because of practical difficulties in questionnaire design and households' willingness to respond, income data are never perfect, and coverage varies among datasets (Smeeding and Weinberg 2001). With respect to household income data for China, certain definitional and coverage issues are noteworthy. Some of these issues arise because of China's socialist institutions and transition path.

The NBS's definition of income, which applies not only in the NBS household surveys but to other surveys that use the NBS methodology, excludes certain important components.[13] Imputed rents from owner-occupied housing are not included. Exclusion of imputed rents was perhaps not so serious an omission earlier in the reform era, but it has become more so with the ongoing reforms in property rights, especially since the implementation of the urban housing reforms in the late 1990s.

In addition, although the NBS income data include the value of some government subsidies and transfers, coverage is incomplete. This is especially

---

[13] For detailed discussion of the calculation of income by the NBS, see Griffin and Zhao (1993), Khan et al. (1992), and Khan and Riskin (1998). Some relevant discussion is also available in Ravallion and Chen (2007), Benjamin, Brandt, and Giles (2005), and Benjamin et al. (forthcoming). One issue raised in this literature is the valuation of in-kind farm income, and in particular the fact that prior to 1990 the NBS valued such income at below-market procurement prices. Since 1990 the NBS has used local market prices to value in-kind farm income.

true of implicit subsidies associated with the distribution of goods and services at low, nonmarket prices. Examples include the implicit value of food ration coupons that gave urban residents the right to purchase low-priced grain and other foods, and the implicit value of public housing for which tenants paid only nominal rents. As urban residents were the main recipients of such implicit subsidies, their exclusion caused understatement of the urban-rural income gap and of overall inequality. The importance of these subsidies, however, has declined substantially as planned allocation of consumer goods and housing was largely eliminated in the 1990s.

The NBS data also do not include the value of household consumption of public services such as health care, education, and sanitation. Once again, in China urban residents benefit disproportionately from such public services, and the exclusion of these services causes understatement of overall inequality. This bias has likely persisted through the reform period as the provision of subsidized public services has continued to a greater or lesser degree, perhaps with some increases in recent years.[14]

The incomplete coverage of the NBS household income definition, and the resulting biases in measurement of inequality using the resulting income data, has been a major concern of the CHIP surveys. From its inception in 1987 and continuing to this most recent 2002 round, the CHIP survey questionnaires have been designed to address key shortcomings in the NBS income data. The CHIP datasets consequently contain not only income as measured according to the NBS definition, but also information on the housing components of income and on subsidies. This allows calculation of income according to alternative definitions.

The contributors to this volume employ this information, and in their analyses they use measures of income that are more comprehensive than that of the NBS. In most cases, this involves adding imputed rents from owner-occupied housing to the NBS measure of income. In Chapter 3 Khan and Riskin take a different approach, which is to add up the underlying components of income. Their approach gives slightly different, but generally consistent, results regarding income inequality. Both approaches give results that

---

[14] A related issue is the treatment of household expenditures on education and health care. For example, households in rural China typically have to pay school fees. These fees can be viewed as user fees and are similar to taxes, and one could argue that the analyst should treat them as such and subtract them in the calculation of disposable income. The same argument can be made for some expenditures on health care. For discussion of this point, see Gustafsson and Li (2004). In this volume such expenditures are not subtracted from income.

differ from those obtained using the NBS definition of income. Key differences are outlined below, with additional discussion in individual chapters.

Note that neither the NBS nor the CHIP dataset contains information on the implicit subsidies associated with public services such as health and education. Such information is desirable from a theoretical standpoint, but it is difficult to collect and absent from almost all income data worldwide.[15]

A final measurement issue arises with respect to the conversion of incomes from nominal values into constant prices. Studies that make comparisons over time, including those in this volume, correct for inflation and deflation in the general price level using consumer price indices. In principle, corrections should also be made for geographic differences in the cost of living, but in practice this is a laborious and complicated exercise with substantial data requirements. Until recently few studies of China's inequality corrected for geographic price differences because of a lack of data on absolute price differences among regions (Brandt and Holz 2006; Benjamin et al. forthcoming; Ravallion and Chen 2007; Sicular et al. 2007). For other countries, too, such adjustments are far from universal. The studies in this volume do not adjust for spatial differences in the cost of living.

IV. Major Findings: China's Winding Path between Increased and Constant Inequality

The chapters of this book contribute new studies, using recent data, of inequality in China. Most of the chapters analyze changes over time, some going back as far as 1988. Some chapters address issues that have been previously examined in the literature, using different data or methods; other chapters examine aspects of inequality that have not been investigated elsewhere. New aspects include, for example, analysis of how rural-to-urban migrants influence the level of nationwide inequality; inequality and the economic situation of the elderly; the contribution of village-specific factors to rural household income distribution; and the distributional consequences of tax reform in rural China.

Overall income inequality is the topic of Chapters 2, 3, and 4. Chapter 2, using surveys for 1988, 1995, and 2002, shows trends in nationwide

---

[15] In their review of income survey data for 25 countries, Smeeding and Weinberg (2001) report that only one country collects information on public education services (Australia), and only three on government-subsidized health care services (Australia, Germany, and the United States).

inequality over time, with an emphasis on spatial differences between rural and urban China, among the eastern, central, and western regions, and at the provincial level. Using data for 1995 and 2002, Chapter 3 examines the contribution to inequality of different types or sources of income, and how the role of different income sources differs between rural and urban sectors. Importantly, this chapter also analyzes income and income inequality among rural-to-urban migrants for 2002. Chapter 4 examines the underlying determinants of inequality in 1995 and 2002. It uses regression-based inequality decomposition to analyze how household characteristics such as family composition and education affect income levels and distribution.

Chapters 5 and 6 continue to look at the national picture, but focus on different aspects. Chapter 5 shifts attention to the distribution of wealth, a topic of increasing relevance following China's reforms of ownership and property rights, including privatization of housing and other assets. Chapter 6 looks at the most vulnerable group, the poor. It analyzes trends in poverty rates between 1995 and 2002 and explores the relationship between poverty, policy, and growth, with attention to migrants.

The remaining chapters look at selected aspects of inequality, some with a focus on the urban or rural sectors. Chapter 7 investigates the changed economic status of the elderly in China, and Chapter 8 analyzes inequality in health care subsidies. Both those chapters cover rural as well as urban China. The three following chapters look at urban China. Chapter 9 analyzes the determinants of urban wages in 1995 and 2002, and Chapter 10 studies gender differences in urban incomes. Living arrangements of the urban elderly are the subject of Chapter 11.

The last two chapters of the book focus on rural topics. Chapter 12 investigates the importance of village-specific factors for the distribution of rural household income. Chapter 13 is an analysis of the recent tax reform and its implications for rural income inequality.

What conclusions emerge from this collection of studies? Here we focus on six central findings that are broad in nature and that, in most cases, cut across the individual chapters. To assist in this discussion, in Table 1.2 we summarize key indicators of inequality for China as a whole, and in urban and rural areas separately, as reported in the various chapters of this book.[16]

---

[16] Indicators are, for the most part, consistent across chapters. For 1995, however, Chapter 2 gives a lower level of inequality within rural areas, and a greater gap between urban and rural income, than does Chapter 3. These two discrepancies reflect the fact that these two chapters calculate income differently (as outlined in the text of the individual chapters), and that Chapter 2's indicators use income in constant 1988 prices whereas Chapter 3 uses income in current prices.

Table 1.2. *Key indicators of inequality and poverty in China*

	1988	1995	2002	Chapter
China as a whole				
Inequality of disposable household	0.395	0.469	0.468	2
income per capita, Gini coefficient		0.452	0.450	3
			Including migrants, 0.448	3
Ratio of urban to rural disposable	2.69:1	3.08:1	3.13:1	2
household income per capita		2.47:1	2.96:1	3
			Including migrants, 2.77:1	3
Contribution of urban-rural income gap to national income inequality (%)	36.5	41.0	46.1	2
Inequality in household wealth per capita, Gini coefficient			0.550	5
Rural China				
Inequality in disposable household	0.325	0.364	0.365	2
income per capita, Gini coefficient		0.416	0.375	3
Inequality in disposable household income per capita among the elderly, Gini coefficient	0.248	0.326	0.302	7
Inequality in household wealth per capita, Gini coefficient	0.311	0.351	0.399	5
				6
Poverty rate (% poor)				
Lower poverty line		12.8	4.4	
Higher poverty line		28.6	12.3	
Urban China				
Inequality in disposable household	0.244	0.339	0.322	2
income per capita, Gini coefficient		0.322	0.318	3
			Including migrants, 0.338	3
			Migrants only, 0.380	3
Inequality of hourly wage earnings per worker, Gini coefficient		0.325	0.370	9
Female mean income as a share of male mean income		0.81	0.76	10
Inequality in household wealth per capita, Gini coefficient			0.475	5
				6
Poverty rate (% poor)				
Lower poverty line		2.7	0.8	
Higher poverty line		8.0	2.2	
Higher poverty line, including migrants			4.4	6
Poverty rate, migrants only (% poor)				
Lower poverty line			5.5	
Higher poverty line			14.4	

Note: The term *migrants* here refers to rural-to-urban migrants who are not formally registered as urban residents. Except where indicated otherwise, the indicators in this table are calculated using the subsamples of rural and urban registered households and do not include rural-to-urban migrants.

Table 1.3. *Alternative estimates of nationwide Gini coefficient for China, 1988, 1995, and 2001/2002*

		Source			
Year	This book	Ravallion and Chen (2007)	World Bank (2005)	OECD (2004)	Wu and Perloff (2005)
1988	0.395	0.330			0.337
1995	0.452–0.469	0.415		0.389	0.382
2001		0.447	0.450		0.415
2002	0.450–0.468				

Finding 1: Because of the emergence of certain equalizing processes, between 1995 and 2002 overall inequality in China remained more or less unchanged.

Chapters 2 and 3 report no increase in overall income inequality between 1995 and 2002, although inequality was at a relatively high level (Table 1.2).[17] This stability of inequality reflects the emergence of equalizing processes that have offset continuing forces toward greater inequality.

Before we turn to a discussion of these processes, some comparison of our estimates of inequality to those reported elsewhere is in order. Table 1.3 provides a selection of recent estimates of China's nationwide Gini coefficient.[18] For 2002 our estimates of the national Gini coefficient are about 0.45–0.47, close to the most recent numbers (for 2000–2001) available in the other sources. This level of inequality is relatively high by international standards. China's Gini coefficient exceeds, for example, those of India and the United States. China is not, however, among the most unequal countries in the world. Countries with higher Gini coefficients include Chile, Honduras, and South Africa, with Gini coefficients exceeding 0.50 or even 0.60; countries with Gini coefficients similar to that of China include Costa Rica and Singapore (World Bank 2005).

[17] According to the analysis presented in Chapter 3, income inequality actually fell somewhat, whereas Chapter 2 using slightly different definitions reports constant inequality.

[18] Note that the estimates shown in this table do not correct for spatial differences in costs of living. Using the NBS survey data, Chen and Ravallion (2007) provide an alternative series of Gini coefficients that is adjusted for urban-rural cost of living differences; using the China Health and Nutrition Survey data, Benjamin et al. (forthcoming) provide inequality estimates that are adjusted for spatial differences in the cost of living, as do Sicular et al. (2007) using the CHIP data. In all cases such corrections lower the measured level of inequality. Such price adjustments, however, do not appear to alter substantially trends over time. Sicular et al. (2007) report that the Theil indices of inequality calculated using incomes both adjusted and unadjusted for spatial price differences do not indicate an upward trend in inequality between 1995 and 2002.

While our 2002 estimates of inequality are similar to those reported in other studies, for earlier years our estimates are higher (Table 1.3). We report a Gini coefficient or ratio in 1995, for example, of about 0.45–0.47. For the same year, the Organisation for Economic Co-operation and Development (2004) reports a Gini coefficient for China as a whole of 0.389, which is almost identical to that of Wu and Perloff (2005). Ravallion and Chen (2007) report a Gini coefficient of 0.415.

Why are our 1988 and 1995 estimates of China's Gini coefficient higher than those in the other studies? The definition of income is relevant here. Most estimates of China's inequality are calculated using income data from the NBS household surveys according to the NBS definition, which excludes the imputed rental value of owner-occupied housing and undercounts subsidies. Our estimates include housing-related income components and more fully capture subsidies. These components of income disproportionately go to urban households, which are relatively rich. Including these income components therefore should, and does, increase the measured level of inequality.

The value of these income components has declined over time. As the reforms have proceeded, China has dismantled its system of planned allocation, and price-based subsidies have declined markedly. As discussed in Chapter 3, these developments have meant that the discrepancy between estimates based on the NBS and our income definitions has narrowed, and so by 2002 our Gini coefficient estimates are similar to those based on the NBS official data.

To investigate this point, in Chapter 2 we use the CHIP data to calculate inequality using two alternative definitions of income, the NBS definition and our definition. With the NBS definition, we find a Gini coefficient of 0.436 in 1995 rising to 0.452 in 2002. In other words, with the NBS income definition, our analysis would, like other studies, have found increasing inequality between 1995 and 2002.[19]

Our findings suggest that rising income inequality in China need not be continuous.[20] Several chapters identify underlying processes that are inequality reducing, and so provide an explanation for why inequality in China could stabilize, or possibly even decline. Inequality-reducing forces

---

[19] The increase is smaller than that reported by Ravallion and Chen (2007) from 1995 to 2001, reflecting perhaps differences in the survey samples or the use of a different end year, 2001 versus 2002.

[20] Other studies based on the official NBS data have also identified such episodes, although the timing is different. Wu and Perloff (2005) find that the Gini coefficient remained essentially unchanged from 1993 to 1998, and Ravallion and Chen (2007) find it unchanged from 1993 to 1999.

emerge in the analyses of different income sources in Chapter 3, of spatial aspects of inequality in Chapter 2, and of the household and individual characteristics that determine income in Chapter 4.

With respect to sources of income, a key change in the underlying structure of income occurred between 1995 and 2002. As shown in Chapter 3, in rural China the proportion of households with income from wage employment expanded substantially. Wage employment, which in 1995 had benefited a relatively small and high-income segment of the rural population, became fairly widespread within rural areas. This wider access to wage income by itself can explain why the nationwide Gini coefficient for household disposable income did not increase between 1995 and 2002.

Trends in the distribution of housing components of income were also equalizing. With the housing reforms, the amount of urban housing subsidies declined. Concurrently, the urban distribution of the rental value of owner-occupied housing became less skewed in favor of richer groups. Housing reform thus reduced income inequality within urban areas.[21]

Along spatial dimensions, inequality-reducing trends were found in the eastern region. Chapter 2 reports that income inequality in the East rose rapidly between 1988 and 1995. This reflected widening gaps among provinces in the East as some provinces took the lead in terms of personal income growth. During the following seven-year period, however, mean provincial incomes in eastern China converged. Income growth in the provinces that grew quickly earlier spilled over to other provinces in the same region. This development is consistent with the historical experience of other countries as they have become more spatially integrated during development.

Trends in income distribution in the East and in rural wage income reflect growth processes that initially caused widening inequality but later became equalizing. Such processes have been noted in the wider literature on economic development, and they underlie Kuznets' prediction of an inverted-U–shaped relationship between growth and inequality in which inequality first rises and then falls during the development process. One reason for the inverted-U–shaped relationship is that growth typically begins in a particular region or sector, and its benefits are enjoyed by a small subset of the population. With time, as people and resources move into the more dynamic sector, or as growth spreads more broadly, the benefits become more widely shared and inequality declines.

---

[21] This is not the entire story of the distributional consequences of housing reform, however, as these reforms made the distribution of wealth less equal. The impact of housing reforms on the distribution of wealth is discussed in Chapter 5.

Further equalizing forces are noted in Chapter 4. The regression-based inequality decomposition reveals that even though inequality associated with education and other individual characteristics increased, overall inequality did not. This was largely because of across-the-board increases in the absolute level of base incomes, likely reflecting widely shared benefits of China's recent macroeconomic growth. Widely shared absolute income increases are by definition inequality reducing.

Despite these equalizing processes, overall inequality did not decline. Key offsetting forces were the urban-rural divide and increasingly differentiated returns to education.

Finding 2: The urban-rural income gap was large, increasing, and an ever more dominant contributor to overall inequality.

In discussions of inequality in present-day China, the urban-rural division figures prominently. The studies in this book underline the importance of, and shed some new light on, the urban-rural gap. Chapters 2 and 3 report that in 2002 urban incomes were three times those in rural areas (Table 1.2). This gap is large by international standards (Sicular et al. 2007) and shows no signs of narrowing.

Not only is the urban-rural gap large, but its impact on overall inequality appears to have risen. Chapter 2 uses inequality decomposition by subgroups to calculate the proportion of inequality in China as a whole contributed by differences in mean income across the registered urban and rural populations. For 1988 this contribution was 37 percent; for 1995, 41 percent; and for 2002, 46 percent. Chapter 3 similarly finds that between 1995 and 2002 the urban-rural income gap became an even more dominant component of overall inequality for China. The disequalizing impact of the urban-rural income gap offset the equalizing forces outlined above.

The continued prominence of the urban-rural income gap is surprising given the growth of rural-to-urban migration. In principle, such migration should help to narrow the gap by increasing the supply of labor in urban areas as well as decreasing the supply in rural areas. Migrant remittances to rural household members can also reduce the urban-rural income gap.

Some might argue that the measured size of the urban-rural gap is substantially overstated because most calculations of the gap exclude rural-to-urban migrants. Findings in Chapter 3, however, do not support this argument. In this chapter Khan and Riskin calculate the urban-rural income ratio excluding and then including the rural-to-urban migrant subsample of the CHIP survey. Including migrants does reduce the income gap, but only by 6 percent. At 2.8, the income ratio remains high by international standards. Including migrants, moreover, has a nearly imperceptible effect on nationwide inequality (see Table 1.2, Finding 6 below, and Chapter 3).

Why do urban households enjoy higher per capita incomes than rural households? Differences in education are certainly part of the story. Differences in other household characteristics such as family composition, age, and Party membership also play a role. Yet even after controlling for these characteristics, the gap remains large. The regression analysis in Chapter 4 controls for observable household characteristics and yields an estimate of the "pure" effect of simply having urban residence of 2,350 yuan in 1995 and 4,606 yuan in 2002 (in constant 2002 prices). These estimates imply that in 1995, 51 percent of the urban-rural income gap was due to the pure effect of simply having urban residence, and in 2002 this pure effect rose to 63 percent of the gap. This "pure" income advantage does not include the effects of differential urban returns to age, household size, and education, nor does it include the effects of differences in household characteristics such as education, household size, and age.

These findings imply that despite substantial migration to date, China's restrictions on household mobility embodied in the *hukou* system and related policies remain a root cause of income inequality. From a policy perspective, then, the pace and nature of further reforms in the *hukou* system will be key to the evolution of inequality.

Also important will be policies that influence the returns to labor and land in rural China. Two of the chapters in the book have bearing on this issue. Chapter 12 highlights the role of village-level governance and infrastructure as factors influencing rural incomes. Findings in this chapter reveal that especially in less-developed regions, small-scale physical infrastructure, social stability, and political connections are significant determinants of income. Thus the development of village-level institutions and investments in poor areas could be an avenue for promoting poverty reduction and equitable growth.

Chapter 13 analyzes the rural tax burden and its consequences for the level and distribution of income. With the object of reducing the urban-rural gap, in recent years China's leaders have announced reforms of and reductions in rural taxes. This chapter reports that China's rural tax reforms have indeed reduced the urban-rural income gap. The magnitude of the rural tax burden, however, is not overly large – the tax burden was only about 5 percent of income in 1995, and about 3–4 percent in 2002. This being the case, rural tax reform cannot be the main road to decreasing urban-rural income disparities.

The urban-rural divide is visible not just in income, but also in other indicators associated with welfare. Chapter 5 reports an urban-to-rural ratio in per capita wealth of 3.6:1 in 2002. This is larger than the gap in income. The wealth gap exists despite the fact that rural households' wealth includes the value of the farmland to which they have use rights. Urban households, however, have benefited disproportionately from a rather long period of rapid income growth, which has enabled many to accumulate financial assets. Housing reforms have also been a factor. Urban residents have had opportunities to buy the apartments in which they live at below-market prices. This has not been an option for rural farmers, who already owned their houses and who have been disadvantaged by their weak property rights to farmland.

Gaps also exist in health and education. When urban citizens pay for medical treatment or buy medicine, they are typically reimbursed to a large degree by their employer. In contrast, rural residents finance such expenditures entirely by themselves. As a consequence, rural residents are at a higher risk of being economically excluded from health care, a basic service relevant to welfare. China is now counted among the countries in the world with the most inequity in health care finance. Chapter 8 shows that this inequity reflects the different systems for funding health care in urban and rural China.

Gaps in education between rural and urban areas in China have been widely reported (Hannum, Behrman, and Wang forthcoming; Knight and Song 1999) and receive some attention in this volume. Chapter 4 finds that by 2002 education had become a major source of inequality in China. The importance of education to overall inequality reflects not only the higher levels of education in urban China, but also differences in the returns to education between urban and rural areas.

Finding 3: Education has emerged as an important influence on incomes and as a growing source of inequality.

Studies worldwide have almost universally found that people with more education earn higher incomes. Education can be the ticket to a job in the formal economy or in a more highly paid occupation. Education can make a person more productive in his or her current job, or allow career enhancement through further training. In pre-reform China egalitarian policies compressed the wage distribution, and education-based earnings differentials were comparatively small. China's movement toward a fully functioning labor market, combined with rising demand for qualified personnel associated with China's rapid growth and globalization, have changed the returns to education. Concurrently, education levels have been rising.

As reported in several chapters of this book, these developments have had implications for the distribution of income. The analysis of earnings in urban China in Chapter 9 shows remarkably rapid increases in the returns to education. The premium for a college degree over primary schooling, for example, was 9 percent in 1988, 39 percent in 1995, and 88 percent in 2002. Other recent studies of urban earnings report similar findings.[22] Additional evidence in Chapters 4, 9, and 10 reinforces the message that wages and incomes in China have become increasingly differentiated on the basis of education. Indeed, Chapter 4 reports that in 2002 more than one-third of China's income inequality was attributable to education, up from about 10 percent in 1995.

Are income differences based on education acceptable? To some extent yes, as higher earnings based on education can be viewed as compensation for investments in human capital or as the result of household choice or merit. Yet, what if access to education is not equal? In China school fees have been increasing and have constituted a growing burden for low-income households, whose children typically complete schooling at a relatively young age to begin work. To what extent do poor children face fewer opportunities to finish primary school and to continue to secondary and higher levels of schooling? To what extent do the odds of receiving a university education differ by parental and geographic background? Are chances for girls equal to those for boys? Do children from minority households have the same opportunities as Han children?

While the studies in this book do not answer these questions, they show why such questions deserve attention. Access to education becomes increasingly important as the private rewards to education rise. The studies here, then, point to the growing relevance of education policy in China. Relevant policy concerns include, but are not limited to, the amount of public funding for education, and the distribution of that funding.

> **Finding 4:** Reversing past trends, between 1995 and 2002 poverty in China declined.

China's record of poverty reduction has been mixed. Initially when the reforms began in the early 1980s, poverty in rural areas decreased rapidly.[23] By the late 1980s, however, poverty reduction had slowed. Indeed, between the first two CHIP surveys (1988 and 1995) China's poverty record was disappointing. Chapter 6, however, finds substantial progress in poverty reduction since 1995. Between 1995 and 2002 poverty rates fell in both rural and urban areas, and in almost all provinces.

---

[22] For example, Zhang et al. (2005), who studied each year from 1988 to 2001, report similar results, and they find that most of the rise occurred during two periods, 1992–1994 and 1997–1999.

[23] See, e.g., Yao (2000) and Ravallion and Chen (2007).

The decline in poverty since 1995 is associated with macroeconomic growth. Chapter 3 analyzes the relationship between growth and poverty reduction and finds that the observed trends in poverty reflect a change from pro-rich growth toward distributionally neutral growth. This conclusion is consistent with Chapter 4's finding of widely shared increases in base income levels. Distributionally neutral growth is desirable from the perspective of poverty reduction, although not as desirable as pro-poor growth.

It is worth noting that poverty rates, and trends in those rates, vary spatially. The incidence of poverty is much higher in the western provinces than in the eastern provinces. Also, the poverty rate is substantially higher in rural than in urban areas. Including migrants in the urban poverty calculation doubles the rate of urban poverty (calculated using a higher poverty line; see Chapter 6) from 2.2 percent to 4.4 percent, but this rate is still much lower than the rural poverty rate of 12.3 percent.

Finding 5: While income inequality remained unchanged, inequality of wealth in China rose.

Analysis of trends in the level and distribution of wealth is of particular interest given recent reforms in property rights and in housing and financial markets. Wealth and income are different, although related, concepts. Income refers to current net flows of income from labor, land, and other assets such as housing, bank deposits, and businesses. Wealth refers to the net value of the stock of owned assets, including land, housing, privately owned productive equipment, consumer durables, bank deposits, and other financial instruments. Income can be used to acquire wealth, and wealth can provide flows of income.

Private ownership of assets is a relatively new phenomenon in China. Until the reforms began in the 1980s, most assets were collectively or publicly owned, and what little wealth was in the hands of households usually took the form of cash, bank deposits, and some consumer durables. Following the rural reforms in the 1980s, rural households have acquired partial property rights to farmland and have had opportunities to accumulate wealth in the form of equipment and consumer durables. In urban areas during the 1990s the privatization of urban housing almost overnight transformed the urban population into a propertied class. The 1990s have also seen the expansion of private enterprise and the development of banking and financial markets, enabling households to accumulate wealth in the form of business assets, stocks, and shares, as well as to borrow and incur debt, a negative form of wealth.

Chapter 5 provides a comprehensive analysis of the level and distribution of per capita household wealth in 2002, with some comparisons to earlier years. As expected, levels of wealth have been rising in both rural and urban areas, but the increase has been uneven. The annual average growth rate in urban wealth between 1995 and 2002 was a remarkable 19 percent, as compared to 2 percent in rural areas. This uneven growth in wealth levels has contributed to an unequal distribution of wealth in China.

China's wealth distribution is unequal, more so than the distribution of income. In 2002 the Gini coefficient for the distribution of wealth was 0.55. Those in the top quintile of the wealth distribution held 59 percent of China's total wealth, while those in the bottom quintile held only 3 percent. By comparison, the top quintile accounted for 51 percent and the bottom quintile 4 percent of total income (Chapter 4).

Is this degree of wealth inequality a cause for concern? Greater inequality in the distribution of wealth than in the distribution of income is fairly common worldwide, and China's level of wealth inequality is not particularly high by international standards (Chapter 5). Still, China's experience is distinct in certain ways. In China wealth inequality has emerged in a very short time span and reflects the outcome of reforms that have not been distributionally neutral. Urban households have gained significant wealth from the privatization of housing and have had greater opportunity to accumulate new forms of financial assets. Rural households have had limited access to financial instruments and own housing of lower value. Farmland is the second most important rural asset after housing, but rural households' rights to their farmland are incomplete and weak.

Even within urban areas the benefits of reforms in property rights have not been shared equally. This is especially true of housing. Housing is the single most important component of urban wealth. The acquisition of housing wealth in urban China has occurred very rapidly through a mechanism under which households purchase apartments at highly subsidized prices that bear little relationship to market values. The resulting distribution of housing wealth is strongly influenced by who happens to have lived where, with a dose of active rent seeking thrown into the mix. Not surprisingly, the distribution of housing wealth is highly unequal, contributing two-thirds of overall urban wealth inequality.

Reports of popular discontent over the distribution of housing and land, then, are not surprising. In general, discontent about inequality in China may be driven more by concerns over the distribution of wealth than of income. With time, though, unequal access to wealth, both physical and human, holds implications for the evolution of income inequality.

Finding 6: Inclusion of rural-to-urban migrants changes the overall levels of inequality and poverty in China in 2002, although the measured impact is relatively modest.

The addition to the survey of a subsample of rural-to-urban migrants provides an unusual opportunity to examine the impact of this group on China's inequality. Economic development typically involves movement of labor from agriculture to nonagriculture, and from rural to urban areas. Such movement occurs as households and individuals respond to differentials in wages and other income. Migration provides an important mechanism through which the benefits of growth can be more broadly shared.

Migration in China has been limited by the *hukou* system and related policies, but such restrictions have been relaxed over time, and the number of rural-to-urban migrants has grown steadily. This raises the question of whether the presence of a larger migrant population in cities has narrowed the urban-rural income gap and moderated inequality.

In the past, researchers have not been able to address this question because the datasets suitable for analysis of inequality in China have not contained unregistered migrants. The CHIP data for 2002, however, include a subsample of migrants. As information on migrants is available only for one year, it is not possible to examine how migration has influenced changes over time in inequality. Also, the subsample of migrants covers only migrants living in urban neighborhoods, and so excludes migrants living on construction sites, in dormitories, or in temporary housing. Still, the survey gives useful information about the situation of migrants in 2002, and it provides some clues about past and future trends.

Analyses of the migrant subsample appear in Chapters 3 and 6, the former examining levels and distribution of income and the latter examining rates of poverty. The average per capita household income of rural-to-urban migrants is higher – nearly double that in rural areas – but about 35 percent below that in urban areas. Although their income falls between that of the urban and rural groups, migrants have the highest rate of poverty. Migrant poverty is higher than that of registered urban households; this reflects the lower mean and greater dispersion of migrant income. Migrant poverty is also higher than that in rural areas, mainly because the poverty threshold used for urban areas where migrants reside is higher than that used for rural areas.

How does including migrants affect overall inequality in China? Including migrants in the calculation of overall inequality reduces inequality, but only by a small amount. The Gini coefficient declines by less than 1 percent, from 0.450 to 0.448. This surprisingly small change in measured inequality reflects three factors.

First, including migrants reduces the urban-rural gap, but it also increases inequality within urban areas. Chapter 3 finds an income ratio excluding migrants of 2.96:1, and including migrants of 2.77:1. This gives a 6 percent reduction in the income ratio. This reduction is not trivial, although the income ratio remains high by international standards. Offsetting this is an increase in inequality within urban areas. The urban Gini coefficient increases by 6 percent, from 0.318 to 0.338.

Second, the difference between the Gini coefficients calculated with and without migrants does not capture the full impact of migration on inequality. This calculation does not take into account the impact of migration on the incomes of rural and registered urban residents. Out-migration from rural areas can increase rural incomes by reducing rural labor supply and increasing land availability per capita. In other words, some of the increase in rural income per capita between 1995 and 2002 could be the result of migration. In urban areas, the presence of more migrants may create downward pressure on the wages of registered urban residents, or perhaps slows increases in those wages. This effect is implicit in measured urban incomes for 2002. As our calculation does not control for such effects, it likely understates the full impact of migration on inequality.

Third, in 2002 the share of migrants in the population was still relatively small. Chapter 3 uses population shares of 7 percent migrant, 32 percent urban, and 61 percent rural. If the relative size of the migrant population continues to rise, their impact on national inequality will likely increase.

V. Concluding Comments

The analyses in this volume yield six major findings regarding inequality in China. First, income inequality remained relatively stable between 1995 and 2002. This stability reflects certain equalizing processes in China's economy, including the spread of wage employment in rural areas, the convergence of personal incomes among provinces in eastern China, and the widely shared benefits of macroeconomic growth. Some of these equalizing trends reflect that China is moving from early to more mature stages of development, in which growth spreads beyond the leading sectors, regions, and groups. Several disequalizing forces, however, have offset these trends. The urban-rural income gap remains wide and shows no signs of diminishing. Due to increasingly differentiated returns to education, differences in human capital are translating into ever greater differences in income.

With respect to poverty, this book contains new and encouraging findings of declining rates of poverty in both urban and rural areas. The unequal distribution of wealth, however, and the fact that the uneven and incomplete reforms of property rights have benefited some groups more than others, is a cause for concern.

The chapters in this book contain many other interesting findings on a range of topics, for example, the rising inequality of wage earnings and a widening male-female wage gap in urban China (Chapters 9 and 10), signs of improved welfare of the elderly, at least in urban areas, reflecting improved pensions and housing availability (Chapters 7 and 11), and inequality in health care expenditures (Chapter 8). We encourage readers to read further for additional discussion on these and other issues.

Together, these studies provide a rich set of perspectives on inequality in China. The book's coverage, however, is not exhaustive. Only two chapters, Chapters 3 and 6, include the migrant subsample in their analysis. More research is needed to shed light on this group. Topics such as housing, education, health, taxation, and social protection are discussed in certain chapters, but they warrant fuller, stand-alone investigation. Gender issues are examined in Chapter 10, but only for urban areas. None of the chapters investigates the ethnic minorities in relationship to inequality.[24] Clearly, additional research is needed to provide a full picture of inequality, its causes and its consequences.

Further work is also needed to improve the empirical basis of research on China's inequality. The studies in this book all make use of the CHIP survey data, which were collected following a strategy that overcame some of the limitations associated with the NBS's household survey data as well as with other datasets that have been used for analysis of inequality in China. The CHIP dataset is large and has wide regional coverage, it contains information that allows for a fuller measurement of income and its components, and analysis of changes over time is possible as comparable data are available from earlier survey rounds. As such, it provides one of the best resources for analysis of inequality in China.

Despite these advantages, the CHIP dataset has certain limitations. Coverage of the rural-to-urban migrants remains an issue. The 2002 CHIP survey makes a step forward in this regard, but further efforts are needed to improve and continue the coverage of this group. In addition, since the CHIP sample is drawn from the NBS household survey sample, it shares some of the same

---

[24] Bhalla and Qiu (2006) give a recent analysis of poverty and inequality among Chinese minorities that makes use of the CHIP 1988 and 1995 survey data.

drawbacks. It would be beneficial if the NBS would document its survey and sampling procedures to allow a clearer understanding of sample and other biases. More generally, the study of inequality in China would benefit greatly if the NBS made the household-level data from its surveys more fully available to researchers.

Most research on inequality in China, including that presented here, uses cross-section data. While the data may be available for several years, they do not follow the same households over time. Panel data that follow households over time would provide a better basis for understanding the dynamics of inequality, as this would permit the study of income mobility and of the relationship between permanent and current income. Some panel datasets have become available for China, but their sample sizes are typically small, and they have not been designed to examine nationwide income inequality (Benjamin et al. forthcoming; Jalan and Ravallion 1998; Morduch and Sicular 2001). A remaining challenge, then, is to collect panel data with broad geographic coverage and suited to the investigation of national income distribution.

Our findings warn against making simple predictions from one period to the next. We have found processes working toward more inequality as well as those working toward less. Public policy can influence both types of processes and alter the relative balance between them. Noteworthy here are policies affecting labor mobility, especially between urban and rural areas, education, public finance, and the provision of social insurance and social welfare programs. In view of the rising importance of asset ownership, steps to strengthen property rights and factor markets will also be key. Finally, policies promoting broad macroeconomic growth remain important so as to promote further progress toward the stage of development where the benefits of growth spread from leading sectors to the broader population.

References

Anand, S. and R. Kanbur (1993), "The Kuznets Process and the Inequality Development Relationship," *Journal of Development Economics,* 40(1), 25–52.

Atkinson, A. B. and F. Bourguignon (2000a), "Introduction: Income Distribution and Economics," in A. B. Atkinson and F. Bourguignon, eds., *Handbook of Income Distribution,* vol. 1, Handbooks in Economics 16, Amsterdam: Elsevier North Holland.

Atkinson, A. B. and F. Bourguignon (2000b), *Handbook of Income Distribution,* vol. 1, Handbooks in Economics 16, Amsterdam: Elsevier North Holland.

Benjamin, D., L. Brandt, and J. Giles (2005), "The Evolution of Income Inequality in Rural China," *Economic Development and Cultural Change,* 53(4), 769–824.

Benjamin, D., L. Brandt, J. Giles, and S. Wang (forthcoming), "Income Inequality during China's Economic Transition," in L. Brandt and T. G. Rawski, eds., *China's Economic Transition: Origins, Mechanisms and Consequences*, New York: Cambridge University Press.

Bhalla, A. S. and S. Qiu (2006), *Poverty and Inequality among Chinese Minorities*, London: Routledge.

Bourguignon, F. and C. Morrisson (2002), "Inequality among World Citizens 1820–1992," *American Economic Review*, 92(4), 727–744.

Bramall, C. (2001), "The Quality of China's Household Income Surveys," *China Quarterly*, no. 167, 689–705.

Brandt, L. and C. A. Holz (2006), "Spatial Price Differences in China: Estimates and Implications," *Economic Development and Cultural Change*, 55(1), 43–86.

Chen, S. and M. Ravallion (1996), "Data in Transition: Assessing Rural Living Standards in Southern China," *China Economic Review*, 7(1), 23–56.

Deaton, A. (1997), *The Analysis of Household Surveys: A Microeconometric Approach to Development Policy*, Baltimore: Johns Hopkins University Press.

Deaton, A. (2005), "Measuring Poverty in a Growing World (Or Measuring Growth in a Poor World)," *Review of Economics and Statistics*, 87(1), 1–19.

Dollar, D. (2005), "Globalization, Poverty and Inequality since 1980," *World Bank Research Observer*, 20(2), 145–175.

Gibson, J., J. Huang, and S. Rozelle (2003), "Improving Estimates of Inequality and Poverty from Urban China's Household Income and Expenditure Survey," *Review of Income and Wealth*, 49(1), 53–68.

Giles, J., A. Park, and F. Cai (2006), "How Has Economic Restructuring Affected China's Urban Workers?" *China Quarterly*, no. 165, 61–95.

Gradín, C., O. Cantó, and C. del Río (2004), "Inequality, Poverty and Mobility: Choosing Income or Consumption as Welfare Indicators," Universidade de Vigo, Instituto de Estudios Fiscales, P.T. No.18/04.

Griffin, K. and R. Zhao, eds. (1993), *The Distribution of Income in China*, London: Macmillan.

Gustafsson, B. and S. Li (2004), "Expenditures on Education and Health Care and Poverty in Rural China," *China Economic Review*, 15(3), 292–301.

Gustafsson, B. and S. Li (2006), "Surveys – Three Ways to Obtain Household Income Data," in M. Heimer and S. Thogersen, eds., *Doing Fieldwork in China*, Copenhagen: NIAS Press.

Hannum, E., J. Behrman, M. Wang, and J. Liu (forthcoming), "Education in the Reform Era," in L. Brandt and T. G. Rawski, eds., *China's Economic Transition: Origins, Mechanisms and Consequences*, New York: Cambridge University Press.

Jalan, J. and M. Ravallion (1998), "Transient Poverty in Postreform Rural China," *Journal of Comparative Economics*, 26(2), 338–357.

Khan, A. R., K. Griffin, C. Riskin, and R. Zhao (1992), "Household Income and Its Distribution in China," *China Quarterly*, 132, 1029–1061.

Khan, A. R. and C. Riskin (1998), "Income and Inequality in China," *China Quarterly*, no. 154, 221–253.

Khan, A. R. and C. Riskin (2001), *Inequality and Poverty in China in the Age of Globalization*, Oxford: Oxford University Press.

Knight, J. and L. Song (1999), *The Rural-Urban Divide: Economic Disparities and Interactions in China*, New York: Oxford University Press.

Li, S. and H. Sato, eds. (2006), *Unemployment, Inequality and Poverty in Urban China*, London: Routledge.

Milanovic, B. (2002), "True World Income Distribution, 1988 and 1993: First Calculation Based on Household Surveys Alone," *Economic Journal*, 112(476), 51–92.

Milanovic, B. (2005), "Can We Discern the Effect of Globalization on Income Distribution? Evidence from Household Surveys," *World Bank Economic Review*, 19(1), 21–44.

Morduch, J. and T. Sicular (2001), "Risk and Insurance in Transition: Evidence from Zouping County, China," in Masahiko Aoki and Yujiro Hayami, eds., *Communities and Markets in Economic Development*, New York: Oxford University Press.

Organisation for Economic Co-operation and Development (OECD) (2004), *Income Disparities in China: An OECD Perspective*, Paris.

Park, A. and S. Wang (2001), "China's Poverty Statistics," *China Economic Review*, 12(4), 384–398.

Ravallion, M. and S. Chen (2007), "China's (Uneven) Progress against Poverty," *Journal of Development Economics*, 82(1), 1–42.

Riskin, C., R. Zhao, and S. Li, eds. (2001), *China's Retreat from Equality: Income Distribution and Economic Transition*, Armonk, NY: M. E. Sharpe.

Sicular, T., X. Yue, B. Gustafsson, and S. Li (2007), "The Urban-Rural Income Gap and Inequality in China," *Review of Income and Wealth*, 53(1), 93–126.

Smeeding, T. M. and D. H. Weinberg (2001), "Toward a Uniform Definition of Household Income," *Review of Income and Wealth*, 47(1), 1–24.

United Nations Development Programme (2005), *China Human Development Report 2005*.

World Bank (2005), *World Development Report 2006*, New York: World Bank and Oxford University Press.

World Institute for Development Economics Research (WIDER) (2005), "World Income and Inequality Database, v. 2.0a: User Guide and Data Sources," June, at www.wider.unu.edu/wiid/wiid.htm.

Wu, X. and J. Perloff (2005), "China's Income Distribution, 1985–2001," *Review of Economics and Statistics*, 87(4), 763–775.

Yao, S. (2000), "Economic Development and Poverty Reduction in China over 20 Years of Reform," *Economic Development and Cultural Change*, 48(3), 447–474.

Zhang, J., Y. Zhao, A. Park, and X. Song (2005), "Economic Returns to Schooling in Urban China," *Journal of Comparative Economics*, 33(4), 730–752.

Zhang, X. and R. Kanbur (2005), "Spatial Inequality in Education and Health Care in China," *China Economic Review*, 16(1), 189–204.

TWO

Income Inequality and Spatial Differences
in China, 1988, 1995, and 2002

Björn Gustafsson, Li Shi, Terry Sicular, and Yue Ximing

I. Introduction

Since the introduction of reforms first in rural areas in the late 1970s and then in urban areas at the beginning of the 1980s, China has moved rapidly toward a market economy. The policy of opening up and marketization has speeded China's economic growth, which was extremely rapid during the 1990s. Growth has been accompanied by China's transformation from a predominantly agrarian economy to an industrial and service-based economy, with a marked increase in urbanization.

Long-run historical examples from the West show that often industrialization goes hand in hand with increased inequality in the distribution of household income, although later this trend reverses (see, e.g., Morrisson 2000). More recently the experiences of countries in Eastern Europe and the former Soviet Union show that the transition from a planned to a market economy is a history of increased income disparities (see, e.g., Milanovic 1998). Thus from different perspectives, rising inequality in China during the 1980s and 1990s was not unexpected.

This chapter presents empirical support for the idea that since the mid-1990s the development of overall income inequality in China has entered a new phase. We show that Lorenz curves and summary measures of income inequality for China as a whole indicate a more or less unchanged inequality in the distribution of income between 1995 and 2002. We also show that this is the net outcome of inequality-increasing and inequality-reducing forces. Urban-rural inequality continued to increase as a proportion of total inequality as it had from 1988 to 1995. In contrast, overall inequality was moderated as economic growth within the eastern region spilled over from the earlier fast-growing provinces to other provinces.

In addition to examining trends in China's overall inequality, in this chapter we analyze spatial aspects of income inequality in China. Our spatial focus is motivated by the common finding in the growing literature on inequality in China that much of China's inequality is associated with geographic differences. In China several features of spatial differences are of interest. Perhaps the first to come to mind is the rural-urban difference. In many parts of the developing world, urban residents on average fare better than their rural counterparts, but in China the urban-rural gap in income has been particularly large. Whereas during the first phase of reform the urban-rural income gap decreased, more recently signs indicate that the gap has widened. One important cause of the large rural-urban divide is China's household registration system, which restricts rural-to-urban migration and thereby limits an important mechanism for income equalization.

Policies of opening up and reform in effect during the 1980s and 1990s have led to increased disparities along a new spatial dimension in China. The move toward a market economy first took place in the East and led to rapid export growth and new investment. Foreign capital and new technology flowed in, accompanied by massive investments in infrastructure. The economy grew more rapidly in the East than in the central and in the western regions of the country. Recent political rhetoric as well as policies introduced at the central level, however, indicate that the preferred scenario now is to narrow the regional dispersion. Policy makers look upon continued widening of inequality between the East, Center, and West as troublesome.

China is a very large country, and policy is made at many territorial levels. Below the central level are (as of 2002) 31 administrative units: provinces, autonomous regions, and large municipalities. The population of those units ranges from less than 3 million to 90 million. Provinces are building blocks when defining the three regions: East, Center, and West. Below the provincial units are smaller administrative units (in rural China prefectures, counties, and villages; in urban China cities at different levels). A disaggregation of China into provinces cuts through the rural-urban divide as each province has rural as well as urban areas.

In this chapter we introduce a framework to disaggregate income inequality in China as a whole into several spatial dimensions. We use four levels in the disaggregation, allowing a rather detailed analysis. Following these disaggregations, we compute the level and composition of inequality using additively decomposable inequality indices. We use data from three years – 1988, 1995, and 2002 – which makes it possible to investigate changes over two subperiods.

Many authors have investigated the contribution of spatial differences to income inequality in China; however, studies using household-level data such as this one are rare. For example, in a survey of 16 studies on spatial income inequality in rural China published since 1991, Gustafsson and Li (2002) noted that only four used household data. None of these four covered large parts of China, and none of them used data collected at different points in time. A recent literature exemplified by Sun and Parikh (2001), Démurger (2001), Zhang and Felmingham (2002), Démurger et al. (2002), Bhalla, Yao, and Zhang (2003), and Fu (2004) examines the contribution of various factors to growth at the provincial level and the extent to which growth in one province spills over to others. The target variable in those studies, however, is an aggregate or macro-income variable, not income measured at the household level.[1]

In the next section we discuss definitions of the spatial levels to be used in the analysis. Section III describes the data and our methodological choices. Section IV reports results on income inequality in China as a whole, in its rural as well as urban parts, and changes over time. In Section V we present findings on how income inequality has developed in the three regions, and in Section VI we present findings breaking down the regions by rural and urban parts. In Section VII we bring the provincial level into the analysis. We conclude in Section VIII with a summary of our findings.

II. Definitions

At the end of the period here studied, the Chinese population numbered almost 1.3 billion persons living in nearly 370 million households. At the first or national level we are interested in income inequality among all these persons.

How to disaggregate this overall inequality along spatial lines is not self-evident. The approach taken here aims to illuminate essential factors that

---

[1] Our approach to spatial disaggregation for China as a whole has two predecessors, both using data for 1988 and 1995, while here we also study 2002. Gustafsson and Li (2001) investigate the importance of the rural-urban income gap and the disparity among the three regions. Unlike this study, theirs does not bring in the provincial level. The present analysis for rural China, however, is not as penetrating as Gustafsson and Li (2002), where rural income inequality was broken down as far as to the county level. Due to changes in the sampling scheme by the NBS, the 2002 samples are no longer representative at the county level.

can be identified using the data we have collected. At the second level, therefore, we disaggregate the population into the three regions that have been commonly identified in the political sphere during transition: the East, Center, and West. Using this breakdown, we decompose income inequality in China as a whole into intraregional income inequality plus interregional income inequality. This decomposition can be expressed mathematically as follows:

$$I(y) = W + B = \sum_{r=1}^{3} s_r I_r(y) + B. \qquad (1)$$

Here subscript i ($i = 1, 2, 3$) is an index for the region, with 1 standing for the West, 2 for the Center, and 3 for the East; s_r and $I_r(y)$ are the population share and inequality index of region r, respectively. The intraregional income inequality, denoted by W in the equation above and usually referred to as within-group inequality, is the weighted sum of the income inequality index measured for each of the three regions. Interregional income inequality, denoted by B and often called between-group inequality, is equal to inequality measured over the mean incomes of the three regions. It reflects inequality arising from differences in mean income levels among the regions.

At the third level we consider the rural-urban division for each region. The inequality index for each of the three regions, then, can be further decomposed into within-region rural income inequality, within-region urban income inequality, and within-region rural-urban income inequality. This can be expressed as

$$I_r(y) = W_r + B_r = \sum_{i=1}^{2} s_{ri} I_{ri}(y) + B_r. \qquad (2)$$

Subscript i ($i = 1, 2$) is an index for rural and urban, with 1 standing for rural and 2 for urban. Thus s_{11} and $I_{11}(y)$ are the population share and inequality index of the rural sector in the West, respectively. Corresponding terms for other regions are defined accordingly. In each of the three regions within-group inequality is the weighted sum of rural and urban inequality, with population shares as weights, while between-group inequality, here measuring within-region rural-urban income inequality, indicates inequality due to differences in mean income between rural and urban areas within the region.

Combining equations (1) and (2), the overall inequality of China can be decomposed in the following way:

$$I(y) = \sum_{r=1}^{3} s_r \left(\sum_{i=1}^{2} s_{ri} I_{ri}(y) + B_r \right) + B$$

$$= \sum_{r=1}^{3} \sum_{i=1}^{2} s_r s_{ri} I_{ri}(y) + \sum_{r=1}^{3} s_r B_r + B. \qquad (3)$$

For region 1, then, the product of s_1 and s_{11} here is the western rural population's share in China's total population. Overall inequality at this level of decomposition contains 16 terms, that is, six terms for population shares, six terms for inequality indices, three terms for between rural-urban inequality with one for each region, and one term for between-region inequality. Between rural-urban inequality in China as a whole can also be expressed as $\sum_{r=1}^{3} s_r B_r$.

At the third level we come to the provinces. In our sample we have rural subsamples in 19 provinces and urban subsamples in 10 provinces. Under this regional breakdown, the inequality index I_{ri} in equation (3) for each of the six provincial groups (rural and urban for each of the three regions) can be further decomposed as

$$I_{ri}(y) = W_{ri} + B_{ri} = \sum_{p=1}^{N} s_{rip} I_{rip}(y) + B_{ri}. \qquad (4)$$

It should be noted that here we make a distinction between rural and urban even for the provinces. Subscript p is an index for province, and the number of provinces, denoted by N in equation (4), differs across rural and urban for each of the three regions.

Substituting equation (4) for $I_{ri}(y)$ in equation (3) and manipulating some terms, we obtain

$$I(y) = \sum_{p=1}^{19} s_{1p} I_{1p}(y) + \sum_{p=1}^{10} s_{2p} I_{2p}(y) + \sum_{r-1}^{3} \sum_{i=1}^{2} s_r B_{ri} + \sum_{r=1}^{3} s_r B_r + B. \qquad (5)$$

In this formula we show the terms for rural and urban provinces separately because of the different number of provinces in our sample for rural and urban areas. We also remove the dimension of regional breakdown for the provincial terms. Here s_{1p} and $I_{1p}(y)$ represent population share in the national total and the level of inequality for the rural sector, respectively, in province p.

The meaning of each of the five terms on the right-hand side of equation (5) is straightforward. The first sum is within-group (or within-province) inequality in rural areas, while the second sum is its counterpart in urban areas. The third sum reflects total inequality among urban provincial groups and rural provincial groups. The last two terms have been introduced above.

The terms obtained in this disaggregation can be used to derive measures of how much of income inequality in rural China is due to differences in mean income among provinces. The procedure we follow is to calculate a weighted sum of the values of the income inequality indices for the provinces, and then take the difference from the income inequality in (total) rural China. Similarly, we can derive a measure of how much of the income inequality in urban China is due to differences in mean income among provinces.

Finally, from our decompositions we can also calculate the proportion of income inequality in China as a whole that is due to differences in income between rural parts of provinces and urban parts of provinces. This is a measure of how much of the income inequality in China as a whole is due to spatial factors. It is a lower-bound estimate, as it does not consider spatial differences in mean income within rural parts of provinces as well as spatial differences within urban parts of provinces. We calculate this proportion by first summing within-province rural income inequality with within-province urban income inequality. The difference with income inequality in China as a whole is due to differences in mean income between rural and urban areas in provinces.

III. Data and Operational Assumptions

The data used for the analysis come from the three waves of the CHIP survey conducted in 1989, 1996, and 2003 for the reference periods 1988, 1995, and 2002. This means that the study covers a period of 14 years of rapid economic growth and can be subdivided into two periods of equal length. More detail about these surveys appears in Chapter 1 and the Appendix.

For this study we use a subsample having the property that each rural province and urban province is present in the survey for all years under investigation. This means that the rural sample covers Anhui, Beijing, Gansu, Guangdong, Guizhou, Hebei, Henen, Hubei, Hunan, Jiangsu, Jiangxi, Jilin, Liaoning, Shandong, Shaanxi, Shanxi, Sichuan, Yunnan, and Zhejiang. The 10 urban provinces are Anhui, Beijing, Gansu, Guangdong, Henan, Hubei, Jiangsu, Liaoning, Sichuan, and Yunnan. Since this study emphasizes the rural-urban divide, not only for China as a whole but also for each of the three regions, we adjust the sample so that the rural-urban weights of the sample equal the population shares within each region. After this adjustment, the sample distribution between the rural and urban areas is consistent with the population distribution between the two areas nationwide.[2]

The target variable for this study is total income calculated as the sum of several components. It covers not only cash income, but also retained in-kind income (rather important in rural China, particularly at the beginning of the period studied) and other income in kind (important in urban China at the beginning of the period). Taxes and fees (on average small) enter with a negative sign.

As discussed in Chapter 1, economists typically believe that a definition of income should include components like subsidies for housing and imputed rents of housing, although they differ on how such components should best be calculated. The National Bureau of Statistics (NBS) does not include these components in its definition of disposable income, a shortcoming we think should be changed. Our estimates of average household income in China are based on the NBS definition but also include housing subsidies and imputed rent, and so mean incomes are higher than those obtained under the NBS definition.

Our analysis uses the household as the income-receiving unit. Disposable income of each household is then divided by the number of household members. Following what is now common practice when analyzing income distributions in the literature on industrialized countries, we assign this value to each member of the household. Individuals are thus the unit of analysis. Using provincial consumer price indices, we express all incomes in 1988 prices.

For our inequality computations we mainly use an index belonging to the generalized entropy family that is additively decomposable, the Mean Logarithmic Deviation (MLD, also known as the Theil L index). It is defined as

$$I(y) = \frac{1}{n} \sum_{i}^{n} \log\left(\frac{\mu}{y_i}\right), \tag{6}$$

where μ is mean income, y_i income of the ith individual, and n the total number of individuals. It can be decomposed as

$$I(y) = \sum_{g}^{k} \frac{n_g}{n} I_g + I(\mu_1 e_1, \ldots, \mu_k e_k), \tag{7}$$

---

[2] We do not make similar population weight adjustments for each sample province, as none of the three waves covers all provinces. This is the case for the rural sample as well as the urban sample.

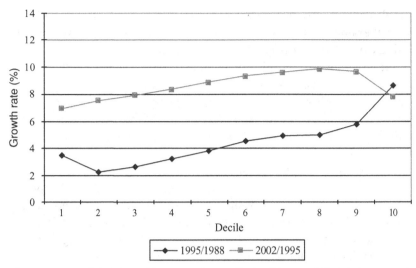

Figure 2.1 Growth in Disposable Income for Deciles in China as a Whole between 1988 and 1995 and between 1995 and 2002.

where n_g is the number of individuals in the gth group, I_g inequality within the gth group, μ_g the mean of the gth group income, and e_g the n_g-vector of ones.

IV. Overall Development

According to our computations, average household income in China as a whole grew rapidly. During the period 1988 to 1995 the annual rate of growth was 5.8 percent, and between 1995 and 2002 it exceeded 8.8 percent. Growth rates of GDP per capita for China as a whole during the same two subperiods were 8.3 percent and 7.2 percent, respectively. Thus the more rapid growth in average household income during the second subperiod is not the consequence of more rapid general growth, but of households on average benefiting more from growth.

Figure 2.1 shows for the first subperiod a clear structure of how growth rates in income differ by decile. The first, or poorest, four deciles had the lowest growth rates, while further up in the income distribution growth rates increased decile by decile. Income for the top decile grew by an impressive 8.6 percent per annum, more than three times the growth rate of the slowest-growing second decile. As a consequence, the Lorenz curve tabulations (Table 2.1) unambiguously indicate more income inequality in 1995 than in 1988. The Gini coefficient rose from 0.395 to 0.469, a rather rapid increase.

The pattern of change during the second subperiod is more complicated. Growth was higher for all deciles with the exception of the top decile.

Table 2.1. *Lorenz curve tabulations and inequality indices for China as a whole, 1988, 1995, and 2002*

	Cumulative percentages of income		
Decile	1988	1995	2002
1	2.12	1.81	1.64
2	5.84	4.73	4.30
3	10.57	8.47	7.84
4	16.26	13.09	12.32
5	23.02	18.79	18.00
6	31.14	25.97	25.42
7	41.34	35.33	35.32
8	54.55	47.86	48.74
9	71.61	65.21	67.02
10	100.00	100.00	100.00
Gini coefficient	0.395	0.469	0.468
MLD	0.280	0.382	0.388
Theil T index	0.267	0.420	0.373
Mean income (yuan)	863	1,294	2,336
(Index)	(100)	(150)	(271)

Note: Mean incomes are in 1988 constant prices. Here and elsewhere, decile 1 is the poorest decile and decile 10 the richest.

Growth has trickled down particularly to deciles 6, 7, 8, and 9. The fastest growth, 9.9 percent per annum, occurred in decile 8, meaning that the income distance to the top decile actually decreased. Thus changes during the second subperiod were both disequalizing and equalizing. As a consequence, the Lorenz curves (Table 2.1) for China as a whole in 1995 and 2002 cross each other. Up until the sixth decile, income in 2002 is more unequally distributed than in 1995, but for the three highest deciles the situation is reversed. Consistent with this, the numerical values of various income inequality indices reported in Table 2.1 do not agree on how to rank inequality between the two years. Although the Theil T index shows decreased income inequality, the Gini coefficient and the MLD index show little change.

Before proceeding further, we comment on our finding of no overall increase in income inequality for China as a whole between 1995 and 2002. This result is at odds with the conventional wisdom that income inequality in China has continued to rise.[3] For example, in the 2002 urban questionnaire

---

[3] For example, Yao et al. (2004) in a study of the development of poverty in China make simulations until 2015. All simulations assume income inequality increases during this period, although the speed of increase varies.

we asked the question "What do you think about income inequality in your city, compared to 1995?" Here we provided the respondent with four choices: (1) reduced, (2) unchanged, (3) increased slightly, or (4) increased notably. In all, 6,823 households answered this question. The proportions of households choosing each of the four choices were 3 percent, 6 percent, 48 percent, and 43 percent, respectively. In other words, more than 90 percent of urban households that responded to this question think that inequality had widened during the prior seven years.

Chapter 1 provides some discussion of why our findings regarding trends in overall inequality differ from the conventional wisdom. To some extent the answer lies in the definition of income. If we use the NBS definition of income, we find increased income inequality, with the Gini coefficient rising from 0.373 in 1988 to 0.436 in 1995 and 0.452 in 2002.[4] Inclusion of subsidies and imputed rents from housing as in our preferred definition changes the picture. When these components are included, income growth at the top of the income distribution does not occur as fast. For all years under study, our definition of disposable income results in a higher level of the Gini coefficient for China as a whole, but the difference in measured inequality between the two definitions narrows over time.

A second explanation could be that changes in income inequality might not take place as smooth trends. During some episodes inequality increases, while during others it remains stable. The NBS has not published a continuous time series for income inequality in China as a whole. Based on tables for rural and urban regions published by the NBS, however, Wu and Perloff (2005) have extracted such a time series for the Gini from 1985 to 2001. Although comparing the first and last year reveals that income inequality was rising, increases did not take place between every pair of years. For example, income inequality in 1998 was almost the same as that in 1993.

A third explanation is that when we discuss income inequality, we follow the mainstream academic thinking about how to conceptualize and operationalize inequality. People might have different concepts in their mind, however, when thinking about income inequality. Economists typically refer to the relative size of the slice, independent of the size of the income cake. Others might take a different view. Take the example of a rapidly growing

---

[4] The NBS has reported a Gini coefficient of 0.341 in 1988, 0.389 in 1995, and 0.417 in 2000 (OECD 2004, p. 20). Wu and Perloff (2005) report a Gini (based on the NBS definition of disposable income) of 0.337 in 1988, 0.382 in 1995, 0.407 in 2000, and 0.415 in 2001. A substantial part, but not all, of the difference in levels between our estimates and the estimates by the NBS and Wu and Perloff (based on the NBS) can thus be attributed to the definition of income.

economy. A constant relative income share means that high-income persons in absolute terms have gained more income than others. Furthermore, it might be that when people think of income inequality, they refer to differences in mean income between different categories or groups: for example, highly educated groups relative to less educated groups. They might pay less attention to inequality within the various groups. As shown in Chapter 4, between 1995 and 2002 China experienced a widening income gap between educational groups.

We now turn to trends in income and income inequality in rural China. Figure 2.2a for the period 1988 to 1995 shows positive but low growth rates of income in deciles 2, 3, and 4, and the highest growth in the top decile. Table 2.2 showing the Lorenz curve computations for 1995 accordingly indicates (with the exception of the first decile) more inequality than in 1988, and the Gini coefficient increased from 0.325 to 0.364. For the period 1995 to 2002, growth rates at the bottom of the distribution caught up with that of the highest decile and were all remarkably similar. The Lorenz curves for rural China in 1995 and 2002 were more or less identical, as were the inequality indices.[5]

Coming to urban China, we find for the subperiod 1988 to 1995 an even clearer structure of the lowest growth rates at the lowest deciles and the highest at the top (Figure 2.2b). Real income of the top decile actually grew more than four times as rapidly as that of the bottom decile. Therefore, the Lorenz curves indicate greater income inequality in 1995 than in 1988, and the Gini coefficient increased from 0.244 to 0.339. Similar to rural China, for urban China we find that the growth rate at the bottom and middle of the distribution gained speed during the second period. Growth at the top was only half as rapid as during the preceding period, and actually lower than for other deciles in the income distribution. The Lorenz curves for urban China in 1995 and 2002 cross. Inequality increases for the first four deciles and decreases for higher deciles. The Gini falls to 0.322, although it remains higher than in 1988.[6]

---

[5] If applying the NBS definition of income, we arrive at estimates of the Gini that are rather close each year and show more or less the same change over time. They are 0.331 in 1988, 0.387 in 1995, and 0.388 in 2002. Compare also with Wu and Perloff (2005), who report very similar Ginis for rural China in 1995 (0.338) and 2001 (0.343). Benjamin et al. (2005) report an increase in rural income inequality from 1995 to 1999 measured by the Gini coefficient based on data from nine provinces.

[6] The latter conclusion is sensitive to the definition of household income. Applying the NBS definition, we arrive at the following Gini coefficients: 0.237 in 1988, 0.284 in 1995, and 0.316 in 2002.

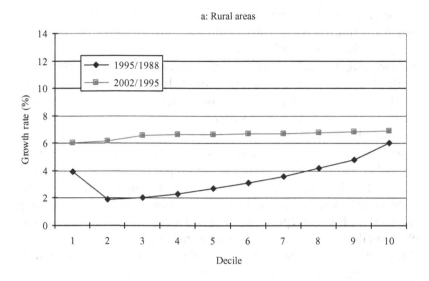

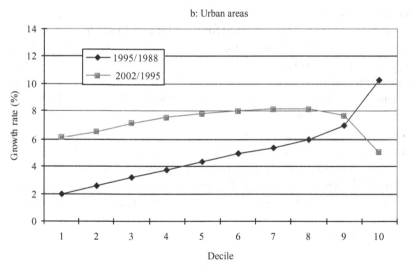

Figure 2.2 Growth in Disposable Income for Deciles in Rural and Urban Areas between 1988 and 1995 and between 1995 and 2002.

Table 2.3 summarizes our findings. Clearly the development of income inequality between 1995 and 2002 is rather different from that between 1988 to 1995. Also, the development of income inequality in China as a whole is somewhat different from that for rural and urban regions, as the increase in overall income inequality from 1988 to 2002 is rather large, while that

Table 2.2. *Lorenz curve tabulations and inequality indices for rural and urban China, 1988, 1995, and 2002*

Decile	Cumulative percentages of income, rural areas			Cumulative percentages of income, urban areas		
	1988	1995	2002	1988	1995	2002
1	2.65	2.69	2.69	4.32	3.20	3.04
2	7.38	6.92	6.85	10.44	7.98	7.63
3	13.28	12.21	12.07	17.45	13.70	13.35
4	20.24	18.45	18.34	25.24	20.31	20.14
5	28.22	25.74	25.69	33.76	27.85	28.06
6	37.30	34.24	34.25	43.04	36.42	37.13
7	47.68	44.23	44.23	53.26	46.15	47.60
8	59.76	56.23	56.25	64.76	57.59	59.90
9	74.70	71.60	71.63	78.43	72.20	75.29
10	100.00	100.00	100.00	100.00	100.00	100.00
Gini coefficient	0.325	0.364	0.365	0.244	0.339	0.322
MLD	0.198	0.224	0.224	0.101	0.196	0.174
Theil T index	0.190	0.237	0.239	0.109	0.250	0.176
Mean income (yuan)	598	806	1,263	1,626	2,486	4,007
(Index)	(100)	(135)	(211)	(100)	(153)	(246)

Note: Mean incomes are in 1988 constant prices.

Table 2.3. *Changes in income inequality in China as a whole, rural China, and urban China, from 1988 to 1995 and 2002*

	1988–1995	1995–2002	1988–2002
China as a whole	++	+−	++
Rural	+	0	+
Urban	++	−	+

Note: + indicates increased income inequality; 0 indicates unchanged income inequality; ++ indicates rapidly increased income inequality; − indicates decreased income inequality; + − indicates increased inequality in some parts of the distribution, decreased income inequality in other parts of the distribution.

for the rural and urban regions separately is more moderate. Reasons for this discrepancy will be further explored below.

V. The Regional Dimension

For the period 1988 to 1995 there is a very clear pattern of increased income inequality in the eastern region of China. Figure 2.3 shows that income

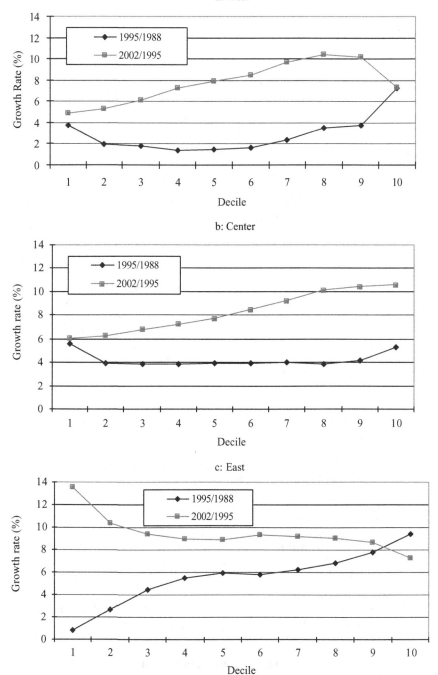

Figure 2.3a, b, and c. Growth in Disposable Income for Deciles in (a) West, (b) Center, and (c) East China between 1988 and 1995 and between 1995 and 2002.

Table 2.4. *Mean incomes and inequality indices for East, Center, and West China, 1988, 1995, and 2002*

	1988	1995	2002
West			
Gini coefficient	0.405	0.472	0.478
MLD	0.279	0.512	0.389
Theil T index	0.290	0.380	0.395
Mean income (yuan)	667	907	1,596
(Index)	(100)	(136)	(239)
Center			
Gini coefficient	0.342	0.363	0.411
MLD	0.198	0.225	0.283
Theil T index	0.210	0.219	0.285
Mean income (yuan)	728	989	1,845
(Index)	(100)	(136)	(253)
East			
Gini coefficient	0.375	0.455	0.431
MLD	0.241	0.374	0.309
Theil T index	0.257	0.385	0.331
Mean income (yuan)	1,150	1,863	3,332
(Index)	(100)	(162)	(290)

Note: Mean incomes are in 1988 constant prices.

growth was rather slow at the bottom of the income distribution, and increasing as one moved up the decile ladder. Income growth for the top decile was 11 times as rapid as for the bottom decile, and the Gini coefficient rose from 0.375 to 0.455 (Table 2.4). For the second subperiod, however, the pattern is totally reversed. Economic growth trickled down, and growth rates at the bottom of the distribution were the highest. Income of the poorest decile grew by an impressive 14 percent per annum. Income inequality in the eastern regions thus fell during the period from 1995 to 2002, although the fall was not as rapid as the preceding increase. The Gini coefficient went down to 0.431.

The development of income and income inequality in the central region shows a somewhat different pattern. Growth was slower in the central than in the eastern region during the first subperiod, especially at the top of the income distribution. Overall inequality increased, but only slightly. This pattern changed completely in the second subperiod, when growth gained speed, particularly at the top of the distribution. The top decile's income grew by an impressive 11 percent per annum and income inequality within the

Table 2.5. *Between-region income inequality and regional income differences,*
1988, 1995, and 2002

Year	Between-region inequality as percentage of total income inequality (as measured by MLD)	Ratio of mean income in the East to mean income in the West	Ratio of mean income in the Center to mean income in the West
1988	10.5	1.70	1.08
1995	14.2	2.07	1.10
2002	13.9	2.09	1.16

central region increased rapidly. The Gini coefficient rose to 0.411, ap-proaching that in the eastern region (Table 2.4).

The western region has the greatest income inequality of all three regions. The proportion of total income accruing to the top decile is higher than that in the two other regions for all years under study. During the first subperiod growth for deciles 2 to 6 was slow, below 2 percent per annum, while income for the top decile grew by 7 percent per annum. Income inequality increased rapidly. Growth accelerated for all deciles during the second period, with growth at the top decile as the exception. Particularly high growth rates of 10 percent per annum are observed for deciles 8 and 9. This growth pattern implies that the Lorenz curves for 1995 and 2002 cross. For the first seven deciles inequality increases, while for higher deciles inequality declines. Consistent with this, inequality indices give different rankings for the two distributions.

What do these regional patterns of change imply for changes in income inequality in China as a whole? To answer this question, we also need to look at the size of between-region inequality. Table 2.5 shows the magnitude of between-region inequality expressed as a percentage of total inequality. In 1988 one-tenth of income inequality in China as a whole was due to differences in mean incomes among the three regions, but this proportion increased to 14 percent in 1995. The widening regional dispersion is one reason why income inequality in China as a whole increased from 1988 to 1995. During the first period, average income in eastern China increased from 170 percent to 207 percent of that in western China. During the second period, however, changes in the regional income gap were marginal.

We summarize the findings on changes in income inequality at the regional level in Table 2.6. While the development in each region as well as the difference in mean income among regions all led to increased income inequality from 1988 to 1995, the pattern of change from 1995 to 2002 is

Table 2.6. *Decomposing changes in income inequality by region*

Region	1995/1988	2002/1995	2002/1988
East	++	−	+
Center	+	+	++
West	++	+−	++
Between-region component	+	0	+
China as a whole	++	+−	++

Note: + indicates increased income inequality; 0 indicates unchanged income inequality; ++ indicates rapidly increased income inequality; − indicates decreased income inequality; + − indicates increased inequality in some parts of the distribution, decreased income inequality in other parts of the distribution.

much different. Only in the central region did the development toward increased income inequality continue. Changes in the western region vary across different parts of the income distribution. The gaps among regional mean incomes remained more or less constant. In the East, income inequality decreased. The trends from 1988 to 1995, however, were strong enough that trends between 1995 and 2002 were insufficient to reduce income inequality for each region compared to 1988.

VI. The Rural-Urban Dimension

It is well known that the rural-urban dimension plays an important role in income inequality in China. Results reported in this section confirm this. We will also show that during the period studied here an increasing share of inequality in China as a whole can be attributed to the rural-urban dimension. The accounting framework presented in Section II makes it straightforward to compute the proportion of total income inequality in China as a whole that is due to the urban-rural income divide. Changes over time in the urban-rural share of inequality are due not only to widening of the urban-rural income gap, but also to changing population weights for rural and urban regions as well as changes in inequality within both rural and urban areas.

A striking change in China during the period here studied is the dramatic increase in urbanization. The exact speed is not measured very accurately, as the definition of urban areas has changed and become more similar to that used in other countries (Chan and Hu 2003). According to official definitions, the urban population increased from 286.6 million in 1988 to 351.7 million in 1995 and 502.1 million in 2002. During the same years, the

Table 2.7. *Urbanization and the urban-rural income gap in the three regions of China, 1988, 1995, and 2002*

Region	1988	1995	2002
Urbanization – share of population in urban areas			
West	21.0	25.1	32.4
Center	24.3	26.1	36.0
East	31.1	34.7	46.9
China as a whole	25.8	29.1	39.1
Urban-rural income ratio			
West	3.34	4.30	4.41
Center	2.45	2.49	2.87
East	2.35	2.69	2.50
China as a whole	2.69	3.08	3.13

Note: Data on urban population shares by region are not available for 1988, so here we show data for 1987. In some years the NBS numbers for the total national population do not equal the sum of the provincial-level populations. In such cases we assume that the national urbanization shares are correct, and we scale up the provincial data so that they are consistent with the national shares. That is, we calculate each province's share of the national urban population as the provincial urban population divided by the sum of the provincial urban populations. To obtain the estimated size of the urban population for each province, we then multiply this provincial urban population share by the national urban population. The regional urbanization numbers in this table are calculated using these estimates of the provincial urban populations.

Source: Urbanization shares for 1988 (1987) are from NBS (1988), for 1995 from NBS (1996), and for 2002 from NBS (2003). Income ratios are calculated using the survey data.

rural population numbered 823.7 million in 1988 and 859.5 million in 1995, but fell to 782.4 million in 2002. The urbanization rate thus increased from 26 percent in 1988 to 39 percent in 2002. The urban share of population is highest in the prosperous eastern region and lowest in the relatively poor western region (Table 2.7). While as few as one out of five lived in urban areas in the West in 1988, in 2002 almost one in two in the eastern region lived in urban areas.[7]

---

[7] One consequence of the rapid urbanization in combination with the widening urban-rural income gap is that mean income in China as whole has increased more rapidly than mean income in rural China and mean income in urban China. The development of per capita income during the period from 1988 to 2002 shows that this is not a trivial effect. During this period rural per capita income grew by 5.3 percent per annum and urban per capita income by 6.5 percent. Per capita income for China as a whole grew by 7.1 percent.

Table 2.8. *Decomposition of income inequality in China along the urban-rural dimension, 1988, 1995, and 2002, using the MLD index*

Contributor to proportion of national income inequality	1988	1995	2002
Rural inequality (%)	53.8	43.7	36.1
Urban inequality (%)	9.7	15.3	17.8
Inequality between urban and rural areas (%)	36.5	41.0	46.1
Total (%)	100	100	100
National MLD index	0.274	0.363	0.377
Proportion of income inequality within regions due to inequality between urban and rural areas			
West (%)	50	62	63
Central (%)	40	48	52
East (%)	33	37	41
West MLD index	0.279	0.512	0.389
Central MLD index	0.198	0.225	0.283
East MLD index	0.241	0.374	0.309

The growth rates reported in Section IV were, with a few exceptions, higher for urban than for rural incomes. The urban-rural income divide increased. Table 2.7 provides further information on this divide for the three regions. The largest urban-rural income gap is found in the western region. Our data show that average urban income in the West is actually slightly higher than that in central China, while average rural income in the West is clearly lower than that in the other two regions. During the first subperiod the urban-rural income gap increased rapidly in the West. The increase in the eastern region was small and followed by a slight decrease during the second subperiod. The increase in the urban-rural income gap in the central region took place during the second subperiod. Putting the regions together we find an increase in the urban-rural income gap for China as a whole from 2.7 in 1988 to 3.1 in 1995, after which it remained relatively stable through 2002.

How much of income inequality in China as a whole is due to rural income inequality, urban income inequality, and rural-to-urban inequality? Table 2.8 shows that the proportion of income inequality attributable to rural inequality diminished from slightly more than half in 1988 to slightly more than one-third in 2002. Opposing this trend are increases in the contributions of urban inequality and inequality between rural and urban areas. The latter component increased from 37 percent in 1988 to 46 percent in 2002. Such a trend also can be seen in each of the three regions. The contribution

Table 2.9. *Percentage of inequality in various rural and urban regions of China due to between-province inequality, 1988, 1995, and 2002*

Region	1988	1995	2002
Rural China			
West	3	5	13
Center	5	6	3
East	11	27	14
Rural China as a whole	22	39	39
Urban China			
West	2	1	5
Center	4	3	1
East	32	25	13
Urban China as a whole	29	26	19

of rural-urban inequality is highest in the western region, where in 2002 it contributed as much as three-fifths of within-region income inequality. Its contribution is lowest (although not trivial) in the eastern region, where in 2002 it stands at two-fifths of regional income inequality.

These trends in urban-rural income inequality are useful for understanding the reasons why income inequality has changed in the various regions during the two subperiods. These trends help explain why income inequality in the western as well as the eastern region of China increased from 1988 to 1995, and why this was also the case in central China from 1995 to 2002. They cannot, however, explain why income inequality in eastern China decreased from 1995 to 2002, a topic we address in the next section when we analyze inequality at the provincial level.

VII. The Provincial Dimension

The provincial dimension provides some additional insights. Results presented in Table 2.9 indicate that differences in mean income among provinces in the central region are of rather limited importance for income inequality in the region; this is also the case for urban parts of the western region.[8] The

---

[8] The number of provinces in the western region is smaller than that in the other regions in our sample. If our sample had covered more provinces in the western region, the between-province component might have been larger than that reported here.

situation is different in eastern China, where changes over time also deserve comment.

Between-province income inequality in the urban East decreased as a proportion of regional inequality between each pair of years, signaling convergence in mean provincial income. For the rural East the first subperiod shows signs of divergence and the second subperiod shows convergence. Taken together, these results imply that convergence in provincial mean incomes in the East has contributed to the decline of inequality in the eastern region during the second subperiod.

Looking at the data reported in Tables 2.A1 and 2.A2 for single provinces, we find that this convergence in mean income from 1995 to 2002 in rural eastern China is due to very rapid income growth in Zhejiang and Shandong, while growth in the most prosperous Beijing and Guangdong was more modest. Also, in the urban sample, income growth in Beijing and Guangdong was slower than that in other provinces in the East. Thus, there is evidence of income growth spilling over from the earlier, fast-growing, and most prosperous provinces to other provinces in the eastern region.

Table 2.9 shows that for rural China and urban China, considerable proportions of income inequality are due to differences in mean income among provinces. As much as one-fifth of income inequality in all of urban China in 2002 is due to differences in mean income among provinces. For rural China the corresponding proportion is twice as high. These shares declined in urban China during the period studied here, while in rural China they increased and then stabilized.[9]

At the provincial level in our sample, the highest mean income observed is for urban Guangdong and the lowest for rural Guizhou. In 1988 the relation between these two means was 6.1:1. Although mean income in rural Guizhou increased in 1995, the increase in urban Guangdong was much more rapid, and so the ratio of their means increased to 11.5:1. This ratio remained fairly constant in 2002 at 11.9:1. Compared to similar comparisons in developed countries, these disparities are very large.[10]

---

[9] In a supplementary analysis, we estimated for rural China and for urban China changes in mean provincial income as a function of mean income during a base year. For rural China we found no relation to be statistically significant at the 10 percent level. For urban China we found that mean provincial income in 1995 was statistically positively (at the 1 percent level) related to mean income in 1988. In contrast, income changes from 1995 to 2002 were negatively related (at the 5 percent level) to mean income in 1995.

[10] For example, in a recent study covering 81 regions in 12 EU countries in 1998, Förster (2004) reports the extremes to be not more than 1:3.1 (between Madeira and Ile-de-France).

Finally, the proportion of inequality in China as a whole that was due to differences in mean income across rural and urban areas in each of the provinces was very large. The proportions were 50 percent in 1988, 63 percent in 1995, and 62 percent in 2002. Thus more than three-fifths of income inequality in China is spatial.

VIII. Summary and Conclusions

In this chapter we have analyzed income inequality in China using household data for 1988, 1995, and 2002, with a focus on spatial differences. We have presented results for China as a whole, rural China, and urban China, as well as for the three regions of eastern, central, and western China. We have further disaggregated each of these regions, as well as each of the provinces, into their rural and urban parts. The results from this exercise confirm that income disparities in China are strongly related to geographic location.

The results confirm previous research showing that the period from 1988 to 1995 was a period of rapidly increasing income inequality, and that income inequality increased along many spatial dimensions. For China as a whole, however, the extent of income inequality in 2002 was remarkably similar to that in 1995. This is consistent with the fact that while average income in the East grew more rapidly than that in the other two regions from 1988 to 1995, thereafter average income grew by approximately the same pace in all three regions of China. For policy makers concerned with regional income differences, this is both good and bad news. The gaps in income between the West, Center, and East did not widen from 1995 to 2002; however, neither did they shrink.

The stability in inequality between 1995 and 2002 for China as a whole hides opposing changes. Larger and larger proportions of income inequality in China as a whole were found to be due to inequality between urban and rural China. The rural-urban income divide has continued to grow mainly because of developments in the central region of China. According to our estimates, as much as 46 percent of income inequality in China as a whole in 2002 would vanish if mean income in rural China were the same as that in urban China. This should put the narrowing of the urban-rural income gap at the top of the policy agenda. The rural-urban income gap is larger in the western region than in the central or eastern regions, making efforts to increase rural income in that region particularly important.

Would easing restrictions on rural-to-urban migration lead to less income inequality in China as a whole? The answer is not self-evident. On the one hand, facilitating rural movement to urban China would put pressure on urban earnings and decrease the oversupply of labor in rural areas. These forces would tend to reduce the urban-rural income gap and thereby reduce income inequality in China as a whole. On the other hand, urbanization means that more people will be at the top of the distribution of income for China as a whole. The net result on income inequality is unclear. Increased migration might also increase inequality in urban areas and create tensions between incoming migrants and urban residents. In this regard also, accelerated urbanization will lead to an increased demand for housing. Housing prices will go up more rapidly, leading to capital gains for the already better-off urban residents. Increased population in existing cities will create pressure on communications and the urban environment, making such movement less attractive.

A force contributing to decreased income inequality in China from 1995 to 2002 was the comparatively slow growth in income for the richest in the urban distribution. Also, inequality in mean household income among provinces, in both rural and urban areas, in the eastern region of China diminished. Income growth in the most prosperous provinces in the East has thus spilled over to other provinces in that region, and the distribution of income at the household level in the eastern region is less unequal in 2002 than in 1995. The decline in inequality observed in eastern China is consistent with the historical experience of other countries as they have become more spatially integrated during the process of economic development.

What does the existence of inequality-reducing forces mean for the future development of income inequality in China? One can think of different scenarios. If spatial differences in mean income decline sufficiently, inequality in China as a whole could possibly decrease in the future. In that case China would have reached the top of the Kuznets curve at the end of the millennium and has now begun moving along the downward slope. Another scenario, however, is that the years from 1995 to 2002 represent only a temporary halt in a development toward ever larger income differences. In that case, forces toward increased inequality will be strong enough to make China even more unequal in the future. It is very much an open question which of these scenarios will be realized.

Appendix Table 2A.1. *Income per capita and its growth rate by province and urban/rural*

Region	Urban or rural[a]	Province	Income per capita (1988 constant prices)			Growth rate of income per capita (% per annum)		
			1998	1995	2002	1988–1995	1995–2002	1988–2002
West	0	Sichuan	471.5	557.5	957.5	2.42	8.03	5.19
	0	Guizhou	440.7	426.0	558.4	−0.48	3.94	1.70
	0	Yunnan	458.4	497.7	631.2	1.18	3.45	2.31
	0	Shaanxi	435.6	479.2	719.9	1.37	5.99	3.65
	0	Gansu	348.9	434.8	666.0	3.19	6.28	4.73
	1	Yunnan	1,442.6	2,017.0	3,692.4	4.91	9.02	6.94
	1	Gansu	1,631.9	2,324.4	2,936.2	5.18	3.39	4.28
Center	0	Shanxi	488.2	588.8	1,040.8	2.71	8.48	5.56
	0	Jilin	721.7	775.5	1,249.8	1.03	7.05	4.00
	0	Anhui	538.9	634.7	970.2	2.37	6.25	4.29
	0	Jiangxi	540.5	762.4	1,135.8	5.04	5.86	5.45
	0	Henan	460.4	834.9	1,187.0	8.88	5.16	7.00
	0	Hubei	550.0	645.0	1,079.6	2.30	7.64	4.94
	0	Hunan	581.5	655.7	1,009.2	1.73	6.35	4.02
	1	Shanxi	1,208.7	1,554.3	2,950.1	3.66	9.59	6.58
	1	Anhui	1,342.9	1,871.7	3,090.1	4.86	7.42	6.13
	1	Henan	1,251.3	1,779.3	3,451.1	5.16	9.93	7.52
	1	Hubei	1,478.3	1,906.2	3,157.6	3.70	7.48	5.57
East	0	Beijing	1,045.9	1,670.1	1,768.0	6.91	0.82	3.82
	0	Hebei	610.9	903.4	1,563.1	5.75	8.15	6.94
	0	Liaoning	793.4	743.6	1,353.6	−0.92	8.93	3.89
	0	Jiangsu	849.0	1,563.3	2,332.2	9.11	5.88	7.48
	0	Zhejiang	1,127.6	1,300.3	2,634.3	2.06	10.61	6.25
	0	Shandong	649.1	662.6	1,499.2	0.29	12.37	6.16
	0	Guangdong	922.9	1,748.1	2,254.0	9.55	3.70	6.59
	1	Beijing	1,991.0	3,451.3	4,886.8	8.18	5.09	6.62
	1	Liaoning	1,517.2	2,371.4	3,983.5	6.59	7.69	7.14
	1	Jiangsu	1,503.9	2,433.8	4,264.5	7.12	8.34	7.73
	1	Guangdong	2,653.7	4,841.0	6,746.7	8.97	4.86	6.89

Note: a. 0 for rural and 1 for urban.

Appendix Table 2A.2. *MLD indexes and population shares by province*

Region	Urban or rural[a]	Province	MLD 1988	MLD 1995	MLD 2002	Provincial shares of total population (%)[b] 1988	1995	2002
West	0	Sichuan	0.119	0.106	0.105	11.51	9.50	6.25
	0	Guizhou	0.142	0.109	0.144	3.07	3.05	3.24
	0	Yunnan	0.137	0.157	0.135	3.73	3.93	3.80
	0	Shaanxi	0.137	0.096	0.144	3.02	2.90	2.98
	0	Gansu	0.131	0.147	0.178	2.30	2.14	2.28
	1	Yunnan	0.070	0.085	0.108	0.90	0.65	1.28
	1	Gansu	0.085	0.439	0.113	0.50	0.66	0.77
Center	0	Shanxi	0.334	0.133	0.129	2.07	2.47	2.45
	0	Jilin	0.111	0.175	0.138	1.00	1.51	1.48
	0	Anhui	0.094	0.084	0.111	5.69	5.58	5.23
	0	Jiangxi	0.094	0.086	0.132	3.86	3.82	3.05
	0	Henan	0.127	0.093	0.113	9.42	8.87	8.33
	0	Hubei	0.079	0.143	0.147	4.55	4.55	4.21
	0	Hunan	0.129	0.123	0.167	6.35	5.65	5.31
	1	Shanxi	0.089	0.111	0.168	1.16	1.08	1.44
	1	Anhui	0.096	0.083	0.131	1.30	1.35	2.28
	1	Henan	0.071	0.136	0.144	1.44	1.59	2.99
	1	Hubei	0.051	0.099	0.107	1.80	2.11	2.88
East	0	Beijing	0.189	0.120	0.210	0.52	0.43	0.28
	0	Hebei	0.214	0.137	0.156	5.55	6.16	5.96
	0	Liaoning	0.202	0.133	0.191	2.04	2.53	2.40
	0	Jiangsu	0.200	0.158	0.161	6.73	5.89	4.69
	0	Zhejiang	0.137	0.146	0.230	3.30	3.34	2.85
	0	Shandong	0.159	0.332	0.188	5.32	6.80	6.31
	0	Guangdong	0.229	0.179	0.166	7.02	4.77	4.55
	1	Beijing	0.062	0.117	0.133	0.56	1.03	1.38
	1	Liaoning	0.037	0.180	0.123	2.14	2.21	2.59
	1	Jiangsu	0.049	0.092	0.153	1.62	2.26	4.06
	1	Guangdong	0.120	0.163	0.173	1.54	3.16	4.70

Notes:
a. 0 for rural and 1 for urban.
b. Sum of provincial shares of population is scaled up to 100.

References

Benjamin, D., L. Brandt, and J. Giles (2005), "The Evolution of Income Inequality in Rural China," *Economic Development and Cultural Change,* 53(4), 769–824.

Bhalla, A., S. Yao, and A. Zhang (2003), "Regional Economic Performance in China," *Economics of Transition,* 11(1), 25–39.

Chan, K. W. and Y. Hu (2003), "Urbanization in China in the 1990s: New Definition, Different Series, and Revised Trends," *China Review,* 3(2), 49–71.

Démurger, S. (2001), "Institutional Development and Economic Growth: An Explanation for Regional Disparities in China," *Journal of Comparative Economics,* 29(1), 95–117.

Démurger, S., J. Sachs, W. T. Woo, S. Gao, and G. Chang (2002), "The Relative Contribution of Location and Preferential Policies in China's Regional Development: Being in the Right Place and Having the Right Incentives," *China Economic Review,* 13(4), 444–465.

Förster, M. (2004), "The Distribution of Income in Different Regions of the European Union," in OECD, *Income Disparities in China: An OECD Perspective,* China in the Global Economy, Paris.

Fu, X. (2004), "Limited Linkages from Growth Engines and Regional Disparities in China," *Journal of Comparative Economics,* 32(1), 148–164.

Gustafsson, B. and S. Li (2001), "A More Unequal China? Aspects of Inequality in the Distribution of Equivalent Income," in C. Riskin, R. Zhao, and S. Li, eds., *China's Retreat from Equality: Income Distribution and Economic Transition,* Armonk, NY: M. E. Sharpe.

Gustafsson, B. and S. Li (2002), "Income Inequality within and across Counties in Rural China 1988 and 1995," *Journal of Development Economics,* 69(1), 179–204.

Khan, A. R., K. Griffin, C. Riskin, and R. Zhao (1993), "Household Income and Its Distribution in China," in K. Griffin, and R. Zhao, eds., *The Distribution of Income in China,* Houndsmills, England: Macmillan.

Milanovic, B. (1998), *Income, Inequality, and Poverty during the Transition from Planned to Market Economy,* Washington, D.C.: World Bank.

Morrisson, C. (2000), "Historical Perspectives on Income Distribution: The Case of Europe," in A. B. Atkinson and F. Bourguignon, eds., *Handbook of Income Distribution,* vol. 1, Handbooks in Economics 16, Amsterdam: Elsevier North Holland.

National Bureau of Statistics (1988), *Zhongguo 1987 Nian 1% Renkou Chouyang Diaocha Ziliao: Quanguo Fence,* Beijing: China Statistics Press.

National Bureau of Statistics (1996), *Zhongguo Renkou Tongji Nianjian 1996,* Beijing: China Statistics Press.

National Bureau of Statistics (2003), *Zhongguo Renkou Tongji Nianjian 2003,* Beijing: China Statistics Press.

OECD (2004), *Income Disparities in China: An OECD Perspective,* China in the Global Economy, Paris.

Sun, H. and A. Parikh (2001), "Exports, Inward Foreign Direct Investment (FDI) and Regional Economic Growth in China," *Regional Studies,* 35(3), 187–196.

Wu, X. and J. Perloff (2005), "China's Income Distribution 1985–2001," *Review of Economics and Statistics,* 87 (4), 763–775.

Yao, S., Z. Zhang, and L. Hammer (2004), "Growing Inequality and Poverty in China," *China Economic Review,* 15(2), 145–163.

Zhang, Q. and B. Felmingham (2002), "The Role of FDI, Exports and Spillover Effects in the Regional Development of China," *Journal of Development Studies,* 38(4), 157–178.

THREE

Growth and Distribution of Household Income in China between 1995 and 2002

Azizur Rahman Khan and Carl Riskin

I. Introduction

This chapter presents a broad overview of income and its distribution in China based on the findings of the CHIP survey of households for 2002 and compares them with the findings of the earlier CHIP surveys of 1995 and 1988.[1] The present survey, like its predecessors, has generated some surprises. Chief among them is the finding that, contrary to expectations, income inequality actually declined somewhat between 1995 and 2002 in both city and countryside, taken separately. Due to a still-expanding gap between average urban and average rural incomes, however, the Gini ratio for urban and rural income taken together remained unchanged from 1995.

This third round of the CHIP survey in 2002 was the first time that a separate survey of migrant households was carried out. This provides an opportunity for the first time to get a more comprehensive picture of income and its distribution in urban China and China as a whole including the migrant population in urban areas. We find that migration had definite effects on income distribution, increasing urban inequality but slightly

---

[1] An independent international group of economists, in collaboration with the Economics Institute of the Chinese Academy of Social Sciences (CASS), first instituted a household survey in 1988 to estimate income and its distribution, in order to get around the problem that official data on household income were available only for highly aggregated groups, not individual households, and that the income definition underlying the official data suffered from numerous deficiencies. The survey was repeated in 1995 and, most recently, in 2002.

The authors wish to thank Sucharita Sinha and Edward Levine, who did almost all the programming and computations; Qin Gao, who did some supplementary computations and helped interpret results; and Li Shi, Yue Ximing, Wei Zhong, and Deng Quheng of the Economics Institute of the Chinese Academy of Social Sciences, who helped clarify many issues. Anil Deolalikar, Gus Edgren, Keith Griffin, and Dorothy Solinger gave very useful suggestions, as did the editors of this volume.

reducing inequality in the overall national distribution of income, and that it helped ease the problem of rural poverty. Continued improvement in rural income distribution is likely to require a combination of policies, including improvement in farm factor productivity, promotion of nonfarm activities in the countryside while improving access of the poor to them, and continuing support for an orderly outflow of rural labor.

The CHIP surveys still remain the only source of household-level data on income and other individual and household characteristics covering most of China. They also provide the only comprehensive database for the application of an income definition that helps overcome the limitations of the official definition that underlies the published income data in China. Our purpose has consistently been to construct household income using a definition that accords as closely as possible with standard international practice, irrespective of the definition used by the National Bureau of Statistics (NBS).[2] We then compare our estimates with those of the NBS and try to analyze the reasons for differences.

Our conclusion that income inequality decreased within the urban and within the rural populations is at odds with the finding of some other studies that inequality continued to increase.[3] Our study differs from such other studies in both methodology and data. We use original household-level data and build our income variable based on our reconstruction of the standard international definition. The others use tabulated official income data as released by the NBS. Perhaps the gold standard for such work is that of Ravallion and Chen (2007). Their study incorporates differences between urban and rural costs of living (COL) going back to 1980. Taking the COL difference into account, they find no trend in the ratio of average urban to rural income between 1980 and 1995. Moreover, they find income inequality rising within both the urban and rural populations between 1995 and 2001.

However, the foundation of our results in the use of disaggregated, household-level data and a definition of income as close as possible to the standard international concept gives them a claim to special attention. For instance, the NBS's exclusion of the imputed rental value of owner-occupied housing, whose share of income grew sharply and the inequality of whose distribution fell sharply, undoubtedly biases estimates of inequality, including of urban-rural inequality, based on the NBS data.[4]

---

[2] These issues have been discussed in detail in the published results of the 1988 and 1995 CHIP surveys. See, e.g., Khan et al. (1992) and Khan and Riskin (1998).

[3] See, e.g., Wu and Perloff (2005); Ravallion and Chen (2007).

[4] See also Section VII of this chapter.

This chapter will focus on an analysis of the change between 1995 and 2002. References to the year 1988 will be made to compare changes between 1995 and 2002 with the corresponding changes between 1988 and 2002. The details of the three surveys and their respective coverage are discussed in the Appendix of this book.

II. Rural Income and Its Distribution

A. The Level, Composition, and Sources of Growth of Income

Table 3.1 shows per capita household (personal) income, as defined by us, estimated from the household survey data, as well as its classification into sources of income. It also shows the corresponding estimates from our 1995 survey.

As in the case of the surveys of 1988 and 1995, the income estimate based on our definition and the survey data is higher than the official estimate by the National Bureau of Statistics, formerly the State Statistical Bureau

Table 3.1. *Per capita disposable rural income (current yuan per year)*

Source	1995		2002		Annual real growth rate
	Amount	Percentage	Amount	Percentage	
Individual wages	516.78	22.38	1,017.88	30.82	8.94
Net farm income	1,072.15	46.44	1,261.74	38.21	1.21
Net income from household nonfarm activities	224.08	9.71	382.61	11.59	6.74
Property income	9.98	0.43	19.54	0.59	8.85
Rental value of owned housing	267.93	11.61	445.97	13.50	6.35
Net subsidies from the state and collective	−10.99	−0.48	−85.52	−2.59	32.56
Other income including private transfers	228.70	9.91	260.21	7.88	0.72
Total	2,308.63	100.00	3,302.43	100.00	4.07
Memo item: Receipts from enterprises	139.89	6.06	2.91	0.09	−43.13

Note: The growth rate in "net subsidies" is actually the growth rate in net taxes because net subsidies are a negative amount.

Table 3.2. *Contribution of different sources to rural income growth (%)*

	Incremental share	Annual growth
Wages	50.4	8.9
Farm income	19.1	1.2
Nonfarm enterprises	16.0	6.7
Property and house ownership	18.9	6.8
Net subsidies	−7.5	32.7
Miscellaneous	3.2	0.7

Note: Net subsidies were negative in the benchmark year. Their positive growth rate indicates that their value became more negative.

(SSB), based on their definition and survey. But the difference for 2002 is lower than it was for 1995 or 1988. The NBS estimate of per capita income for 2002 is 2,475.60 yuan. The difference between our income estimate and the NBS estimate is thus 33 percent for 2002, as compared to 46 percent for 1995 and 39 percent for 1988, in each case our estimate being larger than the official estimate.

One of the consequences of the fall in the ratio of our survey income and the NBS income between 1995 and 2002 is that the rate of increase in real income between 1995 and 2002 is lower according to our estimate than according to the NBS. Using the percentage change in the rural consumer price index of the NBS between 1995 and 2002 – 8.17 percent – as the deflator, the annual growth rate in real per capita rural income is 5.47 percent according to the NBS estimates and 4.07 percent according to our survey estimates.[5]

There have been major changes in the composition of rural income between 1995 and 2002 because of different rates of growth of different sources of income (Table 3.2).[6] Wages were the fastest growing component of income, so that the proportion of income contributed by wages increased sharply. Wages accounted for more than half of the incremental income between the two surveys. This was because of a relatively rapid rate

[5] Note that the growth rate according to the survey estimates would rise to 5 percent if "net individual income from enterprises other than compensation for labor" – an element suspected to have been illegitimately included in the 1995 survey – is excluded from the income estimate for 1995. Space limitations prevent a detailed discussion of these measurement issues.

[6] In view of the fall of "receipts from enterprises" to an insignificant level in 2002, this is abolished as an independent category although retained as a memo item in Table 3.1. This component is now added together with the residual "other income" category.

of growth in rural employment, of which the largest component, employment in family farms, appears to have declined modestly over the period. Per capita rural employment, however, increased by as much as 11 percent[7] because of a decline in the absolute size of the rural population. The year 1995 marks a watershed in China's demographic transition in that the absolute size of the rural population peaked in that year and started declining rapidly thereafter, the annual rate of decline until 2002 being 1.33 percent.

More remarkable, and helpful in explaining the sharp rise in wage income, is the increase in nonfarm wage employment. After several years of stagnation, employment in township and village enterprises (TVEs) started increasing in the late 1990s. Private wage employment in rural China, still a small component of total employment, increased at an extraordinarily rapid annual rate of 17 percent. Together these sources of wage employment increased by 21 percent on a per capita basis over the period.[8] In line with the increase in nonfarm wage employment there was a fairly rapid increase in income from nonfarm enterprises.

Income from family farming (together with income from property and home ownership) constitutes the second largest share of incremental income. The annual rate of growth of this source of income was very small, however. This deserves a closer look. Per capita real agricultural value added, defined as value added in agriculture at constant prices divided by the rural population, increased at an annual rate of 4.7 percent, representing a 3.3 percent growth in real value added in agriculture and a negative 1.33 percent growth in the rural population.[9] Per capita real personal income of rural households from farming, however, increased at only 1.2 percent per year. This suggests a decline in agriculture's terms of trade over the period under review.[10] Note that the meager increase in per capita income from farming, after the erosion due to the decline in the terms of trade, was made possible by the fall in the rural population. With an unchanged or increasing population,

---

[7] See Khan and Riskin (2005).

[8] This information is taken from NBS (2003).

[9] The growth rate in agricultural value added is calculated from table 3–4 in NBS (2003).

[10] Until recently it was possible to make a more direct estimate of agriculture's terms of trade as the ratio of the "General Purchasing Price Index of Farm Products" to the "General Rural Retail Price Index of Industrial Products." Both these indices are shown in NBS (2000), p. 290. The index of the terms of trade for agriculture, thus calculated, had the following values for selected years: 1978: 100; 1988: 177 (steady increase in the intervening period, the index peaking in 1988); 1993: 154 (steady fall between 1988 and 1993, the year in which the index bottomed out); 1994: 184; 1995: 192 (sharp rise for two years, which was followed by only a small decline in 1996); 1999: 151 (steady fall since 1996). After 2000 the NBS stopped publishing the two indices on which these terms of trade estimates are based. The comparison of the change in real growth in value added and real growth in personal income suggests that this decline continued until 2002.

per capita income from farming even might have fallen because of both diminishing returns, given the scarcity of land and the larger number of persons among whom to share the income.

The next two sources of income, in terms of their importance as contributors to the increment in per capita income, are rental value of housing (19 percent of incremental income) and income from nonfarm activities (16 percent of incremental income). This is consistent with the expectation that these are income-elastic components of personal income.

Public intermediation through taxes and subsidies tended to slow down the rate of increase in disposable income. A decrease in net subsidies (increase in net taxes) accounted for a 7.5 percent reduction in personal disposable income. Changes in contributions made by the other sources of income were relatively insignificant as a proportion of incremental income.

B. The Distribution of Rural Income

Inequality is measured, as in the studies reporting the past CHIP surveys, by the Gini ratio, and the contributions of individual components of income to inequality are measured by concentration ratios (also called pseudo-Gini ratios).[11]

Table 3.3 shows the Gini ratio of rural income and the concentration ratios of the sources of rural income for 2002 and the corresponding estimates from our 1995 survey. Rural income inequality declined between 1995 and 2002. Just over half of the increase in the Gini ratio between 1988 and 1995 has been reversed.[12] The decline in the Gini ratio was brought about by the changed distribution of two sources of income and the change in the distribution of net taxes: compared to 1995, wage income became far less disequalizing,[13] farm income became even more equalizing, and net taxes became far less regressive. The contribution of these three sources to the Gini ratio fell by 0.069, far more than the 0.041 decline in the Gini ratio. In other words, every other component of income had a disequalizing effect.

The most important contribution to the reduction in inequality was due to the distribution of farm income, already a strongly equalizing source

---

[11] See Khan and Riskin (2005) or Khan and Riskin (2001) for a detailed explanation of the concentration ratio.

[12] The Gini ratio of rural income distribution estimated from the 1988 CHIP survey was 0.338.

[13] An income source is said to be disequalizing if its concentration ratio exceeds the overall Gini ratio, so that, ceteris paribus, an increase in income from that source would raise the Gini. Conversely, an income source is equalizing if the Gini exceeds the concentration ratio. See sources cited in note 11.

Table 3.3. *Rural Gini and concentration ratios*

	Percentage of income		Gini/concentration ratio		Percentage of Gini contributed	
	1995	2002	1995	2002	1995	2002
Individual wages	22.38	30.82	0.738	0.455	39.7	37.4
Net farm income	46.44	38.21	0.238	0.202	26.6	20.6
Net income from household nonfarm activities	9.71	11.59	0.484	0.558	11.3	17.2
Property income	0.43	0.59	0.543	0.777	0.6	1.2
Rental value of owned housing	11.61	13.50	0.321	0.377	9.0	13.6
Net subsidies from the state and collective	−0.48	−2.59	−1.759	0.106	2.0	−0.7
Other income (including private transfers)	9.91	7.88	0.463	0.515	11.0	10.8
Total	100.00	100.00	0.416	0.375	100.0	100.0

of income back in 1995, but much more strongly equalizing in 2002. Its contribution to the Gini ratio fell by 0.033, more than 80 percent of the total fall in the Gini ratio.

The next most important source of the fall in inequality is the sharp decline in the disequalizing effect of the distribution of individual wages. Wages are still a disequalizing source of income, but much less so than in 1995. The contribution of wages to the Gini ratio fell by 0.025. It is interesting to note that wages derived from local TVEs are far more disequalizing than other wages for 2002, a phenomenon for which there is no comparable information for 1995.

Net subsidies – or rather net taxes, because the average value is negative – are the third source of reduction in inequality. In 1995 its concentration ratio was negative, indicating that the lowest income groups paid more than the total amount of net taxes, while the higher income groups received a net subsidy. The concentration ratio has turned positive, but still is far lower than the Gini ratio, indicating a strongly regressive distribution of net taxes.

The strongly equalizing distribution of farm income must be attributed primarily to the highly egalitarian system of peasant farming established and perpetuated by China's egalitarian distribution of land.[14] Equality of access

---

[14] See Khan and Riskin (2005) for details.

to land has ensured an egalitarian distribution of income from farming and has constituted a strong source of basic income security in rural China.[15]

The reduction in the disequalizing effect of wages is perhaps partly explained by the rapid growth in rural employment and a reduction in the regional inequality of access to wage employment.[16] Cross-sectional evidence for 2002 suggests that the unequal distribution of wage income is largely attributable to the high regional inequality in the distribution of income rather than to the inequality in the distribution of wage income within a given region. The simple average of the concentration ratios of wage income for the 21 provinces is just 0.310 as compared to a concentration ratio of wage income for entire rural China of 0.455, a clear indication that interprovincial inequality dominates inequality within the provinces in the distribution of wage income. Direct comparison of provincial concentration ratios between 1995 and 2002 is not possible because of the absence of comparable estimates for 1995. It appears, however, that much of the impetus for the reduced concentration of wage income was provided by the reduced regional inequality of income – and wage income – among provinces.

There are two kinds of evidence of a reduction in regional inequality in the distribution of rural income.[17] Spearman's rank correlation coefficient between the provincial rank in per capita rural income in 1995 and the provincial rank in the rate of growth in rural income between 1995 and 2002 is –0.44 for the 19 provinces that are common in the two samples, indicating a negative relationship between initial income level and the growth rate of income. The coefficient is not significant at the 5 percent level, but is significant at the 10 percent level. Second, largely as a result of this negative relationship between the initial level and the rate of growth of income, the coefficient of variation of the per capita rural income among the 19 common provinces fell from 0.53 in 1995 to 0.47 in 2002.

The reduction in interprovincial inequality was one of the elements helping the reduction in rural inequality that was broad based. Inequality fell in 14 of the 19 provinces that are included in the surveys of both years.

---

[15] The upsurge in recent years of land disputes due to local government appropriation of farmland for development suggests that the inherited institution of equal access to land is coming into increasing conflict with market incentives in a growing, urbanizing economy with large income and wealth inequalities.

[16] See Chapter 9 of this volume by John Knight and Lina Song for a discussion of the changed wage structure.

[17] Due to a lack of space and the fact that provincial inequality is the subject matter of Chapter 2 in this volume, provincial incomes and Gini ratios are not shown in this chapter. These can be found in Khan and Riskin (2005).

In the above, the important role of the declining rural population in helping both the growth and the favorable change in the distribution of rural income has been emphasized. China's actual rural population in 2002 would have been 911.5 million if it had grown at the same rate as the national population, 0.843 percent per year since 1995. This means that a total of 129 million people moved from rural China to urban areas during this period.[18] They have moved to existing or newly created urban locations. This has been made possible by the de facto flexibility in China's rigid system of residence permits (*hukou*). The growth in rural income might have been lower and the incremental distribution of income might have been worse had all this increased population remained in rural China and competed for the meager land and other rural resources.

III. Urban Residents' Income and Its Distribution

A. The Level, Composition, and Sources of Growth of Income

Table 3.4 shows per capita personal income of urban resident households for 2002 and the corresponding estimates based on the 1995 CHIP survey. As in the prior years, income according to our definition and based on the CHIP sample is higher than the "per capita annual disposable income of the urban households" as estimated by the NBS according to its own definition based on its national survey. This difference for 2002 is 29 percent, as compared to 33 percent in 1995 and 55 percent in 1988.[19] This decline over time is due to the trend decline in the value of subsidies that are included in our definition but mostly excluded from the NBS definition. By 2002 net subsidies had declined to less than 2 percent of income as compared to 11 percent in 1995. Ninety-three percent of the difference between our income estimate and the NBS estimate is explained by the items that are included by us and excluded by the NBS: subsidies and the rental value of housing. The difference in the components that are common in the two income definitions is very small.

---

[18] This is well in excess of the estimated total net rural-urban migration over the period, which is put at about 72 million persons between 1995 and 2000 (inclusive), or about 100.5 million, assuming net migration in 2001 and 2002 was similar in size to that in 2000. The excess loss of rural population of about 28.5 million is probably due mainly to the redefinition of formerly rural places as "towns." The number is, indeed, similar to Chan and Hu's rough estimate of a 30 million increase in the urban population over the entire decade of the 1990s due to new town formation alone. See Chan and Hu (2003); Liang and Ma (2004).

[19] The NBS estimate of per capita income is 7,702.80 yuan. See NBS (2003), table 10–4.

Table 3.4. *Per capita disposable urban income (current yuan per year)*

	1995		2002		Annual real growth rate
	Amount	Percentage	Amount	Percentage	Percentage
Individual wages	3,497.77	61.30	5,814.74	59.54	5.99
Pensions and retirees' income	667.14	11.69	1,443.74	14.78	10.06
Individual enterprises	30.23	0.53	267.90	2.74	34.62
Income from property	72.28	1.27	53.92	0.55	−5.47
Housing subsidies in kind	555.66	9.74	183.09	1.87	−15.89
Other net subsidies	71.12	1.25	7.17	0.07	−28.98
Rental value of owned housing	650.12	11.39	1.723.52	17.65	13.30
Other income	161.87	2.84	271.81	2.78	6.15
Total	5,706.19	100.00	9,765.90	100.00	6.44

For the common components, our income estimate is less than 2 percent higher than the NBS estimate.

Urban per capita income in 2002 is 2.96 times rural per capita income. This ratio was 2.47 in 1995. During the period between 1995 and 2002 the consumer price index is estimated to have increased a little faster for the urban residents than for the rural residents – at 10.59 percent as compared to 8.17 percent for the rural areas over the period as a whole. Even at 1995 purchasing power, the ratio of urban per capita income to rural per capita income is 2.89. Such a staggering level of urban-rural inequality is almost unheard of in the developing world.

The rate of growth in per capita real urban income between 1995 and 2002 was 6.4 percent (Table 3.5), less than the NBS estimate of 7.2 percent. The difference was due to the slower than average growth of the components that are included in our income definition and excluded from the NBS definition. This in turn was due to the sharp absolute fall in subsidies. Still, the rate of growth in urban income was three-fifths faster than the rate of growth in rural income. It was also 44 percent faster than the rate of growth in urban income between 1988 and 1995.

Rapid urbanization during the period under review caused per capita personal income in China to grow at a faster annual rate than either urban or rural personal income. The annual growth rate in per capita personal income was 7.06 percent during this period. The corresponding growth rate

Table 3.5. *Sources of urban income growth between 1995 and 2002 (%)*

Source	Incremental share	Annual real growth
Wages	57.1	6.0
Pensions and retirees' income	19.1	10.1
Individual enterprises	5.9	34.6
Income from property	−0.4	−5.5
Net subsidies	−10.8	−16.9
Rental value of owned housing	26.4	13.3
Other	2.7	6.2
Total income	100.0	6.4

in per capita personal income during 1988–1995 was 5.08 percent per year.[20] The growth rate of per capita real GDP, based on the official NBS estimates, was 8.12 percent during 1988–1995 and a lower 7.22 percent during 1995–2002. Thus, the elasticity of per capita personal income with respect to per capita GDP was 0.63 in the pre-1995 period and 0.98 in the post-1995 period.[21] We do not have enough details to document how this change in the distribution of incremental income in favor of households was brought about. Clearly the policy changes mostly benefited urban households that experienced a much faster growth in income than in the past or than rural households experienced in either period.

A number of significant changes in the composition of urban income took place. There was a fall in the share of wages and a rise in the share of income for the retirees (which includes payments to laid-off workers), while together the share of these two sources of income increased from 73 percent of total income to 74 percent. Housing subsidies in kind – the difference between the market rent and actual rent paid by those occupying public and collective housing – fell sharply, while the rental value of owned housing went up. The contribution of these two sources together fell slightly, from 21 percent of income to 20 percent. Housing reform brought down

[20] These growth rates are based on the weighted averages of rural and urban per capita personal incomes from the CHIP surveys for the three years, the weights being proportional to the actual rural and urban populations (ignoring migrants, for whom no information is available for 1995).

[21] Net exports as a proportion of GDP rose steadily from –1.03 percent in 1988 to 3.81 percent in 1997 and 3.86 percent in 1998, the first full year after the Asian crisis hit some of the East Asian countries. Thereafter it fell steadily to 2.24 percent in 2001. It stood at 2.60 percent in 2002. Final consumption in China as a proportion of GDP fell sharply from 0.64 in 1988 to 0.57 in 1995. It seems that China succeeded in arresting this decline and raising it to 0.58 in 2002. All data for these estimates are from NBS (2003).

Table 3.6. *Urban Gini and concentration ratios*

Source	Percentage of income		Gini/concentration ratio		Percentage of Gini contributed	
	1995	2002	1995	2002	1995	2002
Wages	61.30	59.54	0.247	0.315	45.6	59.0
Pensions and retirees' income	11.69	14.78	0.316	0.307	11.1	14.3
Individual enterprises	0.53	2.74	0.042	0.037	0.1	0.3
Income from property	1.27	0.55	0.484	0.471	1.9	0.8
Housing subsidies in kind	9.74	1.87	0.516	0.316	15.1	1.9
Other net subsidies	1.25	0.07	0.296	−2.158	1.1	−0.5
Rental value of housing	11.39	17.65	0.639	0.378	21.9	21.0
Other income	2.84	2.78	0.371	0.359	3.2	3.1
Total income	100.00	100.00	0.332	0.318	100.0	100.0

the subsidies by widening homeownership, which expanded the share of the rental value of owned housing.[22] The share of income from individual enterprises increased sharply, although it remained low in absolute terms. The shares of property income and nonhousing subsidies, already very low in 1995, fell further.[23]

Wages grew at a slower rate than overall income because of the worsening urban employment situation. Employment per person in urban China fell by more than 9 percent as state and collective enterprises abandoned the use of employment as a method of income maintenance and shed surplus workers. There has been a rapid increase in employment in private, foreign, joint-stock enterprises, and self-employment categories, but these have not been fast enough to offset the fall in state and collective enterprises on a per capita basis.

B. The Distribution of Urban Income

The urban Gini ratio fell by 4 percent between 1995 and 2002 (Table 3.6). Wages, the principal source of urban income, became more disequalizing

---

[22] It should be noted that the estimation of the rental value of urban housing reverted back to the method adopted in 1988, the interest on housing equity. In 1995 we used the direct information on actual house rent. The same information proved unusable for 2002.

[23] It is hard to tell if the fall in the share of property income simply reflects a worsening of the problem of capturing enough income under this heading in the past. It is possible, however, that the main source of income from nonhousing property, interest on savings deposits, actually fell because of the fall in the rate of interest.

over the period, continuing a long-term trend. The impact of this on the distribution of income was blunted somewhat by the fall in the income share of wages. Even so, wages contributed a net increase of 0.036 in the Gini ratio, in absolute terms a full 2.6 times its total decline. Income of retired members is a mildly equalizing source of income. Individual enterprises, a strongly equalizing source of income for urban residents, made a slightly higher absolute contribution to the Gini ratio because of the sharp rise in their share.

All other sources of urban income contributed less to the Gini ratio in absolute terms in 2002 than in 1995. Nonhousing subsidies, though reduced to an insignificant level, had a dramatic improvement in distribution and thus contributed to a lessening of inequality. But the really substantial contribution to the reduction of the Gini ratio, which was large enough to outweigh the disequalizing effect of wages, came from housing reform. Housing subsidies in kind – the difference between market and actual rent paid for public housing – had been largely appropriated by higher income groups in 1995, as reflected in their high concentration ratio (0.516). The sharp reduction in these subsidies – and a better targeting of the remaining subsidies – led to a fall of 0.044 in their contribution to the Gini ratio. Rental value of owned housing also became substantially less disequalizing as homeownership became widespread, its absolute contribution to the Gini ratio falling by 0.006. The inequality of homeownership at the conclusion of housing reform appears to be lower than the inequality of access to housing services under the old system of public ownership of housing. Note that if these findings are right, then income distribution estimates based on the NBS data will not capture the fall in urban inequality because they exclude housing subsidies and the rental value of housing.

Unlike rural inequality, the fall in urban inequality was not broad based. Of the 11 provinces, inequality actually increased in eight and remained the same in one.[24] In only two provinces, Liaoning and Gansu, did urban inequality fall. The reduction in the overall urban Gini ratio, despite the increase in most of the provincial urban Gini ratios, clearly indicates that there was a reduction in interprovincial inequality in income. Support for this is found by the decline in the coefficient of variation for per capita provincial income from 0.39 in 1995 to 0.31 in 2002. Also Spearman's rank correlation coefficient between the provincial rank in per capita income in 1995 and the provincial rank in the growth rate in income between 1995 and 2002 is negative (–0.673) and significant at the 10 percent level.

[24] For similar reasons as in the case of rural China above, provincial incomes and Gini ratios for urban China have not been reported in this chapter. These can be found in Khan and Riskin (2005).

Table 3.7. *Composition and distribution of income of migrants to urban China, 2002*

Income	Per capita income		Gini/concentration ratio
	Amount	Percentage of total	
Wages	2,189.18	34.40	0.250
Individual enterprises	3,758.01	59.04	0.429
Property	18.16	0.29	0.189
Net subsidies	−60.33	−0.95	0.208
Rental value of housing	310.50	4.88	0.658
Other (including pensions)	149.15	2.34	0.408
Total income	6,364.68	100.0	0.380

IV. Migrants' Income and Its Distribution

A. The Level and Composition of Migrants' Income

The 2002 CHIP survey for the first time included a sample of migrant households. The questionnaire used for the enumeration of the migrants' income characteristics was, however, substantially abbreviated as compared to the questionnaire used for the enumeration of the income of the urban residents. Even so, it appears that the coverage of their income has been reasonably comprehensive and comparable to the coverage of the income of the urban residents. There are two categories of urban residents' income for which no information was sought for the migrants: the income of the retirees, and housing subsidies in kind. Since the migrants by and large are not covered by any retirement benefit scheme, it does not seem likely that they would have any income of this type. Similarly, migrant households are unlikely to have received any housing subsidies as they are excluded from any entitlement to public or collective housing.[25]

Table 3.7 shows the migrants' income, its sources, and its distribution, and Table 3.8 shows their sources of employment and comparative data for the urban residents. Per capita income of the migrants is approximately halfway between the per capita incomes of the rural and the urban resident households. By migrating from rural to urban China an average migrant

---

[25] However, only households living in resident communities (*jiedao*) were sampled, which ruled out including migrant workers living on construction sites or in factory dormitories where rudimentary housing may have been part of their compensation. This peculiarity of the sample probably also causes the proportion of wages in migrant income to be biased downward. See below.

Table 3.8. *Employment characteristics of migrants and full status residents of urban China, 2002*

	Migrants	Residents
Percentage of household members in employment	65.0	49.9
Percentage of those employed in:		
Government and institutions	–	30.8
Other nonenterprise institutions	–	9.6
Enterprises:		
State-owned enterprises (including local)	6.7	29.5
Urban collectives	3.6	6.1
Private farms	7.1	3.3
Sino-foreign joint ventures	0.5	1.5
Foreign companies	0.1	0.4
State share-holding companies	0.4	3.3
Other share-holding companies	1.8	7.2
Rural private and individual enterprises	11.8	0.1
Enterprises under other ownership	6.3	0.4
Self-employed	58.3	5.6
Residual	3.5	2.1

Note: – means zero. For urban residents, a two-stage classification is adopted: the first stage consists of (1) enterprises, (2) government agencies, (3) institutions, and (4) "other." The second stage consists of a classification of enterprises into ownership categories. For migrants there is just a one-stage classification into different kinds of enterprises, implying that none are employed in government, institutions (probably organizations like teaching and medical institutions), and "other" categories of nonenterprise employers. The residual category includes those individuals who are shown to be employed without any indication of the employment category.

household nearly doubles its per capita income, although that income remains 35 percent below that of an urban resident household.

By far the highest proportion of the migrants' income, nearly three-fifths, is derived from individual enterprises, a source that contributes less than 3 percent of the income of the residents. This matches the very high proportion of migrants (58 percent) and the very low proportion of residents (less than 6 percent) engaged in self-employment. Wages account for a far smaller proportion of income for the migrants than for the residents, reflecting the difference between the two groups with respect to the composition of employment. The migrants are generally excluded from public sector employment and are heavily concentrated in informal employment. Seventy percent of employment of the urban residents is still derived from government, official institutions, and state-owned enterprises. In contrast, less than 7 percent of employment of the migrants is derived from state-owned enterprises and none from government agencies and institutions.

The proportion employed in the other forms of formal enterprises –
urban collectives, private firms, joint ventures, foreign enterprises, state and
other share-holding companies – is also smaller for the migrants than for the
residents, while the proportion employed in informal (rural) enterprises is
much higher for the migrants than for the residents.[26] The result is a much
smaller share of income derived from wages by the migrants (34 percent)
than by the residents (60 percent).[27]

Other notable differences in the composition of income consist of an
insignificant share of pensions and a much smaller share of the rental value
of housing for the migrants. Their share of the rental value of housing is low
because they have not been the beneficiary of housing reform leading to the
privatization of housing. Their housing assets are derived entirely from their
own investment in construction at market cost, or possibly higher-than-
market cost in order to overcome the disadvantage that is caused by the lack
of residence entitlement. The migrants are subject to a small net tax, while
the residents receive a net subsidy. It is worth noting that the survey has
not fully captured the discriminatory effect of the lack of access to public
services on the migrants' real income.

One final difference between the income of the migrants and the income
of the residents needs to be stressed. Migrants have a higher number of
workers per household member, 0.65 as compared to 0.5 for the residents.[28]
Thus, while the per capita income of the migrants is 65 percent of that of the
residents, the income per working migrant is only 50 percent of the income
per working resident.

B. The Distribution of Migrants' Income

Inequality among the migrants is greater than inequality among either the
urban residents or the rural population. While this is established by a comparison of the respective Gini ratios for China as a whole, the inequality
among the migrants looks worse when comparison is made at the provincial

---

[26] The "rural" enterprises that employ nearly 12 percent of the migrant workers and a negligible 0.1 percent of the urban resident workers may be the "agricultural" enterprises located
in the rural periphery of urban districts. Alternatively, this may mean that periodically a
proportion of urban migrants reverts back to rural areas for employment. The survey is
unclear on this subject.

[27] Nevertheless, the modesty of the incidences of wages and wage employment among
migrants is probably exaggerated by the sampling bias described in note 25.

[28] The reason behind this is not possible for the survey data to illuminate: migrants often
leave spouse and children behind, but it could also be that smaller households with fewer
children are more prone to migration.

level.[29] The Gini ratio for the migrants is almost 20 percent higher than the Gini ratio for the urban residents for China as a whole. The average percentage difference between the provincial Gini ratios for the two groups is much higher, however, at 33 percent. For only two provinces, Sichuan and Guangdong, is the migrants' Gini lower than that of the residents. In the other nine provinces the migrants' Gini ratio exceeds the residents' Gini by an average of 39 percent. The overall inequality among the migrants is less than is the overall inequality among the urban residents[30] because of the interprovincial income difference.

The greater inequality in the distribution of income for the migrants principally derives from the fact that their largest source of income, from individual enterprises, has a strongly disequalizing effect on income distribution. This does not seem to be due to the regional differences in earnings from this source. With the exception of Anhui, this source of income has a disequalizing effect on provincial income distribution everywhere else. Market returns to individual enterprises clearly reflect the considerable difference among the migrants in terms of entrepreneurial ability and resource endowments. Despite a significant increase in its differentiation since the beginning of reforms, the wage structure, on the other hand, still enforces a degree of equality among the residents who derive most of their income from wages. The greater inequality among the migrants is also explained by their lack of access to pensions and unemployment benefits, which serve as redistributive social protection for the residents. Finally, the migrants' homeownership is subject to greater obstacles than the residents' homeownership, which probably explains the greater inequality in the distribution of the rental value of housing for the migrants.

V. National Income Distribution without the Migrants

The overall distribution of income for China as a whole was estimated for the earlier survey years by combining the urban and rural samples in such a way that in the aggregate sample the proportions of rural and urban individuals were the same as their proportions in the actual population.[31]

---

[29] As in the case of rural and urban residents, provincial estimates for the migrants can be found in Khan and Riskin (2005).

[30] The coefficient of variation in provincial per capita incomes is 0.246 for the migrants and 0.308 for the residents. The coefficient of variation in the provincial Gini ratio is higher, however, for the migrants: 0.124 as compared to 0.093 for the residents.

[31] In both 1988 and 1995 the rural population was undersampled so that the combined national sample was formed by augmenting the rural sample by randomly adding the

Migrants were not included in those samples. To arrive at a comparable estimate of national inequality we therefore need to exclude the migrants and construct a national sample by aggregating the rural and urban samples in such a way that the individuals belonging to urban households represent 39 percent of all individuals, which was the proportion of China's urban population in 2002 according to official estimates. The urban sample of the 2002 CHIP survey represents 35.2 percent of all individuals included in the urban and rural samples together. It was therefore necessary to randomly select 1,209 urban households from the urban sample and add them to the original samples to form a new national sample of 8,044 urban households and 9,200 rural households.[32] Table 3.9 shows the Gini and concentration ratios estimated from this national sample.

The first noteworthy feature of the results is that inequality for China as a whole has remained virtually unchanged since 1995, despite the fall in both the rural and urban Gini ratios. The explanation lies in the fact that the inequality between urban and rural China has widened very sharply.

As in previous years, the Gini ratio for China as a whole is greater than the Gini ratios for either rural or urban China, which indicates the dominance of urban-rural inequality over inequality within each of these locations. In 2002 this effect has become much stronger: the national Gini ratio was 21 percent higher than the average of the rural and urban Gini ratios in 1995. In 2002 this difference widened to 30 percent.

Urban income and its distribution contribute more than 98 percent to overall inequality while rural income and its distribution contribute just over 1 percent. This might sound counterintuitive in view of the higher Gini ratio for rural residents than for urban residents. The point, however, is that the national Gini ratio is the weighted average not of the rural and urban Gini ratios but of their concentration ratios. As the rural and urban samples are combined, households with urban income are clustered at the high end of the total distribution, making the concentration ratio of urban income very high, while households with rural income are clustered at the low end, making the concentration ratio of rural income very low. The concentration

---

requisite number of rural households from the original sample, so that in the final sample the randomly drawn rural households were counted twice as two separate rural households.

[32] If the average size of these additional urban households turns out to be the same as the average of the original urban sample, then there would be 37,996 (61 percent of the total) rural individuals and 24,293 (39 percent) urban individuals in the aggregate national sample. The actual numbers turn out to be slightly different because the average size of the additional 1,209 urban households will not be exactly the same as that of the original sample.

Table 3.9. *National income inequality excluding migrants*

Income	Percentage of income		Gini/concentration ratio		Percentage of Gini contributed	
	1995	2002	1995	2002	1995	2002
Total rural	(49.09)	(34.62)	0.192	0.023	(20.9)	(1.8)
Wages	10.71	10.67	0.567	0.100	13.4	2.4
Net farm income	23.04	13.23	−0.001	−0.153	−0.1	−4.5
Net income from nonfarm activities	4.80	4.01	0.266	0.212	2.8	1.9
Property	0.22	0.20	0.327	0.493	0.2	0.2
Rental value of housing	5.74	4.68	0.090	0.026	1.1	0.3
Net transfers from state	−0.26	−0.90	−1.924	−0.224	1.1	0.4
Other	4.84	2.73	0.218	0.172	2.4	1.0
Total urban	(50.89)	(65.38)	0.703	0.677	(79.1)	(98.4)
Wages	31.20	38.85	0.664	0.676	45.8	58.4
Pensions and retirees' income	5.95	9.67	0.698	0.673	9.2	14.5
Individual enterprises	0.27	1.81	0.516	0.516	0.3	2.1
Property income	0.64	0.37	0.776	0.745	1.1	0.6
Housing subsidies in kind	4.96	1.22	0.789	0.676	8.7	1.8
Other net subsidies	0.63	0.07	0.687	−0.268	1.0	–
Rental value of housing	5.80	11.53	0.840	0.707	10.8	18.1
Other	1.44	1.86	0.719	0.698	2.3	2.9
Total	100.00	100.00	0.452	0.450	100.0	100.0

Note: – means negligible.

ratio of rural income is only 5 percent of the Gini ratio, which indicates that it has a strongly equalizing effect on the distribution of overall income. The concentration ratio of urban income is 50 percent higher than the overall Gini ratio, indicating that it has a strongly disequalizing effect on the overall income distribution. Indeed, a one percentage point shift in the share of income from the urban to rural population, with the urban and rural distributions unchanged, would reduce the overall national Gini by 0.007, or by 1.5 percent.

The share of urban income increased from one-half in 1995 to nearly two-thirds in 2002. Of the overall increment in real personal income in China between 1995 and 2002, the increase in rural personal income accounted for only 16 percent, while the increase in urban personal income accounted for the remaining 84 percent.[33] This was partly because of a rise in the

---

[33] These estimates ignore any change due to the change in the number and incomes of the migrants for whom no information is available for 1995.

proportion of the population in urban areas and partly because of the sharp increase in urban-rural inequality. Between 1995 and 2002 rural income has become more equalizing, and urban income has become less disequalizing. Even so, overall inequality has increased because of the large increase in the share of urban income, which, even though less disequalizing in 2002, remains strongly disequalizing.

With the exception of property income, all sources of rural income have a strongly equalizing effect on national income distribution. This applies to wages, income from nonfarm enterprises, and the other components that have a disequalizing effect on rural income distribution. The dramatically equalizing effect of farm income in the overall national context deserves particular notice. With the exception of net subsidies, all the components of urban income have a strongly disequalizing effect on national income distribution, including those, like income from individual enterprises, which have an equalizing effect on urban income distribution. The strongly equalizing effect of nonhousing subsidies in the overall national context deserves to be noted as a dramatic shift in the distributional outcome of such subsidies between 1995 and 2002.

VI. National and Urban Income Distribution Including Migrants

The analysis of urban and national inequality in the preceding sections suffers from neglect of the migrants. The 2002 CHIP survey makes it possible to estimate urban and national inequality by including the migrants. Although there are no comparable estimates for earlier years, a comparison between inequality with and without the migrants should provide useful insights into China's evolving income distribution.

There is considerable uncertainty about the size of the migrant population. A recent study based on the 2000 population census concluded that migrants constituted 17.2 percent of the urban population in that year.[34] In this chapter we have used a slightly higher figure of 18 percent.[35]

---

[34] Liang and Ma (2004).

[35] There are reasons to believe that even this may be an underestimate of the actual number of migrants. Official statistics show an annual decline in the rural population of 1.33 percent and an annual increase of 5.22 percent in the urban population between 1995 and 2002. These demographic figures indicate that the number of migrants from rural to urban areas must have been larger if one simply counts those who have moved since 1995. Assuming the same population share of rural China in 2002 as in 1995, there would have been 129 million more people in rural China than the actual number in 2002.

Table 3.10. *Urban income inequality including migrants, 2002*

Income	Percentage of income	Gini/concentration ratio	Percentage of Gini contributed
Total urban residents	(87.52)	0.381	(98.7)
Wages	51.92	0.379	58.2
Pensions and retirees' income	13.01	0.372	14.3
Individual enterprises	2.48	0.119	0.9
Property	0.48	0.533	0.8
Housing subsidies in kind	1.70	0.377	1.9
Other net subsidies	0.07	−1.446	−0.3
Rental value of housing	15.46	0.436	19.9
Other	2.41	0.421	3.0
Total migrants	(12.48)	0.039	(1.4)
Wages	4.29	−0.143	−1.8
Individual enterprises	7.37	0.111	2.4
Property	0.04	−0.156	−
Net subsidies	−0.12	−0.151	0.1
Rental value of housing	0.60	0.393	0.7
Other	0.29	0.097	0.1
Total	100.00	0.338	100.0

China's population in 2002 is thus classified into three categories: 61 percent rural residents, 32 percent urban residents, and 7 percent migrants into urban areas. The urban and rural samples have been augmented by adding randomly selected households from the respective samples to make the combined sample reflect these population shares.[36]

Tables 3.10 and 3.11 show the distribution of urban income and the overall national distribution of income including the migrants, respectively. The inclusion of the migrants makes the urban income distribution more unequal: the Gini ratio for the urban income distribution including the migrants is 0.338, as compared to the Gini ratio of 0.318 excluding the migrants. Nearly 99 percent of the urban Gini ratio is contributed by the urban

---

[36] Of the total of 63,958 individuals in the three samples, the shares of the three groups are: rural 59.4 percent, urban 32.3 percent, and migrants 8.3 percent. The migrants are most oversampled. By randomly selecting 2,025 rural households and 1,218 urban households and adding them to the original samples we obtain an aggregate national sample with 11,225 rural households (46,360 individuals), 8,053 urban resident households (24,320 individuals), and 2,000 migrant households (5,320 individuals). These give us the desired population shares for the three groups. Note that the number of individuals in parentheses assumes that the average size of the added households is the same as the average household size in the original sample. In practice there is a slight discrepancy.

Table 3.11. *National income inequality including migrants, 2002*

Income	Percentage of income	Gini/concentration ratio	Percentage of Gini contributed
Total rural	(36.03)	0.048	(3.9)
Wages	11.03	0.123	3.0
Net farm	13.82	−0.128	−3.9
Net from nonfarm activities	4.15	0.235	2.2
Property	0.21	0.519	0.2
Rental value of housing	4.89	0.051	0.6
Net transfers from state	−0.93	−0.209	0.4
Other	2.86	0.206	1.3
Total urban residents	(55.99)	0.700	(87.5)
Wages	33.22	0.700	51.9
Pensions and retirees' income	8.32	0.698	13.0
Individual enterprises	1.59	0.550	2.0
Property	0.30	0.761	0.5
Housing subsidies in kind	1.08	0.703	1.7
Other net subsidies	0.04	−0.673	−0.1
Rental value of housing	9.89	0.729	16.1
Other	1.54	0.709	2.4
Total migrants	(7.98)	0.482	(8.6)
Wages	2.75	0.379	2.3
Individual enterprises	4.71	0.522	5.5
Property	0.02	0.338	–
Net subsidies	−0.08	0.344	−0.1
Rental value of housing	0.39	0.697	0.6
Other	0.19	0.504	0.2
Total	100.00	0.448	100.0

residents' income and its distribution. A redistribution of income in favor of the migrants would improve the overall urban income distribution. This sounds paradoxical in view of the greater inequality of the distribution of the migrants' income than of the residents' income, but is explained by the simple fact that the migrants are much poorer than the residents. The only components of urban income that have an equalizing effect on the overall urban income distribution are individual enterprises and net subsidies, both very small. All other components of urban income have a disequalizing effect on the distribution of overall urban income. In contrast, with the exception of the rental value of housing, every component of the migrants' income has an equalizing effect on the distribution of overall urban income. Even income from individual enterprises, which has a disequalizing effect on the distribution of migrant income, has a strongly equalizing effect on the distribution of overall urban income.

The inclusion of the migrants slightly reduces the overall national income inequality. This is because migrants, having an average income that is roughly halfway between the average rural and urban incomes, are clustered closer to the middle of the overall income distribution.

Of the three, rural income is the only one that has an equalizing effect on the overall national distribution, although this effect is less extreme than in the case of the national distribution without the migrants. This is because the inclusion of the migrants has made the rural population less poor relative to the rest of the population.

Migrants' income has a disequalizing effect on the overall national income distribution as shown by its higher concentration ratio than the Gini ratio. This needs careful interpretation. If there is an increase in the share of the migrants' income that is offset by a proportionate reduction in both the rural and urban residents' income, the Gini ratio would rise. If, however, there is an increase in the migrants' income with a corresponding decline in the income of the urban residents, inequality would fall (the concentration ratio being much lower for the migrants than for the urban residents). As argued earlier, the effect of migration on rural income must be positive because it reduces the pressure on the population on limited land and rural resources. Note that although the migrants' income is disequalizing, several of its individual components, including wages, are not.

Urban residents' income and its distribution contribute most of the overall inequality, though a little less than in the case of the national distribution without the migrants. All that was said about the effect of the individual components of rural and urban residents' income on the overall national distribution without the migrants holds in the present case, though in each case the effect is a little less extreme.[37]

VII. Summary and Conclusion

In the period between 1995 and 2002 the inequality in the distribution of rural income in China fell by almost 10 percent as measured by the Gini ratio, recording a reversal of the trend that had characterized much of the period since the beginning of reforms. The reduction in inequality came

---

[37] This statement also holds for the effect of the inclusion of migrant income on urban-rural inequality, a subject we have explored elsewhere. As expected, urban-rural inequality declines somewhat when migrants are included, but remains very high. See Khan and Riskin (2005).

from reductions in both interprovincial and intraprovincial inequality, and from improvements in the distribution of farm and wage income and a reduction in the regressivity of net taxes. The continued improvement in the distribution of farm income was facilitated by the continued equality of access to land. For the first time China experienced a steady absolute fall in the rural population after it peaked in 1995, and this facilitated a growth in per capita rural income.

During this period urban personal income growth was extremely high. The distribution of urban income also became more equal, albeit to a lesser extent than the rural distribution, with a 4 percent decline in the Gini ratio. Much of the impetus for the reduced urban inequality came from a reduction in interprovincial inequality. In terms of the contribution of individual components of income, increased urban equality was mainly a matter of housing reform and the reform of public finance. Housing subsidies, which had been disproportionately appropriated by better-off households, were sharply reduced and the remaining subsidies, especially nonhousing subsidies, were much better targeted to the poorer households. As homeownership became more widespread, its benefits became more broad based and less disequalizing. Together with an increase in social-protection payments to the laid-off urban workers, these changes more than offset the increased inequality of wage distribution. The major factors behind the improved distribution of urban income – the change in the distribution of the rental value of housing, housing subsidies, and other subsidies – are not captured by the official data, which exclude them from the income definition.

On average, the migrants nearly double their income by moving from rural to urban areas, although their income still remains less than two-thirds of the income of the urban residents on a per capita basis and only one-half on a per worker basis. One contribution to this gap undoubtedly comes from discriminatory treatment of the migrants, who are excluded from much of the formal labor market, public services, and asset redistribution programs like the housing reform. Migrants have a higher inequality in the distribution of income than either the rural or the urban residents. There is less interprovincial difference in the migrants' earnings than in the earnings of the urban residents.

The inequality of the overall national income distribution for China, accounting for the rural and urban residents, has changed little between 1995 and 2002. This national Gini ratio of 0.45 continues to make China one of the most unequal of Asian societies. The virtual constancy of the national Gini, despite the fall in both the rural and urban Gini ratios, is due to the sharply widened urban-rural inequality, which is one of the highest among all the countries for which estimates are available (Eastwood and Lipton 2004; Knight and Song 1999). The inclusion of migrants increases the inequality of urban income distribution but slightly reduces the inequality of the overall national income distribution.

In their earlier writings the present authors identified the principal causes of the increased inequality in China between 1988 and 1995 as (1) the increase in interregional inequality, (2) slow and disequalizing rural income growth, (3) regressive transfers to households and reduced transfers from rich to poor provinces, (4) slow growth in employment and a lack of social protection for laid-off workers, and (5) restrictions on and discriminatory treatment of migrants.[38] It appears that there has been an important policy response to deal with a number of these problems in recent years. China's poverty reduction strategy was significantly restructured around the turn of the millennium. In February 2000 the State Council adopted the "Great Western Development Strategy," which promoted economic development in poor western and central provinces. The program has led to a large increase in investment in infrastructure development in these regions. It is likely that increased public expenditure in these poor provinces has worked to reduce interprovincial inequality. While the official system of household registration has continued, there has been a great deal of de facto liberalization of movement of labor out of rural areas.

Programs have also progressed for protection of the urban poor, including a living allowance for laid-off workers; unemployment insurance, which has been replacing the living allowance; and a Minimum Living Standard Scheme, which is a subsistence allowance paid out of the government's general revenue.[39] As discussed above, the increase in the shares of these items in urban household income and the improved distribution of these sources of income have been factors behind the reduction in urban inequality between 1995 and 2002.

There is a need and a scope for further progress in all these areas, as well as in a reduction of the massive disparity between urban and rural income. Indeed, urban-rural income inequality has increased sharply, and this has held the overall inequality for China steady during a period of reduction in the rural and urban Gini ratios. One can think of three kinds of strategies to bring about faster growth in rural income: an improvement in agriculture's terms of trade, a program for the rapid promotion of nonfarm rural activities, and a more rapid and nondiscriminatory system of migration from rural

[38] See Khan and Riskin (1998) and (2001).
[39] For details see Asian Development Bank (2002).

to urban areas. The failure to maintain improved terms of trade for agriculture after 1996 seems to be a complex phenomenon. During this period the reform for WTO accession appears to have limited the sustainability of the high producers' prices for farm products, which had been introduced in 1994. With the exception of rice, domestic prices of grains are currently the same as or higher than the world price. It therefore seems that improving agriculture's net barter terms of trade by raising the producers' prices is not a sustainable policy. Some possibility of reducing input prices may exist insofar as the domestic price of fertilizer appears to be higher than the world price. Future improvement in farm income must, however, be based on improved single factoral terms of trade for agriculture by way of increased labor productivity. The success of this critically depends on the continued liberalization of the labor market so that agriculture can continue to shed its still considerable surplus labor for employment elsewhere.

The promotion of rural nonfarm activities must deal with the problem that this has so far been a strongly disequalizing source of income, and its disequalizing effect on the distribution of rural income has been increasing rather sharply. Thus, the promotion of nonfarm activities must be accompanied by effective measures to improve the access of the poor to these activities.

Migration has helped ease the problem of rural poverty, and its continuation is highly desirable. Political limits on feasible migration are probably close to being reached, especially if one considers the urgency of reducing the discrimination to which urban migrants are now subjected.

Thus, a policy of improved rural income must combine all three policies: improving factor productivity in agriculture, promoting rural nonfarm activities while improving access of the poor to these activities, and continuing an orderly flow of labor out of the rural areas.

References

Asian Development Bank (2002), *Final Report, Urban Poverty in PRC, TAE: PRC 33448*, Manila.

Chan, K. W. and Y. Hu (2003), "Urbanization in China: New Definition, Different Series, and Revised Trends," *China Review*, 3(2), 49–71.

Eastwood, R. and M. Lipton (2004), "Rural and Urban Income Inequality and Poverty: Does Convergence between Sectors Offset Divergence within Them?" in G. A. Cornia, ed., *Inequality, Growth and Poverty in an Era of Liberalization and Globalization*, Oxford: Oxford University Press, pp. 112–141.

Khan, A. R., K. Griffin, C. Riskin, and R. Zhao (1992), "Household Income and Its Distribution in China," *China Quarterly*, no. 132, 1029–1061.

Khan, A. R. and C. Riskin (1998), "Income and Inequality in China," *China Quarterly*, no. 154, 221–253.

Khan, A. R. and C. Riskin (2001), *Inequality and Poverty in China in the Age of Globalization*, New York: Oxford University Press.

Khan, A. R. and C. Riskin (2005), "China's Household Income and Its Distribution, 1995 and 2002," *China Quarterly*, no. 182, 356–384.

Knight, J. and L. Song (1999), *The Rural-Urban Divide: Economic Disparities and Interactions in China*, New York: Oxford University Press.

Liang, Z. and Z. Ma (2004), "China's Floating Population: New Evidence from the 2002 Census," *Population and Development Review*, 30(3), 467–488.

National Bureau of Statistics (2000), *China Statistical Yearbook 2000*, Beijing: China Statistical Publishing House.

National Bureau of Statistics (2003), *China Statistical Yearbook 2003*, Beijing: China Statistical Publishing House.

Ravallion, M. and S. Chen (2007), "China's (Uneven) Progress against Poverty," *Journal of Development Economics*, 82(1), 1–42.

Wu, X. and J. Perloff (2005), "China's Income Distribution, 1985–2001," *Review of Economics and Statistics*, 87(4), 763–775.

FOUR

Explaining Incomes and Inequality in China

Yue Ximing, Terry Sicular, Li Shi, and Björn Gustafsson

I. Introduction

After the mid-1980s income inequality in China increased markedly and has now reached a level that is relatively high by international standards. Underlying this increase was China's transition from a planned to a market economy. Prior to the transition a wide array of policies and programs had depressed income differentials. Wage differentials in urban areas were compressed and based largely on seniority and the ownership classification of the enterprise. In rural areas collective farms distributed earnings in an egalitarian fashion, and income inequality was mainly the result of differences among collective farms in resource endowments. Opportunities for households and individuals to engage in private income-generating activities were severely restricted.

With economic reforms the government has allowed, if not encouraged, some people to get rich first. In urban areas wage differentials and bonuses have increased; in rural areas farming is now household-based, and income differences reflect variation in household resources, abilities, and effort. Restrictions on private economic activities have been lifted, permitting diversification in sources of income and allowing returns to entrepreneurship. Such changes have naturally contributed to greater inequality.

The transition has led not only to a higher level of inequality, but also to a change in the underlying determinants of incomes and inequality. Markets now play a much enlarged role in the determination of incomes. As the scope of markets expands, one would expect incomes, and therefore inequality, to reflect differences in underlying productive characteristics and endowments such as land and labor endowments, education, and so on. That said, substantial government interventions remain, especially in labor and capital markets. In labor markets, for example, government interventions continue to hinder migration and restrict urban wage structures. Also, the Communist Party continues to influence personnel decisions and the implementation of government policies in ways that likely give advantages to those with political status and connections. To the extent that such interventions continue, one would expect variables such as geographic location and political status also to determine incomes and inequality.[1]

With these considerations in mind, in this chapter we try to answer two questions. First, what are the underlying determinants of inequality in China? Second, what explains the fact that inequality, after rising in prior years, remained more or less unchanged between 1995 and 2002? To answer these questions, we analyze empirically the contributions of different household and individual characteristics to inequality in per capita household income. We conduct our analysis using data from the 1995 and 2002 CHIP surveys. The datasets include detailed and rich information on the household and individual characteristics of interest. The use of two years' data permits comparisons over time.

To identify the contributions of different characteristics to inequality, we employ regression-based inequality decomposition. Regression-based inequality decomposition is a relatively new method that identifies the contribution of individual variables to inequality while controlling for variation in other variables. As will be discussed below, this approach has some drawbacks. Nevertheless, it improves on the standard methods that have been used to decompose inequality for China and elsewhere and provides some findings that shed light on recent trends in China's inequality.

Regression-based inequality decomposition has previously been applied to the study of China several times. Examples include Morduch and Sicular (2000), who use data from a single county, and Wan (2004), who uses provincial average per capita incomes rather than household-level data. In both cases the data used were from 1995 or earlier. Knight and Song (2003) employ regression-based inequality decomposition to analyze wage inequality in urban China using the 1988 and 1995 CHIP survey data, and in Chapter 9 of this book they carry out a similar analysis using the 2002 CHIP survey data. The analysis here goes beyond these studies in time frame and scope.

The first step in regression-based inequality decomposition is estimation of income equations using standard regression techniques. The results

---

[1] The market transition could also affect inequality in another regard, by introducing more risk and variability in employment and incomes. This would enlarge income variation, which would widen measured inequality in any given year. This possible impact of markets is not investigated here.

of this step provide answers to the question of how various household and individual characteristics affect income levels. The second step of the decomposition is calculation of the contribution of each characteristic, as well as of the estimated constant term and residuals, to inequality. Here the regression estimates are used to calculate income flows from each characteristic, the constant term, and residuals. These income flows are treated as income from different sources, for example, income from education or from Party membership, and then combined with the standard decomposition of inequality by income source. This second step provides information about the impact of various household and individual characteristics on inequality or the distribution of income.

The results of the analysis are consistent with the notion that markets are playing an increased role in income determination, but at the same time reveal that China's socialist legacy continues to influence income distribution. Education, which was not a major source of inequality in 1995, becomes a significant and large contributor to inequality in 2002. The emergence of education as an important determinant of inequality reflects changes in the returns to education as given by the regression equations. In 1995, and even more so in 2002, the returns to education are increasing with the level of education: that is, the more education one has, the greater the monetary rewards to that education. Furthermore, the gap between the returns to low and high levels of education widens between 1995 and 2002. These changes in the estimated returns to education imply increased inequality. Even if the distribution of education had remained unchanged, the distribution of income derived from education would have become more unequal. The increased importance of education likely reflects the growing role of markets in income determination. As discussed below, our finding that the returns to education have risen is consistent with the story that private compensation has come to reflect more fully differences in productivity arising from education.

While education's contribution to inequality has increased, it is still overshadowed by the contribution of location. We find that location of residence remains the largest single factor contributing to inequality. In view of ongoing restrictions on labor mobility, as well as the fact that location contributes to inequality even in market economies, the importance of location is not entirely surprising. More surprising, perhaps, is that despite the easing of restrictions on labor mobility and increased migration, the importance of location in determining incomes has not declined. Indeed, we find that location's contribution to inequality increased between 1995 and 2002.

Past studies measuring the contribution of location to inequality have, for the most part, used decomposition methods that do not control for other variables that could be correlated with location, such as education, age, and ethnicity. For example, residents in some locations (e.g., cities) have higher levels of education and fewer dependents than residents in other areas (e.g., rural areas). Consequently, differences in education and dependency ratios, not location per se, could explain some of the observed inequality among locations. Our approach controls for such covariates to location; even so, location remains the single most important factor contributing to inequality.

We also find that certain variables that have received considerable attention in the literature as underlying determinants of inequality do not have a large impact. Party membership, health, and ethnic minority status increase inequality, but the size of their contributions is relatively small. These variables jointly explain less than 5 percent of total income inequality. Land, which some have argued plays an important equalizing role, does reduce inequality, but by a small and declining amount. These findings are relevant to understanding the relationship between incomes, inequality, and government policy.

Comparison of the 1995 and 2002 decompositions provides some answers to the question of why inequality remained more or less constant. Our findings suggest that two factors played the largest roles in preventing further increases in inequality. First, the relative income premium enjoyed by urban households with older working-age members, likely reflecting returns to seniority, declined. This income premium was disequalizing in both 1995 and 2002, but less so in 2002. Second, the constant term, which was equalizing in 1995, became much more equalizing in 2002. This change indicates that shared, across-the-board absolute increases in income – the rising of all boats with the tide, so to speak – offset other factors, especially education, that would have otherwise driven inequality up.

In the next section we identify household and individual characteristics that are likely to influence per capita income levels and present some descriptive statistics on these characteristics. Section III contains results from regression estimations of the income equations. In Section IV we explain regression-based inequality decomposition and present findings from the decomposition analysis. We conclude with a discussion of the changing forces underlying China's inequality and implications for public policy.

II. Household Characteristics and Per Capita Incomes

As discussed elsewhere in this volume, household income in China comes from diverse sources, including wage employment, self-employment (in farming or other household-run businesses), earnings on assets, the imputed rental value of housing, and government and private transfers. Income from these various sources depends on the characteristics both of individuals within the household and of the household as a whole. The literature on China and elsewhere identifies a variety of characteristics relevant to the determination of household or household per capita income (Gustafsson and Li 1998, 2001; Knight and Song 1999, ch. 3; Miles 1997; Morduch and Sicular 2000). These include household demographic characteristics such as household size (if economies or diseconomies of scale in income generation exist), the proportion of dependents versus working-age household members, the proportion of male versus female working-age members, the ethnic composition of household members, and the age of household members. The education and experience of household members may also be important, as they influence the returns to labor and to some assets.

Household assets generate income. Holdings of many assets, however, are dependent on the level of household income and so are endogenous. For example, household financial assets are largely a function of household income, especially in China, where intergenerational transfers through bequests are as yet relatively unimportant. One asset that is not dependent on the level of household income is farmland allocated to households by villages under the household responsibility or contracting system. Such land is allocated administratively by the village or township on the basis of household size, and reallocations are infrequent.

Location of residence is commonly thought to affect income levels, and especially so in China, where mobility among provinces and between urban and rural areas is still restricted explicitly and implicitly. In China one set of factors considered potentially important in explaining household incomes is political status and connections (Bian and Logan 1996; Lam 2003; Morduch and Sicular 2000). Political status and connections are difficult to measure directly, but may be associated with the presence of a Communist Party member or cadre within the household. Here we focus on Party membership, as cadre status is often attached to employment, and so disentangling the extent to which political connections as opposed to the wages from cadre employment explain income is difficult. Note that Party membership's relationship with income could reflect not only political connections, but also unobserved ability or ambition that may be associated with Party membership (Gerber 2000; Lam 2003).

Table 4.1 presents descriptive statistics on per capita income and household characteristics from the 1995 and 2002 CHIP surveys. The sample

Table 4.1. *Household characteristics of individuals in the sample, 1995 and 2002*

Variable	1995		2002		Ratio of 2002 to 1995
	Mean	Standard deviation	Mean	Standard deviation	
Income per capita	3,157	4,404	5,731	5,606	1.82
Average education of working-age adults	7.39	2.88	8.54	2.89	1.16
Average age of working-age adults	36.66	6.70	38.24	7.10	1.04
Household size	4.33	1.39	4.04	1.33	0.93
Percentage of household members of working age (16–65)	72.28	20.78	77.04	19.90	1.07
Percentage of working-age members that are male	49.84	14.18	50.03	14.66	1.00
Percentage of working-age members that belong to the Party	10.22	20.65	13.60	23.62	1.33
Percentage of working-age members in poor health			0.49	4.45	
Percentage of family members that are an ethnic minority	4.59	17.31	7.40	22.00	1.61
Contracted farmland per capita (*mu*)	0.83	1.09	0.82	1.51	0.99
Urban location	0.29	0.45	0.39	0.49	1.34
No. of observations	73,649		62,098		

Notes:

[1] The statistics in this table are calculated over individuals rather than households. One can interpret them as weighted household averages, with the weights being the number of household members. The number of observations is the number of individuals in the households surveyed, adjusted to correct for oversampling of urban households in 1995 and of rural households in 2002 (see note 2).

[2] As urban households were oversampled in the 1995 survey and rural households oversampled in the 2002 survey, the samples have been adjusted so that the proportion of urban to rural individuals is equal to the national averages as given by the NBS in each of the two years. This was done by increasing the number of observations in the underrepresented sector through random sampling of the original sample for the underrepresented sector.

[3] Income values for 1995 and 2002 are in constant 2002 yuan. According to the NBS national consumer price index, prices increased 8.1 percent between 1995 and 2002.

[4] Information on health was not collected in 1995. Health status is self-reported.

[5] Farmland is measured in *mu*. Fifteen *mu* equal one hectare; 6.073 *mu* equal one acre.

[6] Provinces covered in the survey are discussed in the Appendix to this book.

we use includes rural and urban households, but not the migrant sample. As the ultimate objective of this chapter is to analyze the determinants of inequality among individuals, this table contains means and standard deviations calculated over individuals in the surveyed households rather than over households (see note 1 to Table 4.1). Income per capita follows the definition used by the National Bureau of Statistics (NBS) plus the rental value of owned housing and in-kind subsidies from public housing. In constant price terms mean per capita household income in 2002 was 82 percent higher than in 1995.

Several variables change between the two years, although in all cases the changes are small relative to their standard deviations and so are not statistically significant. Average education of working-age household members rose by more than a year from 7.4 to 8.5 years. Party membership and minority status also increased in relative importance, although their percentages remained low.[2] Household demographics remained fairly stable between the two years. Average age of household members and the share of working-age members increased slightly; household size decreased slightly. Land allocations per capita remained almost unchanged. Urban residency increased from about 30 percent to nearly 40 percent of the sample (see note 2 to Table 4.1).

One can see from Table 4.2 that many of these characteristics are correlated with income. Table 4.2 contains the mean characteristics for the top and bottom quintiles of the income distribution in 1995 and 2002. In both years the mean income of the top quintile is about 11 times that of the bottom quintile. The richest quintile has education levels of 10 years or higher, compared to only about six years for the poorest quintile. Household demographics in certain regards differ noticeably: the richest households are smaller and older and have a higher proportion of working-age members, but gender composition is not much different from that of the poorest households. The richer households have a higher incidence of Party membership and a lower proportion of members with poor health or minority ethnicity. Richer households are overwhelmingly located in urban areas, and accordingly have less land than poorer households.

The numbers in Table 4.2 suggest that household characteristics such as education, demographic composition, and location influence income levels in the directions expected. These numbers also reveal considerable

---

[2] The proportion of ethnic minorities increased in 2002 largely because of the inclusion of Guangxi and Xinjiang as new provinces in the sample.

Table 4.2. *Household characteristics for the richest and poorest quintiles,*
1995 and 2002

Variable	1995			2002		
	Poorest 20%	Richest 20%	Ratio	Poorest 20%	Richest 20%	Ratio
Income per capita	770	8,068	10.48	1,270	14,495	11.41
Average education of working-age adults	5.76	9.99	1.73	6.41	11.41	1.78
Average age of working-age adults	35.07	40.25	1.15	36.29	41.57	1.15
Household size	5.09	3.37	0.66	5.01	3.12	0.62
Percentage of household members of working age (16–65)	66.34	80.68	1.22	69.84	83.40	1.19
Percentage of working-age members that are male	49.33	49.57	1.00	50.81	48.54	0.96
Percentage of working-age members that belong to the Party	4.39	23.09	5.26	4.59	29.91	6.52
Percentage of working-age members in poor health				0.88	0.09	0.10
Percentage of family members that are an ethnic minority	9.04	2.70	0.30	15.04	3.67	0.24
Contracted farmland per capita (*mu*)	1.24	0.16	0.13	1.24	0.08	0.06
Urban location	0.01	0.81	81.0	0.01	0.91	91.0

Note: Notes to Table 4.1 apply. Income per capita is in constant 2002 prices.

correlation among the various characteristics, which indicates the need to control for covariation in order to identify the effect of the individual variables.

III. The Impact of Household Characteristics on Per Capita Income Levels

Regression analysis provides estimates of the impact of household characteristics on income that control for covariation among characteristics. Table 4.3 contains the results from a linear earnings equation estimated using

Table 4.3. *Per capita income regression estimates (dependent variable: household per capita income)*

Variable	1995		2002	
	Full	Parsimonious	Full	Parsimonious
Average education of working-age adults	95.34***	95.26***	−68.74	−92.66***
Education squared	−4.49**	−4.49*	11.11***	12.72***
Average age of working-age adults	127.82***	122.57***	123.42***	146.11***
Age squared	−1.49***	−1.48***	−1.62***	−1.91***
Household size	−501.92***	−501.49***	−817.74***	−837.23***
Household size squared	25.83***	20.91***	49.61***	51.37***
Percentage of household members of working age (16–65)	12.88***	12.86***	19.39***	19.54***
Percentage of working-age members that are male	−0.16		0.09	
Percentage of working-age members that belong to the Party	9.32***	9.32***	20.96***	20.98***
Percentage of working-age members in poor health			−16.16***	−16.04***
Percentage of family members that are an ethnic minority	−4.39***	−4.39***	0.13	
Contracted farmland per capita (*mu*)	182.52***	182.53***	126.33***	129.79***
Land squared	−20.91***	−20.59***	0.24	
Urban location dummy	2,345.73***	2,350.30***	3,936.45***	4,605.89***
Urban × education	−118.48*	−118.70*	−49.74	
Urban × education squared	16.83***	16.84***	29.18***	26.43***
Urban × age	191.00***	191.02***	180.47***	130.20***
Urban × age squared	−1.52***	−1.52***	−0.60	
Urban × household size	−2,396.54***	−2,397.82***	−3,694.38***	−3,639.15***
Urban × household size squared	276.47***	276.60***	366.05***	360.74***
Observations	73,649	73,649	62,098	62,098
F-statistic	833.70	856.86	2,161.04	2,461.21
Adjusted R^2	0.29	0.30	0.59	0.59

Notes:

[1] The regression equations are linear (not semi-log; see note 3 in text) and estimated using ordinary least squares.

[2] Income per capita for both years is in constant 2002 prices.

[3] The statistics in this table are calculated over individuals rather than households. The number of observations is the number of individuals in households surveyed, adjusted to correct for oversampling of urban households in 1995 and oversampling of rural households in 2002 (see notes to Table 4.1).

[4] Information on health was not collected in 1995. Health status is self-reported.

[5] Coefficients on provincial dummies are not shown because of space limitations. These coefficients were highly significant.

*** indicates significance at the 1 percent confidence level, ** at 5 percent, and * at 10 percent.

ordinary least squares (OLS).[3] As we are ultimately interested in inequality among individuals, observations represent individuals rather than households. The dependent variable is per capita income of the individual's household in constant 2002 prices. This means that we assume that household income is equally shared among household members, which is the usual practice in analyses of income distribution (Gustafsson and Li 2001).

Explanatory variables include characteristics that are likely to influence household per capita income and are not themselves a function of income and so are endogenous in the short term. These include the variables shown in Table 4.1, that is, average education of working-age adults in the household, average age of working-age adults, household size and demographic structure, percentage of household members in poor health (available only for 2002), percentage of working-age adults that belong to the Communist Party, and contracted farmland per capita. In addition, dummy variables are included to indicate province of residence and whether the individual's household is urban (versus rural). Note that poor health may be endogenous, but we include it because it is relevant from a policy perspective, and ultimately the magnitude of its effects on income levels and inequality are small.

Our aim is to analyze incomes and inequality nationwide, and so the sample includes individuals in both urban and rural areas. The process of income determination in urban and rural areas, however, may not be the same. Past studies suggest that the returns to individual and household characteristics differ between rural and urban areas (Knight and Song 1999). Variables where heterogeneity may be important are education, age, and household size. Interactions with the urban dummy variable are included for both the linear and squared terms of these variables, so that the shape of the relationships can differ in the two sectors.

The first two columns in Table 4.3 give estimates for 1995, and the second two for 2002. For each year we present results from a full specification that contains all variables, quadratic terms, and interactions, and also results from a parsimonious specification that eliminates those variables, quadratic terms, and interactions with estimated coefficients that are, individually

---

[3] Earnings equations are typically specified in semi-log form, but regression-based decomposition requires estimates from specifications where the dependent variable – income – has not been transformed. If the decomposition were carried out using results from a semi-log specification, they could be used only to analyze inequality in log income, but we are interested in inequality of income, not of log income or some other transformation of income. To capture potential nonlinearity, we include quadratic terms for several variables that are likely to have a nonlinear relationship with income.

and jointly, not statistically significant. All specifications, full and parsimonious, include dummy variables for location (urban/rural and province of residence); because of space limitations, the tables do not show the estimated coefficients on the province dummy variables. Estimates from the parsimonious specification are used for the inequality decomposition. The discussion below focuses on these parsimonious results.

The regression results show that household characteristics significantly influence per capita income, and for the most part in ways that one would expect. The only variable that is not significant in both 1995 and 2002 is the percentage of working-age household members that are male. This result may seem surprising, as studies of individual wage earnings for China usually find that gender affects earnings. In such studies, however, gender is of the individual, whereas here the gender variable measures the gender composition of working-age household members. If households with different gender compositions adopt different economic strategies, then gender need not have a significant impact on per capita income of the household. Also, while gender may matter when the household is headed by a single mother or when no males of working age are present, the number of such households in the sample is extremely small.

For education, age, and family size, the results show that the relationship with income is nonlinear and differs between urban and rural areas. For age (or, more precisely, average age of working-age household members) and family size, the basic shapes of the relationships are similar in 1995 and 2002, although the magnitudes of the coefficients have increased over time. The relationship between age and income has an inverted-U shape, which is consistent with theories of life-cycle earnings and with empirical findings elsewhere (e.g., Knight and Song 1999; Gustafsson and Li 2001). In rural areas this relationship is stable over time, with maximum income obtained at an average age of working-age household members of about 40 years, slightly higher than the mean in the rural sample. In urban areas the relationship between age and income is not stable over time. The age at which maximum income is obtained rises from 52 years in 1995 to 72 years in 2002, which is in fact beyond the range for this variable, as working age is defined as being less than or equal to 65. This change is consistent with Meng and Luo's finding in Chapter 11 that the income of the older urban residents has grown more rapidly than the average per capita income, largely because of improved pensions. In urban China women typically retire at 55 and men at 60, so pensions begin before age 65.

For family size, the relationship with income is U-shaped. In both rural and urban areas, almost all the sample is to the left of the minimum, so effectively family size reduces per capita income, although at a decreasing rate.[4] Again, this finding is consistent with other studies. In urban areas for small households the negative effect of an extra household member on income is much stronger than in rural areas, but as household size increases this negative effect weakens more quickly in urban than rural areas.

For education, the relationship with income generally has a U shape, with most or all of the samples on the upward sloping portion of the curve. This is the case for the urban samples in both 1995 and 2002 and for the rural sample in 2002. In these cases, more education implies higher income, and the returns to education are increasing with the level of education. The exception to this pattern is for the rural sample in 1995. For this group and year, education and income have an inverted-U–shaped relationship, with most of the samples on the upward sloping portion of the curve. In 1995, then, education increases rural income, with mildly diminishing marginal returns.[5] Thus, the relationship between education and income in rural areas has changed substantially between 1995 and 2002, coming to resemble more closely that in urban areas.

On average the magnitudes of the marginal returns to education were not overly large, especially in rural areas. Table 4.4 gives the marginal returns to education at average levels of education in rural and urban areas. In both 1995 and 2002 an increase in mean education by one year would have increased mean rural income by only about 2 percent, and mean urban income by about 8 percent. In both years the returns to education are higher in urban areas. For example, in 2002 an individual from a household with the mean level of rural education would have a marginal return to education of only 87 yuan in rural areas, compared to 460 yuan in urban areas (see the last column of Table 4.4). Also, the returns to education rose between 1995 and 2002. Even if the mean level of education had not increased between these two years, the marginal return to education would have risen from 40 to 65 yuan in rural areas, and even more so from 230 to 711 yuan in urban

---

[4] In 1995 the rural minimum is at a household size of 12.0, and no rural households are larger than this; in 2002 the rural minimum is 8.15, and only 1.5 percent of the rural sample has a household size larger than this. In 1995 the urban minimum is at a household size of 4.87, and 10 percent of the urban sample has a household size larger than this; in 2002 the minimum is 5.43, and only 1.5 percent of the sample has a household size larger than this.

[5] In 1995 the rural maximum is at 10.62 years of education, and only 1.2 percent of the rural sample has an average education exceeding this level; in 2002 the rural minimum is at 3.64 years, and only 4.99 percent of the sample is below this level. For the urban sample, in 1995 the minimum is at 0.95 years, and the entire urban sample is above this level, while in 2002 the minimum is at 1.18 years, and all but 0.3 percent of the urban sample is above this level.

Table 4.4. *Marginal returns to education at mean education levels, by sector and year (yuan)*

	Rural marginal return to education	Urban marginal return to education	Urban marginal return evaluated at mean rural education level
1995	39.58	230.23	129.70
2002	86.95	756.90	460.14
2002 marginal return evaluated at mean 1995 education level	65.07	711.48	

Note: Marginal returns are calculated using the estimated coefficients from the parsimonious regressions in Table 4.3, and for both years are in constant 2002 prices. They represent the additional per capita income that would result from one additional year of education for a household that has the mean level of education. Mean education levels were as follows: 1995 rural: 6.20; 1995 urban: 10.27; 2002 rural: 7.06; 2002 urban: 10.85.

areas (see the last row of Table 4.4).[6] These results are similar in broad terms to those for education given by other studies for China that use OLS and do not correct for heterogeneity (Heckman 2003; Knight and Song 1999; Li and Luo 2004; Maurer-Fazio and Dinh 2004; Zhang and Zhao 2002).

Aside from age, household size, and education, most other variables also have significant effects on income in the expected directions. In both 1995 and 2002 the percentage of household members of working age has a positive and significant impact on income. Poor health has a negative and significant coefficient in 2002 (the health variable was unavailable in 1995). The presence of household members of ethnic minorities reduces income significantly in 1995, but not in 2002. Land increases income with gradually diminishing marginal returns in 1995 and linearly in 2002.[7]

Party membership has the expected positive and significant effect on income in both years, with the impact increasing substantially between 1995 and 2002. Since the Party variable is defined as the share of working-age

[6] Note that the education variable is defined as the average education for working-age household members. Thus, increasing the education variable by one year would require an additional year of education for every working-age member of the household. For example, in rural households, which on average contained about three working-age members in 1995, this means that three additional years of education distributed among the working-age household members would be needed to increase the education variable by one year.

[7] The relationship in 1995 is quadratic with an inverted-U shape, but the maximum is at land area of 129.79 *mu*, far larger the average land area for the rural sample of 1.16 *mu*, let alone the maximum observed land area of 19 *mu*.

household members who belong to the Party, the magnitudes of the coefficients are, in fact, reasonably large. For example, consider a household with two working-age members, neither of whom belongs to the Party. If one adult in such a two-adult household joins the Party, then the Party variable increases by 50 percentage points. This implies an income increase of 50 times the estimated coefficient, or 466 yuan (15 percent of the average income per capita) in 1995 and 1,048 yuan (18 percent of the average income per capita) in 2002.

Finally, location is a significant determinant of income. The coefficient on the urban dummy variables indicates that urban location increases income by 2,350 yuan or 76 percent of mean income per capita in 1995, and by 4,606 yuan or 80 percent of mean income per capita in 2002. This income advantage does not include the differential urban returns to age, household size, and education discussed above. Province of residence also has significant and large effects on income, although these estimated coefficients are not shown in the table.

IV. The Impact of Household Characteristics on Inequality

Analyzing the impact of household characteristics on inequality requires first measuring inequality, and then identifying how much of the measured inequality is attributable to each characteristic. The most well-known method has been inequality decomposition by population group, which involves dividing the sample into discrete groups (e.g., by urban-rural residence, age group, education category) and then calculating the amount of inequality within each group and between the means of each group. This approach is useful but has several important limitations (Morduch and Sicular 2002). The decomposition must be carried out over discrete categories, even though some characteristics such as age are continuous variables. For continuous variables, the choice of where to divide the sample into categories can affect the results. Also, decomposition by group is not well designed for multivariate analysis that requires holding constant the effects of correlated variables.

In recent years researchers have tried to overcome these limitations by developing regression-based approaches to inequality decomposition. Despite certain limitations, the regression-based decompositions are an improvement over standard group-based decomposition in that they allow for continuous variables and control for covariation among the determinants of income. Here we employ the regression-based decomposition method proposed by Morduch and Sicular (2002). This method is relatively straightforward and can capture the equalizing effect of income sources that are distributed equally among individuals.

A. Regression-Based Inequality Decomposition

Regression-based inequality decomposition begins with the estimation of an income equation along the lines of that discussed in Section III.[8] The income equation can be written as

$$y = X\beta + \varepsilon, \tag{1}$$

where y is income, X is a matrix of explanatory variables, β is a vector of regression coefficients, and ε is a vector of residuals.[9] Using the estimated coefficients from this regression equation, one can calculate income flows attributable to the different explanatory variables. These income flows simply equal the estimated coefficients times the values of their associated explanatory variables, that is,

$$\hat{y}_i^m = \hat{\beta}_m x_i^m, \tag{2}$$

where $\hat{\beta}_m$ is the estimated regression coefficient and x_i^m is the ith individual's value of the mth variable. Total income of the individual is the sum of these flows for all explanatory variables, plus the constant and regression residual. The estimated income flows can be interpreted as income from different sources (from education, age, etc.).

Regression-based decomposition uses these estimated income flows in combination with inequality decomposition by income source. Inequality decomposition by income source is typically used to calculate how much of total income inequality is attributable to income from different sources, such as wages, interest, dividends, and so on. Here we simply define the income flows generated by household characteristics as the "sources" of income. Decomposition by income "source" then tells us how much of total inequality is contributed by income flows from household and individual characteristics, such as education, age, family size, Party membership, and location of residence. The income equation also includes a residual that captures unexplained differences in income. This unexplained component of income also contributes to overall inequality.

As discussed in Morduch and Sicular (2002), and as explained in more detail in the Appendix to this chapter, for most commonly used inequality

---

[8] The discussion in this section is based on Morduch and Sicular (2002). Please refer to that source for additional details and discussion of the method.

[9] X is an $n \times M$ matrix with the first column being the vector $c = (1, 1, \ldots, 1)$.

indices the share of inequality contributed by each explanatory variable can be written as

$$s^m = \frac{\sum_{i=1}^{n} a_i(\mathbf{y})\hat{\beta}_m x_i^m}{I(\mathbf{y})}.$$ (3)

This equation shows that the share s^m of inequality contributed by income flowing from the mth characteristic (e.g., education) is equal to a weighted sum across individuals of their estimated income flows from this variable, all divided by overall inequality $I(\mathbf{y})$. Similarly, the contribution of the estimated residual is

$$s^\varepsilon = \frac{\sum_{i=1}^{n} a_i(\mathbf{y})e_i}{I(\mathbf{y})},$$ (4)

where e_i is the estimated residual.

The weights $a_i(\mathbf{y})$ in these equations depend on the choice of the inequality index. Here we carry out the inequality decomposition using the Theil T index. The Theil T index is commonly used in the literature, and its decomposition has desirable properties. For this index, income flows that are distributed equally among all individuals are inequality reducing: that is, they register a negative contribution to overall inequality. A simple example illustrates why this property is appealing. Consider a population of two people who earn wage income only. The income distribution is ($10; $100). Now, suppose the government gives everyone an equal transfer of $1 million. The income distribution becomes ($1,000,010; $1,000,100). Intuitively this second income distribution is more equal than the first one. With the Theil T inequality decomposition used here, such a government transfer will indeed show up as inequality reducing, as will any positive income flow – large or small – that is equally distributed.[10]

B. Analysis of Income Flows

So as to provide a bridge between the regression results and decompositions, we begin by examining the income flows of selected explanatory variables in the regression equation. Table 4.5 gives average income flows derived from these explanatory variables. Tables 4.6a and 4.6b show the distribution of these income flows among poorer and richer income quintiles in the sample.

---

[10] The decomposition of the Gini coefficient does not have this property, and so we do not discuss it here. We have conducted the decomposition using the Gini, and the results are similar to those for the Theil T except for the constant term and for variables with equally distributed income flows.

Table 4.5. *Average income flows from selected explanatory variables,*
1995 and 2002

	1995		2002	
	Mean value (yuan)	Percentage of mean per capita income	Mean value (yuan)	Percentage of mean per capita income
Average education of working-age adults, total	615	19.5	1,528	26.7
Average age of working-age adults, total	3,907	123.7	4,763	83.1
Household size, total	−3,010	−95.3	−5,486	−95.7
Percentage of household members of working age	930	29.4	1,506	26.3
Percentage of working-age members in the Party	95	3.0	285	5.0
Percentage of working-age members in poor health			−8	−0.1
Percentage of household members that are an ethnic minority	−20	−0.6		
Contracted farmland per capita	112	3.5	107	1.9

Note: Income flows are calculated as the estimated coefficients (from the parsimonious regression specifications in Table 4.3) times the mean values of the explanatory variables. Income flows for education, age, and household size include all squared and interacted effects. Income flows for location variables and the constant term are not shown.

In both tables the income flows for education, age, and household size are calculated as the total flows, including squared terms and urban interaction effects.

The average income flows in Table 4.5 provide information on which characteristics are more or less important relative to mean income. Characteristics that increase income have positive income flows; those that decrease income have negative income flows. In both 1995 and 2002 demographic variables – age, household size, and the percentage of working-age household members – have large average impacts on income. The income flows from age and from the percentage of working-age members are positive, while that for household size is negative. Education also has a relatively large income flow. In 1995 education contributes about 20 percent of mean income, and in 2002, 27 percent.

Party membership, health, minority status, and farmland are, on average, relatively unimportant as sources of income. Income flows from Party

Table 4.6a. *Distribution of income flows from selected variables by quintile, 1995*

	Percentage of income flows					
	Bottom quintile	Second quintile	Third quintile	Fourth quintile	Top quintile	Ratio of top to bottom
Income per capita, total	4.87	8.68	13.30	22.09	51.07	10.49
Average education of working-age adults, total	12.39	13.20	14.96	24.07	35.38	2.86
Average age of working-age adults, total	12.62	13.15	15.29	25.18	33.76	2.68
Household size, total (−)	12.39	12.60	14.94	26.10	33.97	2.74
Percentage of household members of working age	18.36	18.93	19.87	20.53	22.31	1.22
Percentage of working-age members in the Party	8.59	8.67	12.54	25.02	45.19	5.26
Percentage of household members that are an ethnic minority (−)	39.42	20.92	16.71	11.18	11.77	0.30
Contracted farmland per capita	28.88	27.83	25.75	13.54	4.01	0.14

Note: Variables that have negative income flows are indicated by (−) in the first column. Income flows are calculated as the estimated coefficients (from the parsimonious regression specifications in Table 4.3) times the mean values of the explanatory variables. Income flows for education, age, and household size include all squared and interacted effects. Each quintile's percentage of the income flow for a variable is calculated by dividing the sum of the income flow for all individuals in that quintile by the total income flow for the entire sample.

membership on average contribute only 3 percent of mean income in 1995 and 5 percent in 2002. Income flows from health and minority variables contribute less than 1 percent of mean income. Land contributes 3.5 percent of mean income in 1995 and 1.9 percent in 2002.

The income shares of the different variables change somewhat between 1995 and 2002. The relative importance of income flows from the demographic characteristics decreases somewhat. Education's relative importance increases, as does that of Party membership. Land's contribution to average

Table 4.6b. *Distribution of income flows from selected variables by quintile, 2002*

	Percentage of income flows					
	Bottom quintile	Second quintile	Third quintile	Fourth quintile	Top quintile	Ratio of top to bottom
Income per capita, total	4.43	8.24	13.38	23.37	50.58	11.42
Average education of working-age adults, total	0.60	2.18	10.56	33.06	54.14	90.23
Average age of working-age adults, total	11.72	12.63	17.07	26.59	31.99	2.73
Household size, total (−)	10.66	11.39	16.96	28.43	32.56	3.05
Percentage of household members of working age	18.13	19.26	20.25	20.71	21.65	1.19
Percentage of working-age members in the Party	6.76	8.80	14.16	26.31	43.98	6.51
Percentage of working-age members in poor health (−)	35.97	27.70	19.08	13.74	3.51	0.10
Contracted farmland per capita	30.32	32.78	24.67	10.18	2.06	0.07

Note: Please see the note to Table 4.6a.

income declines. Overall, though, the characteristics that are relatively important – have large income shares – in 1995 remain important in 2002.

Tables 4.6a (1995) and 4.6b (2002) show the distribution of income flows from each of the characteristics among quintiles. Perfect equality of income from a particular variable would imply that its income flows are a uniform 20 percent for all quintiles, and that the ratio of the income flow of the richest quintile to that of the poorest quintile equals one (last columns of the tables). A variable that has income flows that are unequally distributed would show smaller percentages of its income flow going to lower quintiles and larger percentages going to higher quintiles, unless that variable has a negative coefficient. If the variable's coefficient is negative, then it decreases with income. In this case the variable is unequally distributed if large percentages of the negative income flow go to lower quintiles. Variables that have negative income flows are household size (in both years), share of household members that belong to an ethnic minority (in 1995), and share of working-age members in poor health (in 2002), as noted by minus signs in these tables.

The first row of the tables shows how total income per capita is distributed among the quintiles. In both years the richest quintile enjoys about half, and the poorest less than 5 percent, of total income. The richest group has about 11 times the income of the poorest group. This pattern changes only slightly between 1995 and 2002.

Several variables have income flows that are relatively equal compared to the distribution of total income. The variable with the most equally distributed income flows in both 1995 and 2002 is the percentage of household members of working age. Household size is also relatively equally distributed, with a negative income flow that goes disproportionately to the richer quintiles. Both these variables have a large impact on average income (Table 4.5), which suggests that they may be important equalizing factors.

The income flows from education, age, Party membership, ethnicity, and health are more unequally distributed. Income from Party membership goes disproportionately to the richer quintiles – the richest quintile's income flow from Party membership is five to seven times that of the poorest quintile. Minority status and health both have negative income flows, and these negative flows go largely to the poorer quintiles in the income distribution. For these three variables, however, the income shares are small (Table 4.5) – for health and minority status less than 1 percent of average income, and for Party membership less than 5 percent. Also, the distribution of income from these variables is more equal than the distribution of total income per capita. This suggests that these variables are likely not the major variables explaining overall income inequality.

Land per capita is also somewhat unequally distributed in both years, but its positive income flow goes disproportionately to the poorer quintiles in the income distribution. Thus, income from land would tend to reduce overall inequality. Land's average income flow, however, is relatively small (2–4 percent), and so its impact on overall inequality may not be large.

Education and age both are unequally distributed and have large income shares. In 1995 the distribution of income flows from these two variables is fairly similar, with that going to the richest quintile about three times that going to the poorest quintile. For age the distribution of income flows remains fairly stable between 1995 and 2002. For education the distribution of income flows changes substantially and becomes extremely unequal. While in 1995 the bottom quintile receives 12 percent of the income flows from education, in 2002 it receives less than 1 percent. In contrast, the richest quintile's share of income from education increases from 35 percent in 1995 to 54 percent in 2002.

The marked increase in inequality of education's income flows reflects the change in the shape of the relationship between education and income. In 1995 for the rural population the marginal return to education is mildly decreasing, so that an increase in years of education generates a less than proportionate increase in income derived from education. In 2002, however, the returns to education are increasing. In other words, an increase in years of education has a more than proportionate increase in income derived from education. Since richer households have more education, this causes education to exacerbate inequality.

With the exception of education in 2002, in both years the distributions among quintiles of income flows from the characteristics shown in Tables 4.6a and 4.6b are more equal than the distribution of total income per capita. Education in 2002 is the only variable shown that is more unequally distributed among quintiles than overall income. All other variables are, relative to overall income, equally distributed.

Not shown in these tables are the distributions of income flows from the location dummy variables and the residual. As will be seen below, location and the residual are key factors contributing to inequality.

C. Regression-Based Inequality Decomposition: Basic Results

Results from regression-based inequality decomposition appear in Table 4.7. The numbers in this table show the contributions to overall inequality of each explanatory variable and of the constant term and residuals. The constant term represents a component of income that is received equally by all individuals. Not surprisingly, then, the Theil T decomposition finds that it reduces inequality. Several household composition variables also generate income flows that are relatively equally distributed (Tables 4.6a, b). Most equal are income flows from the percentage of household members of working age. This variable has a large, negative contribution to inequality of −23 percent in both years. The age variable also has a negative contribution of −10 to −14 percent. Income flows from household size are also fairly equally distributed, but this variable has a negative coefficient and so tends to reduce income. Thus, it tends to increase inequality. Its contribution declines from 9 percent in 1995 to 3 percent in 2002.

Income flows from education are fairly equally distributed in 1995, but because of changes in the shape of returns to education, by 2002 they have become extremely unequally distributed. This change is reflected in

Table 4.7. *Inequality and the contributions (%) of explanatory variables to inequality, 1995 and 2002*

	1995	2002
Overall inequality	0.399	0.361
Average education of working-age adults, total	−1.16	36.14
Average age of working-age adults, total	−14.14	−9.77
Household size, total	8.62	2.63
Percentage of household members of working age	−22.65	−23.18
Percentage of working-age members in the Party	1.39	2.93
Percentage of working-age members in poor health		0.33
Percentage of household members that are an ethnic minority	1.15	
Contracted farmland per capita	−6.53	−4.38
Location dummy variables, total	79.52	90.41
Constant	−15.29	−54.93
Residual	69.10	59.83

Note: Calculated using the Theil T decomposition rule. See the Appendix to this chapter for an explanation of the methodology.

education's contribution to inequality. In 1995 education has a negative, although small, contribution to inequality: that is, it slightly reduces inequality. In 2002 education's contribution to inequality is large and positive, at 36 percent.

As expected, Party membership, poor health, and minority status all tend to increase inequality, but not by much. They all have positive but small contributions to inequality. Land tends to reduce inequality. Its income flows are unequally distributed, but go to poorer individuals. Its contribution is modest, −7 percent in 1995 and −4 percent in 2002.

In both years the residual has a large, positive effect on inequality, contributing 60–70 percent. This indicates that a substantial share of inequality cannot be explained by observed characteristics. Both years also show the overwhelming importance of location of residence. Location is disequalizing and contributes 80 percent to 90 percent of overall inequality, depending on the year.

While overall inequality did not increase substantially between the two years, the decompositions reveal that the factors underlying inequality changed. Most noticeable here is the increase in education's impact as a disequalizing factor. While Party membership's contribution to inequality remained small, it increased between the two years. This could reflect the increased value of political capital and connections, or perhaps of unmeasured ability and ambition that is correlated with Party membership. Land's equalizing effect declined between the two years, which suggests that

Table 4.8. *Contributions of base effects versus urban differentials to inequality (%), 1995 and 2002*

	1995	2002
Average education of working-age adults, total	−1.16	36.14
Of which: base	−10.16	6.32
Urban interaction	8.99	29.81
Average age of working-age adults, total	−14.14	−9.77
Of which: base	−70.08	−49.71
Urban interaction	55.93	39.94
Household size, total	8.62	2.63
Of which: base	58.03	55.47
Urban interaction	−49.41	−52.84
Urban interactions, total	15.51	16.91
Location dummy variables, total	79.52	90.41

Note: Calculated using the Theil T decomposition rule. See the Appendix to this chapter for an explanation of the methodology.

although China's collective land allocation system may have moderated inequality in the past, it may not do so in the future.

D. The Impact of Urban Differentials on Inequality

Table 4.8 shows how much of the sum contributions to inequality of education, age, and household size come from the base effects of these variables versus urban differentials, as captured by urban interaction terms. The base effect reflects how much each variable would contribute to inequality if the rural returns to each variable applied to all individuals. The urban interaction effects capture the impact on inequality of the fact that characteristics yield different returns in urban than in rural areas.

For education and age, the base effects are either inequality reducing or only modestly increase inequality. The urban differentials, however, have large, positive contributions to inequality. For education this is especially true in 2002, when the coefficient for the urban-education squared interaction increases substantially over 1995, providing a large income differential for the urban sector's more highly educated individuals. For age, the contribution of the urban differential to inequality reflects the large, positive coefficient on the urban-age interaction, and thus the significantly higher income enjoyed by individuals in urban households with older working-age members.

In contrast, for household size the base effect increases inequality, while the urban interactions have a large inequality-reducing contribution. These results are the opposite of those for education and age, reflecting that household size is predominately income reducing, and more so for urban than rural segments of the population.

Overall, the urban interaction effects from household size offset those from education and age, so that the net effect of the urban interactions is about 16 to 17 percent, with little change between 1995 and 2002.

The impact of China's urban-rural divide includes these differential returns on household characteristics as well as the pure effect of place of residence measured by the location dummy variables. Unfortunately, the Theil T decomposition does not allow identification of the separate effects of different dummy variables (see discussion in the Appendix to this chapter). Consequently, we cannot identify how much of the sum contribution of the location dummy variables is due to urban location versus province of residence. The sum contribution of location was large, 80 percent in 1995, and increasing to 90 percent in 2002.

It is possible that the rise in the contribution of the location dummy variables shown in Table 4.8 reflects an increased contribution of the urban dummy.[11] The analyses in Chapters 2 and 3 of this volume suggest a narrowing of provincial income differences and widening of the urban-rural gap over time. Their estimates, unlike those here, do not control for differences among locations in household and individual characteristics. Also, the results of our income regressions show that the premium on urban residence, as measured by the estimated coefficient on the urban dummy variable and holding other variables constant, has nearly doubled from 2,350 yuan in 1995 to 4,600 yuan in 2002. This premium is large, in 2002 equivalent to 80 percent of the mean income for our sample. Thus, it seems plausible that the rise in the contribution of location to inequality shown in Table 4.8 reflects an increasing contribution of the urban-rural divide. This, together with the sustained impact of urban differentials for household characteristics, highlights the continued and perhaps increasing importance of the urban-rural divide to overall inequality.

---

[11] Furthermore, decomposition of the Gini coefficient, which permits identification of the separate effects of different dummy variables, finds that the urban location dummy has become more important as a source of inequality. The Gini decomposition, not reported here for reasons discussed elsewhere, shows that the overall contribution to inequality of the location dummy variables remained stable at around 47 percent in the two years, but this was the net effect of a rising contribution of the urban dummy (from 28 to 35 percent) and a declining contribution of the provincial dummies (from 20 to 12 percent).

E. Explaining Why Inequality Remained Constant between 1995 and 2002

Comparison of the 1995 and 2002 decompositions provides some answers to the question of why inequality did not increase between these two years. Since the overall level of inequality remained relatively constant, the answer lies with those factors whose contributions to inequality changed. Education shows the largest increase in contribution to inequality. All else being equal, this would have caused inequality to increase by nearly 40 percent. Location's contribution to inequality has also increased, although less so than education.

The impact of these disequalizing trends from education and location, however, was more than offset by change in the contribution of the constant term. The constant term, which was moderately equalizing in 1995, became very strongly equalizing in 2002. This change reflects the increasing importance of across-the-board absolute increases in income shared by poorer and richer groups alike.

V. Conclusion

In this chapter we have examined the household and individual characteristics that underlie income levels and inequality in China. Our findings suggest that markets may be playing an increased role in income determination, but that government interventions and China's socialist legacy continue to have an influence. Several key results emerge. First, education has become a significant and large contributor to inequality. The emergence of education as an important determinant of inequality reflects changes in the returns to education. By 2002 individuals in households with higher levels of education received substantially greater returns to that education than those in households with lower levels of education. Consequently, even if the distribution of education in China had remained unchanged, the distribution of income derived from education would have become more unequal.

The expanded role of education as a contributing factor to inequality likely reflects the increased role of markets in income determination. Such would be the case if the structure of wages (and other income) has come to reflect more closely underlying productivity differences associated with education. Earlier research on this question has found that through the mid-1990s the private returns to education were lower than the marginal productivity of education. Furthermore, the gap between the productivity of and private returns to education was especially large for highly educated workers (Fleisher, Dong, and Liu 1996; Fleisher and Wang 2001). Our finding of rising returns to education, and especially to higher levels of education, is consistent with the observation that private compensation now more fully reflects differences in productivity arising from education.

Second, location of residence remains the single most important factor contributing to inequality. Moreover, despite reports of increased migration and regional mobility in China, location's contribution to inequality has increased somewhat between 1995 and 2002. A key aspect of location that contributes significantly to inequality is the urban-rural divide. We identify two ways in which the urban-rural divide affects inequality: (a) through differences between the two sectors in the returns to household characteristics, and (b) through differences in the level of income attributable to urban versus rural location, as measured by the contribution of the urban dummy variable to inequality. The first of these contributes more than 15 percent of total inequality. Although we cannot identify the latter effect separately from the effects of province of residence, it is likely to be large. Furthermore, the continued importance of location is visible in the widening premium on urban residency, which by our estimates doubled between 1995 and 2002. Note that our analysis does not include rural-to-urban migrants, so this conclusion does not capture the possible mitigating effects of migration.

Third, we find that certain variables that have received attention in the literature do not have a large impact on inequality. As expected, Party membership, health, and ethnic minority status increase inequality; however, the magnitude of their contributions to inequality is small. Similarly, landholdings reduce inequality, but by a relatively modest and declining amount.

Our findings shed some light on the relationship between government policy and inequality. The continued large role of geographic location, especially urban-rural location, likely reflects government interventions that continue to constrain mobility as well as government policies that favor richer urban locations. The significance and growing role of education points to the importance of government education policies. In the future, public investment in education may be critical from a distributional perspective. That investment should be targeted so as to expand access to education and allow broad-based continuation into higher levels of education.

Much has been written about China's policies on farmland allocation. While in the past China's land tenure policies may have been an important equalizing force, and while these policies may continue to provide a form of social security for poor households, our analysis reveals that the equalizing contribution of land to national income distribution is small. This may reflect the fact that land-based farm income's share of overall income has declined. It may also reflect the fact that the distribution of farmland has become less equal, perhaps because of recent policies that discourage the reallocation of land based on changes in household size or land confiscations or theft (see Chapter 5 of this volume).

Finally, our analysis helps explain the somewhat surprising finding from the CHIP surveys that between 1995 and 2002 inequality in China did not continue to increase. Certain variables, such as education and the urban-rural gap, indeed were forces that would have generated more inequality. Other variables, however, had a mitigating effect. Most important here were two variables. First, the income premium enjoyed by older urban workers, perhaps reflecting the emphasis on seniority in urban wage scales, grew more slowly than average incomes. This premium remains disequalizing, but less so than before. Second, the contribution of the constant term indicates that, after taking into account income flows from other variables, growth in income between 1995 and 2002 was widely shared, with both poorer and richer groups experiencing increases in absolute terms. Whether this was simply the fortuitous outcome of macroeconomic growth or the result of targeted social welfare programs is unclear. Further research is needed to uncover the reasons.

APPENDIX: REGRESSION-BASED INEQUALITY DECOMPOSITION

Inequality decomposition by income source typically employs inequality indices that can be written as a weighted sum of incomes:

$$I(\mathbf{y}) = \sum_{i=1}^{n} a_i(\mathbf{y}) y_i, \qquad (A.1)$$

where $I(\mathbf{y})$ is the inequality index and $a_i(\mathbf{y})$ the weights, both defined over the income vector $\mathbf{y}$. Commonly used inequality measures such as the Gini, variance, and Theil T indices satisfy this property.

Shorrocks (1982) has shown that for inequality measures that satisfy this property, the proportional contribution of income source k to overall inequality can be written as a weighted sum over individuals of income from that source:

$$s^k = \frac{\sum_{i=1}^{n} a_i(\mathbf{y}) y_i^k}{I(\mathbf{y})}. \qquad (A.2)$$

The Theil T index, used here, can be written as

$$I_{TT}(\mathbf{y}) = \frac{1}{n\mu} \sum_{i=1}^{n} \left[\ln \left(\frac{y_i}{\mu} \right) \right] y_i, \qquad (A.3)$$

and the associated decomposition rule gives the proportional share of inequality for source k as

$$s_{TT}^{k} = \frac{\frac{1}{n\mu} \sum_{i=1}^{n} \left[\ln \left(\frac{y_i}{\mu} \right) \right] y_i^{k}}{\frac{1}{n\mu} \sum_{i=1}^{n} \left[\ln \left(\frac{y_i}{\mu} \right) \right] y_i}. \qquad (A.4)$$

Ultimately we are interested in combining the results from regression analysis with income decomposition by source. This is straightforward. Expression (A.2) above giving the shares of inequality from different income sources is simply rewritten using estimated income flows from the regression analysis:

$$s^{m} = \frac{\sum_{i=1}^{n} a_i(\mathbf{y}) \hat{\beta}_m x_i^{m}}{I(\mathbf{y})}. \qquad (A.5)$$

Equation (A.5) gives the share of overall inequality contributed by the income flow from explanatory variable m. Note that the constant is treated as an explanatory variable in this analysis. The contribution of the residual is

$$s^{\varepsilon} = \frac{\sum_{i=1}^{n} a_i(\mathbf{y}) e_i}{I(\mathbf{y})}, \qquad (A.6)$$

where e_i is the estimated residual.

In this chapter we report inequality decompositions using the decomposition rule shown above for the Theil T inequality index. We also calculated inequality decompositions using other indices, but we do not report them here. We do not report findings using the Gini coefficient's decomposition rule because it does not satisfy the property of uniform additions (Morduch and Sicular 2002). The property of uniform additions holds that measured inequality should decline if everyone in the population receives a positive income transfer of equal size. Conversely, inequality should increase if everyone receives an equal, negative income transfer. The property of constant additions is widely accepted in the literature as being desirable, and indeed, the Gini coefficient satisfies the property. The decomposition rule based on the Gini, however, does not satisfy this property, and so we do not use it or other decompositions with this feature.

The Theil T index is also common in the literature, and its associated decomposition rule satisfies the property of constant additions. We also conducted decompositions using the variance and squared coefficient of variation (which satisfy the property of constant additions). As the results are similar to the Theil T, we do not report them here.

Note that the property of constant additions makes the results of the decomposition sensitive to the construction of dummy variables. This problem is avoided by using a standard transformation of the dummy variables. After estimation, we construct a single variable that aggregates all the dummy variables, that is, it equals the sum of the estimated coefficients on the dummy variables times the values of the dummy variables for all observations in the sample. We calculate the mean of this aggregate dummy variable, and then subtract from the aggregate dummy variable its mean. The constant is then adjusted to include the mean of the aggregate dummy variable. Decomposition then is carried out using the normalized aggregate dummy variable and the adjusted constant term.

In the decomposition the contribution of the aggregate dummy variable to inequality captures only deviations around zero caused by dummy variables as a group, and the constant reflects all constant additions (or subtractions) that might otherwise have been attributed to dummy variables. This reconstruction of the dummy variables makes the decomposition produce a consistent result regardless of how the dummy variables are originally constructed in the regression equation. The decomposition so carried out, however, can identify only the aggregate contribution of all dummy variables to inequality, and not the separate effects of individual dummy variables.

References

Bian, Y. and J. R. Logan (1996), "Market Transition and the Persistence of Power: The Changing Stratification System in Urban China," *American Sociological Review,* 61(5), 739–758.

Fleisher, B. M., K. Dong, and Y. Liu (1996), "Education, Enterprise Organization, and Productivity in the Chinese Paper Industry," *Economic Development and Cultural Change,* 44(3), 571–587.

Fleisher, B. M. and X. Wang (2001), "Skill Differentials, Return to Schooling, and Market Segmentation in a Transition Economy: The Case of Mainland China," *Journal of Development Economics,* 73(1), 315–328.

Gerber, T. P. (2000), "Membership Benefits or Selection Effects? Why Former Communist Party Members Do Better in Post-Soviet Russia," *Social Science Research,* 29(1), 25–50.

Gustafsson, B. and S. Li (1998), "Inequality in China at the End of the '80s – Locational Aspects and Household Characteristics," *Asian Economic Journal,* 12(1), 35–63.

Gustafsson, B. and S. Li (2001), "A More Unequal China? Aspects of Inequality in the Distribution of Equivalent Income," in C. Riskin, R. Zhao, and S. Li, eds., *China's Retreat from Equality: Income Distribution and Economic Transition,* Armonk, NY: M. E. Sharpe.

Heckman, J. (2003), "China's Investment in Human Capital," *Economic Development and Cultural Change*, 51(4), 795–804.

Knight, J. and L. Song (1999), *The Rural-Urban Divide: Economic Disparities and Interactions in China*, New York: Oxford University Press.

Knight, J. and L. Song (2003), "Increasing Urban Wage Inequality in China: Extent, Elements and Evaluation," *Economics of Transition*, 11(4), 597–619.

Lam, K. C. (2003), "Earnings Advantage of Party Members in Urban China," Business Research Centre Working Paper, Hong Kong Baptist University.

Li, H. and Y. Luo (2004), "Reporting Errors, Ability Heterogeneity, and Returns to Schooling in China," *Pacific Economic Review*, 9(3), 191–207.

Maurer-Fazio, M. and N. Dinh (2004), "Differential Rewards to, and Contributions of, Education in Urban China's Segmented Labor Markets," *Pacific Economic Review*, 9(3), 173–189.

Miles, D. (1997), "A Household Level Study of the Determinants of Incomes and Consumption," *Economic Journal*, 107(440), 1–25.

Morduch, J. and T. Sicular (2000), "Politics, Growth and Inequality in Rural China: Does It Pay to Join the Party?" *Journal of Public Economics*, 77(3), 331–356.

Morduch, J. and T. Sicular (2002), "Rethinking Inequality Decomposition, with Evidence from China," *Economic Journal*, 112(476), 93–106.

Shorrocks, A. F. (1982), "Inequality Decomposition by Factor Components," *Econometrica*, 50(1), 193–211.

Wan, G. (2004), "Accounting for Income Inequality in Rural China: A Regression-Based Approach," *Journal of Comparative Economics*, 32(2), 348–363.

Zhang, J. and Y. Zhao (2002), "Economic Returns to Education in Urban China," unpublished manuscript.

FIVE

The Distribution of Wealth in China

Zhao Renwei and Ding Sai

I. Introduction

China's reform and openness have now been ongoing for a quarter century. During this important period, while China's economy has developed rapidly and personal incomes have increased, changes in income distribution, especially rising income inequality, have raised social concerns. Income and wealth are closely correlated. The people's well-being depends not only on incomes but also on the level and distribution of wealth (Schneider 2004, pp. vii, 6). Since 1990 China has experienced a period of rapid accumulation of personal wealth combined with unequal distribution of that wealth. The country has established the objective of constructing a well-off society. The issue of wealth distribution thus has become a new focus of concern.

In this chapter wealth, also called property or assets, includes land, housing, and individual savings or holdings of other financial instruments, among other factors. Here the terms wealth, property, and assets are used as synonyms, but in different ways and from different points of view. When we link these assets with ownership we use the term "property rights."

Wealth and income are different concepts. Here income refers to all earnings of a person or a household in a certain period of time (usually a year). Wealth refers to the net monetary value of all assets at a certain point of time. In other words, wealth is the stock of all property at a certain point, while income is a flow of earnings in a time period. Obviously, income and wealth are interrelated. The previous flows of income affect the current stock of wealth; the current stock of wealth affects the flows of future income. Growth of wealth levels and changes in wealth structure and distribution affect

This chapter was written by Zhao Renwei. Ding Sai contributed to the calculations. The authors would like to express thanks to Li Shi and Wei Zhong for their help.

not only macroeconomic stability, but also long-term changes in income distribution.

This chapter presents a general analysis of the distribution of wealth in rural and urban China, and in the nation as a whole, on the basis of the CHIP survey conducted in 2002. We make some comparisons with findings from the 1988 and 1995 surveys (McKinley 1993; Brenner 2001) and with the survey results of urban residents' wealth by the Urban Social and Economic Survey Team of the National Bureau of Statistics (NBS) in 2002. We also examine the relationship between wealth distribution and income distribution, but in-depth analysis of this and other topics is limited by the availability of research materials and references. Except where noted, most of the reference materials come from the 2002 CHIP survey. Details of the calculations and assumptions are given in the Appendix to this chapter.

In the pre-reform period China had nearly no private property or personal wealth. During the reform period many reforms, such as land-use reforms, housing reforms, and financial reforms, have taken place, allowing the Chinese people to become property owners. Perhaps because these changes were so rapid and recent, and because of difficulties in data collection, few studies have examined the distribution of personal wealth in China, with the exception of a small number of works based on the CHIP data. Gustafsson, Li, and Wei (2006), for example, use the CHIP data from earlier survey rounds, but here we provide a more up-to-date analysis using the 2002 survey data. The Urban Social and Economic Survey Team of the NBS conducted a survey of personal wealth in 2002, but it covered only urban areas, and no microdata from this survey are available for analysis.

II. The Distribution of Rural Wealth

To understand the wealth distribution in China fully, we find it useful to begin with descriptive statistics of wealth size and structure in rural and urban areas separately. The wealth of rural residents can be divided into six items: land, housing property, financial assets, fixed production assets, durable consumption goods, and nonhousing liabilities (Table 5.1). Here housing property is defined as the net value, meaning the total value of housing minus unpaid housing debt. Nonhousing liabilities include all debts except housing debt. The total value of wealth is then the sum of all wealth items minus nonhousing debt.[1]

---

[1] For the details of wealth calculations, see the Appendix.

Table 5.1. *Per capita wealth and its components in rural China, 2002*

	Mean value (yuan)	Percentage of total wealth
Total wealth per capita (net value)	12,938	100.0
Land	3,974	30.7
Net value of housing	5,565	43.0
Financial assets	1,593	12.3
Fixed production assets	1,182	9.1
Durable consumption goods	793	6.1
Nonhousing liabilities	−169	−1.3

Great change has taken place in the level and structure of wealth since 1988. The total per capita wealth of rural households in 1988 was 2,870 yuan, which grew to 10,561 yuan in 1995 and 12,938 yuan in 2002. Using constant prices, real growth was 67 percent from 1988 to 1995, 13 percent from 1995 to 2002, and a total of 89 percent from 1988 to 2002.

Of total wealth, land and housing were the two largest assets in 2002, accounting for about 74 percent. The change of land value over time is notable. The land values per capita were 1,698 yuan in 1988, 4,945 yuan in 1995, and 3,974 yuan in 2002. Using constant prices, per capita land value increased by 32 percent from 1988 to 1995, but decreased by 26 percent from 1995 to 2002. As a result, land value occupied a declining share of total wealth. The share of land value in total wealth fell from 59 percent in 1988 to 47 percent in 1995, and declined further to 31 percent in 2002.

Meanwhile, the shares of housing and financial assets increased rapidly. The share of housing value grew from 31 percent to 32 percent and then to 43 percent, and the share of financial assets went from 3 percent to 10 percent and then to 12 percent. The rapid increase of housing and financial assets in total wealth reflects the deepening of market-oriented reform in rural areas and increased savings in a rapidly growing economy.

Land is a scarce resource and carrier for all economic activities. The decline in its value and share in the total wealth seems abnormal. We believe several factors contribute. First, industrialization and modernization of the transportation system have occupied former farmland and caused a reduction in the amount of per capita land belonging to rural residents. Second, the returns to farming have been low. In the 1990s per unit output and the net value of output from land fluctuated at low levels, and farmers reaped little profit. Third, land value is likely underestimated as it is calculated only on the basis of output from agriculture.

We analyze the distribution of rural wealth first by examining decile groups defined according to wealth holdings and then using the Gini coefficient. The decile breakdown of total wealth and its components appears in Table 5.2. The two highest deciles held 46 percent of total wealth, as compared to less than 6 percent for the bottom two deciles. Of total wealth, financial assets were most concentrated in the high wealth deciles. The highest two deciles took 55 percent of total financial assets, while the lowest two deciles had only 5 percent, with the ratio between them at 13:1. Housing was the next component most concentrated in the high wealth deciles. The highest two deciles owned 51 percent of the total housing value, while the lowest two deciles had only 5 percent. The distributions of durable consumption goods and fixed production assets between the top and bottom 20 percent had ratios of 6.6:1 and 6.5:1, respectively. Land was less concentrated in the high wealth deciles. The ratio of land value between the top and bottom 20 percent was 4:1. The distribution of nonhousing debts was quite different from that of other assets, with an irregular pattern across decile groups. Generally speaking, the lowest 10 percent had more debts than the highest 10 percent. The debt ratio between the highest and the lowest 20 percent was 0.4:1.

The dramatic change in rural China's wealth distribution can also be examined using the Gini coefficient (G_i) and the Gini concentration ratio of the i components (C_i). It is generally acknowledged that the distribution of wealth is more unequal than the distribution of income in both developed and underdeveloped countries because of the long-term accumulation of wealth. Consequently, the Gini coefficient for the distribution of wealth is typically larger than that for income. Rural China, however, has been an exception for quite a long period. According to a study conducted by a research team of the Institute of Economics (CASS), the Gini coefficients of per capita income and wealth distribution in rural China were 0.338 and 0.311 in 1988, rising to 0.381 and 0.351 in 1995, respectively. In both these years, then, inequality of wealth was somewhat lower than inequality of income.

The picture changes substantially in 2002. In 2002 the Gini coefficient for wealth of rural residents was 0.399, while the Gini coefficient for income was 0.366. Thus rural China has reached a turning point where per capita wealth is more unequally distributed than per capita income (Table 5.3 and Figure 5.1). Rising inequality in wealth distribution is attributable to the growing share and unequal distribution of assets other than land. This trend suggests that China's rural income and wealth distributions may move in a common direction. Although the equal distribution of land to some extent constrains inequality of wealth, this turning point points toward rising inequality of both income and wealth in the near future.

Table 5.2. *Distribution among decile groups of per capita wealth and its components in rural China, 2002 (%)*

Decile group	Total wealth per capita (net value)	Land	Net value of housing	Financial assets	Fixed production assets	Durable consumption goods	Nonhousing liabilities
1 (lowest)	2.01	3.35	1.73	1.74	3.14	2.91	33.47
2	3.68	5.12	2.98	2.80	3.96	4.07	10.44
3	4.46	6.54	3.99	3.69	4.7	5.54	7.02
4	5.97	7.66	5.24	4.74	5.26	6.01	5.21
5	7.09	8.88	6.25	5.79	6.84	7.23	7.89
6	8.37	9.91	7.77	6.82	7.95	8.13	6.04
7	9.89	11.16	9.36	8.58	9.74	9.49	6.73
8	12.03	12.94	11.77	10.59	11.96	10.86	5.07
9	15.60	15.39	15.74	16.01	14.41	14.67	6.64
10 (highest)	30.51	19.05	35.20	39.24	32.07	31.10	11.49
All	100.0	100.0	100.0	100.0	100.0	100.0	100.0
Ratio of top to bottom quintiles	8.1	4.1	10.8	12.2	6.5	6.6	0.4

Table 5.3. *Inequality in distributions of per capita income and wealth in rural China, 1988, 1995, and 2002*

Gini coefficient	1988	1995	2002
Of income distribution	0.338	0.381	0.366
Of wealth distribution	0.311	0.351	0.399

Sources: Li and Yue (2004), McKinley (1993), Brenner (2001).

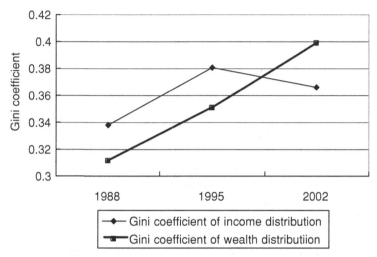

Figure 5.1 Inequality in the Distributions of Per Capita Income and Wealth in Rural China, 1988, 1995, and 2002.

From the Gini coefficients in Table 5.4, one can see that land value was more equally distributed than all other assets; its Gini coefficient was 0.452. Financial assets were most unequally distributed, with a Gini coefficient of 0.681. The concentration ratios of various assets show their correlations with total wealth. The concentration ratio of land was 0.260, much lower than the Gini coefficient of total wealth. This indicates that land was an equalizing factor in the wealth distribution. The concentration ratio for durable consumption goods was marginally lower than the Gini coefficient of total wealth. In contrast, the concentration ratio of financial and housing assets was much higher than the Gini coefficient of total wealth, and so had a disequalizing effect on the overall wealth distribution. The concentration ratio of fixed production assets was almost the same as the Gini coefficient. To some extent the distribution of fixed production assets was probably related to the

Table 5.4. *Inequality of per capita wealth of rural residents, 2002*

	Mean value (yuan)	Percentage of total	G_i	C_i	Contribution to inequality (%)
Total wealth per capita (net value)	12,938	100	0.399		100
Land	3,974	30.72	0.452	0.260	20.02
Net value of housing	5,565	43.01	0.538	0.456	49.15
Financial assets	1,593	12.31	0.681	0.492	15.18
Fixed production assets	1,182	9.13	0.665	0.394	9.02
Durable consumption goods	793	6.13	0.659	0.377	5.79
Nonhousing liabilities	−169	−1.31	0.950	−0.246	0.81

equal distribution of land. Under the current family responsibility system, each household has limited land, which dampens incentives for investment in fixed production assets for agricultural production. Low investment for production on equally distributed land leads to equal distribution of fixed production assets. The equal distribution of durable consumption goods is understandable because high-quality durable consumption goods are of limited availability, and the common durable consumption goods such as TVs now are quite widespread in rural China.

Land because of its equal distribution contributed only 20 percent to the inequality of total wealth, which was obviously lower than its share of wealth, 31 percent. In contrast, financial assets and housing assets contributed 15 percent and 49 percent, respectively, to wealth inequality, with shares higher than their shares of wealth – 12 percent and 43 percent.

In summary, great change has taken place in wealth distribution in rural China in the past 14 years. For instance, in both 1988 and 1995 land was the largest asset and housing the second largest asset in total wealth. By 2002 housing was the largest asset and land the second largest in total wealth. Land is quite equally distributed, but its share of total wealth has fallen, which leads to a decline in its contribution to the inequality of total wealth. In contrast, financial assets occupy a larger share in total wealth and are unequally distributed. Thus they contribute more to the inequality of total wealth.

As for the change of land value, several aspects should be considered. With the deepening of economic reform and development of the rural economy, the nonagricultural sector has become more advanced and market-oriented, which stimulates the development of the finance and real estate sectors. Yet land is a scarce and undeveloped resource. The decline of its significance is deeply rooted in defects of the current land tenure system. At present, the collective owns rural land in name, and land-use rights are contracted to households and individuals.

Some scholars think the rural land system is actually a kind of state-owned system (Zhu 2004). Under this system farmers and local governments have limited incentives to cherish and manage the land. The land is not allocated and managed according to the criteria of a market economy. Frequent land redistribution leads to a situation in which the farmers do not invest in and manage the land as their own property. Meanwhile, more and more cultivated land is converted into urban development with unreasonably low compensation to farmers or is used wastefully. In the 1990s it was quite common for farmers to leave land uncultivated, the result of the prohibition of the entry of rural land into land markets. Since farmers are not motivated to invest in land, they turn to investment in housing and financial assets. Further study on how to "bring the land into full play" and "make good use of all resources" through the reform of the land system is needed.

III. The Distribution of Urban Wealth

As is shown in Table 5.5, the wealth of urban households can be divided into six items as well: financial assets, housing, fixed production assets, durable consumption goods, other assets, and nonhousing liabilities. As above, the net value of housing equals the total value of housing minus unpaid housing debt. Total liabilities minus unpaid housing debt equals nonhousing liabilities. Total wealth is then the sum of all assets minus nonhousing liabilities.

In 2002 the per capita wealth in urban areas was 46,134 yuan, while in rural areas it was 12,938 yuan. The ratio between urban and rural households'

Table 5.5. *Per capita wealth and its components in urban China, 2002*

	Mean value (yuan)	Percentage of total wealth
Total wealth per capita (net value)	46,134	100.0
Net value of housing	29,703	64.4
Financial assets	11,958	25.9
Fixed production assets	815	1.8
Durable consumption goods	3,338	7.2
Nonhousing liabilities	−301	−0.7
Present value of other assets	620	1.3

wealth was 3.6:1. The official statistics' ratio for urban and rural income in 2002 was 3.1:1. Since the official statistical data failed to include the differentials of various subsidies such as housing, medicare, pensions, transportation, and education between urban and rural residents, income inequality between the urban and rural sectors is likely larger than the official number (Li and Yue 2004). Since these subsidies can be accumulated year by year and turned into household assets, they may contribute to the inequality of wealth between urban and rural China.

Comparing the composition of wealth in rural and urban China, one finds that the former includes farmland, while the latter does not. Of all the assets, housing and land were the largest assets for rural households, taking 74 percent of total wealth. For urban households, housing and financial assets were their largest assets, constituting 90 percent of total wealth. Due to rising urban housing values, housing contributed 64 percent of total urban wealth, compared to only 43 percent for rural households. Another difference between the rural and urban households was in fixed production assets, which contributed 9 percent of total wealth in rural areas, but only 2 percent in urban areas. Overall, then, urban household wealth is more highly concentrated in fewer items than is rural household wealth.

As we did for rural wealth, here we adopt the decile approach to examine the distribution of wealth in urban China (Table 5.6). Since for some urban residents the value of debts exceeds that of assets, the lowest decile group owns less than 1 percent of total urban wealth. Wealth of the highest decile group accounts for 34 percent of the total. The two lowest decile groups own only 2.8 percent of total wealth, while the two highest decile groups own 51 percent, 18 times the former. Among all six assets, housing was most concentrated in the top of the wealth distribution. The housing value for the lowest decile was negative, that is, for this group the total value of housing was less than housing liabilities. The richest 20 percent owned 52 percent of housing value, while the poorest 20 percent held only 2 percent of housing value. The ratio between them was 34:1. Fixed production assets and financial assets were the next most concentrated in the top of the distribution. The ratios between the lowest and highest 20 percent were 11:1 for fixed production assets and financial assets, 7:1 for other assets, and 5:1 for durable consumption goods.

Why is the concentration ratio of housing higher than that of any other asset in urban areas, and higher than that of housing in rural areas? The underlying causes can be attributed to the housing system under the old planned economy. As is well known, prior to the reforms basic necessities, such as food, cotton, and edible oil, were rationed on a per head basis.

Table 5.6. *Distribution among decile groups of per capita wealth and its components in urban China, 2002 (%)*

Decile group	Total wealth per capita (net value)	Net value of housing	Financial assets	Fixed production assets	Durable consumption goods	Nonhousing liabilities	Present value of other assets
1 (lowest)	0.20	−0.54	1.62	0.38	4.25	32.32	2.18
2	2.55	2.06	3.14	4.03	4.84	10.31	3.98
3	3.98	3.80	4.17	4.76	5.34	11.89	4.44
4	5.25	5.22	4.89	5.36	6.56	4.28	6.12
5	6.54	6.50	6.37	3.84	7.95	2.98	6.23
6	8.01	8.02	7.78	7.07	8.60	7.75	9.25
7	9.92	9.96	9.78	8.56	9.74	8.80	13.11
8	12.55	12.70	12.22	16.13	11.33	6.33	10.69
9	17.22	17.15	18.17	14.24	14.28	4.09	15.87
10 (highest)	33.85	35.21	31.93	35.69	27.17	11.22	28.22
All deciles	100.0	100.0	100.0	100.0	100.0	100.0	100.0
Ratio of top to bottom quintiles	18.6	34.4	10.5	11.3	4.6	0.4	7.2

Table 5.7. *Difference between urban market housing price and subsidized housing price (Unit: yuan/square meter)*

Province	Market housing price	Public housing sales price	The ratio between market price and public housing sales price
Beijing	3,226.52	403.68	7.99:1
Shanxi	919.06	238.56	3.85:1
Liaoning	1,491.45	272.85	5.47:1
Jiangsu	1,247.26	191.28	6.52:1
Anhui	897.80	105.83	8.48:1
Henan	780.02	166.80	4.68:1
Hubei	2,187.50	98.53	22.20:1
Sichuan	1,050.20	87.04	12.50:1
Guangdong	3,100.00	247.59	12.07:1
Yunnan	1,276.34	201.01	6.35:1
Gansu	1,169.87	241.53	4.84:1
Mean price	1,576.91	204.97	7.69:1

Source: Wang (2001).

Housing was distributed according to one's official rank or political power, and housing distribution standards for individuals in the same rank were set by top-level officials. As a result, housing was unequally distributed based on political considerations.

Since the 1990s the market-oriented housing reform not only inherited the preexisting inequality of housing distribution, but further enlarged that inequality (Zhao and Li 1997). Housing reform in the 1990s failed to follow the basic principles of the market economy. When public housing was sold to individuals, the price was set with only housing space considered, and other factors, such as location and quality, excluded. Consequently, those who occupied high-quality housing in good locations obtained much higher windfall gains. In addition, some cities and work units linked the standard of housing distribution with one's official position, which created opportunities for some officials to obtain better housing. As the price used in the sale of public housing was set artificially, a large gap resulted between the prices paid for public housing and the value of that housing on the market. According to a study of cities in 11 provinces by Wang (2001), in 1995 this price differential was 8:1 (Table 5.7). Such rent-creating activity in the 1990s, in fact, was much more profitable than the rent-seeking activities under the "dual track" for commodity exchange in the 1980s. Due to such institutional arrangements, housing is disproportionately owned by richer groups, more so than other assets (the ratio between the highest and lowest

Table 5.8. *Inequality of per capita wealth of urban residents, 2002*

	Mean value (yuan)	Percentage of total	G_i	C_i	Contribution to inequality
Total wealth per capita (net value)	46,134	100	0.475		100
Net value of housing	29,703	64.39	0.544	0.499	67.62
Financial assets	11,958	25.92	0.596	0.444	24.22
Durable consumption goods	3,338	7.24	0.984	0.323	4.92
Fixed production assets	815	1.77	0.502	0.484	1.80
Nonhousing liabilities	301	−0.65	0.978	−0.260	0.36
Present value of other assets	620	1.34	0.915	0.383	1.08

20 percent was 19:1 for total wealth and 35:1 for housing). Moreover, this pattern is more extreme in urban than in rural areas (the ratio of housing wealth between the highest and lowest 20 percent in rural areas was 11:1).

What explains the high concentration ratio of fixed production assets in urban areas? Such inequality was significant among individuals with different professions and working in different sectors. The reason behind this is that in urban areas only a small group of individuals operate private businesses. According to an NBS survey, only 10 percent of the total urban population had investments in such businesses, while in rural areas fixed production assets were owned and distributed widely among the population.

Compared with housing and fixed production assets, the distribution of financial assets was quite equal. As mentioned earlier, financial assets were more evenly distributed in urban areas than in rural areas.[2] Of all assets, durable consumption goods were the most equally distributed, because most urban households own color TV sets, refrigerators, etc. Private cars are limited to a small group and do not contribute significantly to inequality of wealth. Nonhousing liabilities are worth noting. The lowest decile had 32 percent of the total liabilities, while the highest decile had 12 percent. This perhaps indicates that the poorest have to borrow to get by, while the richest borrow for investment and discretionary consumption.

Table 5.8 gives Gini coefficients and concentration ratios for urban wealth and its components. As discussed in the previous section, the inequality of

[2] In the 2002 CHIP survey 14 percent of urban households refused to fill in the data on bank deposits, which seldom happened in the rural household survey. As a result, the total financial assets of urban households are underestimated, and the distribution of financial assets may be biased.

wealth became larger than the inequality of income in rural areas at the turn of the century. Such a phenomenon did not occur in urban China. The Gini coefficient of wealth distribution was 0.496 in 1995 (Gustafsson, Li, and Wei 2006) and 0.475 in 2002. The Gini coefficient for the urban income distribution was 0.280 in 1995 and 0.319 in 2002 (Li and Yue 2004). Inequality in wealth thus remained substantially higher than that in income.

Of all the assets held by urban households, housing makes the largest contribution to inequality. Housing's net value was 29,703 yuan, or 64 percent of total wealth. Its concentration ratio was 0.499, higher than the Gini coefficient of 0.475 for total wealth. Since housing was a large element and unequally distributed, it contributed 68 percent of the inequality in wealth distribution, exceeding its share in the level of total wealth. The concentration ratio for fixed production assets was 0.484, higher than the Gini coefficient of total wealth. Fixed production assets, however, were relatively small, and so their contribution to inequality of total wealth was only 1.8 percent. Financial assets had a concentration ratio of 0.444, lower than that of total wealth, and so they reduced inequality of wealth. Since they had the second largest share next to housing, their contribution to wealth inequality was the second largest at 24 percent. Durable consumption goods had a concentration ratio of 0.323, much lower than the Gini coefficient of total wealth. Due to their small share of only 7.24 percent of total wealth, they contributed only 4.92 percent to the inequality of wealth distribution.

In 2002 urban residents held total wealth 3.65 times that of rural residents. The distribution of wealth components was quite different for the two groups. Urban financial assets were 7.51 times, housing 5.34 times, and durable consumption goods 4.20 times those of rural residents. Housing was quite unequally distributed in both rural and urban areas, but the urban residents had much higher housing values. Durable consumption goods were relatively equally distributed, but urban residents held more durable goods. As discussed earlier, rural residents had more fixed production assets than urban residents.

Growth over time in urban wealth was rapid. Per capita total wealth in urban areas was 12,385 yuan in 1995 (13,698 yuan in 2002 prices) and 46,134 yuan in 2002. Real growth was 236.8 percent from 1995 to 2002, or 18.9 percent per year. Housing assets increased from 5,412 yuan (5,985 yuan in 2002 prices) to 29,734 yuan over the same period, with growth of 21.7 percent per year in real terms. Financial assets increased from 3,427 yuan (3,841 yuan in 2002 prices) to 11,958 yuan, growing 17.6 percent per year. Meanwhile, the share of financial assets decreased from 28 percent to 26 percent,

Table 5.9. *Composition and distribution of per capita financial assets and liabilities in urban China, 2002*

Assets (liabilities)	Mean value (yuan)	Percentage of total	G_i	C_i	Contribution percentage
Total financial assets	11,958	100	0.596	0.596	100
1. Time deposits	5,975	49.97	0.692	0.602	50.49
2. Demand deposits	1,662	13.90	0.712	0.473	11.03
3. Stocks	1,240	10.37	0.930	0.733	12.74
4. Debt securities	391	3.27	0.974	0.773	4.24
5. Loans	475	3.97	0.953	0.674	4.49
6. Self-invested business capital	366	3.06	0.982	0.670	3.44
7. Business investment (not including stock and debt obligations)	169	1.41	0.985	0.641	1.52
8. Housing funds	1,035	8.65	0.761	0.438	6.36
9. Commercial insurance	469	3.92	0.934	0.616	4.05
10. Market value of collections	176	1.47	0.974	0.662	1.63
Liabilities	1,702	100	0.952	0.952	100
1. Borrowing for construction and purchase of housing	1,401	82.33	0.966	0.960	83.00
2. Business loans	141	8.29	0.994	0.951	8.28
3. Loans for consumption goods	15	0.90	0.997	0.879	0.83
4. Debts for medical care	56	3.28	0.993	0.895	3.08
5. Other consumption debts	29	1.71	0.995	0.870	1.56
6. Education loans	59	3.49	0.991	0.880	3.23

Note: The total sample size was 20,632, and 1,470 observations had zero value of financial assets. In addition, 2,987 observations report zero time or demand deposits.

but the share of housing increased from 44 percent to 64 percent. Together, the percentage of financial and housing assets increased from 72 percent to 90 percent. This indicates that housing and financial assets played a significant role in wealth accumulation at the turn of the century.

The composition and distribution of financial assets and debts reveal some interesting patterns. Table 5.9 shows that of the 10 components of gross financial assets, time deposits were by far the largest with a share of 50 percent. The second largest element was demand deposits at 14 percent, followed by stock shares at 10 percent and housing funds at 9 percent. Together, these four elements constituted 83 percent of the total.

With respect to the distribution of various components of financial assets, time deposits had a concentration ratio of 0.602. The concentration ratio for demand deposits was 0.473. The former had a concentration ratio much higher than the Gini coefficient of gross financial assets, while the latter had a concentration ratio lower than the Gini coefficient of gross financial assets. In other words, time deposits had a disequalizing effect while demand deposits had an equalizing effect on financial assets. Of the financial assets, eight had concentration ratios larger than the Gini coefficient of gross financial assets and were thus disequalizing. Only two elements (demand deposits and housing funds) had concentration ratios smaller than the Gini coefficient of gross financial assets and so were equalizing. Since most of the components had quite small shares, only three components are important: time deposits and stock shares, contributing 51 percent and 13 percent to the inequality of financial assets, and demand deposits, contributing 11 percent.

With respect to liabilities, in 2002 per capita debt in urban China was 1,702 yuan or 14 percent of gross assets. This debt burden was not overly high. Borrowing for housing construction and purchase was the largest component, taking 82 percent of the total, and its concentration ratio was 0.96, only slightly higher than 0.95, the Gini coefficient of gross liabilities. It contributed 83 percent of total inequality in gross liabilities.

In summary, the wealth of urban residents is concentrated in two items, housing and financial assets. The financial assets of urban households are concentrated in bank deposits. Gross liabilities are mainly housing-related debts, which average 4.66 times nonhousing debts.

What story does this structure of wealth in urban China tell? As researchers have pointed out, this structure indicates that for most urban residents, wealth accumulation is mainly driven by living and consumption objectives. Urban residents appear to have no strong initiative or opportunity to accumulate financial assets outside of banks. Savings in the form of bank deposits is the most popular investment tool (Urban Social and Economic Survey Team 2003). We believe many factors contribute to the high dependence on bank savings. First, investment instruments are quite limited in China. High risk in the abnormal stock market depresses interest in stocks as a form of investment. Urban residents' choices are thus narrowed to bank savings. Second, many uncertainties have arisen during the transition. Ongoing reforms affecting pensions, medicare, and education cause people to hold precautionary savings for these purposes. Finally, traditional Chinese culture places value on saving more and spending less. Although such inclinations have a negative effect on the growth of consumption and the economy, they are not easily changed.

Table 5.10. *Mean wealth per capita and its components in China as a whole, 2002*

	Mean value (yuan)	Percentage of total wealth
Total wealth per capita (net value)	25,897	100
Land	2,421	9.35
Financial assets	5,643	21.79
Net value of housing	14,989	57.88
Fixed production assets	1,037	4.01
Durable consumption goods	1,784	6.89
Nonhousing liabilities	−219	−0.84
Present value of other assets	242	0.93

IV. The Distribution of Wealth in China as a Whole

We now turn to an analysis of the distribution of wealth in China as a whole. Table 5.10 contains the basic results for the composition of per capita wealth and its various components nationwide. In 2002 per capita wealth averaged 25,897 yuan. Since most urban residents own no land, average land value was only 2,421 yuan, and its share of total wealth was 9 percent. Durable consumption goods had the smallest difference between the rural and urban samples. They accounted for 7 percent of total wealth, as compared to 6 percent for rural residents and 7 percent for urban residents. Housing, financial assets, and land took 89 percent of total wealth, and housing and financial assets together took 80 percent.

As for the distribution of wealth (Table 5.11), the two highest deciles owned 59 percent of total wealth, while the two lowest deciles had only 3 percent. The ratio between them was 21:1, higher than similar ratios for the rural and urban areas alone. Moreover, the ratio between the highest and lowest decile was 61:1. Obviously, this large gap is closely linked to inequality between the rural and urban areas.

Housing was the asset most concentrated at the top of the wealth distribution. The two highest deciles had 66 percent of total housing value, while the two lowest deciles had only 1 percent. The ratio between them was 63:1. Furthermore, the lowest decile had a negative net housing value, as the value of housing held was lower than the unpaid housing debt.

Table 5.12 shows that in 2002 the Gini coefficient of wealth distribution in China as a whole was 0.550, much higher than the Gini coefficient of income distribution (0.45) and higher than the Gini coefficient of wealth

Table 5.11. *Distribution among decile groups of wealth and its components in China as a whole, 2002*

Decile group	Total wealth per capita (net value)	Land	Financial assets	Net value of housing	Fixed production assets	Value of durable consumption goods	Nonhousing liabilities	Present value of other assets
1 (lowest)	0.68	4.43	1.00	−0.18	2.82	2.84	30.39	0.96
2	2.12	8.67	1.31	1.23	4.52	2.81	8.39	0.78
3	2.95	11.03	1.80	1.93	5.40	3.49	5.97	0.63
4	3.81	13.86	2.12	2.59	8.07	3.88	5.78	1.11
5	4.84	15.01	3.16	3.62	8.90	4.94	6.94	1.55
6	6.23	15.76	4.41	5.09	11.80	6.08	6.82	3.04
7	8.32	14.05	7.16	7.63	10.74	8.96	8.64	6.64
8	11.76	8.34	11.87	12.15	10.12	13.02	5.07	12.35
9	17.89	5.84	19.40	19.30	13.92	18.22	10.95	24.16
10 (highest)	41.41	3.00	47.80	46.54	23.72	35.77	10.80	48.80
All deciles	100.0	100.0	100.0	100.0	100.0	100.0	100.0	100.0
Ratio of top to bottom quintiles	21.18	0.64	29.09	62.70	5.13	9.56	0.56	41.93

Table 5.12. *Inequality of per capita wealth in China as a whole, 2002*

Wealth	Mean value (yuan)	Percentage of total	G_i	C_i	Contribution percentage
Total wealth per capita (net value)	25,897	100	0.550	0.550	100
Land	2,421	9.35	0.669	−0.045	−0.77
Financial assets	5,643	21.79	0.740	0.629	24.92
Net value of housing	14,989	57.88	0.674	0.630	66.32
Fixed production assets	1,037	4.01	0.837	0.296	2.16
Durable consumption goods	1,784	6.89	0.643	0.480	6.01
Nonhousing liabilities	−219	−0.84	0.967	−0.175	0.27
Present value of other assets	242	0.93	0.967	0.689	1.16

distribution in either urban or rural China. This is logical as the gap in wealth levels between rural and urban residents is large. Housing, financial assets, and the estimated present value of other property had concentration ratios larger than the Gini coefficient of total wealth, and so had disequalizing effects. The estimated present value of other property, however, was small (1 percent of total wealth), contributing only 1 percent of the overall inequality of wealth. Housing had a concentration ratio of 0.63, contributing 66 percent, while financial assets had a concentration ratio of 0.63, contributing 25 percent to inequality. Land's role in wealth distribution is notable. It accounted for only 9 percent of total wealth, had a concentration ratio of −0.045, and contributed −0.8 percent of wealth inequality. Durable consumption goods had a concentration ratio of 0.48 and contributed 6 percent, which means they were relatively equally distributed.

In comparison with other countries, a Gini coefficient of wealth distribution that exceeds the Gini coefficient of income distribution is normal. Davies and Shorrock's (2000) research shows that the Gini coefficient of income distribution in developed countries is between 0.3 and 0.4, and the Gini coefficient of wealth distribution is between 0.5 and 0.9. The richest 1 percent of the population in terms of wealth usually holds 15 percent to 35 percent of total wealth, and the poorest 1 percent holds less than 10 percent. According to Smeeding, the Gini coefficient of income distribution in 21 developed countries in the mid-1990s was about 0.3, but the Gini coefficient of wealth distribution was between 0.52 and 0.93 (Schneider 2004, p. 59). By international standards, then, the Gini coefficient of wealth distribution in China is relatively low. The following points, however, should be considered. First, personal wealth in developed countries was accumulated over several hundred years, while personal wealth accumulation in

Table 5.13. *Percentages of decile groups for per capita income and wealth in China as a whole, urban versus rural, 2002*

Decile group	Per capita income		Per capita wealth	
	Rural residents	Urban residents	Rural residents	Urban residents
1 (lowest)	98.73	1.27	75.26	24.74
2	97.26	2.74	89.78	10.22
3	94.96	5.04	89.41	10.59
4	90.64	9.36	90.63	9.37
5	79.36	20.64	83.03	16.97
6	62.18	37.82	72.63	27.37
7	43.87	56.13	55.02	44.98
8	22.48	77.52	29.21	70.79
9	12.69	87.31	18.08	81.92
10 (highest)	6.91	93.09	5.99	94.01

China has taken only about 20 years. This suggests that the speed and trends in personal wealth accumulation in China are unusual. Second, the Gini coefficient of income distribution in China exceeds the developed country averages mentioned above. As we have noted, the current unequal income distribution in China will undoubtedly affect wealth distribution in the future. So, inequality in wealth distribution will likely become larger over time.

The relation between wealth and income in China can be inferred only to a limited extent. Using the 2002 data, we compare per capita wealth and income. We classify the sample for all of China into decile groups according to income and wealth. Table 5.13 gives the results, with Figure 5.2 based on its data.

In Figure 5.2 the vertical axis represents the percentage of the population, and the horizontal axis represents the decile groups of income and wealth. As shown, most rural residents are in low decile groups for both income and wealth, while urban residents fall in high decile groups. This pattern reflects the large gap in income and wealth distribution between rural and urban residents. Turning to the details of the inequality, we find small differences between the rural and urban residents in the low decile groups (from 1 to 4), while in the middle decile groups (from 4 to 7) the urban-rural difference in wealth is larger than that of income. In the high decile groups (from 7 to 9), the urban-rural difference in wealth is again smaller than that of income, and in the highest group the inequality of wealth and income distribution is almost the same.

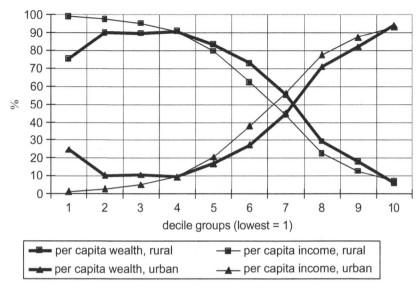

Figure 5.2 The Percentages of Decile Groups for Per Capita Income and Wealth in China as a Whole, Urban versus Rural, 2002. Source: Table 5.13.

The results for the low decile groups are not difficult to understand, because in rural areas the poorest farmers at least have a piece of land. Since income from land is quite low, even if land value is underestimated, the inequality of income distribution is evidently larger than that of wealth. As for the middle decile groups, land is relatively unimportant and is offset by the strong effect of housing and financial assets. The interrelationship between income and wealth distribution deserves further analysis, which we leave for another study.

V. Concluding Remarks: Policy Implications and Suggestions

Since China's economic reform, both rural and urban residents have been transformed from groups with no assets into groups with some assets. In other words, the Chinese people have been transformed from proletariats to property owners. Especially since 1990, the Chinese people have experienced rapid growth and accumulation of wealth. This is one of the great achievements of China's economic reform, in spite of some unsatisfactory results.

Land, housing, and financial assets have become the largest components of total wealth for both urban and rural households. They account for about

89 percent of total wealth and have substantial effects on the distribution of wealth. As outlined above, each of these assets has its own characteristics and problems.

Land seems to present a paradox. Land is a scarce resource, but it is used improperly because of the underestimation of its value. Unclear land property rights are a significant problem, creating a barrier against improving the efficiency of land use. Various forms of land mismanagement are also important reasons for the low efficiency and waste in land use. Deepening the reform of and strengthening the management of land is the first necessary step (Wen 2004).

The high tide of housing construction in both rural and urban areas since the 1980s and market-oriented housing reform in the cities since 1990 have to a certain extent fulfilled the dream that "everyone has a decent home." As outlined in the above analysis, however, the housing reform was carried out in the special circumstances of China's economic transition. For many urban residents homeownership is not the result of long-term accumulation of income. Some have become homeowners overnight. Due to rent-creating activities, housing wealth is disproportionately held by richer groups. In view of this, two solutions are possible. One is to prevent the regeneration of rent-creating activities. The other is to introduce an inheritance tax or other ways to correct inequalities in wealth distribution. Clearly, introducing new taxes in China such as an inheritance tax is not easy; however, a thousand-mile journey starts by taking the first step.

The rapid accumulation of financial assets in China has been a positive development, but some problems remain. Aside from the unequal distribution and irrational structure of these assets, too many uncertainties are present. Bank deposits account for 64 percent of households' financial assets, and they have a strong negative effect on the growth of consumption and domestic demand. This problem can be solved only through deepening the reform and smoothing out various economic relations.

The inequality of wealth distribution in China is larger than that of income distribution. Twenty years ago Chinese residents had little asset income except interest income (World Bank 1981). The present and future conditions, however, are different. In the long run, wealth may become an important determinant of individual income. For instance, in cities more and more residents will have rent income. As a result, the inequality of wealth may exacerbate income inequality. Taxation policies should be adopted to narrow the inequality of income and wealth, which would be beneficial for the stability of society.

The historical problem of "inverse redistribution" must be changed. "Inverse redistribution" means that inequality of income and wealth is enlarged, not diminished, through redistribution, and it goes against the original object of income redistribution. In common terms, it is not the case of "taxing the fat (rich) to subsidize the thin (poor)," but of "taxing the thin to subsidize the fat." Under the planned economy, the policy for rural households was to tax their income and not to provide them with subsidies, while the policy for urban households was to provide them with subsidies and no taxes. This is called the "inverse redistribution" policy, and it has enlarged the gap between rural and urban China. Since the reform and opening began there have been some changes in this situation, but the problem still exists. Indeed, the large inequality of income and wealth between rural and urban areas is closely linked to the "inverse redistribution" policy. The recent reform of agricultural taxes and fees is one step toward changing the situation.

When the government uses tax instruments to change income and wealth distribution, special attention should be paid to whether those taxes are progressive or regressive. For taxes to play a positive role in redistribution, progressive tax rates should be used, and the lump-sum deduction for income tax should also be increased. A prior condition for such policies, however, is a high transparency of income and wealth information. For example, as the real name system of bank deposits in China is imperfect and the transparency of interest income low, a tax on interest income is possible only through a proportional rate, not a progressive rate. Consequently, currently all bank deposits are levied a 20 percent tax on interest income. Of course, this method cannot reduce income inequality. On this Stiglitz would go further and say, "Even though the rich pay more taxes than the poor but not proportionally, the taxation can be thought of as being regressive" (Stiglitz 2000).

According to the notion that "not progressive is regressive," a progressive tax system should be introduced, based on an environment where the transparency of income and wealth is increased. The inheritance tax and wealth tax are clearly two instruments that could be used progressively.

Taxation and transfers can no doubt play a direct role in reducing inequality of wealth and income, but one cannot ignore the role of other macroeconomic policies, some of which may be less direct and effective. Among these are long-term policies for social stability, for example, education policy. Labor is one of the productive factors, and its role in income and wealth distribution depends not only on its quantity, but, more importantly, on its quality as well. To a large extent, improving the quality of the labor force depends on education. Improving the education status of low-income and low-wealth groups is an important way to reduce inequality of income and wealth. In other words, improving education so as to reduce the inequality of human capital can create equal opportunities for people to gain income and wealth.

A second relevant macroeconomic policy is the labor force migration policy. Reductions of the barriers to labor force migration allow people more equal opportunities to take part in the process of income and wealth generation. It has been demonstrated that labor migration, especially between rural and urban areas, can play an obvious role in reducing the inequality of income and wealth. Of course, the systemic barriers put in place under the planned economy cannot all be eliminated in a short time. Although some of the systemic barriers such as the *hukou*, welfare, housing, and employment systems have been reduced, China is still far from a market economy. Making the labor market operate more perfectly, especially in transferring labor between rural and urban areas, thus will be an important and relevant aspect of macroeconomic policies in the future.

A third relevant macroeconomic policy is the transition policy of the industrial structure. In the long term, the basic way to raise farmers' incomes and reduce the income and wealth gap between rural and urban China is to speed up the transition of the industrial structure, develop the secondary and tertiary industries, and improve labor force mobility among industrial sectors, especially from primary industries to secondary and tertiary industries.

APPENDIX

I. Measurement of Per Capita Wealth of Rural Individuals

The rural sample contains 37,969 individuals.

A. Measurement of Land Value

First, land area is adjusted for quality. Here 1 *mu* (666 m^2 or ~0.1647 acre) of paddy field is set equal to 2 *mu* of dry fields. Second, net agricultural income per household is gross income minus production costs. Finally, according to measurements in 1988 and 1995, 25 percent of net agricultural income came from land, and the rate of return on land was 8 percent. We calculate the land value based on these definitions and assumptions. In the 2002 survey the gross agricultural income and production costs are not reported. Using the reported land area and average net agricultural income in the county, we calculate land value per household. Per capita land value is the total land value of the household divided by the number of family members.

B. Measurement of Housing Value

For those who have no ownership rights to housing, the housing value is zero. For a few homeowners housing space is reported, but with no housing value. The value is calculated as the average value per square meter in the county times the reported space. The per capita housing value is the gross housing value divided by the number of family members.

C. Measurement of Fixed Production Assets

The survey contains the value of fixed production assets and their components. The sum of the components is calculated first and then compared with the total value of fixed assets. Where the two are not equal, we use the sum of the components. The gross fixed production asset value is divided by the number of family members to obtain the per capita value.

D. Measurement of Durable Consumption Goods

Some farmers in the survey failed to report the value of durable consumption goods, but they reported the holding of televisions, bicycles, washing machines, etc. We specify a consumer durable function over the rural sample as follows:

The value of durable consumption goods

$$
\begin{aligned}
&= a_1^*(\text{color TVs}) + a_2^*(\text{black-and-white TVs}) + a_3^*(\text{bicycles}) \\
&\quad + a_4^*(\text{refrigerators}) + a_5^*(\text{motorcycles}) + a_6^*(\text{washing machines}) \\
&\quad + a_7^*(\text{sound systems/recorders}) + a_8^*(\text{video recorders/video disks}) \\
&\quad + a_9^*(\text{air conditioners}) + a_{10}^*(\text{cars}).
\end{aligned}
$$

Regression analysis is used to obtain a coefficient for each variable. We then apply the estimated coefficients to the households that held these goods but did not report values. The gross value of durable consumption goods is divided by household size to obtain per capita values.

E. Measurement of Financial Assets

First, we sort out errors in the sample. Then we sum up the value of the components and compare this with the reported gross value of financial assets. To obtain per household financial assets, we divide the gross value by the number of household members.

F. Measurement of Liabilities

Comparing reported gross liabilities with the sum value of debt components, and where the two are not equal substituting the sum of debt components, we get the gross liabilities of the households, which are then divided by the number of family members.

G. Measurement of Per Capita Wealth

Per capita wealth equals the sum of per capita land value, housing value, fixed production asset value, durable consumption goods value, and financial assets minus per capita debt.

II. Measurement of Per Capita Wealth of Urban Individuals

The urban sample contains 20,632 individuals.

A. Measurement of Housing Value

For questions in the survey on housing, where housing ownership is not listed as private housing, commodity housing, or converted public housing, housing assets are given a value of zero. The questionnaire contains three questions on housing value. For purposes of calculating housing value, we use the largest of the three reported values. Some households failed to report housing value. For such cases, housing value is calculated based on the reported square meters times the average price per square meter in the city. Dividing by the number of people in the family, we obtain the per capita housing value.

B. Measurement of Fixed Production Assets and Estimated Present Value

The survey questionnaire asks for the estimated present value of fixed production assets. We use this reported value.

C. Measurement of Durable Consumption Goods Value

Some households do not report the value of durable consumption goods, but do report holdings of televisions, bicycles, washing machines, etc. We estimate a function over the entire urban sample as follows:

The value of durable consumption goods

$$= a_1^*(\text{color TVs}) + a_2^*(\text{black-and-white TVs}) + a_3^*(\text{bicycles})$$
$$+ a_4^*(\text{motorcycles}) + a_5^*(\text{refrigerators}) + a_6^*(\text{washing machines})$$
$$+ a_7^*(\text{sound systems/recorders}) + a_8^*(\text{video recorders/video disks})$$
$$+ a_9^*(\text{air conditioners}) + a_{10}^*(\text{cars}).$$

Separate equations were estimated for the rural and urban samples. Regression analysis is used to estimate the coefficient for each variable. Then we apply these coefficients to the quantities of goods with no reported value. The gross value of durable consumption goods is then divided by household size to obtain the per capita value.

D. Measurement of Financial Assets

First, we sort out errors in the sample. Then we sum up the value of each component and compare this sum with the gross value of financial assets to obtain the household financial assets. This is divided by the number of household members.

E. Measurement of Liabilities

Comparing gross liabilities with the sum value of debt components, and substituting the sum of debt components where there is an inconsistency between the two values, we obtain the gross liabilities of the household, which are divided by the number of family members.

F. Measurement of Per Capita Wealth

Per capita wealth equals the sum of per capita housing value, fixed production assets present value, durable consumption goods value, financial assets minus per capita liabilities, and the present value of other assests.

III. Measurement of Per Capita Wealth in China

The sample contains 20,632 individuals in urban areas and 37,969 in rural areas. The ratio of urban to rural individuals in the sample is different from that reported by the NBS, so we adjust the proportions as follows. We increase the size of the urban sample to 24,367 by randomly selecting and duplicating individuals in the urban sample. Together, then, the total sample size is 62,336 for all of China, and the ratio of urban to rural individuals equals that reported by the NBS.

In the sample the urban individuals have zero value for land. The rural individuals have zero value for "other" assets. Per capita wealth equals the sum of per capita housing value, financial assets value, durable consumption goods, fixed production assets value, land value, and the estimated present value of other assets, minus per capita liabilities.

References

Brenner, Mark (2001), "Reexamining the Distribution of Wealth in Rural China," in Carl Riskin, Zhao Renwei, and Li Shi, eds., *China's Retreat from Equality*, Armonk, NY: M. E. Sharpe.

Davies, James B. and Anthony F. Shorrocks (2000), "The Distribution of Wealth," in A. B. Atkinson and F. Bourguignon, eds., *Handbook of Income Distribution*, vol. 1, Amsterdam: Elsevier North Holland.

Gustafsson, Björn, Shi Li, and Zhong Wei (2006), "The Distribution of Wealth in Urban China and in China as a Whole 1995," *Review of Income and Wealth*, 52(2), 173–188.

Li, Shi, Zhong Wei, and Björn Gustafsson (2000), "The Distribution of Urban Wealth," *Economic Research (Jingji Yanjiu)*, no. 3, 16–23.

Li, Shi and Ximing Yue (2004), "An Investigation on Income Distribution in China," *Finance and Economics (Cai Jing)*, no. 3/4, 30–38.

McKinley, Terry (1993), "The Distribution of Wealth in Rural China," in Keith Griffin and Zhao Renwei, eds., *The Distribution of Income in China*, London: Macmillan.

Schneider, Michael (2004), *The Distribution of Wealth*, Northampton, MA: Edward Elgar.

Stiglitz, Joseph (2000), *Economics*, 2nd ed., vol. 1, Beijing: China People's University Press.

Urban Social and Economic Survey Team, National Bureau of Statistics (2003), *Wealth: The Foundation for a Well-off Society*, Taiyuan: Shanxi Economics Press.

Wang, Lina (2001), "Urban Housing Welfare and Income Distribution," in Carl Riskin, Zhao Renwei, and Li Shi, eds., *China's Retreat from Equality*, Armonk, NY: M. E. Sharpe.

Wen, Jiabao (2004), "Deepening the Reform of the Land Management System: According to Law Truly Strengthen Land Management," *People's Daily (Renmin Ribao)*, Oct.15, 2.

World Bank (1981), *China: Socialist Economic Development*, The World Bank Economic Research Group's Chinese Report on a Study of China's Economy, Beijing: Finance and Economics Press.

Zhao, Renwei and Shi Li (1997), "Increasing Income Inequality and Its Causes in China," *Economic Research (Jingji Yanjiu)*, no. 9, 19–28.

Zhu, Qiuxia (2004), "A Discussion of the State-Owned Character of the Current Land System in Rural China and the Need for Reform," Nanjing Finance and Economics University, Working Paper, November 12.

SIX

Growth, Inequality, and Poverty

A Comparative Study of China's Experience in the Periods before and after the Asian Crisis

Azizur Rahman Khan

I. Introduction

This chapter uses the household-level data to estimate trends in poverty in rural and urban China during 1995–2002 and to compare China's performance in poverty reduction during this period with that in the period prior to 1995, specifically between 1988 and 1995. These time periods are determined by the dates of the three household surveys – respectively for 1988, 1995, and 2002 – that provide the data on which the estimates are based. The two periods have been assigned the designations of the "pre–Asian crisis period" and the "post–Asian crisis period." The Asian crisis hit a number of East Asian countries in 1997, two years after the date of the intermediate survey that separates the two time periods. The logic of the designation is that China's poverty reduction outcome in the second period is largely the consequence of economic performance and policies that took place in the period after the beginning of the Asian crisis, which was also a period of decline in the growth of the world economy. As the chapter will argue, some of the economic policies initiated in response to the crisis had important effects on China's poverty outcome in the second period.

A. China's Poverty Performance as Measured by Official Data

China's performance in poverty reduction during the 1990s has been recognized for both its solid achievements and remaining shortcomings. The World Bank estimates that the number of people living on less than Purchasing Power Parity (PPP) $1 a day fell by 147 million in China between 1990 and 1998, while it increased by 70 million in the rest of the developing countries taken together; this is a remarkable testimony to China's

success in poverty reduction.[1] And yet the World Bank's findings about
China's poverty performance, perhaps the ones most widely quoted, point
out serious blemishes as well. Consider, for example, the issue of regularity
and consistency of China's poverty reduction. World Bank estimates show
that there was indeed some reduction in the incidence of poverty between
1995 and 1999,[2] but the entire reduction in the incidence of poverty took
place in the first year, between 1995 and 1996. Thereafter, between 1996 and
1999, there was no reduction in the proportion of the population in poverty.
For urban China there was no trend of a reduction in poverty during the
entire period. Next, after more than two decades of unprecedented growth,
the proportion of the population below the World Bank's PPP $1 poverty
line in China is higher in the early twenty-first century than in almost any
other country with a comparable PPP$ per capita income. According to this
particular index, China has more than twice the rate of poverty as compared to Indonesia, a country with almost 30 percent lower per capita PPP$
income in recent years.[3]

B. Limitations of Available Estimates

Whatever one might want to conclude about China's poverty performance
from the above estimates must be qualified by the fact that they suffer
from serious problems of measurement. Some of the important sources of
deficiency may be highlighted as follows.[4]

First, published survey data, which serve as the basis of the above estimates, are available only for highly aggregated groups and not for individual
households. This not only leads to an unknown error in the measurement of
poverty indicators but also makes it impossible to analyze the characteristics
of the poor.[5]

Second, the definition employed in the official surveys by the National
Bureau of Statistics (NBS) is inconsistent with standard concepts of income.
It excludes a number of components that are and should be treated as

---

[1] World Bank (2000), Table 1.1.
[2] See Chen and Wang (2001) for these estimates.
[3] These are based on the data reported in recent issues of the World Bank's *World Development Indicators* (see World Bank 2003).
[4] To the best of the knowledge of the author, these apply to World Bank estimates other than the one cited above, e.g., to Ravallion and Chen (2007).
[5] Official Chinese estimates of poverty may actually have used the household level data. They too suffer from the inadequacy of income definition discussed below. Furthermore, they suffer from numerous additional problems concerning the adjustment of the poverty line over time (see Park and Wang 2001).

parts of income. For example, it excludes the rental value of owned housing and incompletely covers nonwage income payments, especially welfare payments, subsidies, and charges levied on households for services. Neglect of the rental value of owned housing not only creates a problem of comparability between groups that own and rent houses but also leads to a problem of comparability over time as homeownership spreads. Neglecting nonwage income payments, subsidies, and charges also creates a serious bias insofar as these payments as a proportion of income have steadily declined as charges have increasingly replaced free services.

Third, the sample for urban China systematically excludes the migrant households that do not have urban residence permits. The number of these migrants, as a proportion of the urban population, has rapidly increased over the last decade. Their living standard is believed to be significantly lower than that of the official urban residents. Their neglect biases not only the estimate of the level of poverty but also its change over time.[6]

The present study uses the data from the CHIP surveys for 1988, 1995, and 2002, which have been described in Chapters 1 and 3 and the Appendix of this book, along with references to the literature relating to the first two rounds of the CHIP surveys. Income data from these surveys are at the level of individual households; they include many of the standard components of income that are excluded from the official estimates. An earlier study by the present author, analyzing the incidence and trend in poverty in China during the 1988–1995 period on the basis of the data from the first two CHIP surveys (Khan 1998; Khan and Riskin 2001) differed from other studies of China's poverty trends insofar as it used comprehensive estimates of income for individual households. For urban China the study found little reduction, or some increase, in the incidence of poverty, depending on the method of adjustment in the poverty threshold for the change in the cost of living, during that period of extraordinarily rapid growth. For rural China the reduction in poverty was significant though at a lower rate than suggested by most other estimates, especially the official ones. The third round of the CHIP survey for the first time included a separate sample of the "floating migrants," the migrant households without official urban residence permits, a group that has hitherto been neglected in official and unofficial estimates of poverty, thereby creating the opportunity to include them in the poverty estimates.

In Section II the method of estimating the poverty threshold is discussed. Section III estimates the changes in rural poverty while Section IV explains the factors behind the difference in China's performance in rural

---

[6] These issues have been discussed in greater detail in Khan (1998).

poverty reduction in the post–Asian crisis period as compared to that in the pre–Asian crisis period. Similarly, Sections V and VI are respectively concerned with the estimation of poverty among those who are registered as urban residents (i.e., the urban population excluding the so-called floating migrants) and the explanation of the difference in the reduction of poverty in this group between the two periods. Section VII estimates poverty among the floating migrants in urban China, while Section VIII explains the causes of the difference in the incidence of poverty between the urban migrants and the urban residents. The concluding section summarizes the broad features of China's performance in poverty reduction in the post–Asian crisis period.

II. The Poverty Threshold

The method of estimating the poverty threshold – the per capita income below which the members of a household are considered poor – involves three steps: (a) setting a normative minimum of food energy requirement in kilocalories per person per day (2,150 kilocalories for rural China and 2,100 kilocalories for urban China), (b) obtaining the value of the minimum food requirement by multiplying the energy requirement by the estimated cost of food energy consumed by the income group that is closest to the poverty threshold (the average for rural China and the lowest income decile for urban China), and (c) making a further allowance for nonfood consumption expenditure on the basis of the consumption pattern of the group that seems to be closest to the poverty threshold (again the average for rural China and the lowest income decile for urban China). Recognizing that, despite the anchoring of the poverty threshold to a minimum food energy requirement, the procedure is not free of arbitrary judgments, not the least because of the lack of agreement among nutritional scientists about what a minimum food energy requirement is, two alternative poverty thresholds are used, the higher one as estimated above and the lower one at 70 percent of the higher estimate.[7]

The result of the above procedure, despite a lower food energy standard for urban areas, is an urban poverty threshold that is nearly twice as high as the rural poverty threshold, a reflection of the higher unit cost of food energy and a lower food-nonfood expenditure ratio in urban areas than in rural areas. The principal justification for using a higher poverty threshold for urban China is that per capita urban income is about three times as high as per

---

[7] In the Khan (1998) study a third, intermediate, threshold was also used. The difference in the procedures between rural and urban areas has been justified in the 1998 study.

Table 6.1. *Poverty thresholds (values in yuan, current prices)*

	1995		2002	
	Value	Percentage of per capita income	Value	Percentage of per capita income
Rural				
Low	810	35	876	27
High	1,157	50	1,252	38
Urban				
Low	1,604	28	1,774	18
High	2,291	40	2,534	26

Note: Percentage change in official CPIs between 1995 and 2002: rural: 8.17, urban: 10.59.

capita rural income. The consequence of using the same poverty threshold for the two areas is to find that urban poverty is virtually nonexistent (see Chen and Wang 2001, Table 6.1). The view that China does not have a significant problem of urban poverty, held by both official Chinese policy makers and the leading international development agencies,[8] is the direct consequence of using for urban China, which has more than three times the per capita income as rural China, the same poverty threshold as that for the latter. A negligible proportion of the urban population is below the PPP $1 poverty line, while a substantial proportion of the rural population is below this level of income.[9] Serious questions, however, have been raised about the

[8] See World Bank (2001). The exclusive preoccupation of this report – the only comprehensive World Bank poverty assessment for the 1990s – with rural poverty implies a presumption on its part that urban poverty is not a problem in China, especially in view of an absence of any work on the urban poor.

[9] The purpose of using the common PPP$ poverty line is to make poverty lines internationally comparable. The national average conversion factor between the domestic currency value and the PPP$ value of consumption is used to arrive at the domestic currency equivalent of PPP $1 (more recently PPP $1.08 which is estimated to be the approximate equivalent of the "national," nutrition-based, poverty line for a set of 10 poor countries for which direct PPP$ national accounts estimates are available) for some benchmark year (1993 in recent estimates). There is, however, no mention in Chen and Wang (2001), the principal document reporting these estimates, that adjustment between urban and rural poverty lines is made to reflect the cost-of-living difference. Indeed, the procedure does not make any adjustment for the difference between the PPP$ conversion factor for the expenditure bundles of different income/expenditure groups. The method uses the average adjustment factor for all income/expenditure groups. It is highly doubtful that the average PPP$ conversion factor is the same as the one for the expenditure bundle of the poor. It has also been reported that recent research at the NBS has shown that the PPP$ conversion rate used by the World Bank diverges by a wide margin from the rate estimated by using recent price data.

appropriateness of this measure as an acceptable living standard for urban China for which, in official discussions, a higher poverty line is commonly used. Perhaps the most careful study of urban poverty in China, prepared for the Asian Development Bank, finds that in 1998 the incidence of absolute poverty, for a rather stringent threshold, was quite significant: 4.7 percent for the income measure and 11.9 percent for the expenditure measure.[10] It finds that small increases in the poverty line lead to large increases in the proportion of the population in poverty.

No claim is being made that the actual difference in "purchasing power parity" between the urban and the rural poverty threshold is as high as is indicated by the ratio of the two thresholds. The large value of the latter is partly due to the difference in consumption preference between the two groups of consumers. Those who are uneasy about this may choose to combine the low urban threshold with the high rural threshold in order to compare poverty incidence in the two locations. Their ratio, at about 1.39, may be much closer to the purchasing power parity difference between the two locations (Brandt and Holz 2006). The rates of change in the rural and urban consumer price indices (CPIs) were used to update the 1995 poverty thresholds for 2002.[11]

Table 6.1 summarizes poverty thresholds for 1995 and 2002. How do these poverty thresholds compare with the ones that are used by others? A simple comparison between the levels of our poverty lines and the levels of the poverty lines used by others would be inappropriate because our income estimates are substantially higher because of the use of a more comprehensive definition. One should compare the ratios between poverty lines and the average of the income estimates to the distribution of which they are applied.

For the benchmark year 1995, the official poverty threshold was 34 percent of official income for rural China, which is about the same ratio as that

---

[10] The study – ADB (2002) by Athar Hussain and others – is yet to be published. It uses the household level data from the 1998 Urban Household Survey by the NBS. It calculates the food-poverty line for each of the 31 provinces by using the consumption pattern of the poorest quintile of the population to obtain the "cost efficient" value of 2,100 kilocalories and, to arrive at the poverty line, adds to it the proportion of non-food expenditure of the typical household that barely attains the minimum food consumption.

[11] This is a departure from the Khan (1998) study which made an adjustment in the CPI for the difference between the average consumption pattern and the consumption pattern of the poor. The reason is that the NBS no longer publishes the data on which the adjustment was based in the earlier study and, in view of the remarkable price stability between 1995 and 2002, such an adjustment would in all likelihood make little difference.

between our low poverty threshold and income. As for the World Bank's "PPP $1" poverty threshold, it appears to represent approximately 45 percent of the official average income for 1995. As a proportion of income this is closer to our high poverty threshold than the low poverty threshold for rural areas.[12] For urban China, the World Bank's "PPP $1" poverty line translates into less than 13 percent of the average income for 1995, a phenomenon to which attention has already been drawn. For urban China, there is no official poverty line comparable to the rural poverty line insofar as there is no comparable recognition of the problem of urban poverty. An official urban poverty line used in the mid-1990s was higher, however, than our high poverty line as a proportion of per capita income.[13]

III. Changes in Rural Poverty between 1995 and 2002

Table 6.2 shows the three standard Foster-Greer-Thorbecke indices of poverty – the head-count rate, the proportionate poverty gap, and the "weighted" (squared) poverty gap – for rural China and for the rural areas of the provinces in the sample for 1995 and 2002 for the upper poverty line.[14] Table 6.3 shows the same for the lower poverty line.

During the period under review, rural China achieved a rapid rate of poverty reduction. There was a 57 percent reduction in the head-count rate according to the upper poverty line (hereafter broad poverty) and an even faster, 64 percent, reduction according to the lower poverty line (hereafter "ultrapoverty"). During the period, China's rural population declined absolutely, according to official estimates, from 859.5 million in 1995 to 782.4 million in 2002. Applying the estimates of poverty head-count rates to the official population figures, one gets an even more impressive reduction in

[12] This is estimated as follows. For 1993 the PPP$ exchange rate for China was about 1.25. Using this, the PPP $1.08 translates into 1.35 yuan per day or 493 yuan per year. Between 1993 and 1995, the increase in the official CPI was 45 percent for rural and 46 percent for urban China. Using these, the 1995 RMB value of the World Bank's poverty line turns out to be 715 RMB for rural China and 720 RMB for urban China.

[13] See Khan and Riskin (2001), p. 61.

[14] The head-count index shows the proportion of the population with income below the poverty threshold. The proportionate poverty gap shows the average, over the entire population, of the income shortfall from the poverty threshold where the shortfall for the nonpoor is defined to be zero. It is the product of the head-count rate of poverty and the average income shortfall of those who are in poverty. The weighted (squared) poverty gap is the average, over the entire population, of the squares of the proportion of the income shortfall of the poor, in which the shortfall for the nonpoor is defined to be zero. For further explanation see Khan (1998) or Khan and Riskin (2001).

Table 6.2. *Indices of rural poverty: Upper poverty line*

	1995			2002		
	HC	PPG	WPG	HC	PPG	WPG
Rural China	28.6	8.2	3.5	12.3	3.2	1.4
Gansu	69.0	26.4	13.0	34.9	9.1	3.4
Guizhou	61.8	19.1	8.3	42.2	10.9	4.0
Shanxi	49.5	16.3	7.7	15.5	5.5	3.1
Shaanxi	58.0	18.5	7.8	22.7	5.5	2.1
Yunnan	45.6	10.6	3.7	27.8	9.2	4.6
Hunan	37.5	12.0	5.1	12.0	2.8	1.0
Sichuan	43.1	12.1	5.0	5.9	1.1	0.4
Jiangxi	27.0	5.9	2.2	10.3	2.7	0.8
Anhui	19.8	4.9	1.8	9.9	2.1	0.7
Henan	20.1	4.2	1.6	6.6	1.2	0.4
Hubei	25.0	8.6	4.3	8.8	2.2	0.9
Hebei	22.7	6.1	2.5	9.0	2.0	0.7
Liaoning	21.9	5.2	1.9	11.7	3.0	1.4
Jilin	18.3	4.4	1.7	5.6	2.2	1.8
Shandong	19.3	4.6	2.0	5.2	1.2	1.2
Zhejiang	4.0	0.7	0.3	4.5	1.8	0.9
Jiangsu	4.7	1.1	0.6	0.5	0.0	0.0
Guangdong	5.2	1.3	0.5	0.9	0.3	0.1
Beijing	1.3	0.8	0.5	0.0	0.0	0.0
Guangxi	–	–	–	16.0	3.2	1.0
Xinjiang	–	–	–	17.7	4.6	2.0

Note: HC = Head-count Rate; PPG = Proportionate Poverty Gap; WPG = Weighted Poverty Gap.

the absolute number of the rural poor: the number in broad poverty declined from 246 million to 96 million – a 61 percent decline – and the number in ultrapoverty declined from 104 million to 34 million – a 67 percent decline.

The rate of reduction in the proportionate poverty gap (PPG) was only slightly faster (61 percent) than the rate of reduction in the head-count index (57 percent) for broad poverty. This means that there was an insignificant reduction in the average income gap of the broad poor. For the ultrapoor the rates of reduction in the head-count index and the PPG are even closer, indicating no improvement in the average income gap of the poor. The rate of decline in the weighted poverty gap (WPG) in each case was about the same as the rate of decline in the PPG, signifying that there was no appreciable change in the distribution of income among the poor.

Table 6.3. *Indices of rural poverty: Lower poverty line*

	1995			2002		
	HC	PPG	WPG	HC	PPG	WPG
Rural China	12.1	3.1	1.3	4.4	1.1	0.6
Gansu	43.9	12.8	5.6	14.0	2.6	0.9
Guizhou	28.5	7.5	2.9	15.9	3.1	0.9
Shanxi	24.3	7.3	3.3	8.1	3.1	1.8
Shaanxi	28.9	7.0	2.5	7.2	1.6	0.7
Yunnan	12.7	2.6	0.9	14.2	4.7	2.1
Hunan	19.2	4.7	1.6	3.9	0.6	0.2
Sichuan	18.5	4.3	1.7	1.4	0.3	0.1
Jiangxi	8.3	1.8	0.7	4.0	0.5	0.1
Anhui	6.4	1.3	0.5	2.6	0.4	0.1
Henan	5.0	1.2	0.6	1.2	0.2	0.1
Hubei	14.1	4.3	1.8	3.0	0.7	0.3
Hebei	7.7	2.0	1.0	3.2	0.4	0.1
Liaoning	7.3	1.4	0.5	3.5	1.3	0.8
Jilin	6.5	1.4	0.6	2.5	1.4	1.9
Shandong	5.9	1.8	0.9	1.0	0.6	1.4
Zhejiang	0.2	0.2	0.2	3.1	0.9	0.4
Jiangsu	1.2	0.6	0.5	0.0	0.0	0.0
Guangdong	2.2	0.4	0.2	0.4	0.1	0.0
Beijing	1.3	0.5	0.2	0.0	0.0	0.0
Guangxi	–	–	–	3.7	0.5	0.1
Xinjiang	–	–	–	5.8	1.8	0.8

Note: WPG should usually be no higher than PPG. The exception in the case of Jilin and Shandong is due to a few cases of negative income. HC = Head-count Rate; PPG = Proportionate Poverty Gap; WPG = Weighted Poverty Gap.

The relationship among growth in income, distribution of income, and poverty reduction for rural China as a whole is brought out in Table 6.4, which compares growth in income, change in inequality, and reduction in poverty between two time periods – the period between 1988 and 1995 ("the pre-1995 period") and the period between 1995 and 2002 (the "post-1995 period").

The annual rate of increase in per capita income was somewhat slower during the post-1995 period than that in the pre-1995 period. Yet the rate of poverty reduction, measured by all three indicators, was a great deal faster during the post-1995 period than during the pre-1995 period. The explanation clearly lies in the fact that inequality increased sharply during the

Table 6.4. *Comparison of growth, inequality, and poverty reduction in rural China, the pre-1995 and post-1995 periods*

	Pre-1995 (Between 1988 and 1995)	Post-1995 (Between 1995 and 2002)
Annual increase in per capita income (%)	4.71	4.07
Change in the Gini over the entire period (%)	+23.08	−9.86
Annual reduction in head-count poverty rate (%)		
High threshold	2.88	11.36
Low threshold	4.66	13.46
Gross elasticity of head-count poverty		
High threshold	0.61	2.79
Low threshold	0.99	3.31
Annual reduction in PPG index (%)		
High threshold	4.72	12.58
Low threshold	7.62	13.76
Gross elasticity of PPG index		
High threshold	1.00	3.09
Low threshold	1.62	3.38

Note: Gross elasticity of poverty reduction is defined as the percentage reduction in the relevant poverty indicator divided by the percentage increase in per capita income.

pre-1995 period, while it fell significantly during the post-1995 period. Inequality, as measured by the Gini ratio, went up by 23 percent during the earlier period, while it fell by 10 percent during the later period.

Gross elasticity of poverty with respect to per capita income, as reported in the table, is simply the ratio of the observed percentage change in an indicator of poverty to the actual percentage change in per capita income. It does not measure the extent of change in an indicator of poverty because of a percentage change in income. The latter is measured by the net elasticity of poverty reduction, which is based on the separation of the effect of income growth from the effect of other factors on the change in an indicator of poverty.[15] A higher gross elasticity of poverty reduction represents a

[15] Consider the following equation explaining the change in the poverty head-count rate: $d(HC)/HC = a_0 + a_1 (dY)/Y + a_2 (dG/G) + a_3 H + \ldots$ in which $d(HC)/HC$ is the proportionate change in the head-count index, dY/Y is the proportionate change in income, dG/G is the proportionate change in the Gini ratio, and H, etc., are other factors having effects on the head-count rate of poverty. The net elasticity of the head-count poverty with respect to

greater effectiveness of economic growth in reducing the incidence of poverty due to favorable changes in the determinants of poverty other than income growth.

As shown in Table 6.4, the gross elasticity of head-count poverty reduction is 4.5 times and 3.3 times as high in the post-1995 period as in the pre-1995 period, respectively, for broad poverty and ultrapoverty. The gross elasticity of PPG reduction is similarly 3.1 and 2.1 times as high for the later period than for the earlier period. Income growth was greatly more beneficial to the poor in the later period than in the earlier period. The immediate explanation of this lies in the fact that growth was inequality reducing in the later period, while it was inequality inducing in the earlier period. Reduction in poverty is caused by an increase in the average income of the poor and an improvement in the distribution of income among the poor. Given the overall rate of income growth, these changes are generally captured by the change in the Gini ratio. Unfortunately, a simple indicator like the Gini ratio does not always capture these changes: a change in the Gini ratio caused by a change in income distribution at the upper end of the income scale leaves the welfare of the poor unchanged, just as an unchanged Gini ratio may hide an unfavorable change in distribution affecting the poor that is offset by a favorable change in distribution at the upper end of the income scale. One hopes, however, that in most cases the change in the Gini ratio captures at least a good part of the change in the distribution affecting the welfare of the poor.

In extending the relationship among income growth, income distribution, and poverty reduction to the provincial data, one can either explain provincial differences in the level of poverty incidence with reference to levels of income and inequality of distribution in any given year (2002 in the present case) or explain provincial differences in the rate of poverty reduction between 1995 and 2002 with reference to provincial differences in the growth rate and change in distribution over the same period. This chapter does both, but focuses on the latter exercise for analytical insights into the determinants of poverty reduction. One reason is one is ideally interested in the interaction among changes in these variables between time periods. To try to read this from cross-sectional differences in variables at a point of

income is a_1 whereas the gross elasticity is $[d(HC)/HC]/(dY/Y)$. Gross elasticity captures the change in the head-count index due not only to the change in income, but also to the other determinants of head-count poverty. Note that a_2 is the net elasticity of head-count poverty with respect to the Gini ratio.

time suffers from the problem that the observed variation among provinces in income levels is far greater than the observed variation in the Gini ratio at any particular time. Thus, the coefficient of variation and the ratio of the highest to the lowest value for 2002 for the 19 common rural provinces that feature in the surveys for both years have been 0.47 and 4.02, respectively, for per capita income, and 0.13 and 1.60, respectively, for the Gini ratio.

In this situation, cross-sectional estimates of levels are more likely to exaggerate the effect of variation in income on poverty reduction than the effect of variation in inequality on poverty reduction.[16] Table 6.5 shows that this problem does not exist in the case of rates of change in the variables between 1995 and 2002.

In discussing the pattern of poverty reduction in the provinces, it is useful to distinguish those provinces that had a substantial incidence of poverty in 1995 from the four high-income provinces (Zhejiang, Jiangsu, Guangdong, and Beijing), where in 1995 there was very little poverty: 5.2 (2.2) percent in broad (ultra-) poverty in Guangdong and less in the other three. Their per capita rural income in 2002 was from 58 percent (Guangdong) to 128 percent (Zhejiang) higher than the per capita income for rural China. Due to the low benchmark poverty in these provinces, small absolute change in poverty performance becomes magnified in terms of the percentage change in the poverty indicators. Of these provinces, Zhejiang had a much higher than average growth in per capita income but a modest increase in inequality. The result was a small absolute rise in the head-count rate of broad poverty but a more substantial increase in the head-count rate of ultrapoverty, which translates into a massive percentage increase in poverty. Guangdong and Jiangsu each attained very high rates of poverty reduction with only a modest absolute fall in poverty, thanks again to the very low base poverty rates. Both these provinces had very low rates of income growth, but both of them had high rates of reduction in the Gini ratio of income distribution. Beijing's negligible head-count rate of 1.3 percent poverty was wiped out with the help of a low rate of income growth despite a sharp rise in inequality.

---

[16] A linear regression to explain provincial head-count poverty (upper poverty line) by provincial per capita income and the provincial Gini for 2002 gives the following fit: $HC = -12.80 - 0.0076Y + 165.78$ Gini in which both the coefficients are significant at the 1 percent level and the adjusted R^2 is 0.62. The double logarithmic fit is however log $HC = 31.10 - 3.60 \log Y + 0.28 \log$ Gini, in which the coefficient of income is significant at the 1 percent level but the coefficient of the Gini is not significant at any reasonable level. The adjusted R^2 is 0.59.

Table 6.5. *Gross elasticity of poverty reduction: Rural China*

	Percentage change in the Gini 1995–2002	Annual percentage change in per capita income	Annual percentage reduction in poverty HC		Gross elasticity of HC poverty reduction	
			Upper	Lower	Upper	Lower
Rural China	−9.86	4.09	11.36	13.46	2.78	3.29
Gansu	−6.69	7.23	9.28	15.06	1.28	2.08
Guizhou	−0.99	3.51	5.30	8.00	1.51	2.28
Shanxi	−3.40	8.59	15.28	14.52	1.78	1.69
Shaanxi	−23.12	4.26	12.54	18.01	2.94	4.23
Yunnan	+0.33	1.93	6.83	−1.61	3.54	−0.83
Hunan	+9.27	9.34	15.02	20.36	1.61	2.18
Sichuan	−24.71	6.89	24.73	30.84	3.59	4.48
Jiangxi	−1.74	5.04	12.86	9.90	2.55	1.96
Anhui	−2.57	3.61	9.43	12.07	2.61	3.34
Henan	−5.45	4.64	14.71	18.44	3.17	3.97
Hubei	−7.72	5.30	13.86	19.83	2.62	3.74
Hebei	+7.09	6.36	12.38	11.79	1.95	1.85
Liaoning	−2.67	4.67	8.57	9.97	1.84	2.13
Jilin	−18.34	2.56	15.56	12.76	6.08	4.98
Shandong	−21.30	3.61	17.08	22.40	4.73	6.20
Zhejiang	+6.08	7.22	−1.70	−47.93	−0.24	−6.64
Jiangsu	*−16.27*	*2.17*	*27.39*	*63.68*	*12.62*	*29.35*
Guangdong	−17.44	0.93	22.16	21.61	23.83	23.24
Beijing	*+34.10*	*2.45*	*64.10*	*64.10*	*26.16*	*26.16*

Note: In the last four columns, the heading "Upper" refers to the upper poverty line, and the heading "Lower" refers to the lower poverty line. Jiangsu and Beijing, for which the entries are italicized, reduced poverty to zero, from very low initial poverty levels, for the given poverty thresholds. The rates of poverty reduction for these provinces have been calculated by making the assumption that the head-count rate in 2002 was 0.001. Their high rates of poverty reduction and elasticities of poverty reduction should be viewed in this context.

Beijing is clearly a special case in view of its virtually nonexistent initial poverty. In the other three high-income provinces, the change in income distribution seems to have acted as a stronger determinant of the poverty outcome than the rate of income growth. In Zhejiang poverty increased despite a high rate of income growth, which seems to have been offset by the increase in inequality. In Jiangsu and Guangdong poverty declined despite low rates of income growth; an obvious reason seems to be the significant reduction in inequality.

Guangxi and Xinjiang were not included in the 1995 survey. In the remaining 15 provinces the head-count rate of broad poverty ranged between 18 percent in Jilin and 69 percent in Gansu. Of these provinces, Sichuan achieved the fastest rate of reduction in poverty. It had a rate of income growth that was two-thirds faster than rural China as a whole and a reduction in the Gini ratio that was two and a half times as fast as the reduction of the Gini ratio for rural China. Thus a combination of high growth and a large reduction in inequality resulted in the best performance in poverty reduction. The next most impressive reduction in poverty occurred in Shandong and Jilin, both of which had significantly lower rates of income growth than the national average but a significantly faster reduction in inequality. Hunan and Hebei represent a different combination of growth rates and changes in inequality. Both of them experienced a moderate increase in inequality, which appears to have weakened the effect of their very high rates of income growth – more than twice as high as the national average for Hunan and more than 50 percent higher for Hebei – on poverty reduction, which was at about the same, or only a little faster, rate than the national average. The head-count rate of broad poverty declined in all provinces, and the head-count rate of ultrapoverty declined in all provinces except Yunnan, where it increased a little. Yunnan had little growth in per capita income and no improvement in income distribution.

Table 6.5 shows the gross elasticities of head-count poverty reduction for the provinces. Discounting the high-income provinces with little initial poverty, the highest elasticities are observed for Shandong and Jilin, provinces with low growth but a large reduction in inequality. Some of the most rapidly growing provinces with rising inequality or very low reduction in inequality – for example, Hunan, Hebei, and Shanxi – on the other hand had relatively low gross elasticities of poverty reduction.

Table 6.6 shows the results of the regressions explaining the differences in the provincial rates in poverty reduction. Regressions have been limited to the 15 provinces with significant rates of benchmark poverty. The four high-income provinces with insignificant benchmark poverty have been excluded for reasons discussed earlier.[17]

The dependent variable in the equations reported in Table 6.6 is the annual rate of reduction in broad head-count poverty during 1995–2002. The explanatory variables are (a) percentage change in the Gini ratio – reported as ratios, not indices, with values well below one – between 1995 and 2002; (b) annual percentage change in per capita income; (c) the initial,

---

[17] Their inclusion in the regressions weakens the results that are reported below.

Table 6.6. *Regression results: rural poverty reduction (15 provinces)*
(dependent variable: annual percentage reduction in poverty)

Regressor	1	2	3	4
Change in the Gini	−0.247		−0.324	−0.484
	(−2.344)		(−3.819)	(−6.292)
Income growth		0.861	1.312	1.835
		(1.512)	(3.158)	(6.613)
Gini				−59.076
				(−3.405)
Income				0.005
				(3.802)
Intercept	11.212	8.443	3.911	10.307
	(8.700)	(2.662)	(1.555)	(1.896)
R^2	0.297	0.149	0.616	0.881
Adjusted R^2	0.247	0.084	0.552	0.833

Notes:
Change in the Gini = Percentage change in the provincial Gini ratio between 1995 and 2002.
Income growth = Annual percentage growth in per capita provincial income.
Gini = Initial (1995) level of the provincial Gini ratio.
Income = Initial (1995) level of the provincial per capita income.
Dependent variable = Annual percentage reduction in the provincial head-count poverty (upper poverty line).
Figures in parentheses are *t*-values.

1995, level of the Gini ratio; and (d) the initial, 1995, level of per capita income. The equation that best explains the variation in the rate of poverty reduction includes all four explanatory variables. More than 83 percent of the variation in the rates of poverty reduction is explained. The signs of the coefficients are all as expected. A rise in inequality (Gini ratio) reduces the rate of poverty reduction. A high initial level of inequality (high benchmark Gini ratio) slows down the rate of poverty reduction. Faster income growth accelerates the rate of poverty reduction. High initial income facilitates poverty reduction. All the coefficients are significant at the 1 percent level.

Net elasticity of poverty with respect to income is 1.835, while the net elasticity of poverty with respect to inequality is −0.484. In judging the relative magnitudes of these elasticities it is necessary, however, to consider the units in which the variables are specified: income growth is shown as a percentage change per year, whereas the change in inequality is shown as a percentage change in the benchmark Gini ratio (the average in 1995 for the provinces was 0.324) over the seven-year period ending in 2002. A 5 percent fall in the Gini ratio over the seven-year period – from the average value of

0.324 to 0.308 – would reduce the head-count rate of broad poverty by 2.42 percent per year (about 18 percent over the seven-year period) and bring down the average of the provincial head-count rates of broad poverty from 36 percent in 1995 to 29.5 percent in 2002. Thus, controlling for other variables, a relatively modest absolute fall in the Gini ratio would bring about a substantial reduction in poverty. A 5 percent growth in income over the seven-year period means a 0.7 percent income growth per year, which would lead to 1.28 percent annual reduction in poverty, or just over 9 percent reduction in poverty over the seven-year period. Once again, the return to growth in terms of reduction in poverty is very substantial, although a 5 percent faster income growth would not result in as much a reduction in poverty as a 5 percent reduction in inequality. A high initial value of the Gini ratio makes it more difficult to reduce poverty. The rate of poverty reduction would be higher by 0.95 percent per year, or a total of 6.8 percent over the seven-year period, if the initial Gini ratio were 5 percent lower, say, 0.308 instead of the average of 0.324. Higher initial per capita income helps poverty reduction. In 1995 the (unweighted) average of the 15 provincial per capita incomes was 1,776 yuan. Comparing the effect of a 5 percent higher initial income with that of this average shows that the rate of poverty reduction would be higher by 0.09 percent per year, a total of 3.5 percent over the seven-year period. Comparing a given percentage change in different explanatory variables is arbitrary: it does not signify the equality in the magnitude of the effort in bringing those changes about, nor the relative desirability of those changes. But the ranking of a 5 percent change in each of the explanatory variables in the right direction, in terms of the magnitude of their effect on poverty reduction, puts the reduction in inequality at the top, followed by income growth, initial inequality, and initial income, in that order.

IV. An Explanation of the Faster Rate of Reduction in Rural Poverty in the Post–Asian Crisis Period

The above clearly brings out the two principal sources of rapid poverty reduction in rural China during 1995–2002, the post–Asian crisis period: a moderately rapid rate of growth in per capita income and a significant reduction in the inequality of income distribution. Although the rate of income growth was somewhat slower than in the pre–Asian crisis period, the vastly improved performance in the distribution of income made the rate of reduction in poverty much faster during the later period. This section analyzes the factors behind the performance in the growth of income and the reduction of inequality.

Table 6.7. *Contribution of different sources of income to rural income growth (%)*

	Incremental share	Annual growth
Wages	50.4	8.9
Farm income	19.1	1.2
Nonfarm enterprises	16.0	6.7
Property and homeownership	18.9	6.8
Transfers and miscellaneous	−4.3	−4.2

A. Growth in Income

During the period under review the growth in per capita personal income in rural China was just over 4 percent per year, somewhat lower than that in the preceding seven-year period and low by the standard of the rate of growth in urban per capita income (6.7 percent per year) and per capita GDP (7.2 percent per year). And yet this growth in income should be judged high by any absolute and international standard. What have been the sources of this income growth?

The incremental shares in the change in personal income (in percentage of the total) and the annual percentage rates of real growth of different income sources between 1995 and 2002 are shown in Table 6.7. The most important source of income growth was due to wages, which accounted for more than half of the increase in personal income and achieved a nearly 9 percent annual real rate of growth, the highest of all the components of income. This was due to a reasonably rapid growth in per capita employment in rural China (Table 6.8).

The accuracy of the numerical estimate and the conceptual basis of total rural employment, reported from the NBS estimates, are uncertain. The largest component of employment is employment in family farms,[18] which appears to have declined modestly over the period. Per capita rural employment, however, increased by as much as 11 percent.[19] This was due to a

[18] This is not shown separately in Table 6.8, but this probably accounts for almost the entire difference between total employment and nonfarm wage employment.

[19] Change in employment per member of the labor force, rather than per capita, is a more accurate indicator of an improvement in the demand-supply balance for labor. Unfortunately, labor-force estimates are not separately available for rural and urban China. The NBS (2003) shows that the economically active population, as a proportion of the total population in China, increased from 56.8 percent in 1995 to 58.7 percent in 2002. If the ratio of the rural labor force to the rural population increased at about the same rate, then there was a fairly rapid increase in employment per member of the labor force.

Table 6.8. *Changes in rural employment*

	1995	2002
Rural population (million)	859.5	782.4
Total rural employment (million)	490.3	489.6
Employment per person	0.57	0.63
Nonfarm wage employment (million)	133.3	147.0
TVE	(128.6)	(132.9)
Private	(4.7)	(14.1)
Nonfarm wage employment per person	0.155	0.188

Note: Data have been obtained from NBS (2003).

decline in the absolute size of the rural population. The year 1995 marks a watershed in China's demographic transition in that the absolute size of the rural population peaked in that year and started to decline rapidly thereafter, at an annual rate of 1.33 percent.

More remarkable, and helpful in explaining the sharp rise in wage income, is the increase in nonfarm wage employment. After several years of stagnation, employment in township and village enterprises (TVEs) started increasing in the late 1990s. Private wage employment in rural China, still a small component of total employment, increased at an extraordinarily rapid annual rate of 17 percent. Together these sources of wage employment increased by 21 percent on a per capita basis over the period. In line with the increase in nonfarm wage employment there was a fairly rapid increase in income from nonfarm enterprises.

Income from family farming constitutes the second largest share of incremental income. The annual rate of growth of this source of income was very small, however. This deserves a closer look. Per capita real agricultural value added, defined as value added in agriculture at constant prices divided by the rural population, increased at an annual rate of 4.7 percent, representing a 3.3 percent growth in real value added in agriculture and a –1.33 percent growth in the rural population.[20] Per capita real personal income of rural households from farming, however, increased at only 1.2 percent per year. This suggests a decline in agriculture's terms of trade over the period under review.[21] Note that the meager increase in per capita income from farming,

[20] The growth rate in agricultural value added is calculated from table 3–4 in NBS (2003).

[21] Until recently it was possible to make a more direct estimate of agriculture's terms of trade as the ratio of the "General Purchasing Price Index of Farm Products" to the "General Rural Retail Price Index of Industrial Products." Both these indices are shown in NBS (2000), p. 290. The index of the terms of trade for agriculture, thus calculated, had the following

despite the erosion due to the decline in the terms of trade, was made possible by the fall in the rural population. With an unchanged or increasing population, per capita income from farming might even have fallen because of both diminishing returns from scarce land and a larger number of persons among whom to share the income.

Public intermediation through taxes and subsidies tended to slow down the rate of increase in disposable income. Per capita net taxes increased at nearly 33 percent per year.

B. Change in Inequality

As argued above, much of the accelerated reduction in poverty was due to the reduction in inequality of the distribution of income. Sources of change in inequality between 1995 and 2002 are shown in Table 3.3 of Chapter 3. Only three of the income components – wages, farm income, and net subsidies (taxes) – became less disequalizing or more equalizing over this period.[22] All other sources of income became more disequalizing.

Wages were a very strongly disequalizing source of income in 1995. In 2002 they remain a disequalizing source of income, but much less strongly so. The concentration ratio of the distribution of wages fell sharply but is still above the Gini ratio. The evidence for 2002 suggests that the unequal distribution of wage income is largely attributable to the high regional inequality in the distribution of income rather than to the inequality in the distribution of wage income within a given region. The simple average of the concentration ratios of wage income for the 21 provinces is just 0.310 as compared

values for selected years: 1978: 100; 1988: 177 (steady increase in the intervening period, the index peaking in 1988); 1993: 154 (steady fall between 1988 and 1993, the year in which the index bottomed out); 1994: 184; 1995: 192 (sharp rise for two years which was followed by only a small decline in 1996); 1999: 151 (steady fall since 1996). After 2000 the NBS stopped publishing the two indices on which these terms of trade estimates are based. The comparison of the change in real growth in value added and the real growth in personal income suggests that this decline continued until 2002.

[22] For the ith component of income, one can derive a pseudo-Lorenz distribution in which the cumulative shares of the ith source of income are plotted against the cumulative deciles of the population in which the latter is obtained from a ranking of individuals according to per capita overall income rather than per capita income from the ith source. As the Gini ratio is estimated from the Lorenz distribution of income, so is the pseudo-Gini ratio or the concentration ratio for the ith source of income estimated from the pseudo-Lorenz distribution of the ith income component. The Gini ratio is the weighted average of the concentration ratios of the components of income where the weights are the shares of the respective components in total income. A component of income is considered equalizing (disequalizing) if its concentration ratio is lower (higher) than the Gini ratio; a rise in its income share reduces (increases) the Gini ratio.

to a concentration ratio of wage income for entire rural China of 0.455, a clear indication that interprovincial inequality dominates inequality within the provinces. Direct comparison of provincial concentration ratios between 1995 and 2002 is not possible because of the absence of comparable estimates for 1995. It appears, however, that much of the impetus for reduced concentration of wage income was provided by the reduced regional inequality of income – and wage income – among provinces.

There are two kinds of evidence for a reduction in regional inequality in the distribution of rural income. Spearman's rank correlation coefficient between the provincial rank in per capita rural income in 1995 and the provincial rank in the rate of growth in rural income between 1995 and 2002 is -0.44 for the 19 provinces in common in the two samples, indicating a negative relationship between the initial income level and the growth rate of income. The coefficient is not significant at the 5 percent level, but is significant at the 10 percent level. Second, largely as a result of this negative relationship between the initial level and the rate of growth of income, the coefficient of the variation of per capita rural income among these 19 provinces fell from 0.53 in 1995 to 0.47 in 2002. This may reflect the early results of the government's recent policy to shift the focus of poverty reduction toward the promotion of a greater regional balance in development.

Farm income was a strongly equalizing source of income distribution in 1995. By 2002 it became even more strongly equalizing. Its concentration ratio fell absolutely and as a proportion of the Gini ratio. The strongly equalizing distribution of farm income must be attributed primarily to the highly egalitarian system of peasant farming established and perpetuated by China's egalitarian distribution of land. Table 6.9 shows land distribution and its association with inequality in China in 1988, 1995, and 2002.

The Gini ratio of land distribution is remarkably low by the standard of all available international estimates. Even this low inequality is almost certainly due to regional differences in land endowment rather than to inequality in any region with a given land endowment per rural household. Over the period as a whole, there has been some reduction in the Gini ratio. By 2002 the "concentration" ratio of adjusted land had fallen close to zero, indicating that land in irrigated units was absolutely equally accessible to all income groups. The "concentration" ratio for unadjusted land had turned slightly negative, indicating that the amount of land, unadjusted for the proportion irrigated, was a little more accessible to the lower-income groups than to the higher-income groups. Equality of access to land has ensured an egalitarian distribution of income from farming and has constituted a strong source of basic income security in rural China.

Table 6.9. *Distribution of per capita landholdings*

	1988	1995	2002
Gini ratio			
Unadjusted land	0.499	0.431	0.488 (0.478)
Adjusted land	0.465	0.414	0.458 (0.443)
"Concentration ratio"			
Unadjusted land	0.021	0.001	−0.013 (−0.019)
Adjusted land	0.063	0.051	0.018 (0.012)

Note: "Unadjusted" land is total land area irrespective of the proportion irrigated, while "adjusted" land counts an irrigated hectare as equivalent to 2 ha of unirrigated land. The Gini ratio is estimated from the Lorenz distribution of per capita land, in which individuals are ranked according to per capita landholding. The "concentration ratio" is estimated from the Lorenz distribution of per capita land, in which individuals are ranked according to per capita income. Figures in parentheses for 2002 are estimates based on the same 19 provinces that were in the 1995 sample (i.e., excluding Xinjiang and Guangxi). For the sources of the 1988 and 1995 estimates see Khan and Riskin (2001), p. 108.

Net taxes continued to be disequalizing in 2002 but not as massively as in 1995. In 1995 the concentration ratio of net taxes was negative: the poorest income groups paid more than the entire net taxes, while the richest income groups received a net subsidy. By 2002 the tax-subsidy system had become less disequalizing. Its concentration ratio, however, remained far below the Gini ratio, indicating that taxes are highly regressive. The tax-subsidy system still has a long way to go before it begins to improve the distribution of income.

C. Rural-Urban Migration

In the above the important role of the declining rural population in helping both the growth and the favorable change in the distribution of rural income has been emphasized. China's actual rural population in 2002 would have been 911.5 million if it had grown at the same rate as the national population, 0.843 percent per year, since 1995. This means that a total of 129 million people moved out of rural China to urban areas during this period.[23] They

---

[23] This is far in excess of the estimated increase in the number of floating migrants over the period. The total level of floating migrants is estimated to have increased from about 60 million in 1995 to about 80 million in 2000 (Liang and Ma 2003). It seems that for a large proportion of those who have ceased to remain rural residents, the formerly rural locations of their residence have been converted into new urban locations. Be that as it may, they have ceased to claim land and employment resources of the rural economy.

have moved to existing or newly created urban locations. This has been made possible by the de facto flexibility in China's rigid system of residence permits (*hukou*).

V. Changes in Urban Residents' Poverty
in the Post–Asian Crisis Period

Table 6.10 shows the poverty indices both for the urban residents for the sample as a whole and for the 11 provinces. Between the two years poverty

Table 6.10. *Indices of urban poverty*

Index	1995			2002		
	HC	PPG	WPG	HC	PPG	WPG
The Upper Poverty Line						
Urban China	8.0	2.0	0.8	2.2	0.5	0.2
Shanxi	20.7	5.3	2.1	5.3	1.3	0.5
Henan	21.1	5.8	2.3	2.9	0.7	0.3
Anhui	6.9	1.3	0.4	1.9	0.3	0.1
Yunnan	6.1	0.9	0.3	1.2	0.3	0.1
Hubei	5.3	1.3	0.8	2.1	0.5	0.2
Sichuan	7.3	1.8	0.7	4.1	0.9	0.3
Liaoning	5.7	1.1	0.3	1.6	0.3	0.1
Gansu	12.9	3.4	1.2	2.3	0.5	0.2
Jiangsu	1.8	0.5	0.2	1.0	0.1	0.0
Beijing	0.6	0.1	0.0	0.3	0.1	0.1
Guangdong	0.9	0.2	0.0	0.3	0.1	0.0
The Lower Poverty Line						
Urban China	2.7	0.6	0.3	0.8	0.1	0.0
Shanxi	7.9	1.8	0.7	2.3	0.3	0.1
Henan	9.0	1.9	0.7	1.2	0.2	0.1
Anhui	1.7	0.2	0.1	0.2	0.1	0.0
Yunnan	0.9	0.2	0.1	0.3	0.1	0.0
Hubei	1.6	0.7	0.6	1.0	0.2	0.1
Sichuan	2.1	0.6	0.3	1.1	0.3	0.1
Liaoning	1.2	0.1	0.0	0.6	0.0	0.0
Gansu	4.4	0.9	0.3	0.6	0.2	0.1
Jiangsu	0.8	0.2	0.1	0.2	0.0	0.0
Beijing	0.0	0.0	0.0	0.3	0.0	0.0
Guangdong	0.3	0.0	0.0	0.2	0.0	0.0

Note: HC = Head-count Rate; PPG = Proportionate Poverty Gap; WPG = Weighted Poverty Gap.

Table 6.11. *Comparison of growth, inequality, and poverty reduction in urban China, the pre-1995 and post-1995 periods*

	Pre-1995 (Between 1988 and 1995)	Post-1995 (Between 1995 and 2002)
Annual increase in per capita income (%)	4.48	6.44
Change in the Gini over the entire period (%)	+42.49	−4.22
Annual reduction in head-count poverty rate: high threshold (%)	0.35	16.84
Gross elasticity of head-count poverty: high threshold	0.08	2.61

Note: Gross elasticity of poverty reduction is defined as the percentage reduction in the relevant poverty indicator divided by the percentage increase in per capita income.

declined for every entity and for every indicator, with the unusual exception of the ultrapoverty head count in Beijing.[24] The rate of decline has often been quite dramatic in the provinces in which the incidence of urban poverty was significant. This is in sharp contrast with China's performance in poverty reduction in the period between 1988 and 1995, when urban poverty showed little decline and, indeed, some increase according to certain indicators.

Because of the very low incidence of ultrapoverty in the benchmark year, the discussion of change in poverty in what follows is carried out with reference to broad poverty, measured in terms of the upper poverty line. The difference between the pre-1995 period (the period between 1988 and 1995) and the post-1995 period (the period between 1995 and 2002) for the residents of urban China as a whole is summarized in Table 6.11.

Growth in per capita income was faster in the post-1995 period than in the pre-1995 period: 6.44 percent per year as compared to 4.48 percent.[25]

[24] In Beijing five individuals, out of a total of 1,456, fell below the lower poverty line in 2002, while none was below the lower poverty line in 1995. In several cases very low poverty rates according to certain indicators remained the same in 2002 as in 1995 due to what appears to be a rounding error.

[25] It is worth noting that the rate of growth in personal income does not have a stable relationship with the rate of GNP or GDP growth. Annual growth in per capita GNP for China was 8.1 percent during 1988–1995 and a lower 7.3 percent between 1995 and 2002 according to official data. Growth in per capita personal income, for China as a whole, as measured by the CHIP surveys, was 5.1 percent in the first period and a higher 7.1 percent during the second period. Clearly, public policy with respect to the distribution of income among households, business, and the government changed in favor of the households in the second period. The faster growth in personal income in the second period was partly

Yet the truly remarkable change occurred in the distribution of income. In the pre-1995 period the Gini ratio increased by more that 42 percent, while in the post-1995 period it fell by a modest 4 percent. The poverty outcome – measured as the change in the head-count rate for the upper poverty line – was a tiny reduction of a third of a percent per year in the pre-1995 period and a dramatic fall of 17 percent per year in the post-1995 period.

The difference was due to the very different outcome with respect to the change in inequality. In the pre-1995 period the gross elasticity of poverty reduction – the percentage change in poverty divided by the percentage change in per capita income – was an insignificant 0.08. In the post-1995 period it rose to 2.61. In the first period the potential poverty-reduction effect of income growth was largely offset by the increase in inequality. In the second period the poverty-reduction impact of income growth was accentuated by the improvement, albeit modest, in income distribution.

An econometric analysis of the relationship among poverty reduction, inequality, and growth suffers from the limitation that the number of provinces in the urban sample is much smaller than that in the rural sample. Furthermore, in several provinces urban poverty in the initial period was too low to permit a meaningful measurement of its change. The exclusion of those provinces would further reduce the already limited degrees of freedom. The results reported below need to be interpreted in the context of these limitations.[26]

Table 6.12 shows the percentage change in the provincial urban Gini ratios between 1995 and 2002. It is noteworthy that in 8 of the 11 provinces the Gini ratio actually increased. It fell in just two, while in one (Henan) it was unchanged. The reduction in the overall urban Gini, despite the increase in the large majority of provincial urban Gini ratios, indicates that there was a reduction in interprovincial inequality in income. Support for this is found by the decline in the coefficient of variation for per capita provincial

---

due to the rising share of the urban population whose personal income was higher and increasing faster than that of the rural population.

[26] As in the case of rural provinces, a regression was fitted to explain the level of broad head-count poverty (HC) by the levels of the provincial per capita income (Y) and the provincial Gini ratio (Gini): $HC = -1.539 - 0.0005Y + 28.868$ Gini, which had an adjusted $R^2 = 0.65$, the coefficients of Y significant at 1 percent and the coefficient of the Gini significant at 5 percent. In the double log fit, $\log HC = 34.842 - 3.474 \log Y + 2.039 \log$ Gini, the coefficient of the Gini is not significant at any reasonable level of probability, while the coefficient of income is significant at 1 percent and the adjusted $R^2 = 0.90$. Once again, the insignificance of the coefficient of the Gini, especially in the logarithmic fit, seems to be due to the very low variability in provincial inequality at any given time. The coefficient of variation of the provincial Gini for 2002 is 0.09, while the coefficient of variation for the provincial per capita income is 0.31.

Table 6.12. *Gross elasticity of poverty reduction in urban China*

	Percentage change in the Gini 1995–2002	Annual percentage change in per capita income	Annual percentage reduction in poverty head count	Gross elasticity of HC poverty reduction
Urban China	−4.22	6.44	16.84	2.61
Shanxi	+19.92	9.18	17.69	1.93
Henan	0	8.10	24.69	3.05
Anhui	+22.87	7.14	16.83	2.36
Yunnan	+12.11	8.37	20.73	2.48
Hubei	+7.73	6.55	12.39	1.89
Sichuan	+14.77	6.15	7.91	1.29
Liaoning	−12.04	7.12	16.60	2.33
Gansu	−46.89	2.80	21.83	7.80
Jiangsu	+27.97	7.42	8.05	1.08
Beijing	+5.68	6.60	9.43	1.43
Guangdong	+3.80	3.32	14.52	4.37

Note: Poverty reduction and gross elasticity of poverty reduction are with respect to the upper poverty threshold.

income from 0.39 in 1995 to 0.31 in 2002. Also, Spearman's rank correlation coefficient between the provincial rank in per capita income in 1995 and the provincial rank in the growth rate in income between 1995 and 2002 is negative (−0.673) and significant at the 10 percent level. Table 6.12 also shows the annual percentage reduction in poverty head count and the annual percentage growth in per capita income for the provinces. The ratio of the two, shown in the last column of the table, is the gross elasticity of poverty reduction.

Table 6.13 shows the results, for urban areas of the provinces, of the same four regression equations that were employed to explain the rate of rural poverty reduction. Equation (1) shows that, as the sole explanatory variable, the change in the Gini ratio has the right sign: a higher rate of increase in the Gini ratio results in a decline in the rate of poverty reduction. The coefficient is, however, not significant at any convincing level of confidence. Income growth, as the sole explanatory variable, also has the expected sign for the coefficient, but the coefficient again is not significant at any reasonable level of confidence (eq. [2]). Equation (3) employs both the rate of change in the Gini ratio and the rate of income growth as explanatory variables. Both the coefficients have the right sign. While the coefficient of the change in the Gini ratio is significant at the 5 percent level, the coefficient of income growth is

Table 6.13. *Regression results: Urban poverty reduction (dependent variable: annual percentage reduction in poverty)*

Regressor	1	2	3	4
Change in the Gini	−0.131		−0.241	−0.167
	(−1.632)		(−2.581)	(−0.789)
Income growth		0.171	1.792	1.529
		(0.178)	(1.832)	(0.850)
Gini				19.311
				(0.273)
Income				−0.001
				(−0.431)
Intercept	16.184	14.386	4.889	3.475
	(9.915)	(2.186)	(0.772)	(0.109)
R^2	0.228	0.004	0.456	0.485
Adjusted R^2	0.143	−0.107	0.320	0.141

Notes:
Change in the Gini = Percentage change in the provincial Gini ratio between 1995 and 2002.
Income growth = Annual percentage growth in per capita provincial income.
Gini = Initial (1995) level of the provincial Gini ratio.
Income = Initial (1995) level of the provincial per capita income.
Dependent variable = Annual percentage reduction in provincial head-count poverty (upper poverty line).
Figures in parentheses are *t*-values.

just short of being significant at a 10 percent level of confidence. Together they explain a third of the variation in the rate of poverty reduction. Introduction of the initial levels of income and inequality as additional variables in equation (4) renders the coefficients of the explanatory variables insignificant and reduces the explained proportion of the variation in the dependent variable as compared to equation (3), perhaps because of the lowering of the degrees of freedom.

VI. An Explanation of the Faster Reduction in Urban Poverty in the Post–Asian Crisis Period

The faster reduction in urban poverty during the post-1995 period, as compared to the pre-1995 period, has been due to the faster growth in personal income and, more notably, the reversal of the sharp increase in income inequality in the past. As already noted, the faster growth in personal income during the period was not due to a faster overall economic growth. Indeed, official estimates suggest that the rate of growth in per capita GDP was slower in the post-1995 period than in the pre-1995 period. There was, however, a

Table 6.14. *Urban employment (millions except where noted otherwise)*

	1995	2002
Total employment	190.40	247.80
Total population	351.74	502.12
Employment per person (ratio)	0.54	0.49
Employment categories:		
State and collective enterprises	144.08	82.85
Cooperative and joint enterprises	0.53	2.06
Limited liability and shareholding	3.17	16.21
Private	4.85	19.99
Foreign including Taiwan, Macao, and Hong Kong funded	5.13	7.58
Self-employment	15.60	22.69

Source: NBS (2003). A cryptic note states that the components do not add to the totals, which "have been adjusted in accordance with the data obtained from the 5th National Population Census." This probably means that the components are from independent labor-force–type surveys that incompletely count individual employment in informal activities that are captured by the population census.

change in macroeconomic policies permitting a higher incremental share of GDP to accrue to the households, especially the urban households, perhaps as a conscious policy to promote a high rate of growth in consumer demand during this period of sluggish growth in the rest of East Asia and the world economy.

As analyzed above, the difference in the rates of urban poverty reduction between the two periods perhaps has been even more powerfully influenced by the change in income distribution performance between the two periods. The effect of change in inequality on poverty reduction is more complex in urban areas than in rural areas. It is hard to see the effect of the change in inequality on poverty reduction in individual provinces, except in a few outstanding cases such as Gansu, because most of the provinces registered an increase in inequality. Overall urban poverty reduction came about because of the faster than average rate of income growth for poor provinces with high initial poverty (notably Shanxi and Henan) – which led to a reduction in inequality for urban China as a whole though not for urban areas of individual provinces – and because of the fall in inequality in provinces with high initial poverty (notably Gansu).

Table 6.14 and Tables 3.5 and 3.6 of Chapter 3 provide some idea about the factors behind income growth and the change in income distribution between 1995 and 2002. Wages as a source of income have grown at a slower rate than overall income. This is due to the worsening urban employment situation. Employment per person in urban China fell by more than 9 percent because of a dramatic fall in employment in state and collective enterprises caused by the restructuring away from the past system of using employment in these enterprises as a concealed method of unemployment insurance. There has been a rapid increase in employment in private, foreign, and joint-stock enterprises and self-employment categories, but these have not been fast enough to offset the fall in state and collective enterprises on a per capita basis. Net subsidies, which represented mostly housing subsidies in kind in 1995, have drastically declined as a source of personal income. Income from property has also declined though it was very small to begin with. In contrast to the above declining components of income, there was an increase in three components: income from pensions and related earnings of retirees, income from individual enterprises, and rental value of housing.

The change in the composition of income has a close relationship to the change in the concentration of individual components of income. Reduction in employment per capita appears to have been accompanied by a change in the structure of earnings, making wages a more disequalizing source of income. This was almost certainly because of the decline in the enforced egalitarianism of the structure of wages that dominated the overwhelmingly important state and collective enterprises in the past. Thus, despite the fall in the share of wages in total income, the contribution of wages to the Gini ratio went up from 46 percent in 1995 to 59 percent in 2002.[27]

All other sources of income became more equalizing or less disequalizing. Pensions and payments to retirees, including payments made to laid-off workers, have increased significantly as a proportion of income, and their concentration ratio has fallen. It appears that compensatory public action to protect the laid-off workers, however inadequate, is behind these changes. Net subsidies were highly disequalizing in the past, their benefits mainly appropriated by the nonpoor groups. They have not only been drastically reduced, but their redistributive effect has changed from regressive to progressive. Income from individual enterprises, though still small as a proportion of income, has grown at the fastest rate and has become even more strongly equalizing than before. Finally, housing reform has shifted income away from in-kind housing subsidies (public and collective housing rented out at nominal rent, which was highly disequalizing) to broad-based

---

[27] The percentage contribution of a component to the Gini ratio is the product of the income share of the component and its concentration ratio divided by the Gini ratio.

Table 6.15. *Income, inequality, and poverty, 2002: Residents, migrants, and combined urban population*

	Residents	Migrants	Combined urban
Per capita income (RMB per year)	9,766	6,365	9,160
Gini ratio	0.318	0.380	0.338
Poverty head count (%): Upper poverty line	2.2	14.4	4.4

Note: Estimates for the combined urban population are directly made from the combined urban sample. That explains why the per capita income for the combined urban population is not exactly the same as the weighted average of the per capita incomes of the residents and the migrants.

homeownership, which is less disequalizing than the distribution of subsidized public housing was in the past. Note that the rental value of housing, though still significantly disequalizing in 2002, is far less so than in 1995. This perhaps signifies that housing reform initially enabled the better-off households to attain ownership, which became broad based only after the reform was fully implemented.

To summarize, the decline in employment and the disequalizing change in the distribution of wages were offset by a combination of factors: public action in providing some protection to the laid-off workers by an increase in pension provisions, a reduction in wasteful subsidies to the rich, a rapid growth in small enterprises, and a broadening of homeownership.

VII. Poverty among the Floating Migrants

Table 6.15 shows income, inequality, and poverty for residents, migrants, and the entire urban population.[28] On average a migrant, by moving out of a rural area, nearly doubles the per capita income of his or her household

---

[28] Combined urban estimates, reported in this section, are based on a sample of urban resident and urban migrant households that make migrants approximately 18 percent of the urban population. There is little consensus about the size of the migrants. Liang and Ma (2003) put the figure at 17.2 percent of the urban population for 2000. In this chapter we use a slightly higher figure of 18 percent for 2002. In view of the fact that official statistics show an annual decline of 1.33 percent in the rural population and an annual increase of 5.22 percent in the urban population between 1995 and 2002, this figure appears to be an underestimate, unless one allows for the possibility of a substantial number of migrants receiving residence permits and/or substantial areas of former rural locations being designated as urban. Since the CHIP sample for the migrant households oversamples the migrants relative to the residents, the sample for the residents has been augmented by randomly drawing a certain number of households from the original sample and adding them to it to make the proportion of the resident population in the aggregate urban sample approximately 82 percent.

in an urban location (not counting any member who might have been left behind in the rural areas). Still, their per capita income remains more than a third below that of the urban residents. Given the fact that the poverty threshold for residents and migrants is the same, this alone would indicate a higher incidence of poverty among migrants. Migrants, however, also have a substantially higher inequality in the distribution of income than residents, which exacerbates this effect. As a result, the incidence of poverty is far greater among migrants than among urban residents. Note also that the combined incidence of urban poverty for residents and migrants is twice what it is for residents alone.

Interestingly, poverty incidence for migrants is very similar to that among the rural population. This is because the poverty threshold for urban areas is about twice as high as the rural poverty threshold. The migrant in China attains a higher income, but, relative to the poverty threshold of his or her adopted society, is no better off than he or she was as a member of the rural society.[29]

The upper rural poverty threshold is 38 percent of the per capita rural income, while the upper urban poverty threshold is just under 40 percent of the migrants' per capita income. The Gini ratio of income distribution for migrants is slightly higher than the rural Gini ratio. It is thus quite plausible that the incidence of poverty among migrants is a little higher than it is among the rural population.

The observation that the incidence of poverty is much higher among migrants than among urban residents is also borne out by the evidence for individual provinces (Table 6.16). For each province the average income of migrants is lower than the average income of residents, the ratio ranging from 0.53 for Guangdong to 0.84 for Jiangsu. With the exception of Guangdong and Sichuan, the Gini ratio is higher for migrants than for residents in each province. Unlike those for rural and urban residents, the estimates of poverty for migrants are available at only one point of time. We can therefore only try to explain the difference in provincial levels of poverty in 2002. In explaining the difference in provincial poverty levels at a point of time for rural and urban residents, we cited as a major obstacle the fact that, of the two explanatory variables, variability among provinces was far smaller in inequality than in income. This problem is fortunately less serious for migrants, for whom the variability in per capita provincial income is substantially smaller

---

[29] This is a common phenomenon in international migration. An educated Asian, for example, often increases his or her income very substantially by migrating to the United States, while often accepting a lower relative economic and social rank in the United States than he or she had in his or her country of origin.

Table 6.16. *Income, inequality, and poverty among migrants*

	Per capita income	Gini ratio	Broad poverty			Ultra poverty		
			HC	PPG	WPG	HC	PPG	WPG
All China	6,365	0.380	14.4	4.4	2.5	5.5	2.3	1.6
Shanxi	4,768	0.370	27.4	7.2	3.8	8.9	3.5	2.4
Henan	5,435	0.362	16.4	4.7	2.7	5.4	2.5	1.8
Anhui	5,078	0.362	22.3	7.1	3.5	10.8	3.4	1.8
Yunnan	5,885	0.447	20.0	8.0	5.9	10.6	5.7	4.9
Hubei	5,192	0.323	17.0	4.5	2.2	4.4	1.8	1.4
Sichuan	6,282	0.292	8.0	3.0	2.0	3.5	1.8	1.5
Liaoning	6,711	0.365	11.3	3.0	1.4	3.1	1.3	0.7
Gansu	5,001	0.409	29.3	7.8	3.2	9.8	2.7	1.1
Jiangsu	9,135	0.384	5.1	1.5	1.0	1.6	1.1	0.8
Beijing	8,668	0.391	7.5	3.0	1.6	4.9	1.5	0.7
Guangdong	8,077	0.306	3.4	1.6	1.1	1.6	1.1	0.8

Note: HC = Head-count Rate; PPG = Proportionate Poverty Gap; WPG = Weighted Poverty Gap.

and the variability in provincial inequality is substantially greater, as compared to the residents.

Table 6.17 shows the linear and logarithmic regression equations in which income and inequality explain the head-count rate of broad poverty. All the regression coefficients have the expected sign and are highly significant. They explain a very high proportion of the variation in provincial poverty of the migrants. The logarithmic equation, explaining virtually all the variation in the dependent variable, shows high elasticity of the poverty head count with respect to both income and inequality. Indeed, the logarithmic regression explaining the level of the head-count rate of broad poverty by per capita income and inequality for the pooled provincial averages for the urban residents and migrants together has an equally good fit.[30]

VIII. Factors Explaining the Higher Incidence of Poverty among Migrants than among Residents

Since higher poverty among migrants than among residents is explained by their lower income and the higher inequality of the distribution of income, it is necessary to turn to an analysis of the sources of their income and the

[30] The fitted equation for the 22 observations is as follows: log (poverty HC) = -3.179 log $Y + 2.773$ log Gini. Adjusted $R^2 = 0.952$ and both the coefficients are highly significant.

Table 6.17. *Regression results explaining the level of provincial poverty of migrants*

Dependent variable	Broad head-count poverty	Log broad head-count poverty
Regressor		
Per capita income	−0.005	
	(−7.770)	
Gini ratio	80.883	
	(3.784)	
Log per capita income		−2.659
		(−14.666)
Log Gini ratio		2.244
		(6.637)
Intercept	16.242	28.037
	(1.817)	(17.552)
R^2	0.907	0.972
Adjusted R^2	0.883	0.965

inequality of their distribution. The relevant story is told by Tables 3.7 and 3.8 in Chapter 3, which describe the sources of income and its distribution and the distribution of employment for migrants and contrast these characteristics with those of residents.

By far the highest proportion of migrants' income, nearly three-fifths, is derived from individual enterprises, a source that contributes less than 3 percent of residents' income. This matches the very high proportion of migrants (58 percent) and very low proportion of residents (less than 6 percent) engaged in self-employment.

Wages account for a far smaller proportion of income for migrants than for residents. This reflects the difference between the two groups with respect to the composition of wage employment. Migrants have very limited access to public-sector employment. They are heavily concentrated in informal employment. Seventy percent of the employment of the urban residents is still derived from government, official institutions, and state-owned enterprises, whereas less than 7 percent of migrants' employment is derived from the state-owned enterprises and none from the government agencies and institutions.

The proportion employed in the other forms of formal enterprises – urban collectives, private firms, joint ventures, foreign enterprises, and state and other share-holding companies – is also smaller for migrants than for residents, while the proportion employed in informal (rural) enterprises is much higher for migrants than for residents.[31] The result is a much smaller share of income derived from wages by migrants (34 percent) than by residents (60 percent).

Other notable differences in the composition of income consist of a much lower share of pensions and rental value of housing for migrants. Indeed, migrants derive insignificant pension income. Their share of the rental value of housing is low because they have not been the beneficiary of housing reform leading to the privatization of housing. Their housing assets are derived entirely from their own investment in construction at market cost, or possibly higher than market cost in order to overcome the disadvantage that is caused by the lack of residence entitlement. Migrants are subject to a small net tax, while residents receive a net subsidy. It is worth noting that the survey has not fully captured the discriminatory effect on migrants' real income due to their lack of access to public services.

One final difference between the income of migrants and the income of residents needs to be stressed. Migrants have a higher number of workers per household member, 0.65 as compared to 0.5 for the residents. Thus, while the per capita income of migrants is 65 percent that of the residents, the income per working migrant is only 50 percent that of the income per working resident.

The greater inequality in the distribution of income for migrants principally derives from the fact that their largest source of income, from individual enterprises, has a strongly disequalizing effect on income distribution. This does not seem to be due to the regional difference in earnings from this source. With the exception of Anhui, this source of income has a disequalizing effect on provincial income distribution everywhere. Market returns to individual enterprises clearly reflect the considerable difference among migrants in terms of entrepreneurial ability and resource endowment. Despite a significant increase in its differentiation since the beginning of reforms, the wage structure, on the other hand, still enforces a degree of equality among residents, who derive most of their income from wages. The greater inequality among migrants is also explained by their lack of access to pension and unemployment benefits, which serve as redistributive social protection for residents. Finally, migrants' homeownership is subject to greater obstacles

---

[31] The "rural" enterprises that employ nearly 12 percent of the migrant workers and a negligible 0.1 percent of the urban resident workers may be the "agricultural" enterprises located in the rural periphery of the urban districts. Alternatively, this may mean that periodically a proportion of urban migrants reverts back to rural areas for employment. The survey is unclear on this subject.

than residents' homeownership, which probably explains the greater inequality of the distribution of the rental value of housing for migrants.

To summarize: the greater poverty among migrants, relative to residents, is due to their lower income and the higher inequality of the distribution of income. The lower income is a common phenomenon for most migrant groups. In the case of urban China this is exacerbated by the numerous discriminations that migrants are subject to because of the system of residence permits, which excludes migrants from more remunerative sectors of wage employment and access to public services. The greater inequality among migrants is due to the predominance in their income of individual enterprises in which rewards are market-based and hence differentiated according to individual abilities and endowments. It is also due to the exclusion of migrants from the safety nets that provide a degree of protection to the residents.

IX. Conclusions

China's performance in poverty reduction was incomparably superior – nearly four times as fast in rural China and a staggering 50 times as fast in urban China in terms of annual rates of reduction in broad poverty head count – in the post–Asian crisis period compared to that in the pre–Asian crisis period. This happened in spite of a lower rate of growth in per capita GDP in the post–Asian crisis period than in the pre–Asian crisis period. The difference in performance in poverty reduction was primarily due to (a) a faster growth in personal income, albeit highly skewed in favor of the urban areas, during the second period and (b) more importantly, much better performance with respect to the distribution of income in the second period.

The reason that most other studies fail to capture the faster reduction in poverty in the post-1995 period is that they also fail to capture the reduction of inequality within rural and urban areas. This is primarily because their estimates of income, based on official definitions, exclude components – for example, taxes, urban subsidies, and the rental value of owned housing – that contribute far less to inequality now than before, a point discussed in detail in Chapter 3 and in this chapter.

The faster growth in personal income in recent years may have been due to policy changes in direct response to the Asian crisis. Policy makers in China were clearly concerned about their ability to maintain an increasing incremental share of growth in aggregate demand from external sources, and this may have induced them to take measures to redistribute income in favor of households in the hope of inducing them to increase their

Table 6.18. *Growth rates in GDP, personal income, and related data (annual compounded, %)*

Real growth rate in per capita GDP	1988–1995	8.12
	1995–2002	7.22
Real growth rate in per capita personal income	1988–1995	5.08
	1995–2002	7.06
Final consumption as percentage of GDP at current price	1988	0.64
	1995	0.57
	2002	0.58
Household consumption as percentage of GDP at current price	1988	0.52
	1995	0.46
	2002	0.45

Note: Real growth rates in per capita GDP are based on GDP and population data in NBS (2003). Final consumption and household consumption rates are also based on data in NBS (2003). Real growth rates in per capita personal income are based on weighted averages of rural and urban residents' per capita incomes from the CHIP surveys. The weights are the actual population shares of the rural and urban areas. The values on which the growth rates are based are in 1995 prices; real growth rates shown in this chapter are used to calculate values for other years.

consumption. Table 6.18 summarizes some of the basic facts. Growth in personal income, as a proportion of GDP growth, was far slower in the pre-1995 period than in the post-1995 period. The policy seems to have paid off insofar as the precipitous decline in the ratio of final consumption to GDP and the ratio of household consumption to GDP between 1988 and 1995 was arrested over the period between 1995 and 2002. Net exports as a proportion of GDP peaked in 1997 and 1998 and thereafter started to decline.[32] China might not have succeeded in maintaining as high a growth in aggregate demand as actually occurred in this period if the ratio of domestic consumption had continued to fall, as it did in the pre-1995 period.

As noted earlier, the principal beneficiaries of this policy of redistributing the incremental product in favor of households were the urban residents. During this period the gap between the growth in urban and rural incomes greatly widened. Per capita personal income growth in rural China was slower in this period than in the preceding period. The much faster rate of the reduction in rural poverty was due to a significant decline in the inequality of income during this period, as compared to a sharp rise in inequality in the pre-1995 period.

---

[32] Table 3–11 of NBS (2003) shows that net exports as a proportion of GDP rose steadily from −1.03 percent in 1988 to 3.81 percent in 1997 and 3.86 percent in 1998. Thereafter, they started a steady decline to 2.24 percent in 2001. In 2002 they stood at 2.60 percent.

The decline in rural inequality was broad-based. The rural Gini ratio declined in 15 of the 19 provinces included in the samples of both years. There was also a decline in interprovincial inequality. For rural China as a whole the Gini ratio declined by almost 10 percent. The three main sources of reduction in rural inequality were (1) the stronger equalizing effect of the distribution of farm income due largely to the continued equality of distribution of land; (2) a decline in the disequalizing effect of the distribution of wage income, which was probably due largely to an improvement in the regional distribution of this source of income; and (3) a decline in the degree to which taxes were regressive.

Underlying both the growth of rural personal income, albeit much slower than the growth of urban personal income and indeed slower than the growth of rural personal income in the past, and the decline in inequality was the overwhelmingly important factor of the rapid decline in the rural population. This could not have taken place unless public policy changed in favor of de facto toleration of migration.

In urban China the remarkably faster reduction in poverty in the post-1995 period was due to a much faster growth in personal income than in the previous period and a modest decline in inequality in contrast to a sharp increase in inequality in the previous period. The decline in inequality in urban China was due to a decline in interprovincial inequality. Of the 11 provinces in the sample, inequality actually increased in eight and remained unchanged in one. For urban China as a whole, in terms of sources of income, the decline in inequality was due principally to three factors: (1) a sharp fall in the disequalizing effect of public subsidies, which actually became an equalizing factor in the distribution of income, though declining sharply as a proportion of income; (2) an increase in unemployment and pension benefits, which helped provide at least partial protection to the laid-off workers; and (3) a decline in the inequality of homeownership as housing reform was brought closer to completion. These factors outweighed the increased inequality of wage distribution, which was due to a reform of wage structures in a period of declining urban employment.

Urban migrants, for whom poverty can be estimated only for 2002, had about the same incidence of poverty as rural residents, but only because of the much higher poverty threshold by which their poverty was measured than the rural poverty threshold. The incidence of poverty among migrants might have been lower if they were subjected to less discrimination, which would have increased their income and reduced the inequality of the distribution of their income. Had migrants remained in rural areas, the overall poverty in China would have been worse: these migrants would have remained poor by the standard of a lower poverty threshold and would almost certainly have dragged down a higher proportion of the remainder of the rural population into poverty by competing with them for the meager supply of land and other rural resources.

Reduction in rural and urban inequality at the turn of the century was largely brought about by major changes in policy. These have been discussed in this chapter, and a summary is excluded to save space (a brief summary can be found in the conclusion of Chapter 3). One major area of failure that has persisted is China's massive disparity between urban and rural income. Its persistence explains why inequality for China as a whole has failed to decline despite the fall in rural and urban inequalities. The need for its reduction is strongly underlined by the far higher incidence of poverty in rural China than in urban China.

References

Asian Development Bank (ADB) (2002), *Final Report, Urban Poverty in PRC, TAE: PRC 33448*, Manila.

Brandt, L. and C. A. Holz (2006), "Spatial Price Differences in China: Estimates and Implications," *Economic Development and Cultural Change*, 55(1), 43–86.

Chen, S. and Y. Wang (2001), *China's Growth and Poverty Reduction: Trends between 1990 and 1999*, Washington, D.C.: World Bank.

Khan, A. R. (1998), *Poverty in China in the Period of Globalization: New Evidence on Trend and Pattern*, Issues in Development Discussion Paper 22, Geneva: International Labour Office.

Khan, A. R. and C. Riskin (2001), *Inequality and Poverty in China in the Age of Globalization*, New York: Oxford University Press.

Liang, Z. and Z. Ma (2003), "China's Floating Population: New Evidence from the 2002 Census," Department of Sociology, SUNY at Albany, unpublished manuscript.

National Bureau of Statistics (NBS) (2000), *China Statistical Yearbook 2000*, Beijing.

National Bureau of Statistics (NBS) (2003), *China Statistical Yearbook 2003*, Beijing.

Park, A. and S. Wang (2001), "China's Poverty Statistics," *China Economic Review*, 12(4), 384–398.

Ravallion, M. and S. Chen (2007), "China's (Uneven) Progress against Poverty," *Journal of Development Economics*, 82(1), 1–42.

World Bank (2000), *World Development Report 2000/2001: Attacking Poverty*, New York: Oxford University Press.

World Bank (2001), *China: Overcoming Rural Poverty*, Washington, D.C.: World Bank.

World Bank (2003), *World Development Indicators 2003*, Washington, D.C.: World Bank.

SEVEN

What Has Economic Transition Meant for the Well-Being of the Elderly in China?

Edward Palmer and Deng Quheng

I. Introduction

Since reorientation to a market economy in 1978, China has experienced remarkably high economic growth. Growth has most certainly been both an effect of and a motor for the transition process and has raised the living standard, especially of the segments of the country participating directly in growth-related activities. At the same time growth has created greater inequality in incomes between regions and between the rural and urban populations (see Chapters 2 and 3 of this volume). The question addressed in this chapter is how has the economic well-being of the elderly, a large group that does not benefit directly from the growth process, been affected by the past two decades of rapid growth and development? To answer this question, this chapter examines the determinants of the income status of both the rural and urban elderly in China.

From the outset it is important to note that there is a big difference in how old age security is provided in rural and urban China. In 2003 around 60 percent – 800 million – of China's population of almost 1.3 billion persons lived in rural China, where the older generation relies almost exclusively on the family network for income support in old age. In contrast, workers in urban China who have been employed in state-owned enterprises (SOEs) or as civil servants are covered by a pension plan. The percentage of the urban population covered by pensions has decreased since the reorientation toward a market economy in 1978, however, from 78 percent (Lin 2002) to around 50 percent in 2000 (Takayama 2003). Hence, a large and increasing percentage of the older urban population has had to rely on their own means or the family network to cover consumption needs in old age.

Given that most Chinese are not covered by a pension plan of any sort, it is of considerable interest to analyze how the Chinese elderly have managed

Table 7.1. *Living arrangements of persons aged 60+ (%)*

	1988		1995		2002	
	Urban	Rural	Urban	Rural	Urban	Rural
Living with children	70.83	94.59	59.26	91.87	60.50	84.14
Living with spouse only	25.29	4.46	39.41	7.73	37.53	14.86
Other arrangements	3.88	0.94	1.33	0.40	1.97	1.00
Number of observations	2,453	3,609	2,408	2,484	2,382	3,103

during the period of rapid economic transition. In addition, the composition of household income in urban and rural China has been affected in other ways in the process of transformation into a market economy. For example, in urban China considerable subsidies of household consumption have been almost eliminated. In rural China the economy has become increasingly more formal, as farming has been privatized.

The overwhelming majority of persons 60 and older live either with their spouse or their children (Table 7.1). The living arrangements of this group, which we define as the "elderly" in this study, have nevertheless changed considerably in the 1988–2002 period. The elderly in the rural areas living with their children declined from about 95 to 84 percent between 1988 and 2002 and in urban areas from 71 to 61 percent. Hence, although the majority of the elderly still lived with their children in 2002, the trend is clearly toward living in single generation households.

An important question is whether the erosion of intergenerational households has affected the income of the elderly. There are at least two processes behind the creation of households where older parents no longer live with their children. First, this is a result of the migration of the younger generation to where the economic opportunities are: from rural to urban areas, but also between urban areas. Migration per se does not necessarily imply a substantial decline in welfare because the migrant generation can make monetary transfers to their parents – or vice versa. Also, in a general growth setting, both generations can benefit directly from the fruits of economic growth, and the marginal disadvantage of splitting up the household will be less of a burden and may even lead to an overall economic gain for the two separate households viewed together. What we can and will analyze is the effect of private money transfers on the income status of the elderly.

A second driving force behind the increase in the percentage of the elderly living with only a spouse may simply be the positive choice of the elderly with higher incomes to establish independent households. In this case the erosion of intergenerational households is the result of increasing affluence. If it is this process that lies behind the trend in the independence of the elderly from their children, then one can conclude that China is simply following the pattern of Western cultures.

The data examined in this study come from the 1988, 1995, and 2002 rounds of the CHIP survey. The surveys include separate samples covering both the rural and the urban populations.[1] Note that defining the "elderly" as persons 60 years old and older adheres to the pension age for men who qualify for benefits in the urban areas. It is above the benefit age for urban women under the pension system, however, which is 55 for female cadres and 50 for female workers. In rural China, since there is no benefit system, there is no pension age. Hence, setting the cutoff age at 60 throughout is a practical way to create a standard for comparison of the rural and urban population on equal grounds.

The disposition of the chapter is as follows. Section II discusses the support systems of the elderly, and Section III takes a closer look at intergenerational households and the income of the elderly. Section IV examines the changing composition of income during the transition, and Section V analyzes the group mean income of the elderly and the likelihood for persons 60 and older to end up in the bottom three deciles, controlling for a number of individual and household characteristics. Section VI draws conclusions.

II. Background – Support Systems in Old Age

China introduced disability and old-age pensions for employees of government and state-owned enterprises in the early 1950s. Replacement rates were high,[2] but the system covered only employees of SOEs and civil servants in the urban population. The residual urban population and the much larger rural population, with the exception of a few rural civil servants and rural employees in SOEs, were not covered at all. Hence, from the very outset in

---

[1] For detailed descriptions of the first two surveys, see Eichen and Zhang (1993) and Khan and Riskin (1998). Chapter 1 and the Appendix to this book provide details on the 2002 data.

[2] Takayama (2003) calculates a replacement rate of around 75–80 percent, defined as the ratio of mean pension benefits for males age 60–64 or females age 55–59 to the mean wages for males 50–54 or females 40–44. This is substantiated by Ding et al. (2001), according to which the average replacement rates in the 1990s were at least 80 percent.

the 1950s, the Chinese pension system has covered only a small portion of the population.

In 1978 policy was reoriented in the direction of a market economy. This new framework had some repercussions that were potentially important for the well-being of the elderly. First, during the period examined in this study, the financing of pensions of older urban workers was far from given. A system developed for pooling of commitments was disrupted during the Cultural Revolution, after which enterprises had to finance pension expenditures on their own (Dong and Ye 2003; Song 2001). For some time, however, SOEs faced soft budget constraints so that in practice financing was covered by the public budget and was nevertheless still close to pooling commitments (West 1999). From 1984 onward, SOEs were forced to adopt independent accounting rules, and this brought hard budget constraints. A consequence of this was, however, that it became difficult or impossible for SOEs with financial problems to pay pensions (West 1999; Dong and Ye 2003).

Second, both the absolute number and relative proportion of people working in SOEs has decreased constantly since 1978. According to the National Bureau of Statistics (NBS) (2004, table 5–4), 27 percent of the employed urban population worked in SOEs at year-end 2003, which can be compared with 78 percent in 1978. The decline in persons working in SOEs is, by definition, a major cause of the decline in the percentage of the covered population through 2002.

Third, since benefits are employer related, the question of what to do with pension commitments to employees who are laid off has been an issue during most of the period examined. Many enterprises have resolved the issue by making lump-sum severance payments (Hurst and O'Brien 2002). The question is whether this method of resolving commitments provides the same stream of future income as the counterfactual of a life benefit, especially in a setting with increasing life expectancy.

In 1991 pooling of the financing of pension commitments was introduced nationwide following trials at the county or prefecture level beginning in 1984 (Ding et al. 2001; Dong and Ye 2003). Initially pooling was mainly at the county level, which limited the scope of risk sharing (Song 2001).[3] However, by the end of 2000 all provinces except Tibet had set up social pooling at the

---

[3] The Circular on Implementing the Pooling of Pensions for Enterprise Employees at the Provincial Level and Transferring the Industry-Based Pooling of Pensions to Local Administration was issued by the State Council in 1998. See also Ding et al. (2001); Song (2001), p. 42; Dong and Ye (2003).

provincial level or created a fund for paying pensions within the individual province (MOLSS and NBS 2001), with the source of finance being a levy on the wage bill. Benefits are still financed largely with a transfer to the appropriate fund of whatever monies are available at the time of retirement (Dong and Ye 2003).

The rural population was also affected by the reorientation toward a market economy in 1978. Goods and services were increasingly traded for money and as a result income became an increasingly more important measure of well-being. Even in the period of collective farming before 1978, most of the rural population relied largely on traditional intergenerational family support in old age. Consequently, the shift into a market-oriented economy and decollectivization of agriculture after 1978 meant, first, that the rural family once again became both a production and consumption unit (Lee and Xiao 1998) and, second, that social policy was explicitly shifted to the family. Since the traditional intergenerational family was, in fact, the reigning model anyway, the de facto result of this change was probably more to relieve the collective and the community of the eventual responsibility of providing health and other care in kind to the rural elderly. For this reason it probably had little direct effect on their income status.

Migration from rural to urban economic centers has come about in response to a high rate of growth and the relaxation of restrictions on mobility.[4] When the younger rural generation migrates, the older generation's cost of living rises because of the absence of economies of scale from the sharing of consumption, though this negative effect could be counteracted to some extent by money transfers from migrant children to their parents.

Surviving spouses are particularly vulnerable to the break-up of intergenerational households. Taking care of an older family member is a deep-rooted social convention in China, and the data used in this study indicate that the family is still the dominant form of survivor benefit, since so few persons are living on their own (Table 7.1).

In sum, the 1978 reform led to the introduction of profit criteria in the urban industrial and business environment and a shift from collective to family-based market-oriented agriculture in the rural sectors of the country. At the time when the first wave of data was collected for this study in 1988, the transition to the market economy had been going on for a decade. With

---

[4] Chapter 2 of this volume finds that the ratio of per capita income in urban China to that in rural China increased from 2.69 in 1988 to 3.13 to 2002, and that the contribution of income inequality between urban and rural China to income inequality in China as a whole climbed from 36.5 percent in 1988 to 46.1 percent in 2002.

Table 7.2. *Relative status of the elderly (%)*

Decile group	Urban			Rural		
	1988	1995	2002	1988	1995	2002
1 (lowest)	8.33	8.60	8.44	9.71	9.86	10.38
2	9.72	8.39	8.44	10.07	10.06	11.15
3	7.27	8.31	9.66	10.34	11.35	9.96
4	8.17	8.80	7.85	9.60	10.99	10.05
5	9.44	8.72	9.19	10.29	9.70	9.76
6	8.09	10.71	8.94	10.93	9.90	9.51
7	9.27	9.55	11.75	9.12	9.74	9.18
8	10.99	11.17	10.62	10.15	9.02	9.76
9	14.05	13.37	13.69	10.65	9.98	10.12
10 (highest)	14.67	12.38	11.42	9.15	9.38	10.12

Note: Decile groups are for the entire population, elderly and nonelderly.

data from 1988 to 2002, we examine in the following sections the effects of the transition on the economic well-being of the elderly after almost 25 years and in a setting where security in old age has become increasingly and highly reliant on individual resources.

III. The Relative Income Status of the Population Aged 60 and Older

In this section, we begin our examination of the development of the income status of the elderly by taking a look at what has happened to their relative status in the distribution of income from 1988 to 2002.[5] We examine the urban and rural populations separately.

A. The Urban Population Aged 60 and Older

The data show that the urban elderly not only started out with a better relative position, but have maintained this position throughout the transition period (Table 7.2). Here we see that the urban population aged 60 and older constitutes a smaller share of the lower income deciles and a larger share of the higher deciles throughout the period examined. In 1988 57 percent, and in 2002 56 percent, were in deciles 6–10.

---

[5] Relative income status is defined here as the income situation of the elderly compared with that of the nonelderly as shown in the income deciles. Throughout the text the unit of analysis is persons instead of households, and income is household income per capita without consideration of equivalence scales.

Table 7.3. *Relative status of the elderly living with children (%)*

Decile group	Urban			Rural		
	1988	1995	2002	1988	1995	2002
1 (lowest)	10.38	11.77	11.73	9.62	10.56	11.57
2	11.48	11.49	12.49	10.03	10.47	12.03
3	8.71	10.37	11.94	10.23	11.44	10.76
4	9.98	11.49	8.74	9.67	10.34	10.57
5	10.15	9.18	8.81	10.38	9.73	9.77
6	8.82	10.93	10.62	11.23	9.55	10.23
7	8.25	8.69	11.17	9.15	9.95	9.15
8	10.27	8.90	10.27	10.20	9.07	8.85
9	11.59	7.22	10.06	10.47	9.60	8.39
10 (highest)	10.38	9.95	4.16	9.03	9.29	8.69

Note: Decile groups are for the entire population, elderly and nonelderly.

Table 7.4. *Relative status of the elderly living with spouse (%)*

Decile group	Urban			Rural		
	1988	1995	2002	1988	1995	2002
1 (lowest)	3.23	4.00	3.58	9.32	2.08	4.34
2	5.49	3.90	2.13	6.83	4.17	6.94
3	4.04	5.37	6.15	14.29	10.94	5.64
4	4.04	4.74	6.60	9.32	18.23	7.16
5	7.59	8.11	10.18	9.94	9.90	10.2
6	6.30	10.54	6.26	4.97	14.06	5.64
7	12.28	10.22	12.75	8.70	7.81	8.46
8	12.76	14.44	11.19	10.56	8.33	15.18
9	20.03	22.55	19.35	14.29	14.58	19.31
10 (highest)	24.23	16.12	21.81	11.80	9.90	17.14

Note: Decile groups are for the entire population, elderly and nonelderly.

Separating the urban elderly into those living solely with their spouses and those living with their children shows that those living with their children (Table 7.3) are more likely to be in the lower deciles and that those living solely with their spouses are more likely to be in the upper half of the income distribution (Table 7.4). In fact, over 52 percent of persons 60 and older living solely with their spouses were in the top three deciles in 2002, which nevertheless was a decline from 1988, when 57 percent were in the top three deciles.

Less than 25 percent of the elderly living with their children were in the top three deciles in 2002, while over 36 percent were in the lower three deciles.

In addition, there is a dramatic decline between 1988 and 2002 in the proportion of the elderly living with their children in the highest (tenth) decile.

In sum, the urban elderly are on the whole better off than the urban population in general, and they have maintained this relative advantage from 1988 to 2002. The picture for the entire urban elderly population disguises, however, two separate trends. Compared with 1988, a larger percentage of the elderly lived with their spouses in 2002, and they are more likely to be among the better off in urban China. However, urban households where the elderly live with their children have become worse off between 1988 and 2002. From analysis of the data, two conclusions can be drawn. First, the affluent urban elderly choose to create independent households. Second, the urban elderly who keep with tradition and live with their children are more likely to live in households that are relatively poorer, where choice is limited by smaller resources.

B. The Rural Population Aged 60 and Older

As opposed to the urban elderly, in rural areas the elderly are fairly evenly distributed among the deciles in Table 7.2. However, the picture resembles that for the urban elderly when the rural elderly are separated into those living with their children and those living with spouses.

There is a clear tendency for the elderly who live with their children to be in the lower deciles, which became more pronounced from 1988 to 2002. On the other hand, the elderly living solely with spouses are more concentrated in the upper deciles. In addition, there is a clear trend between 1988 and 2002 away from the lower and toward the upper deciles for elderly living alone.

In sum, the pictures are similar for the urban and rural populations. Households with the elderly are at least as well off as households without elderly persons. Furthermore, the elderly living solely with their spouses are more likely to be better off than those living in households with their children. To help understand what is behind this phenomenon, in the next section we examine the components of the income of households containing the elderly.

IV. The Changing Composition of Income during the Transition

Tables 7.5 and 7.6 present a picture of the composition of total income of the elderly.[6] We examine data for the elderly in both the urban and rural

---

[6] The unit of analysis and definition of income are the same as in the previous section. See note 5 for detailed information.

Table 7.5. *Decomposition of urban income of the elderly by source of income*

	Share of total income (%)			Gini or concentration ratio			Contribution to Gini (%)		
	1988	1995	2002	1988	1995	2002	1988	1995	2002
Individual wages	21.74	22.74	18.29	0.100	0.194	0.164	8.81	13.54	9.92
Income of retired members, of which:	28.84	46.40	56.35	0.269	0.288	0.334	31.34	41.03	62.25
Pensions	17.50	30.11	53.49	0.221	0.245	0.329	15.64	22.63	58.33
Income from individual enterprises	0.99	0.27	0.95	0.440	−0.160	−0.071	1.76	−0.13	−0.22
Income from property	0.62	1.00	0.49	0.534	0.476	0.458	1.34	1.46	0.75
Housing subsidies in kind	18.34	12.43	2.35	0.334	0.492	0.343	24.77	18.74	2.67
Other net subsidies	14.53	1.02	0.45	0.166	0.341	0.094	9.72	1.07	0.14
Rental value of owned housing	6.35	10.60	18.14	0.302	0.581	0.352	7.74	18.90	21.11
Other income	8.59	5.55	2.97	0.418	0.317	0.343	14.51	5.39	3.38
Total	100.00	100.00	100.00	0.248	0.326	0.302	100.00	100.00	100.00

Table 7.6. *Decomposition of rural income of the elderly by source of income*

	Share of total income (%)			Gini or concentration ratio			Contribution to Gini (%)		
	1988	1995	2002	1988	1995	2002	1988	1995	2002
Individual wages, of which:	9.14	20.63	29.78	0.670	0.716	0.501	18.75	36.19	39.35
Pensions	0.96	1.58	2.53	0.421	0.621	0.791	1.24	2.41	5.27
Net farm income	72.62	50.49	37.40	0.276	0.258	0.164	61.26	31.94	16.12
Net nonfarm income		8.74	8.54		0.514	0.523		11.01	11.77
Income from property	0.15	0.44	0.96	0.505	0.508	0.788	0.24	0.55	1.99
Rental value of owned housing	10.26	12.04	13.48	0.203	0.304	0.374	6.38	8.96	13.29
Net transfers from state and collective	−2.05	−2.66	−2.18	−0.004	0.016	0.053	0.02	−0.10	−0.31
Other income, of which:	9.87	10.32	12.03	0.442	0.453	0.561	13.36	11.46	17.79
Private transfers	3.89	2.52	5.44	0.547	0.400	0.530	6.52	2.47	7.60
Total	100.00	100.00	100.00	0.327	0.408	0.379	100.00	100.00	100.00

Note: Net farm and net nonfarm income cannot be separated for 1988, so in that year the two are combined.

populations. The tables show the Gini coefficients and the contributions to the Gini coefficients of the various sources of income, which enables us to examine the profile of inequality.

Overall, inequality among both the urban and rural elderly increased considerably from 1988 to 2002. According to the Gini coefficient, inequality among the urban elderly increased between 1988 and 2002 from 0.248 to 0.302, with a peak of 0.326 in 1995.[7] The rural elderly had a much higher Gini coefficient in 1988 than their urban counterparts, with a value of 0.327. It increased to 0.408 in 1995, but fell to 0.379 in 2002 – which is still on a much higher level than in 1988.[8] The nonlinearity appears, however, to be a result of the income definition used. The increase in the Gini coefficient between 1988 and 2002 for both the entire urban and entire rural populations is also a finding of Khan and Riskin (Chapter 2 of this volume), who employ the same income definition as used in our study – itemized in our Tables 7.5 and 7.6. If another definition of income (NBS + housing subsidies + imputed rent, see Chapter 2) is used, the nonlinearity for the entire rural population disappears.

A. The Urban Elderly

According to Table 7.5, in the approximately 15-year period covered by this study, pensions have gone from being a relatively minor component of the total income of urban elderly to constituting over half of their income. At the same time, the share of wages in the total average income of pensioners declined from around 22 to 18 percent between 1988 and 2002, reflecting the decreased dependence of the elderly on wage-earning children.

The increased importance of pension income probably also reflects the increase in the institutionalization of pensions. As we have already discussed, pooling of commitments has become much more common. In addition, the practice of automatically paying pensions through public institutions, such as banks and post offices, makes it more difficult for employers to default on these commitments.

Housing and other net subsidies accounted on average for about a third of the total income of the elderly in 1988, whereas in 2002 subsidies were almost abolished, accounting for less than 3 percent of total income. At the same time, the rental value of owned housing increased dramatically in

---

[7] Similar calculations for the urban nonelderly show an even greater increase in the Gini coefficient from 0.231 to 0.318 between 1988 and 2002. The Gini was slightly higher at 0.332 in 1995.

[8] The Gini coefficients for the rural nonelderly are 0.331 (1988), 0.419 (1995), and 0.375 (2002).

importance, from a little over 6 percent of total income in 1988 to about 18 percent in 2002. Both examples clearly signal the transition from providing consumption support in kind to the market economy. Furthermore, the increase in independent living of the elderly would not have been possible in the absence of available housing, which has indirectly contributed to the trend toward independent living (Chapter 11 of this volume).

The overall picture of the increasing importance of individual resources is confirmed when we examine the picture for urban-area spouses living alone in 2002.[9] In 2002 pension income constituted on average about 70 percent of the total income of urban spouses living alone, a dramatic increase from only about 27 percent in 1988. Subsidies declined in importance from constituting about 30 percent of the income of spouses living alone in 1988 to less than 3 percent in 2002. After pension income, the next most important component of income of spouses living alone was the rental value of owned housing.

Pension income is even the dominant form of income, however, for the elderly living with their children. This suggests that the elderly are also contributing to the income status of intergenerational households. Generally, the trends for intergenerational families are similar to those for spouses living alone, with a significant decline in the relative importance of subsidies and an increase in the relative importance of the rental value of owned housing.

B. The Rural Elderly

Pension income hardly exists in the rural setting. Instead, the income of the elderly consists of wage and farm income, the rental value of housing, and private transfers from outside the immediate household – normally children not living in the same household as their parents – and other transfers. With the transition to a market economy in the rural areas, the relative importance of wage income has increased, while the relative importance of farm income has decreased (Table 7.6).

Private transfers have increased as a share of total income from 3.89 percent in 1988 to 5.44 percent in 2002 for all the rural elderly (Table 7.6). A closer examination of the data reveals that it is only in nonintergenerational households where this change has occurred, where the share of transfers in total income increased from 6.36 percent in 1988 to 9.60 percent in 2002.[10]

---

[9] Due to a space limit, we do not report decompositions of income of the elderly living with spouses and children. These are available upon request.

[10] The share of other income in the total income of the elderly living with children increased from 3.77 percent in 1988 to 4.22 percent in 2002.

This is a clear indication that younger family members continue to provide income support for their parents even when they do not live with them.

Also noteworthy is that the rental value of owned housing for spouses living alone was greater than that for those living with children, which is consistent with an overall picture in which the more wealthy spouses live alone in their own homes. The share of the rental values in the total average income for the elderly living with children has remained approximately unchanged, however. Also, note that farm and nonfarm income are less important for the elderly living with a spouse than for those living with children. This is logical if the main provider of this income is the younger generation. Finally, in 2002 the income of the rural elderly living with a spouse was 1,896 yuan compared with 1,274 yuan for those living with children, a difference of 622 yuan compared with 38 yuan in 1995 and 57 yuan in 1988.[11]

C. Conclusions on the Development of Income of the Elderly

The overall picture for the urban elderly suggests that China is going the way of Western cultures, where the more affluent elderly live in independent households. Pensions create a basis for independence for the elderly as well as an additional source of income for traditional intergenerational households. This suggests that in the urban setting transfers from the elderly constitute an important component of the total income of urban intergenerational households, and thus that many intergenerational urban families still need the resources of both the young and the old.

In the rural setting, pensions are not a significant source of income. Market (wage) income has become more important and farm income less important as an income source for the rural elderly. Also, the data support the hypothesis that children who migrate transfer considerable amounts to their parents, as is evidenced by the increase in the relative importance of transfers in the overall income of spouses living alone. Even in the rural setting, the trend is toward creating independent households for the elderly who are more affluent, with the rental value of houses becoming an important component of total income.

V. The Development of the Income of the Elderly by Population Groups and the Probability of Falling into the Lowest Three Deciles

This section begins by examining the development of per capita income of the elderly based on individual characteristics of the elderly. Those examined

---

[11] These figures are all in 1988 prices.

Table 7.7. *Group mean income of the elderly in urban and rural China (yuan, 1988 prices)*

Characteristic	Urban			Rural		
	1988	1995	2002	1988	1995	2002
Gender:						
Male	2,123	2,783	4,243	774	940	1,422
Female	1,900	2,558	4,008	763	999	1,320
Age group:						
60–64	2,190	2,894	4,317	815	943	1,513
65–69	2,002	2,650	4,010	742	910	1,330
70–74	1,766	2,422	4,299	701	930	1,248
75–79	1,815	2,147	3,730	761	981	1,212
80–84	1,777	2,433	3,768	789	1,181	1,269
85+	1,762	2,180	3,324	800	1,260	1,477
Education:						
Less than primary school	1,879	2,139	2,837	794	951	1,241
Primary school	2,025	2,404	3,451	869	1,055	1,481
Junior high school	2,227	2,690	4,107	940	1,007	1,600
Senior high school	2,308	3,157	4,731	1,169	959	1,892
Technical school	2,414	2,737	4,767	1,027	911	1,997
College and above	2,876	3,625	5,813	855	844	1,461
Living arrangement:						
Living with children	1,832	2,393	3,443	766	967	1,274
Living with spouse	2,394	3,099	5,120	823	1,005	1,896
Other	2,656	2,842	6,166	739	1,155	1,888
Political status:						
CPC member	2,529	3,222	4,788	931	1,112	1,683
Non-CPC	1,893	2,420	3,754	751	960	1,336
Region:						
Eastern	2,286	3,448	5,007	940	1,478	1,893
Central	1,678	2,112	3,574	670	726	1,090
Western	1,891	2,156	3,687	606	593	951
All elderly	2,003	2,677	4,126	768	971	1,373

are gender, age, educational background, living arrangements, political status, and the region where the household lives. The section then closes with an analysis of the probability of falling into the lowest three deciles for persons in different categories within these characteristics.

Table 7.7 shows the mean income of the elderly for both the urban and rural populations by group. In the urban population, the income of elderly males was, on average, about 12 percent higher than the income of elderly females in the first survey year, 1988. The difference declined to 6 percent in 2002. In the rural population, men and women 60 and older had practically the same average income in 1988. In 2002 the average income of men aged 60 and older was about 8 percent higher than that of women. Hence, in 2002, in both the urban and rural populations, the average income of men aged 60 and older was 6–8 percent higher than that of women aged 60 and older.

In the urban population, the average income of the elderly tends to decline with increasing age. This tendency is not observable for the rural elderly, however. It is possible that this rural-urban difference is driven by the need-based nature of transfers as discussed in Lee and Xiao (1998). This would suggest that the single urban elderly are more likely to be able to support themselves, even at age 85+, with relatively small amounts of money, whereas their rural counterparts to a large extent have to live on private transfers.

Education gives a premium in the urban population, which carries over from working years into old age. The education premium is connected to the education of the elderly themselves, which is how they are classified in Table 7.7, but it may also reflect the fact that persons with more education tend to live with spouses and children who also have more education. Knight and Li (1996) have found that parents with more education have better-educated and hence better-paid children. This in turn can contribute to larger intergenerational transfers to parents.

It is not surprising then that, in all three survey years, persons in the urban population 60 years old and older with more education lived in households with higher per capita incomes. This is most pronounced in 2002. At the time of the first survey year in this study, returns to education were much lower in rural than in urban China (Li and Lee 1994). As Table 7.7 indicates, this is still the case in 2002. In the rural areas the difference in average income for different levels of education is much smaller than in the urban setting.

Political status is also a determinant of the income status of the elderly. Those members of the Communist Party of China (hereafter CPC members) have a higher income level than their counterparts in both urban and rural China, with a larger effect in the former area. This finding is similar to the results of Raymo and Xie (2000), who find that being a former cadre leads to more income separately from reemployment and from public support. However, their study did not analyze explicitly the effect of political status on the total income of the elderly, a finding in the present study.

As has already become clear, in both the urban and rural populations older persons living with their spouses had higher per capita incomes than persons living with their children. What we see here is that in the urban population the average income of persons 60 and older living with their spouses was 30–50 percent higher than that of those living with their children. In the rural population persons over 60 living with their spouses had an average income about 50 percent higher than those living with their children in 2002.

It makes a difference where people live, too. Persons in the eastern region are better off in both the urban and rural areas and during all three measurement years from 1988.[12]

The income differences among different groups of the elderly are also confirmed in the logistic models (Appendix Table 7A.1 on pp. 202–203), which estimate the probabilities of falling into the lowest three deciles of the whole population. Table 7.8 gives estimated probabilities for the elderly of ending up in the lowest three deciles, which, generally speaking, are consistent with the findings above. Note, however, that males 60 years old and older are now more likely than their female counterparts to be in the lowest three deciles when individual characteristics, especially education and political status, are controlled for. This suggests that education and political status give a premium, which is consistent with the result that CPC members and the better educated among the elderly are less likely to be in the lowest three deciles. In addition, the older among the elderly are more likely to be worse off than their younger counterparts. These results also confirm that the elderly living alone with spouses are better off than the elderly living with children. Finally, the elderly in eastern China have a lower probability of falling into the lowest three deciles than those living elsewhere.

VI. Conclusions

This study has examined the development of the income of the elderly – defined as persons 60 years old and older – during the 1988–2002 period in both the urban and the rural areas of China. The data show a large and increasing gap in the income of the elderly between the rural and the urban areas. This is an expected result, given the large difference in the rural-urban incomes of workers and the prevalence of institutional support systems in the urban but not the rural areas, with pensions being the most important institutional form of support for the urban elderly.

---

[12] The geographic inequality may be caused by the unequal distribution of personal income or the overall financial situation associated with the local residence of the elderly. For example, Joseph and Phillips (1999) note generous resources other than family-based resources for the care of the elderly provided by a prosperous community in Zhejiang province in eastern China.

Table 7.8. *Predicted probabilities of the elderly falling into the lowest three deciles of the whole population*

Type of individual	1988		1995		2002	
	Urban	Rural	Urban	Rural	Urban	Rural
1. Male, 60–64, non-CPC member, less than primary school education, living with children, central region of China	0.443	0.317	0.598	0.358	0.754	0.209
2. Female, 60–64, non-CPC member, less than primary school education, living with children, central region of China	0.384	0.304	0.477	0.346	0.568	0.213
3. Male, 70–74, non-CPC member, less than primary school education, living with children, central region of China	0.590	0.354	0.778	0.342	0.869	0.211
4. Male, 60–64, CPC member, less than primary school education, living with children, central region of China	0.225	0.254	0.425	0.288	0.592	0.222
5. Male, 60–64, non-CPC member, college education and above, living with children, central region of China	0.143	0.484	0.260	0.292	0.249	0.257
6. Male, 60–64, non-CPC member, less than primary school education, living with spouse, central region of China	0.236	0.372	0.310	0.237	0.399	0.119
7. Male, 60–64, non-CPC member, less than primary school education, living with children, eastern region of China	0.159	0.158	0.286	0.174	0.423	0.119
8. Male, 60–64, CPC member, college education and above, living with children, central region of China	0.058	0.408	0.149	0.230	0.135	0.273
9. Male, 60–64, non-CPC member, less than primary school education, living with spouse, eastern region of China	0.069	0.193	0.108	0.105	0.137	0.065
10. Male, 60–64, non-CPC member, college education and above, living with spouse, eastern region of China	0.006	0.263	0.014	0.059	0.008	0.089

Note: For all types of individuals, property income is at the sample mean.

Older workers in urban state-owned enterprises or public institutions leave the labor market with a pension, and pension income is a large and growing component of the income of the elderly in urban China. On the other hand, there is no pension coverage to speak of in rural China. Instead, the elderly in rural China rely on income from work and transfers, both within intergenerational households and in households where elderly spouses live independently from their children. As younger generations migrate and become wage earners, parents are left behind to manage agricultural plots. In the rural setting wages and farm income have become increasingly important with the transition to a market economy. The trend shown in the data here suggests that wages can be expected to weigh increasingly more than farm income in the near future. Also, transfers, including transfers from children, are an important income source for the elderly in the rural areas.

Another important finding is that especially in the urban areas, but also in the rural population, the trend is for persons 60 and older to live solely with their spouses rather than in intergenerational households with their children. This trend is pronounced for persons with higher incomes. Although the migration of younger household members is certainly one determinant of this trend, the results of this study indicate that the increase in economic prosperity is the main driving force behind the creation of independent households with elderly spouses. It is still primarily the case that single elderly live to a large extent with their children, which is indicated by the fact that there are so few households that are not living either with children or with a spouse.

The individual characteristics behind the income distribution of the elderly reflect mainly individual characteristics that have determined life income, largely before age 60. Education has a positive effect on earnings in the urban setting and, as a result, is important for the income of the elderly. In the rural setting, our results show that technical education influences income, probably through off-farm employment but not through farm income. Pensions are important in the urban setting, and these are a result of previous employment with a state-owned enterprise or as a civil servant. Generally there is a gender gap among the elderly that reflects the earnings gap between male and female workers. Political status also plays a significant role in determining the income of the elderly.

A main conclusion of this study is that economic growth and prosperity are behind the erosion of the traditional multigenerational household. On the other hand, one's children still seem to provide survivor insurance, especially when the elderly person is in an unfavorable financial situation, as is also discussed in Lee and Xiao (1998). There is little evidence that the transition to a market economy in either the urban or rural areas has led to a worse economic situation for the elderly when, as in this study, income is used as the measuring rod. The population in general has benefited from growth, although the upper deciles have benefited more, leading to less equality in income in 2002 compared with 1988 among not only the population at large, but also the elderly.

References

Asian Development Bank (2002), *People's Republic of China – Old Age Pensions for Rural Areas: From Land Reform to Globalization*, Manila: Asian Development Bank.

Ding, Ningning, Yanfeng Ge, Keyong Dong, and Yansui Yang (2001), "Reforms on China's Pension Systems," in Mengkui Wang, ed., *Restructuring China's Social Security System: Funding, Operation and Governance*, Beijing: China Development Press (in Chinese).

Dong, Keyong and Xiangfeng Ye (2003), "Social Security System Reform in China," *China Economic Review*, 14(4), 417–425.

Eichen, Marc and Ming, Zhang (1993), "The 1988 Household Sample Survey – Data Description and Availability," in Keith Griffin and Zhao Renwei, eds., *The Distribution of Income in China*, 331–346, London: Macmillan.

Hurst, William and Kevin J. O'Brien (2002), "China's Contentious Pensioners," *China Quarterly*, no. 170, 345–360.

Joseph, Alun E. and David R. Phillips (1999), "Aging in Rural China: Impacts of Increasing Diversity in Family and Community Resources," *Journal of Cross-Cultural Gerontology*, 14(2), 153–168.

Khan, Azizur, R. and Carl Riskin (1998), "Income Inequality in China: Composition, Distribution and Growth of Household Income, 1988 to 1995," *China Quarterly*, no. 154, 221–253.

Knight, John and Li Shi (1996), "Educational Attainment and the Rural-Urban Divide in China," *Oxford Bulletin of Economics and Statistics*, 58(1), 83–117.

Lee, Yean Ju and Zhenyu Xiao (1998), "Children's Support for Elderly Parents in Urban and Rural China: Results from a National Survey," *Journal of Cross-Cultural Gerontology*, 13(1), 39–62.

Li, Shi and Lee Travers (1994), "Estimates of Returns to Education in China," in Renwei Zhao and Keith Griffin, eds., *Study on Income Distribution of Chinese Households*, 442–456, Beijing: China Social Sciences Press (in Chinese).

Lin, Ge (2002), "Regional Variation in Family Support for the Elderly in China: A Geodevelopmental Perspective," *Environment and Planning*, 34(9), 1617–1633.

Ministry of Labor and Social Security (MOLSS) and National Bureau of Statistics (NBS) (2001), "Statistical Bulletin on the Development of China's Labor Situation and Social Security," http://www.molss.gov.cn/gb/zwxx/2005-12/14/content_99530.htm.

National Bureau of Statistics (2004), *China Statistical Yearbook 2004*, Beijing: China Statistics Press.

Raymo, James M. and Xie Yu (2000), "Income of the Urban Elderly in Postreform China: Political Capital, Human Capital, and the State," *Social Science Research*, 29(1), 1–24.

Song, Xiaowu (2001), *Reforms on China's Social Security Systems*, Beijing: Tsinghua University Press (in Chinese).

Takayama, Noriyuki (2003), "Overview of PRC Pension Development and Economic Status of the PRC Elderly," Paper prepared for the workshop on Pension Reform of the PRC, jointly organized by the MOLSS and ADB Institute in Dalian, January 10.

West, Loraine (1999), "Pension Reform in China: Preparing for the Future," *Journal of Development Studies*, 35(3), 153–183.

Appendix Table 7A.1. *Logistic regression on the probability of the elderly falling into the lowest three deciles of the whole population*

	1988		1995		2002	
	Urban	Rural	Urban	Rural	Urban	Rural
Gender:						
Male						
Female	0.707**	0.875	0.653***	0.904	0.648***	1.101
Age group:						
60–64						
65–69	1.381*	1.047	1.133	0.952	1.425***	1.137
70–74	1.759***	1.393*	1.471**	0.881	1.191	1.039
75–79	1.744**	1.404	1.490*	0.715**	0.977	0.923
80–84	3.459***	1.047	1.139	0.622**	0.578**	0.900
85+	1.474	8.375***	0.957	0.928	0.551*	0.608**
Political status:						
CPC member	0.366***	0.736	0.497***	0.719	0.473***	1.082
Non-CPC						
Education:						
Less than primary school						
Primary school	0.760	0.882	0.911	0.857	0.711**	0.902
Junior high school	0.657**	0.684	0.508***	1.141	0.475***	1.084
Senior high school	0.410***	0.215	0.378***	1.179	0.174***	0.557*
Technical school	0.421***	0.895	0.350***	1.301	0.170***	0.133***
College and above	0.210***	2.024	0.236***	0.740	0.108***	1.309

Living arrangements:						
With children						
With spouse	0.389***	1.280	0.302***	0.556***	0.216***	0.512***
Other	0.415**	3.188***	0.147***	1.437	0.201***	0.150***
Income from property	0.981***	0.981	0.998***	0.994**	0.998***	0.978***
Region:						
Eastern	0.238***	0.404***	0.268***	0.377***	0.239***	0.512***
Central						
Western	0.565***	1.017	1.261*	2.668***	0.737**	1.851***
Log likelihood	−718.5	−878.7	−1,116.3	−1,353.3	−1,077.2	−1,731.1
Prob > chi^2	0.0000	0.0000	0.0000	0.0000	0.0000	0.0000
Pseudo R^2	0.1604	0.0488	0.1800	0.1137	0.2100	0.0943
Predicted correctly (%)	82.10	74.15	78.65	72.61	78.37	69.66
No. of observations	1,749	1,609	2,407	2,457	2,358	3,075

Note: Odds ratio reported. ***, **, and * indicate statistical significance at the 1 percent, 5 percent, and 10 percent levels, respectively.

EIGHT

Inequity in Financing China's Health Care

Wei Zhong and Björn Gustafsson

I. Introduction

The health status of the population is of central importance to any country. At the beginning of the new millennium, China had a relatively healthy population. Life expectancy at birth in 2002 was 71 years, exceeding the world average by four years (World Bank 2006). This represents great improvement for a country that experienced a disastrous famine resulting in high mortality in the late 1950s. China's recent health record, however, is not just due to the performance of the health sector but is an outcome of China's favorable economic development. With decreasing proportions of the rural population living in extreme poverty, levels of nutrition and general health have improved.

A country's health care system can be assessed from different perspectives. Economic analyses typically examine levels of efficiency and costs as well as access to the services provided and how the sector is financed. This last issue, the financing of health services, is the focus of this chapter. According to recent reports, the performance of the Chinese health sector in terms of how it is financed has been very poor indeed. When the World Health Organization (2000) in its World Health Report ranked health care systems in 191 countries according to fairness in financial contributions, China ranked near the bottom at 188 (WHO 2000).

Currently a large body of literature addresses questions on inequity in health care funding around the world. Methods of study have been developed, some making use of advances in the literature on income distribution and taxation. Individual country studies as well as studies examining many countries are available. When turning to China, however, issues of equity in health care financing have attracted almost no attention in the research literature, making our study unique.[1]

In contrast to the typical situation in developed Western economies, the household's outlays play a rather important role for funding health care in present-day China. Households can, however, be reimbursed for health care outlays by their employers, social insurance agencies, or other public agencies. It is the distributional profile of such reimbursements or subsidies – making up approximately three-fourths of public expenditures on health care – that are the focus of this chapter. Our method of analysis is to estimate income-based concentration coefficients. To understand inequity in health finance in China as a whole, we also analyze the importance of spatial factors. Our examination of spatial factors is motivated by the observation that public subsidies for health care in China are geographically concentrated in urban areas. The urban population has considerably higher income than the rural population, which receives almost no subsidies for health care expenditures. Another spatial dimension we consider is the difference between the most developed eastern region and the less developed western region, with the central region assuming a position somewhere in between.

Several key findings emerge from our analysis. We find that the distribution of health care subsidies strongly benefits the better-off segments of the population. This is much less the case for the households' unreimbursed out-of-pocket payments. These findings contrast to the situation in OECD countries, where public subsidies tend to have small positive redistributive effects, while private health spending is generally more unequally distributed. Further, we report that within urban China subsidies disproportionately benefit those better off; for example, subsidies are on average larger for the wealthy eastern region than for the other regions.

We believe these findings deserve attention in the policy debate on health care in China. They constitute arguments for changing the profile of subsidies for the health care sector. Rural China, particularly the western region, should receive a larger proportion of the subsidies, while urban China, particularly the eastern region, should receive a smaller proportion. Such a redistribution would improve fairness in funding the health sector in China. In a rapidly growing economy it could mean freezing subsidies to urban areas, while increased resources for health care are targeted to rural

---

[1] Bogg (2002) studied inequity in health finance among households in six counties in Jiangsu, Anhui, and Jiangxi based on data collected during the mid-1990s. The results indicate extreme regressivity in the financing of health care services.

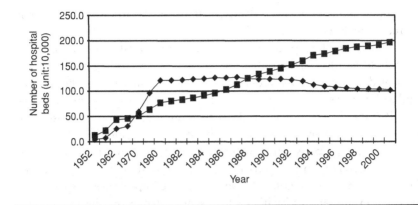

Figure 8.1 Number of Hospital Beds in Urban and Rural China, 1952–2001. *Source:* National Bureau of Statistics (2002).

regions, especially the western region. In addition to decreased inequality in health finance, such a policy could also narrow regional differences in health outcomes.

The rest of the chapter is laid out as follows: In the next section we provide background on the Chinese health care sector. Section III presents our research strategy and Section IV our data. Section V reports the results. Finally, Section VI summarizes the study and draws relevant conclusions.

II. China's Changing Health Sector

China's health care sector in 2002, the year of our study, is a highly fragmented system. It is still publicly dominated, but the private sector has developed rapidly, particularly in the rural areas. As in many other spheres of life in China, very large differences exist between rural and urban regions. In this regard the health sector has experienced radical changes in the past 50 years. Figure 8.1, which reports the total number of hospital beds in urban and rural China, indicates the need to discuss three episodes.

The first episode began in 1950 and ended in 1958, when the collective movement began. During this episode, spending on health care in urban areas was much greater than in rural areas. This is in contrast to the second episode (1958–1980), when the Cooperative Medical Systems (CMSs) were established in rural areas during the collective movement. During this episode new hospitals were established at the rural county and township levels and new clinics at the village level in the three-class primary health care network. In addition, some villagers became barefoot doctors after short training courses. Figure 8.1 illustrates that during this period the number of hospital beds in rural areas overtook the number of beds in urban areas. While the 1960s and 1970s are not remembered as years of increased material living standards in rural China, the verdict on changes in access to health care is more positive. In addition, during this episode in urban China all employees in state- and collective-owned institutions were covered by medical insurance systems.

During the third episode starting in 1980, expenditures on health care increased more rapidly in urban areas than in rural areas. Importantly, in rural China the CMSs collapsed, and the coverage of rural health insurance decreased from about 80 percent of the rural population in 1980 to only 6.6 percent in 1998. Consequently, the typical rural resident has to carry all costs for health care, which in most cases means a rationing according to economic resources, with potentially negative health consequences.[2] Although several health indicators such as the infant mortality rate, under-five mortality rate, maternity mortality rate, and life expectancy at birth have shown improvement, these changes are generally believed to be driven by improved nutrition.

In urban China, the Government Employee Health Insurance System (GIS) for many years has covered government employees and retirees, teachers, university students, and disabled veterans, but not dependents. The Labor Health Insurance System (LIS) covered state-owned enterprise employees, retirees, and their dependents. The LIS is a self-insurance scheme, meaning that each enterprise is responsible for financing its own health insurance. In reform China, however, many state-owned enterprises have experienced losses and as a consequence face problems financing the health care of their employees. In some instances, state-owned units have been closed and have left their former employees without health care coverage. The movement from a planned system to a market system has led to the development of new social insurance programs, a process in which Social Insurance Bureaus have been set up by local governments. This reform intends to cover all urban employees and to solve the problem of risk pooling by mandating risk pooling at the city level. Implementing these reforms,

---

[2] There have been efforts to introduce new rural cooperative medical schemes (RCMSs) to promote better equity. Jackson et al. (2005) compare such a scheme with the out-of-pocket system in Henan province. The authors conclude that although the effects of the RCMS on hospital charges were unclear, health care utilization in RCMS areas was twice that in non-RCMS areas.

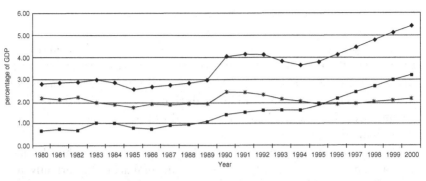

Figure 8.2 Total Health Care Expenditures in China, 1980–2000 (% of GDP). *Sources:*
1980–1989 data from Hossain (1997); the data source of Hossain (1997) is also the
Chinese Ministry of Health. The data of the statistical yearbook came from the estimates
of the MOH as well. 1990–1994 data from Institute of Health Economy, Ministry of
Health (1997); 1995–2000 data from National Bureau of Statistics (2002).

however, has been difficult so far, and only part of basic health care is reimbursed, so that a large potential remains for households to purchase private
health insurance voluntarily (see Liu and Yi 2004).

In Figure 8.2 we provide an illustration of the changes during the third
episode by showing expenditures on public health care since 1980 as a share
of GDP. In the figure, separate curves are shown for two exhaustive subcomponents, unreimbursed out-of-pocket expenditures by the households,
and government or employer expenditures, respectively. When examining
these, it is important to understand that GDP increased rather rapidly in
China during this period. This makes the expansion of total health care
from less than 3 percent in 1980 to 5.3 percent in 2000 quite remarkable.
The figure shows that growth in total health care's relative share began in
the early 1990s and was driven by growth in out-of-pocket payments, which
rose from less than 1 percent of GDP in 1980 to more than 3 percent in
2000. Out-of-pocket payments have become the major source of health
care financing in China, while government and employer expenditures have
remained relatively unchanged as a share of GDP.

The rapid growth in out-of-pocket payments for health care has many
explanations. Looking at the demand side, as residents have became wealth-
ier the demand for health care has increased. On the supply side, there have
been technical developments as new medicine and treatments have become
available.

Policy changes have been adopted within the health care sector as well. Public health services have been decentralized, which has led to increased autonomy of health facilities. Freedom of movement by health workers has increased, and political control has decreased. Such steps were aimed at increasing productivity in the health sector.

One important feature of the transition in the health care sector has been that the government has retreated from funding health care institutions. Only a small number of expenses in public hospitals are covered directly by the various levels of government. Consider, for example, the payments made by a typical patient visiting a public hospital. First, he or she pays a doctor's fee, which might be topped off with under-the-table payments in order to be treated better and quicker. Though wage costs for medical personnel in hospitals and clinics are paid for by public sector funds, this does not apply to other equally important costs covered by private spending.

Examination fees apply when being X-rayed, for example. Often a patient receives a prescription for medicine. The level of consumption of pharmaceuticals in China is very high, and in 1999 over 45 percent of total health expenditures was on drugs (Liu and Yi 2004). Often medicines are bought at the hospital pharmacy where they are often sold with a considerable mark-up. The hospital pharmacy is typically an important revenue generator for the hospital.

At the household level, the typical urban employee saves receipts for all medical outlays. Annually he or she checks to see if the year's total is over a predefined level. If it is, the receipts are handed in to the work unit, and the worker is reimbursed according to a formula, typically unique for each work unit. Rural inhabitants and the self-employed do not receive such reimbursements.

One can obtain a direct measure of how the Chinese government prioritizes health expenditures by inspecting changes in the share of the public budget for health expenditures. In 1991 it was 2.6 percent but it decreased to 1.6 percent in 1999. In contrast, the budget share for education was around 12 percent in 1991 and has remained at this level. Expressed differently, while the public budget for education was 4.7 times higher than the budget for health care in 1991, it was 7.2 times higher in 1999.

These trends raise concerns as to how the Chinese health system is performing after the onset of reform. Bloom and Gu (1997), for example, write about growing inequity in access to health services, increases in costs of medical care, and the deterioration of preventive programs in some poor areas. Liu and Mills (2002) draw attention to distorted provision of public health inspections and reduced demand for utilization of preventive services

Table 8.1. *Households' out-of-pocket per capita health
expenditures in rural and urban areas (yuan)*

Year	Rural	Urban	Urban/Rural
1978	11.34	12.66	1.12
1980	13.55	14.45	1.07
1985	22.20	25.80	1.16
1990	34.81	63.38	1.82
1991	37.78	66.59	1.76
1992	42.72	84.54	1.98
1993	42.71	116.36	2.72
1994	39.13	134.47	3.44
1995	48.72	158.69	3.26
1996	65.81	189.37	2.88
1997	72.86	227.74	3.13
1998	84.80	266.98	3.15

Source: China Total Health Expenditure Accounting Group (2000).

with positive externalities (for example immunization services and treatment of infections). Smith (1998) states that the reforms of the 1980s and 1990s appear to have widened the gaps in the spatial provision of health care services. Results from a detailed study by Akin et al. (2005) based on data on health access from 155 counties in 1989 and 1997, however, present a mixed picture in terms of changes in access experienced by the poorest.

Finally, we draw attention to changes in the urban-rural gap in out-of-pocket expenditures on health care. Table 8.1 shows that at the beginning of the third episode, per capita out-of-pocket expenditures for health care were similar in rural and urban areas. A disparity in expenditures, however, became visible and increased rapidly after 1985. Per capita out-of-pocket expenditures in 2002 (the year of our survey) indicate that urban residents, on average, had expenditures 3.6 times as large as rural residents. Chinese sources indicate that since 1988 urban households benefit from the majority of public and occupational expenses on health care.[3]

III. Research Strategy

Our research strategy for studying inequity in financing health care in China is to focus on and analyze the empirical relation between household income

---

[3] Health Care Financing and Organization in Poor Rural Areas of China Project Team (1998).

and household out-of-pocket expenditures on health care, and decompose the expenditures by components as well as population group. Our study does not cover the approximately one-fourth of expenditures for health care that is transmitted to the health sector (hospitals, clinics) directly from public budgets at various levels.[4] Reliable information on such direct funding is difficult, if not impossible, to obtain.

The households' out-of-pocket expenditures on health care are decomposed into two components, that which is reimbursed by the employer, social insurance agencies, or other public agencies, which we label as subsidies. The other is the unreimbursed component. We consider information on this second component useful, as it can be thought to represent the household's demand for health care and provide information on the income elasticity of health care expenditures.

The relation of central interest can be summarized in the concentration coefficient for health expenditures, which measures the inequality of health expenditures when sorted by total income; its values range from -1 to $+1$. The concentration coefficient is defined as[5]

$$CI_H = \frac{2}{\mu^h} \sum_{i=1}^{n} f_i \mu_i^h R_i - 1, \tag{1}$$

where f_i and μ_i^h are the proportions of the population and health care expenditure, respectively, belonging to the ith group ($i = 1 \ldots n$), and μ^h is the mean health care expenditure of the entire population. Finally, R_i is the relative rank of the ith income group, which is defined as

$$R_i = \sum_{\gamma=1}^{i-1} f_\gamma + \frac{1}{2} f_i, \tag{2}$$

which indicates the cumulative proportion of the population up to the midpoint of each group interval.

To better understand the importance of the two components, we decompose the concentration coefficient of total health expenditures between the unreimbursed and subsidized portions as follows:

$$CI_H = w_o CI_o + w_s CI_s, \tag{3}$$

---

[4] According to Figure 8.2, public expenditures on health care amounted to 2.10 percent of GDP in 2000, and residents' payments were 3.23 percent. From Table 8.2 we also know the relation (in 2002) between subsidies and out-of-pocket expenditures and can thus estimate that subsidies amounted to 1.53 percent of GDP. From this we estimate that ($1.53/2.10 \times 100$), or 73 percent of public expenditures on health are covered in our analysis.

[5] See Clarke et al. (2003).

where w_o is the unreimbursed out-of-pocket share of the households' total health care expenditure, w_s is the subsidies' share of the households' total health care expenditure, and so $w_o + w_s = 1$. CI_o is the concentration coefficient of unreimbursed out-of-pocket expenditures, and CI_s, the concentration coefficient of subsidies. From the formula we can see that this formula gives a complete decomposition of household expenditures on health care.

To investigate the importance of spatial differences we decompose the concentration coefficient of the households' health expenditures by various subgroups of the population. The overall concentration coefficient can be divided into three components:

$$CI_H = CI_B + CI_w + R, \tag{4}$$

where CI_B is the "between group" component, that is, the concentration coefficient on the average value of different groups. The second term is the "within group" component, which is the weighted sum of the subgroup concentration coefficients, where the weights are the health care expenditure share (w_i) multiplied by the population share (p_i):

$$CI_w = \sum_{i=1}^{i} w_i\, p_i\, CI_i. \tag{5}$$

The final term R is a residual caused by the overlap of the groups. Usually it is non-zero unless there is no overlap among the groups.

When decomposing by subgroups we will work in two steps. First, we decompose by the two categories, rural and urban, as this is deemed to be the most important spatial difference (see, e.g., Chapter 2 of this volume). In the second step we divide rural and urban China into the eastern, central, and western regions.[6] This means we will provide information on mean values and concentration coefficients for household health expenditures and its two components for each of the regions in rural and urban China, respectively.[7]

---

[6] In this research, the total survey samples were divided into three regions by the standard Chinese definition. The eastern region includes *Beijing, Liaoning, Jiangsu,* Zhejiang, Shandong, and *Guangdong*; the central region includes Jilin, Hebei, *Shanxi,* Jiangxi, *Anhui, Henan, Hubei,* and Hunan; and the western region includes Guangxi, *Sichuan, Chongqing, Yunnan,* Guizhou, Shaanxi, *Gansu,* and Xinjiang. Provinces covered in both the urban and rural surveys are in italics; provinces covered only by the rural survey are in regular type.

[7] When designing the analysis we considered the alternative of standardizing households' health care expenditures by age and gender, but refrained from doing so. Only small differences in such characteristics, however, exist across the spatial units we are analyzing here.

IV. Data

Our data are taken from the 2002 CHIP urban and rural surveys. The urban survey covers two municipalities and 10 provinces, from which a sample of 7,000 households was drawn. The rural survey covers 22 provincial-level units comprising 122 counties or towns, from which 9,200 households were selected. The questionnaires were designed by the project team to meet the needs of the project's research objectives. Information on total health care expenditure was investigated in both the urban and rural surveys. More details on the surveys are provided in Chapter 1 and the Appendix to this book.

With respect to the variables used in the analysis here, the definition of household income that we use in this chapter is the official National Bureau of Statistics definition and is obtained directly from the survey. When visiting a hospital or clinic, the household typically pays all of the health care expenses, but may later be reimbursed, as discussed above. This allows measurement of total out-of-pocket expenditures, as well as of reimbursements. The survey collected information on both these variables for the urban sample, but was not successful in measuring reimbursements to rural households. With no information on rural residents' reimbursements, we assume that there are no such subsidies in rural areas. This assumption is reasonable as very few rural households (e.g., some governmental officials) have received reimbursements, and health insurance coverage in rural areas is very low (6.6 percent in 1998).

In the analysis we divide total income by the number of household members. This value is then assigned to each member of the household, and we perform the analysis using individuals as the unit of analysis. Health care expenditures are measured at the household level and then divided by the number of people in the household and then assigned to each person.

V. Results

According to our survey, average household per capita expenditures on health care in China were 347 yuan (Table 8.2). The urban-rural divide is rather large. Urban households had expenditures of 726 yuan per capita, while rural households had expenditures of only 118 yuan per capita, meaning a ratio of 1 to slightly more than 6. This is much higher than the corresponding ratio for total per capita income, which, according to our sample and definitions, is 1:3. According to Table 8.2, the average urban resident receives health care subsidies (reimbursements) amounting to 297 yuan. Subsidies make up two-fifths of the households' total health care

Table 8.2. *Average per capita health care expenditure for various inhabitants of China, 2002 (yuan)*

Region	Sample size	Total household health care expenditure	Unreimbursed out-of-pocket health care expenditures	Subsidies	Subsidies as percentage of total household health care expenditures
Nationwide	54, 235	347.22	235.46	111.76	32.19
Urban	20, 433	725.92	429.27	296.65	40.87
Rural	33, 802	118.30	118.30	0.00	0.00

Note: Based on individuals as unit of analysis.

Table 8.3. *Concentration coefficients of per capita health care expenditure, 2002 (%)*

Region	Total household health care expenditures	Unreimbursed out-of-pocket expenditures	Subsidies
Nationwide	48.33	37.32	71.52
Urban	25.35	16.31	38.43
Rural	22.30	22.30	0.00

Note: Based on individuals as unit of analysis.

expenditures in urban China and one-third of the health expenditures in China as a whole.

Table 8.3 reports our estimates of income-related concentration coefficients. The concentration coefficient for household total health expenditures per capita is 48 percent, so health expenditures are positively related to income. The concentration coefficient is close to the Gini coefficient of 45 percent for total income per capita; the difference does not appear to be great. The two subcomponents of health expenditures, however, are distributed very differently. Unreimbursed out-of-pocket expenditures increase with total per capita income, but the increase is much less than that for subsidies. The concentration coefficient for subsidies is very high at 72 percent, indicating a profile that considerably favors those better off. These numbers indicate a situation that is different from that in the OECD countries, where public health care funds have small redistributive effects in favor of poorer groups, while private financing sources generally have

Table 8.4. *Decomposition of concentration coefficients of per capita health care expenditure by urban and rural, 2002 (%)*

	Total household health care expenditures		Unreimbursed out-of-pocket expenditures	
	Score	Share	Score	Share
Between urban and rural	35.99	74.47	28.40	76.09
Within group	10.47	21.67	5.81	15.58
Residual	1.87	3.86	3.11	8.33
Total	48.33	100.00	37.32	100.00

Note: Based on individuals as unit of analysis.

relatively large, negative redistributive effects, meaning that richer segments of the population spend more on health care (Wagstaff et al. 1999).

Examining the categories urban and rural separately, we observe that within urban areas the concentration coefficient of subsidies is 38 percent. Although much smaller than the corresponding coefficient for China as a whole, it is larger than the Gini coefficient for total income per capita, which in urban areas is 32 percent. Thus, it is also true for urban areas that subsidies disproportionately benefit those better off. Note that although unreimbursed out-of-pocket payments have positive concentration coefficients in rural as well as urban areas, they are lower than the Gini coefficients for income in each region. Thus, unreimbursed out-of-pocket expenditures increase with income, but not at a high rate.

We now turn to the results of the decomposition between rural and urban groups of total household per capita health expenditures as well as per capita unreimbursed out-of-pocket expenditures (Table 8.4). As much as three-fourths of the concentration coefficient for households' expenditures on health care can be attributed to the between-group component, and only a very small part can be attributed to the residual component. The within-group component is relatively small. Therefore we can conclude that most of the inequity in health finance in China reflects differences between rural and urban areas.

We now turn to the results from decomposing inequity in health finance within urban and rural regions, respectively, by the three regions – East, Center, and West. Table 8.5 shows the expected pattern of highest average household expenditures in the eastern region. Total per capita household health care expenditures vary within urban China, with those in the East being three times those in the West, primarily due to differences in subsidies.

Table 8.5. *Average per capita health care expenditure in different regions of China, 2002*

Region	Sample size	Total household health care expenditures (yuan)	Unreimbursed out-of-pocket expenditures (yuan)	Subsidies (yuan)	Subsidies as percentage of total household health care expenditures
East urban	7, 462	951.37	493.69	457.68	48.11
Center urban	7, 427	575.64	391.88	183.76	31.92
West urban	5, 544	623.77	392.66	231.11	37.05
East rural	9, 335	183.64	183.64		
Center rural	13, 253	101.76	101.76		
West rural	11, 232	83.48	83.48		

Note: Based on individuals as unit of analysis.

Table 8.6. *Concentration coefficients of per capita health care expenditure by region, 2002 (%)*

Region	Total household health care expenditures	Unreimbursed out-of-pocket expenditures	Subsidies
East urban	20.95	15.14	27.21
Center urban	22.71	13.10	43.19
West urban	23.19	16.21	35.05
East rural	13.09	13.09	0
Center rural	18.76	18.76	0
West rural	15.64	15.64	0

Note: Based on individuals as unit of analysis.

On average, urban residents in the wealthiest eastern region receive as much as 2.5 times more subsidies than people living in the central region. Turning to rural China, we find that persons living in the eastern region spend twice as much on health care as those living in the western region. We thus report considerably smaller variations among regions than between rural and urban areas. When combining the two spatial dimensions, however, we find that average household per capita health expenditures in the rich, urban East are as much as 11 times larger than in the poor, rural West.

Table 8.7. *Decomposition of per capita household health care expenditure in China as a whole (by six regions)*

	Total household expenditures		Unreimbursed out-of-pocket expenditures	
	Contribution to the concentration coefficient for China as a whole	Share	Contribution to the concentration coefficient for China as a whole	Share
Between group	41.66	86.20	31.69	84.93
Within group	2.92	6.05	2.32	6.21
Residual	3.75	7.76	3.31	8.87
Nationwide	48.33	100.00	37.32	100.00

Note: Based on individuals as unit of analysis.

Table 8.6 reports the concentration coefficients by region and sector. We find them all to be positive and not markedly different from those for all of urban China and all of rural China as reported in Table 8.3. For example, while the concentration coefficient for subsidies in urban China was 38 percent, for western urban China it was 35 percent. The concentration coefficient for subsidies is lowest in the eastern region, and highest in the central region.

We have decomposed inequality in health care finance first by rural and urban, then for each of the regions – East, Center, and West. Now we work with the six regions East urban, East rural, Center urban, Center rural, West urban, and West rural. Table 8.7 shows that as much as 86 percent of the inequality in total household per capita expenditures can be attributed to differences in means across regions, while only 6 percent can be attributed to differences within the six regions. We thus conclude that a large proportion of the inequity in health finance in China is spatial.

To further explore this finding, we repeat the analysis but use geographic units as the unit of analysis. This means we aggregate total household per capita income and total household per capita health expenditures and per capita unreimbursed out-of-pocket expenditures to the geographic unit. For urban China we use 77 cities, and for rural China we performed the analysis at both the village level (961 villages) and the county level (122 counties). Once again, the results from our analysis show that much of the inequality in household health care expenditures in rural as well as urban China is spatial in nature.

VI. Conclusions

The health system in China has changed over time, and the public sector's role in health care provision and financing has declined. Among different problems facing the sector, here we have focused on the distribution of and fairness in financial contributions. To better understand this issue we examined the empirical relation between household income and expenditures on health care paid by the households. The latter was decomposed into subsidies and unreimbursed out-of-pocket expenditures. Subsidies make up roughly three-fourths of total public expenditures on health care in China. We used a new survey covering large parts of China in 2002 to estimate income-related concentration coefficients. In the analysis we paid particular attention to spatial differences represented by the rural-urban dimension as well as regional divisions among East, Center, and West China.

We find that the concentration coefficient for subsidies is as high as 72 percent, much higher than the Gini coefficient for income of 45 percent. Thus subsidies disproportionately benefit those who are better off. The concentration coefficient for the household's unreimbursed out-of-pocket payments is much lower, 37 percent. These results are in marked contrast to the situation in OECD countries, where public sources tend to have small redistributive effects and private financing sources generally have larger negative redistributive effects.

Much of the inequity in health care finance in China was found to be due to spatial differences. First, the rural-to-urban difference is rather important. The much better-off urban residents are the sole beneficiaries of subsidies, while the rural majority is excluded. This profile of favoring those who are better off applies also in that subsidies are generally larger for urban inhabitants in the prosperous eastern region than for urban residents living in the other two regions.

An argument against our conclusion would be that health needs are higher among households with higher incomes. We do not believe that this is the case and base our opinion on the recent study by Li and Zhu (2006). The authors based their study on self-reported health in China from the 1993 China Health and Nutrition Survey collected in eight provinces. They find a concave relation between self-reported health and per capita income; income and health are positively related but at a decreasing rate.

Our results should be of interest to the debate surrounding China's future health care system, particularly its funding. Our findings can be used as arguments for changes in the profile of subsidies to the health care sector. Rural China, particularly the western region, should receive a larger proportion of the subsidies. At present, the question of health insurance in rural China is a hot issue. Our results can provide an argument for allocating public funds to such programs. From another viewpoint, our results can be used as arguments for decreasing subsidies for health care in urban China, particularly in the eastern region. Such a redistribution of public funds from the urban East would improve fairness in funding China's health sector. This could be achieved in China's rapidly growing economy by freezing subsidies to urban areas, while increasing resources for health care targeted at rural regions, primarily in the western region. Increased public resources for health care in the rural West, if skillfully targeted, could also lead to better health outcomes in that region, thereby narrowing regional differences in health outcomes. Thus not only equity in health care funding, but also equity in health care outcomes, provide arguments for policy changes.

References

Akin, J., W. Dow, P. M. Lance, and C.-P. A. Loh (2005), "Changes in Access to Health Care in China, 1989–1997," *Health Policy and Planning*, 20(2), 80–89.

Bloom, G. and Gu Xingyuan (1997), "Health Sector Reform: Lessons from China," *Social Science and Medicine*, 45(3), 351–360.

Bogg, L. (2002), *Health Care Financing in China: Equity in Transition*, Stockholm: Karolinska University Press (Division of International Health, Department of Public Health Sciences).

China Total Health Expenditure Accounting Group (2000), "A History Review and Development Forecasting of Total Expenditure of Health in China," *Soft Health Sciences*, 14 (5), 202–213.

Clarke, P., U. G. Gerdtham, and L. B. Connelly (2003), "A Note on the Decomposition of the Health Concentration Index," *Health Economics*, 12(6), 511–516.

Health Care Financing and Organization in Poor Rural Areas of China Project Team (1998), *Health Care Finacing and Organization in Poor Rural Areas of China: Literature Review and Analytical Report on 114 Poor Countries*, Beijing: People's Medical Publishing House.

Hossain, S. I. (1997), "Tackling Health Transition in China," World Bank Policy Research Paper No. 1813, Washington, D.C.: World Bank.

Institute of Health Economy, Ministry of Health (1997), "Research Report on China Total Health Expenditure, 1990–1995," *China Health Economy*, 16(12), 34–37 (in Chinese).

Jackson, S., A. Sleigh, P. Li, and X.-L. Liu (2005), "Health Finance in Rural Henan: Low Premium Insurance Compared to the Out-of-Pocket System," *China Quarterly*, no. 181, 137–157.

Li, H. and Y. Zhu (2006), "Income, Income Inequality, and Health: Evidence from China," *Journal of Comparative Economics*, 34, 668–693.

Liu, X. and A. Mills (2002), "Financing Reforms of Public Health Services in China: Lessons for Other Nations," *Social Science and Medicine*, 54(11), 1691–1698.

Liu, X. and Y. Yi (2004), "The Health Sector in China: Policy and Institutional Review," background paper for the World Bank China Health Study, Available at http://siteresources.worldbank.org/INTEAPREGTOPHEANUT/Resources/502734-1129734318233/policyandinstitutionalreview-final.pdf.

National Bureau of Statistics (2002), *China Statistical Yearbook 2002*, Beijing: China Statistics Press.

Smith, C. J. (1998), "Modernization and Health Care in Contemporary China," *Health and Place*, 4(2), 125–139.

Wagstaff, A., E. van Doorslaer, H. van der Burg, S. Calonge, T. Christiansen, G. Citoni, U.G. Gerdtham, M. Gerfin, L. Gross, U. Hakinnen, P. Johnson, J. John, J. Klavus, C. Lachaud, J. Lauritsen, R. Leu, B. Nolan, E. Peran, J. Pereira, C. Propper, F. Puffer, L. Rochaix, M. Rodriguez, M. Schellhorn, G. Sundberg, and O. Winkelhake (1999), "Equity in the Finance of Health Care: Some Further International Comparisons," *Journal of Health Economics*, 18(3), 263–290.

World Bank (2006), *World Development Indicators*, Washington, D.C.: World Bank.

World Health Organization (WHO) (2000), *World Health Report 2000*, Geneva: World Health Organization.

NINE

China's Emerging Urban Wage Structure, 1995–2002

John Knight and Lina Song

I. Introduction

Since the mid-1990s the pace of economic reform in China's urban labor market has accelerated. One contributing factor was the draconian labor retrenchment program in the state sector: many previously secure workers were thus thrown into a new labor market. Another contributing factor was the corporatization or privatization of much of the state sector. This institutional change brought with it less state control and more concern with profits. Nevertheless, various obstacles to the creation of a functioning labor market continued. The social and collective nature of the Chinese work unit (*danwei*) remained powerful, and the rate of labor mobility between employers remained extremely low. In this chapter we examine the ways in which the urban wage structure changed over the 1995–2002 period, and in particular the extent to which wages came to be determined by market forces.

We draw on the two strictly comparable cross-section CHIP surveys relating to the years 1995 and 2002, described in Chapter 1 and the Appendix to this book. Owing to the administrative and economic divide between urban and rural China, reflected also in the organization of survey work by the National Bureau of Statistics (NBS), separate survey instruments were employed in the urban and rural areas. In this chapter we analyze the two urban samples, which covered 11 provinces in 1995 and 12 provinces in 2002 (effectively the same number, as Sichuan and Chongqing had been divided in 1999).

We are grateful to Du Qianqian for research assistance and to the editors for comments.

The 2002 survey was the third of three comparable surveys, each conducted seven years apart. We have already analyzed the changes in the urban wage structure that took place between 1988 and 1995 (Knight and Song 2003). The new survey enables us to take the story forward by another seven years. There are similarities in the trends during the two periods, but also some sharp and revealing differences. In Section II, therefore, we review the findings of the earlier study. Section III provides information on the ways in which labor market policies and practices evolved over the seven-year period. Section IV documents the changes in various measures of the central tendency and dispersion of real wages between 1995 and 2002. Section V presents earnings functions for 1995 and 2002 so as to analyze and interpret the changes in wage structure. Section VI decomposes the rise in real wages to examine its underlying causes. In Section VII an equivalent decomposition is conducted of wage inequality and its rise over the seven years. Section VIII presents a quantile regression analysis in order to throw light on the relationships between the observed and the unobserved determinants of wages. Section IX concludes.

II. Wage Behavior, 1988–1995

In this section we briefly review the findings of Knight and Song (2003) from the comparable analysis for the earlier seven-year period. We concentrate on those aspects that explain the starting point for this chapter, and those that contrast with the analysis to come. More detailed comparisons of the two periods are made at relevant points later in the chapter.

In the mid-1980s China had a centrally planned urban economy. Labor was allocated bureaucratically, and movement from one work unit to another was extremely rare. Wages were administered according to a nationally prescribed pay scale, and the wage structure was highly egalitarian. The data from the 1988 survey, conducted near the start of the urban reform process, reflected this administered and egalitarian wage system. The following seven years witnessed some decentralization of decision making in labor matters. Government and its state-owned enterprise (SOE) agents were willing to trade off some wage equality in return for more efficiency through the provision of incentives.

Wage inequality rose sharply: the Gini coefficient of wages increased by more than one percentage point per annum, from a low value of 0.229 in 1988 to 0.307 in 1995. Whereas the median real wage rose by 5.8 percent per annum, the corresponding increases for the tenth and ninetieth percentiles were 0.8 and 8.3 percent per annum, respectively. Given the extreme disequilibrium in the urban labor market in 1988, this rise in wage inequality probably represented a move toward market equilibrium.

From the wage function analysis it was found that the rewards for human capital increased from very low levels. The returns to education and the returns to occupation-based skills both rose. The initially slightly inverted-U shape of the age-earnings profile – reflecting institutionalized payments for seniority – became more pronounced and peaked earlier. However, there was also evidence of greater wage discrimination – against women and minorities and in favor of Communist Party members. Moreover, the market forces operating in the growing private sector and the relative immunity of the state sector from those forces generated greater wage segmentation among types of ownership. Provincial differences in the pace of reform and in economic growth created spatial segmentation in wages that could not be removed by the equilibrating movement of labor owing to restrictions on and impediments to such movement.

Decomposition of the rapid increase in the mean wage showed that, whereas the unskilled wage rose very little in real terms, the impetus came especially from the rising returns to education and the growing gap between the low-paying local private sector and other ownership sectors. Decomposition of the growth in wage inequality into the contributions of particular characteristics found that the segmentation variables made the greatest contribution, and that was mainly due to growing wage dispersion among provinces. Some but not all components of human capital were disequalizing. These included education beyond secondary school and the most skilled occupations, which might represent the stirring of labor market forces.

Only part of wage inequality, and of its increase, could be explained: the unobserved determinants of wages were clearly important. Quantile regression analysis was employed to shed light on the relationships between the observable and the unobservable determinants. Those employers who, by virtue of their low conditional pay, appeared more subject to market discipline were also more prone to reward the human capital variables. The locally and foreign-owned private sectors, and the most reformed province, were the most sensitive to the unobservables, suggesting that marketization increases the importance of the unobserved influences on wages, whether they be employee or employer characteristics.

Overall, the earlier research presented a mixed pattern. Some of the new inequalities appeared justifiable in terms of the greater incentives or efficiency to which they gave rise. Other emerging inequalities were more difficult to justify in terms of output objectives. Indeed, the greater discrimination and sharper segmentation implied by some rising coefficients suggested new sources of inefficiency. Will the same be true of the succeeding seven years? As the pace of labor market reform appeared to accelerate in several dimensions in the years between 1995 and 2002, our hypothesis is that the importance in wage determination of productive characteristics grew and that of nonproductive characteristics declined.

III. The Evolution of the Labor Market, 1995–2002

The pace of reform of the urban labor market – slow in the early reform period – quickened in the subsequent seven-year period, 1995–2002. The planning quota for recruitment by state-owned enterprises was gone, and the state no longer took responsibility for matching the supply and demand for labor. In 1995 there were 11.1 million job vacancies at (urban) labor exchanges, whereas in 2002 there was double that number, 22.5 million. In the former year there were 9.1 million urban registered labor assignments, and in the latter year 13.9 million (MOLSS 1997, pp. 91,123; 2003, pp. 126, 156). The growth in these proxies for mobility should have made the labor market more flexible. Whereas in the earlier period most employers had limited autonomy in wage setting – their control being extended to bonuses and subsidies but not to basic wages – in the latter period all employers effectively determined the wages of their employees. Wages were therefore open to market forces.

The most important change came with respect to employment. In the mid-1990s the government finally decided to push state-owned enterprises into the market, holding them responsible for their losses even to the point of bankruptcy. It was accepted that unemployment could not remain disguised in the factories, but would have to become open on the streets. This change of policy was forced on government by the worsening finances of the state-owned enterprises, which threatened both continued economic growth and government revenue. In 1995 the profits of state-owned industry were down to 4 percent of the net value of fixed assets, and the losses of loss-making enterprises represented 49 percent of the profits of profit-making enterprises (NBS 1998, p. 461). The ensuing large-scale redundancy program created much urban unemployment.

Between 1995 and 2002 inclusive, no fewer than 78 million workers were laid off (Knight and Xue 2006). Whereas total urban employment increased by 58 million, from 190 to 248 million, employment in "urban units" (corresponding to the formal sector) fell by 43 million, from 153 to 110 million. The falls were in state-owned units (by 40 million) and urban collective units

(20 million), whereas employment in "other ownership" categories rose by 17 million, from 9 to 26 million. The main increase, however, occurred beyond registered urban units, in the sector "private enterprises and individuals": 43 million were reported in 2002 whereas none had been recorded in 1995 (MOLSS 1996, p. 17; 2003, pp. 7, 12, 20). The urban unemployment rate rose sharply: Knight and Xue (2006, Table 9.5) suggest that the true figure was 3.2 percent in 1988, 7.7 percent in 1995, and 11.5 percent in 2000. Li and Gustafsson (Chapter 10 of this volume, Tables 10.2a and 10.2b) using the 1995 and 2002 data sets, show the combined unemployment and *xiagang* rate as rising from 3.1 percent in the former year to 13.1 percent in the latter.

The redundancy program might be thought of as a controlled experiment, having the effect of creating a labor market overnight! However, Appleton et al. (2002, p. 272), using a 1999 urban household survey comparable to the 1995 and 2002 surveys, showed that laid-off workers faced a narrow, tough labor market. More than half of them remained unemployed in 1999, and the expected duration of their unemployment was almost four years. Moreover, Appleton et al. (2004) adduced evidence that the urban labor market was segmented, with those urban *hukou* employees who had not been laid off experiencing higher wages and different wage functions from the "retrenched and reemployed" workers and the rural-urban migrants. The urban *hukou* residents who had retained their jobs appeared to be protected from labor market competition. Using the panel component of the dataset, Appleton et al. (2004, p. 200) estimated the real wage increase of this group to be 9.7 percent per annum over the 1995–1999 period. More generally, average real wages in urban units rose by 10.7 percent per annum on average between 1995 and 2002 (NBS 2003, pp. 151, 313).

Knight and Li (2005) suggest that the lack of competition reflects in part the nature of the Chinese *danwei*, which retains collectivist features and continues to differ from an enterprise in the Western sense. Wages of members depend on the profitability of the *danwei*, and this relationship grew stronger over the 1995–1999 period. The authors' interpretation is that this represents a form of efficiency wage behavior: managers need to share profits with members of the *danwei* to gain and maintain their cooperation. Labor market competition remained too weak to iron out the growing interfirm wage differences. Knight and Yueh (2004, p. 643), also using the 1999 survey, showed that the labor mobility of urban *hukou* residents remained remarkably low: 78 percent were still in their first job, 16 percent were in only their second, and the average duration of first job tenure (including incomplete tenure) was 21 years.

Table 9.1. *Measures of the central tendency and dispersion of wages per worker, 1995 and 2002, at 2002 prices: Urban China*

	Hourly wage				Annual wage	
	1995	2002	2002 minus 1995	2002 (1995 = 100)	2002 (1995 = 100)	1995 (1988 = 100)
Mean	3.55	5.96	2.41	168	179	152
Median	3.07	4.84	1.77	158	170	148
10th percentile	1.34	1.83	0.49	137	160	106
90th percentile	6.04	10.57	4.53	175	188	175
Ratio of 90th to 10th percentile	4.50	5.77	1.27	128	117	166
Ratio of 90th percentile to median	1.97	2.18	0.21	111	110	119
Ratio of median to 10th percentile	2.29	2.64	0.35	115	106	140
Gini coefficient	0.325	0.370	0.045	114	113	134
Coefficient of variation (%)	71	93	22	131	118	109
Log variance	0.27	0.47	0.20	174	118	270
Number of observations	10,880	9,951				

Notes:

1. The data refer to the urban sample of employed individuals aged 16 and over and receiving earned income.

2. 1995 wages are converted to 2002 prices by means of the urban consumer price index, which rose by 10.6 percent over the seven years.

Source: 2002 urban survey for this and the following tables; also Knight and Song (2003), Table 1.

In summary, a labor market was being created in urban China during the period in which the wage structure is to be reviewed, yet the process appeared to be far from complete (Knight and Song 2005, chs. 2, 10). Our hypotheses, therefore, are that the urban wage structure became more market-determined than before, but that elements of discrimination and segmentation remained important and may even have grown. An implication is that the inequality and dispersion of wages continued to widen in the second seven-year period. Such growth in wage inequality would, however, be contrary to the finding, from the same surveys, of Khan and Riskin (Chapter 3 of this volume, Table 3.6) that the Gini coefficient of income per capita in urban China fell, from 0.332 to 0.318, between 1995 and 2002. They interpreted this fall as the result of a decline in interprovincial inequality in mean income per capita.

IV. The Rise in Wage Inequality

We see from Table 9.1 that over the 1995–2002 period the real hourly wage rose by 58 percent (6.8 percent per annum) at the median, 37 percent (4.6 percent per annum) at the tenth percentile, and 75 percent (8.3 percent per annum) at the ninetieth percentile (column 4). Thus the wage structure widened both above and below the median. The Gini coefficient rose from 0.325 to 0.370. In fact, all three of our measures of wage inequality rose. When the analysis is conducted in terms of the annual wage (as was necessarily the case for the 1988–1995 study), the results are very similar (the penultimate column). When a comparison is made with the earlier period, the real wage is seen to rise more rapidly in the later period, but the increase in wage inequality is somewhat smaller on all but one measure (the final two columns).

Can this rise in wage inequality be justified in terms of increased output? In the case of the employees there can be improved incentives to apply more effort and to acquire more skills. In the case of the employers, wages based on productive characteristics can provide incentives to use labor more efficiently. Given that these are household surveys, we lack direct information on the productivity of workers. Our indirect test is to estimate wage functions and to inquire whether productive characteristics were increasingly and nonproductive characteristics decreasingly rewarded.

V. The Change in Wage Structure

We estimate wage functions of the form $y = f(x)$, where y is the logarithm of individual wages and x is the vector of explanatory characteristics. Table 9.2 presents estimates for the two years using the individual urban samples.

Table 9.2. *Wage functions for individual workers in urban China, 1995 and 2002*

	Mean value		Ln wage	
	1995	2002	1995	2002
Intercept	1.000	1.000	1.200***	1.281***
Female sex	0.461	0.442	−0.055***	−0.090***
Minority status	0.043	0.042	−0.063***	0.010
Party membership	0.258	0.292	0.053***	0.052***
Local SOE	0.542	0.189	−0.161***	−0.183***
Urban collective	0.142	0.069	−0.235***	−0.389***
Private firm	0.003	0.042	−0.464***	−0.213***
Individual	0.009	0.081	−0.370***	−0.410***
Sino-foreign joint venture	0.012	0.000	0.120***	−
Foreign-owned	0.001	0.006	0.061***	0.026***
Other ownership	0.005	0.103	−0.327****	−0.200***
Beijing	0.074	0.085	0.125***	0.435***
Shanxi	0.090	0.085	−0.330***	−0.284***
Liaoning	0.108	0.106	−0.197***	−0.049***
Anhui	0.068	0.067	−0.265***	−0.186***
Henan	0.077	0.094	−0.376***	−0.324***
Hubei	0.104	0.101	−0.155***	−0.194***
Guangdong	0.093	0.096	0.406***	0.384***
Sichuan	0.124	0.124	−0.188***	−0.171**
Yunnan	0.102	0.089	−0.228***	−0.078***
Gansu	0.051	0.055	−0.406***	−0.276***
College or above	0.081	0.105	0.205***	0.447***
Professional school	0.160	0.230	0.129***	0.258***
Middle professional school	0.172	0.126	0.104***	0.177***
Upper middle school	0.242	0.281	0.048***	0.098***
Primary school	0.047	0.025	0.121***	−0.184***
Less than primary school	0.004	0.002	−0.288***	−0.430***
Owner of enterprise	0.013	0.044	0.050	0.066*
Professional	0.228	0.215	0.127***	0.267***
Top manager	0.037	0.026	0.132***	0.246***
Section manager	0.081	0.081	0.118***	0.302***
Office worker	0.206	0.206	0.076***	0.164***
Skilled worker	0.214	0.188	0.056***	0.170***
Other occupations	0.045	0.006	0.027	−0.076**
Age younger than 21	0.016	0.008	−0.319***	−0.274***
Age 21–25	0.078	0.059	−0.167***	−0.126***
Age 31–35	0.156	0.146	0.067***	0.133***
Age 36–40	0.204	0.200	0.155***	0.181***
Age 41–45	0.211	0.178	0.208***	0.204***
Age 46–50	0.126	0.189	0.218***	0.255***

	Mean value		Ln wage	
	1995	2002	1995	2002
Age 51–55	0.069	0.098	0.252***	0.283***
Age 56–60	0.035	0.032	0.278***	0.227***
Age 61–65	0.004	0.005	−0.225***	0.327**
Age 66+	0.001	0.002	−0.268***	0.368***
Adj. R^2			0.347	0.360
F-value			127.65***	134.01***
Dependent mean	1.168	1.539		
No. of observations	10,058	9,951		

Notes:
1. The dependent variable is the logarithm of the wage per hour, expressed in 2002 prices.
2. The urban consumer price index is used to convert 1995 values to 2002 prices.
3. The number of hours is obtained from the number of hours worked per day, the number of days worked per week, and the number of weeks in employment during the year.
4. The sample contains all individuals aged 16 or over who were employed or working for at least part of the year and received positive earned income.
5. The omitted categories in the dummy variable analysis are male sex, Han status, not a Communist Party member, state ownership, Jiangsu province, completed lower middle schooling, unskilled occupation, and age 26–30.
6. ***, **, and * denote statistical significance at the 1 percent, 5 percent, and 10 percent levels respectively.
7. The results obtained from use of the annual instead of the hourly wage are very similar.

There are 10,058 observations in 1995 and 9,951 in 2002 after selection of relevant wage earners (aged 16 or older, working at least part of the year, and receiving positive earned income). The specifications are identical so as to facilitate comparisons, and the wage per hour in both years is expressed in 2002 prices. The explanatory variables that might represent discrimination are gender, minority status, and Communist Party membership; those that might represent segmentation are ownership status of employer and province; and the potential human capital variables are educational level, skill-based occupation, and age group.

There are some important differences in the coefficients for the two years. Consider the variables that might represent discrimination. The coefficient on female sex, significantly negative in 1995, remained significantly negative in 2002 and was nearly doubled in size. Women then earned 9 percent less than men, ceteris paribus. The significant disadvantage of minority status in 1995 had been eliminated by 2002. Similarly, the significant advantage of Party membership in 1995 remained the same, at 5 percent, in 2002. Whereas all three potential forms of discrimination had risen over the previous seven years, the evidence for 1995–2002 suggests that gender discrimination rose again, political discrimination remained constant, and ethnic discrimination fell. However, these results are no more than hypotheses for further examination as they cannot eliminate alternative explanations associated with selectivity or unobserved heterogeneity.

With nonlocal state ownership being the omitted category in the dummy variable analysis and, along with foreign ownership, the highest-paying category, we see that the coefficients on the other forms of ownership, extremely large and negative in 1995, were still significantly negative and not consistently smaller in 2002. However, if we think of the growing private, individual, and "other" sectors as the employers most likely to set market wages, the average wage premium in the remaining, "nonmarket" sector was 27 percent in 1995 but 15 percent in 2002.

With Jiangsu as the omitted province, eight of the provinces had smaller coefficients, whether positive or negative, in 2002 than in 1995. The two exceptions were Beijing, which experienced a sharp increase, and Hubei. All the province coefficients were significant in both years, but there was a slight widening, in contrast to the dramatic widening that had occurred in the earlier period. In 1995 the standard deviation of the province coefficients had been 2.3 times its 1988 level; in 2002 the standard deviation was 0.9 times its 1995 level. Since the dependent variable is expressed in logarithmic terms, this implies a slight fall in the coefficient of variation of the standardized mean wage across provinces.

The human capital variables were increasingly rewarded over the seven years. By comparison with lower middle school completion, in 2002 those with college education or above earned 56 percent more, professional school 29 percent more, middle professional school 19 percent more, upper middle school 10 percent more, and primary school 17 percent less. The percentage point increases over 1995 at each of these levels were 27, 14, 8, 5, and −6, respectively. Over the 14 years the returns to education grew remarkably: the premium, over primary schooling, for a college degree was 9 percent in 1988, 39 percent in 1995, and 88 percent in 2002; and for completed secondary schooling the corresponding figures were 4, 17, and 42 percent, respectively.

A very similar story can be told about the returns to occupational skills. With unskilled labor as the reference group, and of course standardizing for education, in each case the coefficient rose. In 2002 professionals earned 31 percent more than unskilled workers, office workers 18 percent more, and skilled labor 19 percent more. The additional premiums over 1995 were 15, 9, and 12 percentage points, respectively.

The coefficients on age groups present an interesting pattern. In 1988 wages were strongly age-related, with a continuous rise, ceteris paribus, until the 56–60 age group, and then a slight fall. In 1995 the age-wage profile was much more bowed, with those under 26 years of age earning a great deal less, the wage peak occurring at 41–55, and wages falling precipitously after 60. The 2002 pattern is closer to that of 1988, showing an almost monotonic rise right up to the oldest age group (for which group selectivity may have been important). Youth and old age were no longer at so great a disadvantage as in 1995. In 1995 the labor market may have been segmented by age cohort, with the young and the old being more subject than the middle-aged to competitive forces, whereas in 2002 there may have been more competition across the age cohorts.

In summary, the general rise in the rewards for human capital suggests that the labor market became more competitive between 1995 and 2002. The main qualification was the high degree of segmentation by ownership and by province, and the continued advantage of men and of Party members, which remained even in 2002.

Knight and Li (2005) used the 1995 survey and a smaller 1999 survey to examine the influence of profitability on wages in the enterprise sector. We conduct the same analysis for the enterprise sector in 1995 and 2002. The additional variable is whether the worker reported that the employer is profit making or loss making. The authors explained why the respondents are likely to be well-informed and to report without bias on this issue. They also tested for sample selectivity of the profits variable and were unable to reject the null hypothesis. This is not surprising in view of the random allocation of workers to enterprises in the past and the very low rate of labor mobility between employers. Similarly, they could not find evidence of endogeneity.

Table 9.3 reports the resulting wage functions. There is no notable difference in the coefficients on the other explanatory variables: we concentrate on the new variable. In 1995 the coefficient on profit making (with loss making the omitted category) was 0.196, and in 2002 it was 0.259, both highly significant. Thus, being employed in a profit-making firm raised pay by 21 percent in 1995 and by 32 percent in 2002.

Knight and Li (2005) argue that this de facto profit sharing is likely to represent the cooperative and communal nature of the Chinese *danwei*. Profit sharing and efficiency wage behavior may well be intertwined if members of the *danwei* expect to share profits and will relax their efforts if sharing does not occur. The rise in profit sharing may reflect the greater ability of reformed enterprises to pay their remaining employees, on the one hand, and the continuation of the *danwei* culture despite the withdrawal of soft budgets and the stiffening of product market competition, on the other.

Table 9.3. *Wage functions for individual workers in the
enterprise sector of urban China, 1995 and 2002*

	1995	2002
Profit making	0.196***	0.259***
Female sex	−0.079***	−0.092***
Minority status	−0.051***	0.010
Party membership	0.064***	0.042**
Local SOE	−0.175***	−0.142***
Urban collective	−0.273***	−0.297***
Private firm	−0.499***	−0.249***
Individual	−0.141	−0.428***
Sino-foreign joint venture	−0.158***	−
Foreign-owned	0.162	−0.065
Other ownership	−0.210***	−0.158***
Beijing	0.152***	0.532***
Shanxi	−0.296***	−0.276***
Liaoning	−0.180***	−0.009
Anhui	−0.257***	−0.148***
Henan	−0.356***	−0.277***
Hubei	−0.151***	−0.103***
Guangdong	0.384***	0.450***
Sichuan	−0.167***	−0.079***
Yunnan	−0.247***	0.031
Gansu	−0.368***	−0.264***
College education or above	0.158***	0.401***
Professional school	0.120***	0.244***
Middle professional school	0.093***	0.146***
Upper middle school	0.039***	0.098***
Primary school	−0.097***	−0.200***
Less than primary school	−0.297***	−0.486***
Owner-manager	−0.075	0.180***
Professional	0.092***	0.213***
Top manager	0.113***	0.270***
Section manager	0.089***	0.245***
Office worker	0.029*	0.188***
Skilled worker	0.047***	0.171***
Other occupation	0.029	−0.041
Age younger than 21	−0.298***	−0.284***
Age 21–25	−0.171***	−0.101***
Age 31–35	0.099***	0.148***
Age 36–40	0.177***	0.194***
Age 41–45	0.244***	0.220***
Age 46–50	0.238***	0.248***

	1995	2002
Age 51–55	0.257***	0.244***
Age 56–60	0.273***	0.163***
Age 61–65	−0.169*	0.383***
Age 66+	−0.225	0.649***
Constant	1.051***	1.146***
Adj. R^2	0.348	0.342
F-value	82.58	71.10***
Dependent mean	1.109	1.454
No. of observations	6,740	5,814

Notes:
1. The notes to Table 9.2 apply also to Table 9.3.
2. The sample is restricted to workers whose work unit is an enterprise.
3. The additional profitability variable has "loss making" as the omitted category.

Whatever the reason, the evidence suggests that labor market segmentation among firms was accentuated over those years when the SOE sector was being drastically reformed.

VI. Decomposing the Wage Increase

Why did mean real wages increase so rapidly – by 7.7 percent per annum – over these years? Was it due to an improvement in the quality of the labor force, a change in the wage structure, or a rise in wages generally? Using the wage functions of Table 9.2, the growth of wages can be decomposed as

$$\bar{y}_1 - \bar{y}_0 = f_1(\bar{x}_1 - \bar{x}_0) + (f_1 - f_0)\bar{x}_0, \qquad (1)$$

where the first term reflects the effect of differences in characteristics and the second the effect of differences in coefficients. The alternative decomposition is

$$\bar{y}_1 - y_0 = f_0(\bar{x}_1 - \bar{x}_0) + (f_1 - f_0)\bar{x}_1. \qquad (2)$$

Table 9.4 presents a decomposition of the growth in mean real wages over the seven years, using the two alternative decomposition formulae. An advantage of this simple decomposition over more complicated methods is that the assumed counterfactuals have a readily understood economic meaning. When the coefficients of 1995 are used to measure the effect of the change in mean characteristics, the effect is slight: 84 percent of the growth

Table 9.4. *Decomposition of the increase in mean real wages, urban China, 1995–2002*

Percentage due to:	1	2
Mean characteristics		
Total	16.2	22.9
Discrimination variables	0.5	0.9
Segmentation variables	7.6	12.9
Of which: ownership	7.3	11.3
Province	0.3	1.6
Human capital variables	8.1	9.2
Of which: education	3.5	8.1
Occupation	−0.3	−4.6
Age	4.9	5.7
Coefficients		
Total	83.8	77.1
Discrimination variables	−3.5	−3.8
Segmentation variables	16.4	11.0
Of which: ownership	−3.2	−7.3
Province	19.6	18.3
Human capital variables	49.1	48.0
Of which: education	20.5	15.9
Occupation	19.4	23.7
Age	9.2	17.4
Intercept term	21.8	21.8

Notes:

1. The variable being explained is the difference in (geometric) mean wages (in 2002 prices) (= 100.0 percent).
2. The decompositions are based on Table 9.2.
3. Column 1 shows the decomposition based on the means of 2002 and the coefficients of 1995, and column 2 the decomposition based on the means of 1995 and the coefficients of 2002.

in wages is due to change in the income-generation mechanism. Using the coefficients of 2002 – when skill is better rewarded – the improved characteristics of the labor force account for 23 percent of the wage increase, and the education variables contribute 8 percent.

Table 9.4 shows some changes in the wage function raised and some lowered the mean wage. The contribution of a variable or set of variables is arbitrary because the choice of an omitted category in a dummy variable analysis alters the relative contributions of the intercept and the dummies. It is therefore important to choose an economically meaningful intercept.

The intercept term relates to the pay of those possessing the characteristics of the omitted categories (lower middle school, Han, 26–30-year-old, male, non-Party member, unskilled worker, in the state sector, in Jiangsu). This might be thought of as the unskilled market wage except in two respects: it is better measured at the national level than in Jiangsu and in all sectors than in the state sector. Correcting for this, the standardized unskilled market wage lagged behind the average wage. Nevertheless, it represented 32 percent of the overall increase. The rise in the returns to education and to occupational skills had a positive effect, accounting for 40 percent of the entire increase. Thus, two factors dominated the remarkable growth in real wages: a rise in the unskilled wage and a rise in the quantity of and reward for human capital.

VII. Decomposing the Rise in Wage Inequality

It is possible to help explain the rise in wage inequality by measuring the contribution of particular characteristics, or sets of characteristics, that determine wages. We choose the Gini coefficient of wage per hour, which rose by 14 percent, from 0.325 to 0.370 over the period under study. The methodology for decomposing inequality and its change is well known (see, e.g., Jenkins 1995; Fields 1996; Ravallion and Chen 1999). Knight and Song (2003) used it to analyze the rise in wage inequality in urban China between 1988 and 1995. Briefly, the contribution of income source k to the change in inequality over time is

$$\mu_k = \frac{\pi_{k1} I_1 - \pi_{k0} I_0}{I_1 - I_0}, \tag{3}$$

where I_j ($j = 1, 0$) is a measure of inequality, π_k is the share of inequality contributed by income source k, and $\sum_k \mu_k = 1$, where the characteristics determine wages through a stochastic process $y_i = \sum_k \beta_k x_{ik}$, x_k being characteristic k. The contribution of characteristic k to inequality of wages is

$$\pi_k = \frac{\beta_k cov(x_k, y)}{var(y)}. \tag{4}$$

The decomposition is based on the equations reported in Table 9.2. Table 9.5 shows the percentage contribution of each variable to inequality in 1995 and in 2002, and its contribution to the increase in inequality over the seven years. It also provides corresponding information for the sets of

Table 9.5. *Decomposition of wage inequality by the determinants of wages:
Urban China (%), 1995, 2002, and 1995–2002*

	1995	2002	1995–2002 Total increase	1995–2002 Explained increase
Human capital	12.4	17.6	55.1	102.1
Education	3.1	8.4	46.7	86.7
Occupation	2.2	6.5	37.5	68.8
Age	7.1	2.7	−29.1	−53.4
Discrimination	1.7	1.6	0.9	1.7
Gender	0.7	0.8	1.5	2.8
Communist Party membership	0.9	0.8	0.1	0.2
Minority status	0.1	0.0	−0.7	−1.3
Segmentation	20.8	18.1	−1.5	−2.8
Ownership form	4.0	7.0	28.6	52.5
Province	16.8	11.1	−30.1	−55.2
Residual	65.1	62.7	45.5	

Note: The decomposition of the change in inequality is based on the Gini coefficient of the wage
per hour.

variables representing productive characteristics and market imperfections.
Only a minority of wage inequality can be explained by the independent variables available; that is, the sum of π_k for all the explanatory variables is 34.9
percent in 1995 and 37.3 percent in 2002: the unexplained residual is important in both cases. Only 54.5 percent of the increase in inequality is accounted
for (this is the net figure as some variables have an equalizing effect). The
final column of the table decomposes the part that can be explained.

The discrimination variables as a group make very little contribution to
inequality in either year or to the rise in inequality. In 1995 the most important contribution was spatial (arising from the large wage differences among
provinces), followed by age (reflecting the extremely bow-shaped age-wage
profile). By 2002, however, the component attributable to the provinces
(although still large) and to age had fallen, whereas education and occupation had grown in importance. We see the changes more clearly in the
components of the rise in inequality. The segmentation of the labor market makes little net contribution as the positive effect of differentiation by
ownership is offset by the negative effect of differentiation by province. The
human capital variables, education and occupation, can themselves account
for the entire rise in explained inequality. The decomposition analysis suggests that there is indeed an efficiency-equity trade-off to be made.

VIII. The Rise in Wage Inequality: Quantile Regression Analysis

In Section VII more than 60 percent of wage inequality, and more than 40 percent of the increase in wage inequality, could not be explained by the explanatory variables at our disposal. The unobserved determinants of earnings are clearly important and deserve investigation. Quantile regression analysis might be able to provide the means: it can be used to compare the wage function at different points in the conditional wage distribution. The conditional wage distribution represents measurement error, or chance, or unobserved individual characteristics attracting payments ("ability" for short) or unobserved characteristics of the employer or of the locality that affect the wage. Quantile differences in the coefficients on an explanatory variable may therefore reveal a relationship between it and the unobserved influences. Quantile regressions are estimated for values of the quantile $q = 0.125, 0.375, 0.625$, and 0.875 (corresponding to the midpoints of the quarters). A full set of explanatory variables (those in Table 9.2) is included, but only those coefficients that reveal interesting patterns are shown in Table 9.6. We concentrate on two variables that might be interpreted as representing human capital (education, skill-based occupation) and a proxy for the extent of economic reform (province).

It is plausible that individuals of higher unobserved "ability" acquire more cognitive skills in education and more vocational skills in the workplace. Insofar as conditional wages represent unobserved ability, therefore, we might expect education and occupational skill to be more productive in the case of workers who are higher up the conditional wage quantile and, in a competitive labor market, therefore better rewarded.

Consider education: in both years and at each quantile, the coefficients on the education terms (lower middle education being the omitted dummy variable) are almost all highly significant and ranked according to educational level. In 1995 the coefficient on each educational level tends to decline toward zero as we move up the quantiles. The coefficient is consistently numerically greater at the 0.125 than at the 0.875 quantile. For instance, the coefficient on college education is 0.257 at the lowest and 0.170 at the highest quantile. Between 1995 and 2002 the coefficients on education beyond lower middle school rose generally but especially at the higher quantiles. Contrary to our hypothesis that the coefficient of education rises with the quantile, in 1995 we find the reverse. A possible explanation is that in 1995 firms paying higher conditional wages did so through profit sharing, and that profits were shared equally among their employees, thus reducing the returns to education for their workers. In 2002, by contrast, the association

Table 9.6. *Coefficients on selected variables in quantile regressions, 1995 and 2002*

	Quantile											
	0.125			0.375			0.625			0.875		
	1995	2002	2002 minus 1995	1995	2002	2002 minus 1995	1995	2002	2002 minus 1995	1995	2002	2002 minus 1995
College education or above	0.257	0.427	0.170	0.230	0.429	0.199	0.174	0.453	0.279	0.170	0.498	0.328
Professional school	0.185	0.228	0.043	0.135	0.244	0.109	0.112	0.277	0.165	0.101	0.276	0.175
Middle professional school	0.114	0.143	0.029	0.107	0.184	0.077	0.093	0.193	0.100	0.079	0.215	0.136
Upper middle school	0.073	0.078	0.005	0.047	0.103	0.056	0.049	0.120	0.071	0.055	0.125	0.070
Primary school	-0.117	-0.213	-0.096	-0.125	-0.199	-0.074	-0.092	-0.185	-0.093	-0.069	-0.154	-0.085
Professional worker	0.141	0.336	0.195	0.148	0.312	0.164	0.124	0.250	0.126	0.067	0.219	0.152
Top manager	0.166	0.290	0.124	0.141	0.257	0.116	0.118	0.184	0.066	0.095	0.219	0.124
Office worker	0.082	0.231	0.149	0.111	0.179	0.068	0.070	0.131	0.061	0.026	0.114	0.088
Skilled worker	0.040	0.217	0.179	0.061	0.179	0.118	0.050	0.154	0.104	0.026	0.145	0.119
Guangdong	0.368	0.337	-0.031	0.368	0.375	0.007	0.429	0.422	-0.007	0.538	0.513	-0.025

Notes:

1. The specification is precisely the same as in Table 9.2; only selective coefficients are reported.

2. The omitted categories in the dummy variable analyses are completed lower middle education, unskilled worker, and Jiangsu.

3. All coefficients are significantly different from zero at the 1 percent level, except primary school at the 0.875 quantile (significant at the 5 percent level).

across the quantiles is generally positive. The implication is that – although we have seen that profit sharing became even stronger – profits were shared in a less egalitarian manner in 2002. The evidence is now consistent with the theoretical hypothesis.

Turning to occupation, we see that the returns to occupational skill (with unskilled labor as the omitted category) rose almost consistently between 1995 and 2002 at each of the four quantiles. Ignoring nonsignificant coefficients, in both years the returns fell almost consistently as the quantile rose. Whereas our hypothesis is that the returns rise with the quantile, we find the opposite. We prefer an explanation in terms of unobserved employer characteristics rather than unobserved employee characteristics. It is consistent with the evidence that firms paying lower conditional wages are in a more competitive labor market, in which skills are more fully rewarded, and those paying higher conditional wages are in a less competitive market, in particular raising the pay of less skilled occupations above the competitive level.

The table also shows the coefficient on the Guangdong province dummy. Guangdong holds the reputation of having the most reformed, competitive, and developed provincial economy. This may well have implications for the wage structure. The coefficient on the dummy variable is significantly positive and large in both years and at each quantile. Moreover, in both years the coefficient rises at an accelerating rate as we move up the quantiles. This suggests either that unobserved worker ability is more rewarded in Guangdong or that enterprises in Guangdong are more varied in their ability or willingness to pay their workers.

The upshot of the quantile regression analysis is, first, that there are clear patterns in the results, implying that the unobservables do not simply represent chance or measurement error, and that there is indeed something to be explained. Second, the pattern of coefficients on the education (in 1995) and occupation (in both years) variables suggests that the unobserved characteristics of the employer rather than of the employee are relevant, and that employers paying high conditional wages treat their workers with little human capital relatively well. Third, the results for education in 2002 suggest that unobserved ability, correlated with education, is now rewarded. Fourth, where economic reform is well advanced, unobserved characteristics, whether of the employer or the employee, appear to fetch a higher market price.

IX. Conclusions

This chapter has provided a descriptive account of the evolution of the wage structure in urban China over the 1995–2002 seven-year period. It has not dealt with the econometric issues, such as potential endogeneity and selectivity, that beset attempts to establish causal relationships. For that, each of the explanatory variables – such as education, occupation, gender, Party membership, or ownership – would require a separate paper in which, for instance, alternative explanations are also tested by examining the patterns of results for various subgroups. Rather, the associations that have been found should be seen as providing hypotheses for further testing and a framework within which such analysis can be conducted.

In a complementary paper Appleton, Song, and Xia (2005) made some progress in establishing causal relationships. They used some recall information in the 2002 data set to create a panel for the 1998–2002 years. This allowed the authors to control for time-invariant unobserved determinants of wages. The most interesting differences with our results concerned the effects of the ownership sector and Communist Party membership. Examination of workers who changed from one ownership type to another during the five-year period suggested that some of the wage differences by ownership were due to the selectivity of more productive workers into foreign firms and of less productive workers into urban collectives. The wage premium on Communist Party membership was lower when estimated from the panel, suggesting that part of this premium is due to members' possession of unobserved characteristics such as "ability."

In some respects, the trends in wage structure observed between the 1988 and 1995 surveys have continued in the period between the 1995 and 2002 surveys, and in other respects the trends have stopped or have been reversed. Wage inequality continued to rise around a rapidly increasing median wage. Also as before, the increase in real wages had two main components: a general rise, as reflected in the unskilled wage, and an increase in the quantity of and reward for human capital.

As in the earlier period, it appears that discrimination based on gender increased. However, discrimination based on Party membership remained constant and that based on ethnicity was eliminated. The human capital variables, education and occupational skill, were increasingly rewarded over the seven years. These two variables may also account for the entire explained increase in wage inequality, suggesting that there is indeed a trade-off between efficiency and equity considerations. Age continued to be remunerated but the extreme bowing of the age-wage profile in 1995, reflecting the greater labor market competition faced by the young and the old, was weaker in 2002, suggesting greater competition among age cohorts.

Conditional wage differences based on ownership category and on province remained important. Moreover, segmentation among firms appeared to increase as wages within enterprises became more dependent on profits over the seven years. The quantile regression analysis showed interesting relationships between the observed and the unobserved determinants of wages, and it was plausible to interpret some of these results in terms of unobserved employer rather than employee characteristics.

In summary, there is a good deal of support for the main hypothesis that the rewards for productive characteristics rose during this period of growing labor market competition. However, there is also evidence inconsistent with the view that a competitive labor market emerged over these years, such as the continued labor market segmentation and the rapid increase in unskilled real wages despite rising urban unemployment. In 2002 China still did not possess a well-functioning labor market.

As Knight and Song (2005, ch.10) have argued, public policy should be directed at the creation of such a labor market; but, at the same time, it should provide a social safety net – redistributive mechanisms that ensure that people who lose from the arrival of a competitive urban labor market receive fair and equitable treatment.

References

Appleton, S., J. Knight, L. Song, and Q. Xia (2002), "Labor Retrenchment in China: Determinants and Consequences," *China Economic Review*, 13(2–3), 252–275.

Appleton, S., J. Knight, L. Song, and Q. Xia (2004), "Contrasting Paradigms: Segmentation and Competitiveness in the Formation of the Chinese Labour Market," *Journal of Chinese Economic and Business Studies*, 2(3), 185–205.

Appleton, S., L. Song, and Q. Xia (2005), "Has China Crossed the River? The Evolution of Wage Structure in China," *Journal of Comparative Economics*, 33(4), 644–663.

Fields, G. S. (1996), "Accounting for Differences in Income Inequality," Cornell University, mimeo.

Jenkins, S. P. (1995), "Accounting for Inequality Trends: Decomposition Analysis for the UK, 1971–1986," *Economica*, 62(245), 29–63.

Knight, J. and S. Li (2005), "Wages, Firm Profitability and Labor Market Segmentation in Urban China," *China Economic Review*, 16(3), 205–228.

Knight, J. and L. Song (2003), "Increasing Urban Wage Inequality in China: Extent, Elements and Evaluation," *Economics of Transition*, 11(4), 597–619.

Knight, J. and L. Song (2005), *Towards a Labour Market in China*, Oxford: Oxford University Press.

Knight, J. and J. Xue (2006), "How High Is Urban Unemployment in China?" *Journal of Chinese Economic and Business Studies*, 4(2), 91–107.

Knight, J. and L. Yueh (2004), "Job Mobility of Residents and Migrants in Urban China," *Journal of Comparative Economics*, 32(4), 637–660.

Ministry of Labor and Social Security (MOLSS) (annual), *China Labor Statistical Yearbook*, Beijing: China Statistics Press.

National Bureau of Statistics (NBS) (annual), *China Statistical Yearbook*, Beijing: China Statistics Press.

Ravallion, M. and S. Chen (1999), "When Economic Reform Is Faster than Statistical Reform: Measuring and Explaining Income Inequality in Rural China," *Oxford Bulletin of Economics and Statistics*, 61(1), 33–56.

TEN

Unemployment, Earlier Retirement, and Changes in the Gender Income Gap in Urban China, 1995–2002

Li Shi and Björn Gustafsson

I. Introduction

Urban China was an egalitarian society in the 1980s and even the early 1990s. Income inequality among urban residents was extremely low compared to other developing countries (Adelman and Sunding 1987; Khan et al. 1992; Gustafsson and Li 1998). Wage inequality among urban workers was also very low (Knight and Song 1993). In explaining total inequality of earnings in urban China the gender gap in earnings between urban male and female workers was observed as relatively unimportant compared to other explanatory variables such as ownership structure, economic sector, and location (Knight and Song 1993; Gustafsson and Li 2000). The narrow gender gap was related partly to the implementation of a full employment policy, which was firmly considered as an advantage of the socialist system, and partly to a political ideology that emphasized equalizing earnings between male and female workers.[1]

Since the mid-1990s urban reforms have speeded up in terms of reconstructing urban industries and enterprises, changing the employment system and retirement arrangements, and remodeling social security. As a result of implementation of the *xiagang* (layoff) policy, large numbers of urban workers have been laid off and have become unemployed or *xiagang* workers. At the same time, some early retirement programs were introduced to reduce redundant workers in enterprises. Several studies examine the

[1] "Same work and same pay for men and women."

The first draft of the chapter was presented at the International Research Conference on Poverty, Inequality, Labor Market and Welfare Reform in China, Canberra, Australia, August 25–27, 2004, and the Project Workshop in Beijing, September 10–11, 2004. The authors are grateful to Andrew Leigh, Terry Sicular, and Lina Song for useful comments, to Meng Xin for providing programs for decomposition analysis, and to the Ford Foundation and SIDA for financial support.

number of unemployed and *xiagang* workers and the adverse consequences they have encountered after being laid off, such as difficulties becoming reemployed and their reduced wages upon being reemployed (for examples, see Appleton et al. 2002; Knight and Li 2002). Studies also find that the increasing number of unemployed and laid-off workers contributed to rising income inequality in urban China in the late 1990s (Meng 2004).

A notable consequence of the increasing number of unemployed/*xiagang* workers in urban China is a decline in the female participation rate. At the turn of the new century, relatively more female labor-market participants have retreated from increasingly competitive labor markets, and some have become housewives. Our two surveys for 1995 and 2002 indicate that the participation rate of urban females aged 16–60 fell from 77 percent in 1995 to 70 percent in 2002, while the participation rate for males fell from 88 percent to 85 percent during the same period. This change is larger for less-educated females. Between 1995 and 2002 the participation rate for females with only lower middle school education decreased from 79 percent to 62 percent.

Against the background of the remarkable changes in urban labor markets and reforms in urban enterprises, several studies have examined the magnitude of the gender earnings (wage) gap (Dong and Bowles 2002; Gustafsson and Li 2000; Kidd and Meng 2001; Liu, Meng, and Zhang 2000; Maurer-Fazio and Hughes 2002; Meng 1998; Meng and Miller 1995; Rozelle et al. 2002). Few studies, however, have investigated the effects of those reforms on the gender gap in income in urban China. This chapter makes an effort to examine this issue. Obviously, our approach differs from the conventional one, which concentrates on the gender earnings gap in the sense that the coverage of the population group in our analysis is extended to all the labor-market participants' successes (the employed) and failures (the unemployed/laid off) in the job-seeking process. In our view, incorporating the unemployed and laid off into the gender gap analysis is meaningful, particularly under the circumstances of the economic transition and industrial restructuring that have taken place in urban China.

One should note that *xiagang* is a different state for workers who have lost their jobs than the standard state of unemployment. While the *xiagang* workers have lost their work, their work units are required by the government to take responsibility for their reemployment and to provide an allowance. Significant differences exist in the levels of allowances among *xiagang* workers, partly because of different standards of allowances among regions, and partly because allowances depend on the profitability of the work units. For *xiagang* workers in enterprises in financial difficulty, the allowance is much lower. As some *xiagang* workers are engaged in temporary jobs, the total income of *xiagang* workers can be higher than the allowance received from their work units, but it still tends to be lower than the income of employed workers.

Earlier retirement includes two different states in our analysis. The first refers to retirement before the mandatory retirement age, which is normally 60 and 55 for white- and blue-collar males and 55 and 50 for white- and blue-collar females. The second refers to a situation in which women retire earlier than men because of the earlier mandatory retirement age for women workers. From our data, it is hard to identify to which state a retiree belongs, so in our analysis we simply regard all the workers in the two states as a single group.[2] Our data show that for female retirees under age 60, 66 percent are under 55 and 18 percent under 50, while for male retirees, the corresponding figures are 40 percent and 10 percent. It is possible for some retirees to be reemployed, and 13.4 percent of the retirees in our analysis were reemployed in 2002.

This chapter attempts to explore to what extent the widening income gap between male and female labor-market participants can be explained by gender differences in unemployment/laid-off status and earlier retirement. Using the datasets from the two CHIP surveys, we address the following question: What would the gender income gap be if female workers had enjoyed the same probability of unemployment and layoff, and the same retirement arrangements, as male workers?

The results in this chapter indicate that unemployment/laid-off status and earlier retirement explain a substantial part of the gender income gap in 1995 and even more of the gap in 2002. Moreover, findings from a decomposition analysis show that the more rapid increase in the number of unemployed/laid-off females than males became a major cause of the widening income gap between males and females. The widening income gap between 1995 and 2002 can be largely explained by both the increasing number of unemployed/laid-off females over time and the increasingly higher population share of females compared to their male counterparts.

If the gender income gap is decomposed into two parts, the explained one and the unexplained one as suggested by Juhn, Murphy, and Pierce (1991), our results show that the overall gap becomes wider along with labor market liberalization and deep reform of state enterprises, but at the same time the unexplained gap as a percentage of the overall gender gap declines. We should, however, be very cautious about concluding from this that discrimination against women declined over these years. The results from

---

[2] Although the central government has set the mandatory retirement age, which is younger for female workers, local governments and enterprises sometimes implement earlier retirement ages in order to shed more redundant labor.

our decomposition analysis also indicate that an overall increase in income inequality had quite a significant impact on the change in the gender gap between 1995 and 2002.

This chapter is organized as follows. The next section discusses the analytical framework and decomposition methods employed. The third section presents the estimation results and gives some interpretations. The final section makes some concluding remarks.

II. Analytical Framework and Decomposition Methods

Our research questions require that we include all labor-market participants in the analysis. These include working or employed people, the unemployed, the laid-off, and earlier retirees. The conventional approach is to focus on the gender earnings gap, with the assumptions that unemployment has an equal impact on men and women and that earlier retirement does not exist. These assumptions do not apply to the current situation in urban China. Female workers were hit more seriously by the tide of unemployment and layoffs, which caused their income to decrease more than that of their male counterparts. Moreover, in China during the period of study, becoming laid off or going on earlier retirement was a forced outcome rather than the result of private choice. As many studies indicate, the increasing number of laid-off workers had a negative impact on inequality. Our reasoning is that if the impact was greater for females than for males, we should examine the size of the gender difference.

For working and employed people, income comes from their earnings or wages. Unemployed and laid-off persons receive as income unemployment benefits or allowances; the earlier retired receive pensions as their income. For all observations in all three groups combined, income consists of three components: earnings, unemployment benefits, and pensions.[3] Table 10.1 illustrates how our approach differs from the conventional one. Clearly we have broader coverage of people in the analysis. In addition to working and employed people, the unemployed/laid off and the earlier retired are also included in our analytical framework.

Two elements have effects on the gender income gap for labor-market participants. Since the working/employed have higher income on average than the other two groups, the share of the unemployed/laid off and the

---

[3] Incomes included here are those that can be attributed to each individual in a household, so earnings (from wages and self-employment), unemployment benefits, and pensions are included. Other income components that can be attributed only to the entire household such as property income and imputed housing income are excluded from the analysis.

Table 10.1. *Types of income for groups covered in the analysis*

| Urban groups | Three types of income | | |
	Earnings	Unemployment benefits and allowances	Pensions
Working or employed	O		
Unemployed/laid off (*xiagang*)		O	
Earlier retired			O

earlier retired among females is one of two explanatory factors. If the female share is higher than that of males, the gender gap in income would be larger. The second factor is how high the average unemployment benefits received by the female unemployed/laid off and the average pensions received by the female earlier retirees are compared to those received by their male counterparts. Several studies show that laid-off workers receive much less allowance than that to which they are entitled because of enterprises going bankrupt and local governments' lack of sufficient unemployment funds (Institute of Labor Science 2000; Appleton et al. 2002).

Bearing the framework above in mind, we estimate income functions for both male and female observations. With the regression results we use two decomposition methods, the method initially proposed by Oaxaca (1973) and Blinder (1973), and the method developed in Juhn, Murphy, and Pierce (1991).

Following the first method, the gender income gap in year t can be expressed as

$$Y_{m,t} - Y_{f,t} = \beta_{m,t} X_{m,t} - \beta_{f,t} X_{f,t}, \tag{1}$$

where X is the vector of explanatory variables adopted in the income function and β is the vector of estimates of their coefficients. Subscriptions m and f here refer to the male and female groups, respectively.

The difference $(Y_{m,t} - Y_{f,t})$ can be decomposed into two components:

$$Y_{m,t} - Y_{f,t} = \beta_{m,t}(X_{m,t} - X_{f,t}) + X_{f,t}(\beta_{m,t} - \beta_{f,t}) \tag{2a}$$

or

$$Y_{m,t} - Y_{f,t} = \beta_{f,t}(X_{m,t} - X_{f,t}) + X_{m,t}(\beta_{m,t} - \beta_{f,t}). \tag{2b}$$

To decompose the change in the gender gap over time, the following formula can be applied:

$$\Delta Y_{t+1} - \Delta Y_t = \beta_{m,t}(\Delta X_{t+1} - \Delta X_t) + \Delta X_{t+1}(\beta_{m,t+1} - \beta_{m,t})$$
$$+ X_{f,t}(\Delta \beta_{t+1} - \Delta \beta_t) + \Delta \beta_{t+1}(X_{f,t+1} - X_{f,t}), \tag{3}$$

where ΔY_{t+1} and ΔY_t refer to the gender income gap in time $t+1$ and time t, and

$$\Delta X_t = X_{m,t} - X_{f,t}, \Delta X_{t+1} = X_{m,t+1} - X_{f,t+1}, \Delta \beta_t$$
$$= \beta_{m,t} - \beta_{f,t}, \text{ and } \Delta \beta_{t+1} = \beta_{m,t+1} - \beta_{f,t+1}.$$

The weakness of this method is that it is not able to capture the effect of changes in the income distribution of females. If income inequality among females becomes wider than that for males, the second method is strongly recommended.

According to Juhn, Murphy, and Pierce (1991), the gender income gap at time t can be shown as

$$Y_{m,t} - Y_{f,t} = \beta_{m,t}(X_{m,t} - X_{f,t}) + \sigma_t(\theta_{m,t} - \theta_{f,t})$$
$$= \beta_{m,t}(X_{m,t} - X_{f,t}) + \sigma_t(-\theta_{f,t}), \tag{4}$$

where $\theta_{m,t}$ and $\theta_{f,t}$ are the standard error terms of the residuals in the male and female income functions; σ_t is the standard deviation of the residuals. The second equation in (4) follows given $\theta_{m,t} = E(u_{m,it}|X_{m,it}) = 0$.

When the decomposition analysis is applied to explore changes in the gender income gap over time, formula (4) can be developed into the following equation:

$$\Delta Y_{t+1} - \Delta Y_t = \beta_{m,t}(\Delta X_{t+1} - \Delta X_t) + \Delta X_{t+1}(\beta_{m,t+1} - \beta_{m,t})$$
$$+ \sigma_t(\Delta \theta_{t+1} - \Delta \theta_t) + \Delta \theta_{t+1}(\sigma_{t+1} - \sigma_t). \tag{5}$$

The first two terms in formula (5) have the same interpretations as those in formula (3). The third term represents changes in the relative position of males and females within a given distribution of the unobservable income components. The fourth term represents changes in the income distribution.

III. Surveys, Data, and Descriptive Statistics

The data used for our analysis in this chapter come from the CHIP urban sub-samples for 1995 and 2002. For these two years the urban surveys cover the same provinces and cities, and almost the same number of households. However, the data are cross-sectional rather than panel type. Eleven provinces are included: Anhui, Beijing, Gansu, Guangdong, Henan, Hubei, Jiangsu, Liaoning, Shanxi, Sichuan, and Yunnan. In the second year rural-urban migrant households were included in the urban survey, but we do not use them in our analysis as the 1995 survey contains no such households. For

Table 10.2a. *Employment and unemployment of urban labor-market participants, 1995*

Employment status	Male		Female	
	Observations	Percentage	Observations	Percentage
Working or employed	6,362	93.23	5,796	83.55
Unemployed/*xiagang*	192	2.81	217	3.13
Earlier retired	270	3.96	924	13.32
Total	6,824	100.00	6,937	100.00

Source: 1995 urban household survey.

more information on the surveys, see Chapter 1 and the Appendix to this volume.

The instruments in the two surveys are very similar, although not identical. Most questions raised in the first survey were repeated in the second survey. This allows us to generate exactly the same explanatory variables in the income function for the two years. The two samples are rather large as there are 7,483 males and 7,827 females aged 16–60 in the first year and 7,531 males and 7,783 females in the same age group in the second year of the survey. For our research purposes, we exclude students and housewives and assume that they are out of the labor market.[4] After excluding these two groups of individuals, the 1995 sample contains 6,824 males and 6,937 females, and the 2002 sample contains 6,741 males and 6,636 females.

The proportions of workers, the unemployed/laid off, and the earlier retired in each year are presented in Table 10.2a and Table 10.2b.[5] Compared to the 1995 sample, the proportion of male employees in the 2002 sample declines nearly 9 percentage points. The drop is even larger for females, 15 percentage points. The sharp decrease of employment rates for both the males and females can be partly explained by the substantial rise in the proportion of the unemployed/*xiagang*, which jumps from 2.8 percent in 1995 to 10.1 percent for males and from 3.1 percent to 13.1 percent for females. It can also be partly explained by the rise in the proportion of the earlier retired, especially for females.

---

[4] Self-reported housewives as a percentage of all female individuals aged 16–60 in our data increased from 2.8 percent in 1995 to 4.2 percent in 2002. This reflects stronger supply-side competition in the labor market for females and a declining participation rate of women (Cai et al. 2004).
[5] The official retirement age is 60 for male workers and 55 for female workers. This arrangement obviously discriminates against women, as retirees receive less income than when they work. We define a person as an earlier retiree if he or she retires before the age of 60.

Table 10.2b. *Employment and unemployment of urban labor-market participants, 2002*

	Male		Female	
Employment status	Observations	Percentage	Observations	Percentage
Working or employed	5,678	84.23	4,542	68.44
Unemployed/*xiagang*	683	10.13	8,70	13.11
Earlier retired	380	5.64	1,224	18.44
Total	6,741	100.00	6,636	100.00

Source: 2002 urban household survey.

Table 10.3 presents the average income of males and females and the ratios of female to male income by different subgroups. These ratios reflect the gender income gap for each subgroup. The ratio decreased from 0.81 in 1995 to 0.76 in 2002 for the entire sample, reflecting that on average female incomes declined relative to male incomes. The gender gap for the employed group increased slightly. To find out whether this increase was due to changes in working hours, we checked average working hours for male and female workers and found that in 2002 women worked 3.3 percent more hours than men. For some subgroups, the gender gap changed more dramatically during the period of study. As shown in Table 10.3, the ratio for the unemployed/laid off drops substantially, from 0.95 to 0.65, while for the employed whose ratio measures the gender gap in earnings, it decreases only slightly from 0.82 to 0.80. The earlier retired group has a modest decline in its ratios from 0.89 in 1995 to 0.81 in 2002, but this drop is still greater than that for the employed.

With respect to age groups shown in Table 10.3, some age groups experienced a larger drop in the gender income ratio. The 36–40 and 41–45 age groups gender income ratios fall by 14 and 10 percentage points, respectively. These two groups have a higher concentration of unemployed/laid-off people and earlier retired people in 2002. Gender income ratios also differ by educational level. Groups with low educational attainment have a lower gender ratio of income, because females with less education are usually affected more seriously by rising unemployment than their male counterparts. As shown in Table 10.3, the three groups with educational levels below professional school experienced declines of 6, 7, and 6 percentage points in their gender income ratios between 1995 and 2002.

Table 10.3 also shows that the gender income ratio for ethnic minorities and for the Han majority were the same in 1995. In 2002, however, it had increased to 0.85 for the minorities but fallen to 0.75 for the Han majority.

Table 10.3. *Average income of urban labor-market participants by population group, 1995 and 2002 (yuan, in 2002 prices)*

	1995			2002		
	(1) Male	(2) Female	(3) = (2)/(1)	(1) Male	(2) Female	(3) = (2)/(1)
All samples	7,726	6,255	0.81	12,069	9,118	0.76
1. By employment status						
Working or employed	7,996	6,576	0.82	13,069	10,513	0.80
Unemployed/*xiagang*	911	866	0.95	4,295	2,809	0.65
Earlier retired	6,222	5,508	0.89	10,307	8,300	0.81
2. By age group						
16–20	2,228	2,490	1.12	2,928	3,901	1.33
21–25	4,554	4,360	0.96	6,728	7,279	1.08
26–30	6,337	5,398	0.85	10,350	7,886	0.76
31–35	7,208	6,142	0.85	11,442	9,218	0.81
36–40	7,997	7,039	0.88	12,971	9,545	0.74
41–45	8,623	7,192	0.83	12,714	9,261	0.73
46–50	8,944	7,000	0.78	12,925	9,550	0.74
51–55	9,174	6,182	0.67	12,991	9,532	0.73
56–60	9,481	6,165	0.65	13,121	9,628	0.73
3. By education						
4-year college and above	9,988	8,460	0.85	18,357	15,660	0.85
2-year college	8,491	7,875	0.93	14,371	12,004	0.84
Professional school	7,807	7,063	0.90	11,868	10,720	0.90
Upper middle school	7,081	5,886	0.83	10,875	8,340	0.77
Lower middle school	7,136	5,655	0.79	9,406	6,816	0.72
Primary school and below	6,738	4,683	0.70	8,817	5,603	0.64
4. By minority status						
Ethnic minority	7,182	5,793	0.81	11,560	9,778	0.85
Han majority	7,750	6,276	0.81	12,091	9,090	0.75
5. By Party membership						
Party member	9,279	8,206	0.88	14,911	9,866	0.66
Non-Party member	6,991	5,920	0.85	10,628	8,311	0.78
6. By province						
Beijing	10,402	8,895	0.86	19,546	15,183	0.78
Shanxi	6,164	4,389	0.71	10,403	7,416	0.71
Liaoning	6,979	5,437	0.78	11,702	7,700	0.66
Jiangsu	8,341	6,642	0.80	12,290	9,330	0.76
Anhui	6,514	5,079	0.78	10,578	7,224	0.68
Henan	5,812	4,427	0.76	9,025	6,706	0.74
Hubei	7,041	6,130	0.87	10,408	8,213	0.79
Guangdong	14,129	10,870	0.77	18,949	14,473	0.76
Sichuan	7,140	6,138	0.86	9,847	7,638	0.78
Yunnan	7,050	6,173	0.88	10,992	9,748	0.89
Gansu	5,766	4,372	0.76	10,132	7,705	0.76

Source: 1995 and 2002 urban household surveys.

With respect to Party membership, both Communist Party members and non-Party members had substantial declines in their gender income ratios, indicating wider gender income gaps for the two groups in 2002. For Party members the gender income gap becomes wider largely because of the slow income growth for the female Party members rather than the more rapid income growth for the male members.[6] The causes behind these trends need to be investigated further. Finally, the provincial differences in the gender income ratio give a clue as to where the females face disadvantages in the labor market. Liaoning province, a traditional heavy industry base and deeply struck by rising unemployment during this period, shows a big decline in the gender ratio of income.

IV. Estimation Results and Interpretations

The gender gap of earnings and income in urban China has been widening since the late 1980s. Gustafsson and Li (2000) report that average female earnings were 15.6 percent lower than male earnings in 1988, and the gap increased to 17.5 percent in 1995. Our data show a wider gender gap of earnings in 2002, increasing to 20 percent.

This ongoing rise in the gender gap can also be found for labor-market participants, the focus of our analysis. As shown in Table 10.3, the gender income gap for labor-market participants increased from 19 percent in 1995 to 24 percent in 2002. The increase will be explained in detail in the rest of this chapter.

Our analysis proceeds in two directions. First, we run income functions for both 1995 and 2002, in which male and female dummies are introduced with a number of controlling variables such as employment status, age . group, educational attainment, ethnic minority status, Communist Party membership, and province dummies. The dependent variable is the logarithm of annual income. Descriptive statistics for these variables are given in Appendix Tables 10A.1 and 10A.2 on pages 263 and 264. The purpose of this analysis is to find out how large a gender gap remains in each year after controlling for other explanatory variables. Second, we apply the decomposition methods introduced in Section II. This requires that we run income functions for males and females separately for each year. The dependent variable is again the logarithm of annual income, and the explanatory variables are the same as the control variables used in the previous regressions.

---

[6] Average income grew by 20 percent over the 1995–2002 period for female Party members, while it rose 46 percent for all females.

Table 10.4a. *Results from regression analysis on log income of urban labor-market participants, 1995 and 2002*

	1995		2002	
	Coefficient	*t*-value	Coefficient	*t*-value
Male	0.1372	7.5	0.1836	6.98
Female	–	–	–	–
Working or employed	–	–	–	–
Unemployed/*xiagang*	−5.4166	−99.23	−3.4897	−85.35
Earlier retired	−0.3957	−10.33	−0.4204	−8.5
Age 16–20	−1.5802	−26.55	−2.2183	−18.33
Age 21–25	−0.5447	−13.46	−0.7993	−11.73
Age 26–30	–	–	–	–
Age 31–35	0.2135	5.82	0.3875	6.8
Age 36–40	0.3166	8.99	0.5799	10.67
Age 41–45	0.3854	10.79	0.7071	12.7
Age 46–50	0.3888	10.07	0.9189	16.72
Age 51–55	0.4312	10.04	1.0304	16.79
Age 56–60	0.5218	10.74	1.0269	13.88
4-year college and above	0.1281	3.25	0.2764	4.82
2-year college	0.0389	1.21	0.0964	2.08
Professional school	–	–	–	–
Upper middle school	−0.1285	−4.49	−0.2472	−5.64
Lower middle school	−0.1973	−7.22	−0.4003	−9.07
Primary school and below	−0.4683	−11.53	−0.6436	−8.97
Ethnic minority status dummies	Yes		Yes	
Party membership dummies	Yes		Yes	
Province dummies	Yes		Yes	
Constant	8.6587	198.95	8.8365	95.18
Adj-R^2	0.570		0.440	
F-value	652.6		437.8	
Observations	13,761		13,377	

Source: 1995 and 2002 urban household surveys.

After obtaining the estimated coefficients of the explanatory variables, we calculate how large a part of the gender gap is due to the differences in the mean values of the explanatory variables and how large a part is due to the differences in the coefficients.

Table 10.4a presents the results from income functions for 1995 and 2002. The coefficients on the male dummies imply that the income difference between males and females purely due to the gender effect is 0.14 in 1995 and 0.18 in 2002. Comparatively, the crude gender gap, as shown in Table 10.3, is 24 percent in 1995 and 32 percent in 2002. In other words, the control

Table 10.4b. *Results from regression analysis on log income of urban labor-market participants with a different specification, 1995 and 2002*

	1995		2002	
	Coefficient	*t*-value	Coefficient	*t*-value
Working or employed male	–	–	–	–
Working or employed female	−0.1456	−7.59	−0.1365	−4.68
Unemployed/*xiagang* male	−5.4488	−69.66	−3.2477	−54.03
Unemployed/*xiagang* female	−5.5350	−76.31	−3.8194	−70.92
Earlier retired male	−0.4730	−7.03	−0.4717	−5.35
Earlier retired female	−0.5149	−12.39	−0.5579	−10.79
Age 16–20	−1.5779	−26.47	−2.2418	−18.53
Age 21–25	−0.5444	−13.44	−0.8165	−11.98
Age 26–30	–	–	–	–
Age 31–35	0.2131	5.81	0.3891	6.83
Age 36–40	0.3165	8.99	0.5841	10.76
Age 41–45	0.3853	10.79	0.7111	12.78
Age 46–50	0.3874	10.03	0.9202	16.75
Age 51–55	0.4291	9.99	1.0190	16.6
Age 56–60	0.5237	10.78	1.0219	13.8
4-year college and above	0.1272	3.23	0.2812	4.91
2-year college	0.0389	1.21	0.0958	2.07
Professional school	–	–	–	–
Upper middle school	−0.1279	−4.47	−0.2452	−5.6
Lower middle school	−0.1970	−7.2	−0.3975	−9.01
Primary school and below	−0.4708	−11.58	−0.6358	−8.87
Ethnic minority status dummies	Yes		Yes	
Party membership dummies	Yes		Yes	
Province dummies	Yes		Yes	
Constant	8.7999	198.47	8.9932	96.06
Adj-R^2	0.571		0.442	
F-value	609.2		410.4	
Number of observations	13,761		13,377	

Source: 1995 and 2002 urban household surveys.

variables are able to explain part of the crude gap, but a large part of the gap remains unexplained.

Our analysis also shows that employment status plays an important role in explaining the crude gender gap of income. If the employment status dummies were excluded from the income functions, the coefficient of the male dummy would rise to 0.16 in 1995 and 0.30 in 2002. This implies that including the employment status dummies narrows the pure gender gap by nearly 3 percentage points and 12 percentage points, respectively, in the two functions.

Table 10.4b presents the results from regression analysis with a different specification of employment status, where employed males are treated as the omitted variable and the dummies represent employed females, unemployed/laid-off males and females, and earlier retired males and females. The coefficient of these dummies for other employment status, for example, employed females, reflects the income difference between employed females and the omitted group. The results indicate that the relative income of the employed females did not change in 2002, and that income of earlier retired women declined.

Tables 10.5a and 10.5b give the results from our decomposition analyses. These estimates are based on the results of regressions of log income functions for men and women separately in the two years (see Appendix Tables 10A.3 and 10A.4 on pp. 265 and 266). Let us first turn to Table 10.5a. The crude difference in log income between males and females in 1995 is decomposed into two parts, one part due to the gender differences in the mean values of the explanatory variables, and one part due to the gender differences in the estimated coefficients. The first part reflects the changes in the shares of the two population groups, and the second part captures the effects of changes in rewards to personal characteristics. Table 10.5a reveals that 46–49 percent of the gender gap can be explained by differences in the mean values of the explanatory variables. The above employment status dummies account for over half of this difference because of the means in the first simulation analysis, and for one-third in the second simulation analysis. In addition, the gender difference in mean levels of education variables also explains a large part of the crude gender gap of income: 11 percent and 21 percent in the two simulation analyses, respectively.

Over half of the crude gender gap of income is due to differences in the estimated coefficients. Among the coefficients, those on education, province, and age group have the largest contributions to the gap. The large contribution of the education coefficient arises because the returns to education are higher among females than among males (Appendix Table 10A.3). The same interpretation can be applied to the province dummies, which show larger differences in the coefficients between rich and poor provinces in the female function than in the male function. The coefficients on the age group dummies, however, show the opposite pattern. The age profile of income is steeper among males than among females.

Table 10.5b presents results from our decomposition analysis for year 2002. The contribution of the differences in means increases as a percentage of the crude gap to 56–58 percent. Moreover, gender differences in the employment status dummies contribute a significantly larger part of the explained gender gap for 2002 than for 1995. These results imply strongly

Table 10.5a. *Decomposition of the gender gap in log income of labor-market participants, 1995 (% of the total difference)*

	Simulation I		Simulation II	
	$\beta_m(X_m - X_f)$	$X_f(\beta_m - \beta_f)$	$\beta_f(X_m - X_f)$	$X_m(\beta_m - \beta_f)$
Employment status	25.50	−13.51	16.29	−4.29
In which: unemployed/*xiagang*	6.54	−0.47	6.49	−0.42
Earlier retirement	18.96	−13.04	9.80	−3.87
Age	5.35	26.75	3.33	28.77
Education	11.13	46.47	20.57	37.03
Ethnic minority	0.01	−0.40	0.00	−0.39
Party membership	5.73	−4.33	10.89	−9.50
Province	−1.31	25.11	−1.99	25.79
Constant	0.0	−26.48	0.0	−26.48
Total	46.40	53.60	49.08	50.92

Source: 1995 urban household survey.

Table 10.5b. *Decomposition of the gender gap in log income of labor-market participants, 2002 (% of the total difference)*

	Simulation I		Simulation II	
	$\beta_m(X_m - X_f)$	$X_f(\beta_m - \beta_f)$	$\beta_f(X_m - X_f)$	$X_m(\beta_m - \beta_f)$
Employment status	39.15	6.62	37.07	8.70
In which: unemployed/*xiagang*	23.14	13.90	26.42	10.63
Earlier retirement	16.01	−7.28	10.65	−1.93
Age	5.54	−46.53	6.66	−47.66
Education	8.03	42.57	12.88	37.72
Ethnic minority	0.01	7.26	0.03	7.24
Party membership	3.70	2.52	1.82	4.40
Province	−0.64	11.64	−0.94	11.94
Constant	0.0	20.14	0.0	20.14
Total	55.78	44.22	57.51	42.49

Source: 2002 urban household survey.

that the gender income gap widened over the period largely because proportionately more women than men became unemployed/laid off and earlier retired. Specifically, the more rapid rise in the number of the female unemployed and laid off greatly contributed to the widening of the gender gap.

The percentage of the overall gap due to the differences in the coefficients of employment status changes from negative in 1995 to positive in 2002. This change results mainly from the changes of relative income of the

unemployed/*xiagang* males and females compared to their employed counterparts. In 2002 relative income increased for all the unemployed/*xiagang*,
but it increased faster for males than for females.

If the gender income gap is decomposed into two parts, the explained and
the unexplained parts, our results show that the overall gap becomes wider
along with labor market liberalization and deep reform of state enterprises,
but at the same time the unexplained gap as a percentage of the overall gender
gap declines. This finding is consistent with those of other researchers, such
as Knight and Song's contribution in this volume (Chapter 9). It indicates
that stronger competition in the labor market has eroded nonmarket wage
differentials. This outcome is also reflected in our findings that the differences between males and females in the coefficients of education and
province dummies decline between 1995 and 2002.

The gender income gap in urban China almost doubled in constant prices
over the 1995–2002 period, an astonishing increase indeed. Naturally one
would like to know how large a part of the increase can be explained by the
increase in the number of unemployed and laid-off females. Applying equation (3) from Section II to our data, we produced the decomposition results
in Table 10.6. In equation (3) the first term captures the changes in the gender
gap due to the changes in gender differences of personal characteristics over
time, holding the coefficients in the 1995 male function constant. The fourth
term captures the changes in the gender gap due to the changes in female
personal characteristics over time, holding the differences of the coefficients
between the male and the female function constant. Therefore, both term 1
and term 4 reflect the contribution of changes in the personal characteristics of females over time, compared to their male counterparts. As shown in
Table 10.6, term 1 explains 94 percent of the overall change in the gender gap
of income in the 1995–2002 period. Interestingly, the unemployment/laid-
off variable and the earlier retirement variable play a dominant role within
this term. Similarly, while term 4 explains one-third of the overall change,
the unemployment/laid-off variable is the greatest contributor.

Our data show that concurrently with the widening of the gender income
gap, overall income inequality increased among males and females over the
1995–2002 period. The Gini coefficient of income increased from 0.32 to
0.37 for the males and from 0.34 to 0.40 for the females under study. This
implies that the approach of Juhn, Murphy, and Pierce (1991) (JMP) has
some advantage for investigating the effects of rising income inequality on
the gender gap, which is denoted by $\Delta\theta_{t+1}(\sigma_{t+1} - \sigma_t)$, that is, the fourth
term of formula (5) in Section II. The term is also labeled as the gender gap
attributable to unobserved prices (Juhn, Murphy, and Pierce 1991).

Table 10.6. *Decomposition of changes in the gender log income gap of urban labor-market participants over 1995–2002 (% of the total difference)*

	Term 1	Term 2	Term 3	Term 4
Employment status	103.57	−42.58	16.24	22.62
In which: unemployed/*xiagang*	91.31	−41.58	9.47	27.45
Earlier retirement	12.27	−0.99	6.77	−4.83
Age	−1.34	7.17	−169.08	5.18
Education	−6.40	9.47	52.55	−16.24
Ethnic minority	0.04	−0.02	1.49	18.02
Party membership	−1.63	2.08	11.93	1.57
Province	−0.47	0.89	−12.20	2.27
Constant	0.0	0.0	94.82	0.0
Total	93.78	−22.99	−4.24	33.43

Source: 1995 and 2002 urban household surveys.

Table 10.7. *Decomposition using JMP's approach for urban labor-market participants over 1995–2002*

	Log income	Percentage
Total difference between 1995 and 2002	0.1629	100.0
1. Observed quantities	0.1528	93.8
Unemployed/*xiagang*	0.1487	91.3
Earlier retirement	0.0200	12.3
Other	−0.0160	−9.8
2. Observed prices	−0.0375	−23.0
Unemployed/*xiagang*	−0.0678	−41.6
Earlier retirement	−0.0016	−1.0
Other	0.0319	19.6
3. Gap	0.0023	1.4
4. Unobserved prices	0.0453	27.8

Source: 1995 and 2002 urban household surveys.

The results from application of the JMP approach are presented in Table 10.7. It shows that 28 percent of the change in the gender gap between 1995 and 2002 can be attributed to increased inequality of the income distributions, as represented by the item labeled "unobserved prices." This item holds the mean difference in male/female unobservables constant at $\Delta\theta_{t+1}$. Since σ_t and σ_{t+1} represent the standard deviations of the unexplained residuals in 1995 and 2002, this result can be further interpreted as reflecting that the distribution of the unexplained residuals became more unequal between 1995 and 2002.

Table 10.8. *Economic dependency of women in urban China, 1995 and 2002, with international comparisons (%)*

Country and year	Mean dependency	Woman has no earnings	Woman earns less than man	Equality in earnings	Woman earns more than man	Woman sole earner
Denmark 1992	0.22	12.2	50.4	21.3	10.5	5.6
Finland 1995	0.15	12.1	44.5	17.7	16.7	9.1
Norway 1995	0.22	13.4	53.4	14.0	10.1	9.1
Sweden 1995	0.23	8.7	57.9	15.5	12.3	5.5
Germany 1994	0.39	33.5	39.2	9.6	6.3	11.5
The Netherlands 1994	0.53	39.8	41.2	7.6	2.5	7.8
U.K. 1995	0.36	25.8	46.3	12.5	5.0	10.3
Urban China 1995	0.124	1.0	32.2	59.9	7.9	0.1
Urban China 2002	0.163	7.6	40.5	47.7	12.0	1.2

Note: Equality is defined as each partner contributing between 40 percent and 60 percent of combined earnings.
Source: Sørensen (2001) and 1995 and 2002 urban household data.

V. A Consequence: Rising Women's Economic Dependency

Does the change in the gender income gap mean that married women have become more economically dependent on their husbands than before? How dependent are Chinese urban women as compared to women in some other countries? Dependency is interesting to study as it is one measure of bargaining power between spouses. Keeping other factors constant, a high dependency means lower bargaining power.

We build our analysis on work by Sørensen and McLanahan (1987) and Sørensen (2001). The analysis focuses on households with husbands and/or wives. The economic dependence of women is measured as the difference between the husband's and wife's relative contributions to family earnings:

$$DEP = (his\ earnings - her\ earnings)/(his\ earnings + her\ earnings) \quad (6)$$

The measure DEP ranges from $+1$ to -1. If the woman is completely dependent on her partner, DEP is 1; if they contribute equally it is zero; and if they are completely dependent on her, DEP is -1. There is a direct relationship between this measure of dependence and the wife's contribution to the couple's earnings ($REL = (1 - DEP)/2$).

The values of DEP computed from the 1995 and 2002 surveys are presented in Table 10.8. This table shows that average dependency among wives rose despite the fact that the proportion of wives earning more than husbands or being the sole earner increased slightly. The numbers in the table also indicate that economic dependency among women in urban China is relatively similar to what is observed in Scandinavian countries. This situation is rather different from that in Germany and the Netherlands, as in those countries a large proportion of wives have no earnings at all.

VI. Conclusions

Using the data from two large-sample surveys we have investigated the gender income gap in urban China. The data allow comparisons between 1995 and 2002. During this period urban China experienced a rising tide of unemployment along with a deep reform of the employment scheme and unexpectedly rapid industrial restructuring. As a result, large numbers of urban workers became unemployed and laid off (*xiagang*). At the same time, a large number of urban workers were retired early in order to reduce the pressure of unemployment. These circumstances affected female workers more heavily than male workers and led to a declining income status for urban Chinese females as a whole compared to their male counterparts. Given this background, this chapter attempts to answer the question: How and to what extent did the tide of unemployment affect the relative income status of urban females? Therefore, our approach, differing from the conventional analysis of gender earnings gaps, focuses on the gender income gap for three groups of people: workers, the unemployed/laid off, and the earlier retired, inclusively, rather than simply investigating the gender earnings gap.

Our analysis indicates that unemployment/laid-off status and earlier retirement explain a substantial part of the gender income gap in the 1995 income function and have a yet more powerful contribution in the 2002 function. Moreover, decomposing the average crude income gap between women and men in urban China, we find that nearly half in 1995 and almost 60 percent in 2002 can be attributed to differences in the mean values of the personal characteristics between genders.

Our findings indicate that the more rapid increase in the number of unemployed/laid-off females than males was a major cause of the widening of the gender income gap between 1995 and 2002. The gender income gap, measured as the difference between male and female incomes as a percentage of female income, increased from 24 percent to 32 percent. This widening gap can be sufficiently explained by both the increased number of unemployed/laid-off females and the increasingly higher population share of females who were unemployed/laid off compared to their male counterparts. When applying the decomposition approach of Juhn, Murphy, and Pierce

(1991), we find that increased inequality in the income distribution also had a quite substantial impact on the change in the gender gap between 1995 and 2002. The story of the rising gender income gap in urban China between 1995 and 2002 is to a large extent a story of economic restructuring leading to a more rapid decline in labor-market participation among women than among men. As a consequence, the economic dependency of women within urban households has increased, and their bargaining power has weakened.

References

Adelman, I. and D. Sunding (1987), "Economic Policy and Income Distribution in China," *Journal of Comparative Economics*, 11(3), 444–461.

Appleton, S., J. Knight, L. Song, and Q. Xia (2002), "Labor Retrenchment in China – Determinants and Consequences," *China Economic Review*, 13(2–3), 252–275.

Blinder, A. (1973), "Wage Discrimination: Reduced Form and Structural Estimations," *Journal of Human Resources*, 8(4), 436–455.

Cai, Fang, Du Yang, and Wang Meiyang (2004), "Employment, Wage Differentials and Labor Market in China," unpublished background paper for *China Human Development Report 2005*.

Dong, X. and P. Bowles (2002), "Segmentation and Discrimination in China's Emerging Industrial Urban Market," *China Economic Review*, 13(2–3), 170–196.

Gustafsson, B. and S. Li (1998), "Inequality in China at the End of the 1980s: Locational Aspects and Household Characteristics," *Asian Economic Journal*, 12(1), 35–63.

Gustafsson, B. and S. Li (2000), "Economic Transformation and the Gender Earnings Gap in Urban China," *Journal of Population Economics*, 13(2), 305–330.

Institute of Labor Science (2000), "Analytical Report of the Situation of *Xiagang* Workers in Shenyang and Wuhan Using Sample Data," *Research Forum*, 19, August (in Chinese).

Juhn, C., M. Murphy, and B. Pierce (1991), "Accounting for a Slowdown in Black-White Wage Convergence," in M. Kosters, ed., *Workers and Their Wages*, Washington, D.C.: American Enterprise Institute Press.

Khan, A., K. Griffin, C. Riskin, and R. Zhao (1992), "Household Income and Its Distribution in China," *China Quarterly*, no. 132, 1029–1061.

Kidd, M. and X. Meng (2001), "The Chinese State Enterprise Sector: Labour Market Reform and the Impact on Male-Female Wage Structure," *Asian Economic Journal*, 15(4), 405–423.

Knight, J. and S. Li (2002), "Unemployment Duration and Earnings of Re-employed Workers in Urban China," unpublished manuscript.

Knight, J. and L. Song (1993), "Why Urban Wages Differ in China," in K. Griffin and R. Zhao, eds., *The Distribution of Income in China*, Houndsmills, England: Macmillan.

Liu, P., X. Meng, and J. Zhang (2000), "Sectoral Gender Wage Differentials and Discrimination in the Transitional Chinese Economy," *Journal of Population Economics*, 13(2), 331–352.

Maurer-Fazio, M. and J. Hughes (2002), "The Effects of Market Liberalization on the Relative Earnings of Chinese Women," *Journal of Comparative Economics*, 30(4), 709–731.

Meng, X. (1998), "Male-Female Wage Determination and Gender Wage Discrimination in China's Rural Industrial Sector," *Labor Economics*, 5(1), 67–89.

Meng, X. (2004), "Economic Restructuring and Income Inequality in Urban China," *Review of Income and Wealth*, 50(3), 357–379.

Meng, X. and P. Miller (1995), "Occupational Segregation and its Impact on Gender Wage Discrimination in China's Rural Industrial Sector," *Oxford Economic Papers*, 47(1), 136–155.

National Bureau of Statistics (annual), *China Statistical Yearbook*, Beijing: China Statistics Press.

Oaxaca, R. (1973), "Male-Female Wage Differentials in Urban Labor Markets," *International Economic Review*, 14(3), 693–709.

Rozelle, S., X. Dong, L. Zhang, and A. Mason (2002), "Gender Wage Gaps in Post-Reform Rural China," *Pacific Economic Review*, 7(1), 157–179.

Sørensen, A. (2001), "Gender Equality in Earnings at Work and at Home," in M. Kautto et al., eds., *Nordic Welfare States in the European Context*, London: Routledge.

Sørensen, A. and S. McLanahan (1987), "Married Women's Economic Dependency, 1940–1980," *American Journal of Sociology*, 93(3), 659–687.

Appendix Table 10A.1. *Mean and standard deviation of characteristics of labor-market participants by gender, 1995*

	Male		Female	
	Mean	Std. Dev.	Mean	Std. Dev.
Working/employed	0.932	0.251	0.836	0.371
Unemployed/*xiagang*	0.028	0.165	0.031	0.174
Earlier retired	0.040	0.195	0.133	0.340
Age 16–20	0.029	0.168	0.031	0.173
Age 21–25	0.092	0.288	0.090	0.287
Age 26–30	0.170	0.376	0.180	0.384
Age 31–35	0.132	0.339	0.139	0.345
Age 36–40	0.170	0.376	0.180	0.384
Age 41–45	0.177	0.381	0.188	0.391
Age 46–50	0.129	0.336	0.118	0.323
Age 51–55	0.100	0.300	0.086	0.281
Age 56–60	0.079	0.270	0.063	0.243
4-year college and above	0.098	0.298	0.048	0.213
2-year college	0.174	0.379	0.111	0.314
Professional school	0.159	0.366	0.167	0.373
Upper middle school	0.228	0.420	0.243	0.429
Lower middle school	0.290	0.454	0.334	0.472
Primary school and below	0.050	0.218	0.098	0.298
Ethnic minority	0.043	0.202	0.043	0.204
Han majority	0.957	0.202	0.957	0.204
Party member	0.321	0.467	0.147	0.354
Non-Party member	0.679	0.467	0.853	0.354
Beijing	0.071	0.256	0.072	0.258
Shanxi	0.094	0.292	0.087	0.282
Liaoning	0.106	0.308	0.102	0.302
Jiangsu	0.112	0.315	0.117	0.321
Anhui	0.067	0.251	0.071	0.257
Henan	0.086	0.281	0.085	0.279
Hubei	0.109	0.311	0.108	0.311
Guangdong	0.084	0.277	0.085	0.279
Sichuan	0.121	0.326	0.122	0.327
Yunnan	0.094	0.292	0.095	0.294
Gansu	0.057	0.231	0.056	0.230
Log income	8.585	1.514	8.324	1.593

Source: 1995 urban household survey.

Appendix Table 10A.2. *Mean and standard deviation of characteristics of labor-market participants by gender, 2002*

	Male		Female	
	Mean	Std. Dev.	Mean	Std. Dev.
Working/employed	0.854	0.354	0.692	0.462
Unemployed/*xiagang*	0.099	0.299	0.130	0.336
Earlier retired	0.047	0.212	0.179	0.383
Age 16–20	0.014	0.116	0.011	0.106
Age 21–25	0.059	0.235	0.062	0.240
Age 26–30	0.071	0.257	0.082	0.274
Age 31–35	0.118	0.323	0.135	0.341
Age 36–40	0.169	0.375	0.179	0.383
Age 41–45	0.153	0.360	0.164	0.370
Age 46–50	0.200	0.400	0.189	0.392
Age 51–55	0.144	0.351	0.126	0.332
Age 56–60	0.073	0.260	0.053	0.224
4-year college and above	0.109	0.312	0.057	0.232
2-year college	0.211	0.408	0.174	0.379
Professional school	0.106	0.308	0.133	0.340
Upper middle school	0.267	0.442	0.288	0.453
Lower middle school	0.271	0.444	0.296	0.457
Primary school and below	0.036	0.185	0.051	0.221
Ethnic minority	0.043	0.203	0.041	0.198
Han majority	0.957	0.203	0.959	0.198
Party member	0.336	0.473	0.193	0.394
Non-Party member	0.664	0.473	0.807	0.394
Beijing	0.065	0.247	0.067	0.250
Shanxi	0.092	0.289	0.083	0.277
Liaoning	0.112	0.316	0.115	0.319
Jiangsu	0.105	0.307	0.107	0.309
Anhui	0.073	0.260	0.071	0.258
Henan	0.094	0.291	0.094	0.292
Hubei	0.103	0.304	0.102	0.303
Guangdong	0.089	0.284	0.091	0.288
Sichuan	0.124	0.330	0.125	0.331
Yunnan	0.085	0.278	0.090	0.286
Gansu	0.058	0.234	0.054	0.225
Log income	8.852	1.922	8.429	2.184

Source: 2002 urban household survey.

Appendix Table 10A.3. *Results from regression analysis on log income of labor-market participants by gender, 1995*

	Male		Female	
	Coefficient	*t*-value	Coefficient	*t*-value
Working/employed	–	–	–	–
Unemployed/*xiagang*	−5.4260	−71.96	−5.3869	−68.5
Earlier retired	−0.5283	−8.23	−0.2729	−4.98
Age 16–20	−1.6453	−20.31	−1.5322	−17.64
Age 21–25	−0.5314	−9.8	−0.5607	−9.38
Age 26–30	–	–	–	–
Age 31–35	0.2486	5.04	0.1886	3.5
Age 36–40	0.3553	7.47	0.2939	5.7
Age 41–45	0.4181	8.69	0.3568	6.81
Age 46–50	0.4390	8.62	0.3310	5.68
Age 51–55	0.4984	9.13	0.3291	4.78
Age 56–60	0.5967	9.97	0.4002	4.93
4-year college and above	0.1683	3.58	0.1016	1.48
2-year college	0.0418	1.04	0.0710	1.37
Professional school	–	–	–	–
Upper middle school	−0.0762	−2.01	−0.1806	−4.23
Lower middle school	−0.1013	−2.77	−0.2872	−7.11
Primary school and below	−0.2567	−4.25	−0.6017	−10.74
Ethnic minority	−0.0387	−0.66	−0.0148	−0.22
Han majority	–	–	–	–
Party member	0.0855	3.16	0.1626	4.12
Non-Party member	–	–	–	–
Beijing	0.2025	3.66	0.1015	1.61
Shanxi	−0.3107	−6.11	−0.4996	−8.45
Liaoning	−0.2248	−4.57	−0.3849	−6.8
Jiangsu	–	–	–	–
Anhui	−0.2139	−3.83	−0.2595	−4.16
Henan	−0.3441	−6.61	−0.4796	−8.09
Hubei	−0.2991	−6.12	−0.2344	−4.22
Guangdong	0.4720	9	0.3307	5.57
Sichuan	−0.1863	−3.92	−0.2299	−4.27
Yunnan	−0.2455	−4.69	−0.1871	−3.17
Gansu	−0.4369	−7.38	−0.5438	−8.03
Constant	8.6897	151.55	8.7588	138.03
Adj-R^2	0.610		0.532	
F-value	396.0		293.0	
Number of observations	6,824		6,937	

Source: 1995 urban household survey.

Appendix Table 10A.4. *Results from regression analysis on log income of labor-market participants by gender, 2002*

	Male		Female	
	Coefficient	*t*-value	Coefficient	*t*-value
Working/employed	–	–	–	–
Unemployed/*xiagang*	−3.2092	−56.28	−3.6635	−62.28
Earlier retired	−0.5160	−6.08	−0.3434	−4.79
Age 16–20	−2.6530	−17.2	−1.8408	−9.76
Age 21–25	−1.1692	−12.76	−0.5070	−5.05
Age 26–30	–	–	–	–
Age 31–35	0.3318	4.28	0.4393	5.3
Age 36–40	0.5677	7.74	0.6103	7.66
Age 41–45	0.6209	8.28	0.8009	9.78
Age 46–50	0.7331	10.04	1.1045	13.4
Age 51–55	0.9201	11.79	1.0706	10.76
Age 56–60	0.9331	10.1	1.0539	8.58
4-year college and above	0.3045	4.26	0.3022	3.18
2-year college	0.1170	1.89	0.0973	1.4
Professional school	–	–	–	–
Upper middle school	−0.1131	−1.89	−0.3565	−5.6
Lower middle school	−0.2647	−4.4	−0.5169	−8.03
Primary school and below	−0.2914	−2.86	−0.9150	−9.05
Ethnic minority	−0.0205	−0.24	−0.0525	−0.53
Han majority	–	–	–	–
Party member	0.1091	2.83	0.0536	1.03
Non-Party member	–	–	–	–
Beijing	0.3141	3.85	0.2506	2.69
Shanxi	−0.2785	−3.78	−0.5045	−5.81
Liaoning	−0.2457	−3.5	−0.5313	−6.65
Jiangsu	–	–	–	–
Anhui	−0.1589	−2.02	−0.2643	−2.92
Henan	−0.5265	−7.18	−0.4933	−5.88
Hubei	−0.3034	−4.24	−0.2436	−2.96
Guangdong	0.1084	1.46	0.0835	0.98
Sichuan	−0.3223	−4.72	−0.3584	−4.6
Yunnan	−0.2125	−2.73	−0.1141	−1.29
Gansu	−0.3624	−4.31	−0.3096	−3.12
Constant	8.9534	73.84	8.8681	63.95
Adj-R^2	0.441		0.436	
F-value	223.0		221.8	
Number of observations	6,741		6,636	

Source: 2002 urban household survey.

ELEVEN

What Determines Living Arrangements of the Elderly in Urban China?

Meng Xin and Luo Chuliang

I. Introduction

The welfare of the elderly is an important issue in the study of income equality, as old age is often associated with low incomes and income insecurity, especially in the developing world where the social security system is not well established. When income distribution widens it is often the elderly who are among the increasingly disadvantaged. In China economic transition has adversely changed the economic well-being and social stratification of the elderly through health care and pension reforms (Raymo and Yu 2000; Saunders et al. 2003). Due to these reforms, many old workers lost their expected pensions and are currently under limited health and income protection. In addition, demographic changes brought about by the one-child policy have led China to join developed countries prematurely in becoming an aging society. Rapid aging has cast doubt on the ability of the newly established Pay-as-You-Go (PAYG) pension scheme (Cai and Meng 2003). If the current PAYG system fails, which has been argued by many studies (World Bank 1997; Whiteford 2003; Murton 2002), the elderly population will suffer significantly. Under these circumstances, a question naturally arises as to how China can adjust its policy to assist its aging population in this particularly difficult period. In this chapter we investigate one of the most effective ways through which the elderly's well-being may be improved – coresiding.

Some studies argue that coresiding with adult children and other relatives is beneficial to both the elderly and society (Palloni 2001; Palloni and De Vos 2003; Andrade and DeVos 2002; Hoerger, Picone, and Sloan 1996). Families provide emotional comfort and physical care, and informal care provided by family members is more efficient. In addition, coresiding reduces unit living costs, and when coresiding, adult children may financially supplement the elderly. Ulker (2003) found that elderly who coreside on average consume more than those who live alone.

Elderly living with, and being financially and emotionally supported by, adult children is regarded as a good Eastern tradition. Japanese elders, for example, are more likely to live with their children and relatives than their counterparts in most Western developed countries at a similar level of income (Palloni 2001). In China adult children being financially and emotionally responsible for elderly parents is stipulated as a responsibility in the Elderly Rights and Security Law (Zhang 2000).

Recent literature has found that the proportion of the elderly living with adult children or other relatives has been declining, both in the West and in the East (Costa 1997; Palloni 2001). Such a decline may be due to different reasons. For example, an increase in income of the elderly (assuming privacy is a normal good), reduction in fertility, improvement in both elderly health status and the technology of household production, and changing social values may all contribute. The erosion of the traditional norm of elderly coresiding with family members is most threatening to the elderly's well-being where public transfers to the elderly are unlikely to increase in the near future, such as in developing countries.

The literature on elderly living arrangements in Western countries is mainly focused on the effect of an increase in income or social security payments on the elderly's living arrangements choices. These issues are directly related to public policy as to the level of public pensions and the extent to which governments should subsidize institutionalization of the elderly (Schwartz, Danziger, and Smolensky 1984; Borsch-Supan et al. 1992; Hoerger, Picone, and Sloan 1996; Costa 1997, 1999; Pezzin and Schone 1999; Engelhardt, Gruber, and Perry 2002).

Studies of elderly living arrangements in the non-Western world are limited. A comprehensive review of such studies is found in Palloni (2001), where summary statistics of living arrangements in some Asian and Latin American countries are provided. The general picture indicates that in most non-Western countries the proportion of elderly living alone is lower than in Western society but the trend toward increased living separately is similar. Given that in most Asian and Latin American countries public transfers are limited, the declining trend in intergenerational coresiding may be worrisome. In addition, some studies find that on average elders living alone are poorer than their counterparts who coreside (Agree 1993; Saunders and Smeeding 1998), although other studies find that income (or pensions) contributes positively to the probability of the elderly living alone (Chan and Da Vanzo 1996; Kan, Park, and Chang 2001).

Elderly living arrangements in China have mostly been studied in a descriptive manner. Davis-Friedmann (1991) finds that in China the elderly and their adult children keep close contact even when they live independently. Benjamin et al. (2000) compare the living arrangements of the rural elderly in the 1930s and 1995 and find a marked decline in the proportion of elderly living in extended or multiple family households, although the majority of the elderly (around 60 percent) was still living in extended or multiple family households in 1995. When comparing rural and urban households they found modest differences. Using 1982, 1990, and 2000 census data, Zeng and Wang (2003) find a decline of around 8 percentage points of the elderly who coreside between 1990 and 2000 for rural and urban combined data, whereas, relative to rural households, urban elderly in 2000 are 6 percentage points more likely to live alone. The reasons for such a change, however, are not investigated in either study. Palmer and Deng in Chapter 7 of this book using CHIP 1988, 1995, and 2002 data describe the declining trend of elderly living with children or others in both urban and rural China over the 14-year period, but reasons for the trend are not provided.

This chapter outlines the change in living arrangements of the elderly in urban China during the last 14 years of fast economic reform and growth, and then examines the determinants of elderly living arrangements and the changes over time. Over this period, household income increased significantly, and the Chinese economy experienced important institutional reform. The reform most relevant to the change in the elderly's living arrangements is the housing reform initiated in the early 1990s. Although the State Council announced the housing reform experiment in 1988, the formal nationwide reform that allowed state-owned enterprises (SOEs) and other government institutions to sell their housing to employees was not introduced until 1991 (State Council 1991). The 1991 introduction also stated that any new housing put into use beginning in 1992 should first be sold to employees, and the remainder that cannot be sold can then be rented and should follow the market rent.

The housing reform dramatically increased households' housing ownership, as well as housing availability. The most significant increase in housing availability was during 1992 and 1993 and then after 1998. According to the *China Statistical Yearbook*, in 1988 per capita residential floor space in urban China was 13.0 square meters, increasing to 16.3 in 1995, and 22.8 in 2002 (National Bureau of Statistics 2003).[1] Furthermore, residential housing sales increased rapidly, from 255 million square meters in 1988 to

---

[1] Data on living space are not available after 1988.

679 million square meters in 1995, and further to 2.2 billion square meters in 2002 (National Bureau of Statistics 1999, 2003). It would be expected that individuals previously constrained by housing availability to stay in an extended family may be able to live alone now that housing availability has increased so much. In addition, as a result of the increase in income and the introduction of privatization, the economic and political system is continually stressing the role of individual responsibility, and this may have had some impact on family values. Thus, the impact of the increase in income, housing reform, and the change in social norms may all have contributed to the change in the elderly's living arrangements. Understanding these issues may be helpful in formulating economic policy to prevent Chinese tradition from eroding.

The chapter is organized as follows. The next section discusses the data and summary statistics with regard to living arrangements. Section III formulates the model and Section IV presents the empirical results. Conclusions and policy implications are drawn in Section V.

II. Data and Summary Statistics

The data used in this study are from the CHIP surveys for 1988, 1995, and 2002. These surveys are comparable, were conducted in 1989, 1996, and 2003, respectively, and comprise 10, 11, and 12 provinces for the three survey years, respectively.[2] The sample size of each survey is reported in Appendix Table 11A.1. The full samples are between 6,835 and 9,009 households, depending on the year of the survey, while the total sample of individuals ranges from 20,632 to 31,827. For a detailed description of these surveys, see Eichen and Zhang (1993) and the Appendix to this book. As this chapter is interested only in the elderly population, the working sample includes only households that have at least one member aged 60 years or older. With this restriction, the sample sizes are reduced to between 1,574 and 1,855 households, and contain between 2,382 and 2,453 elderly individuals.[3] The proportion of households with at least one elderly member increased from 20 percent in 1988 to 24 and 23 percent in 1995 and 2002, respectively.

All three surveys include basic information on individual characteristics, different components of income, and household expenditure. Living arrangements are categorized according to the information on the household

---

[2] By 2002 Chongqing, formerly part of Sichuan, had become a separate province. For consistency with earlier years, we treat it as part of Sichuan.

[3] The definition of the elderly household used in this chapter is the same as that in Chapter 7 of this book.

Table 11.1. *Living arrangements of the urban elderly, 1988, 1995, and 2002*

	1988		1995		2002	
	Frequency	Percentage	Frequency	Percentage	Frequency	Percentage
Live alone	692	28.2	949	39.4	883	37.1
Coreside with child or others	1,761	71.8	1,434	59.6	1,458	61.2
Total number of elderly	2,453	100	2,408	100	2,382	100

Note: "Live alone" includes elderly who live singly and elderly who live with a spouse only.

relationships provided in the surveys. Living arrangements are defined in three categories: living alone, living alone with spouse, and living with children or others. Hereafter the first two categories are both classified as "live alone."[4] Table 11.1 presents the distribution of elderly living arrangements over the three survey years. It shows that the proportion of elderly who coreside was 72 percent in 1988, declining by around 10 percentage points between 1988 and 2002. The reduction occurred mainly between 1988 and 1995. By 1995 only 60 percent of the elderly coreside, a 12 percentage point reduction in seven years, whereas between 1995 and 2002 almost no change is detected. The change between 1988 and 1995 is much faster than figures presented in the literature for some other countries. For example, Costa (1997) presents data showing that male elderly coresidence in the United States changed from 55 percent in 1880 to 16 percent in 1990. The most significant changes occurred in the 20 years between 1940 and 1960, when the ratio was reduced by 15 percentage points. Kan, Park, and Chang (2001) show that in Taiwan the ratio of elderly aged 65 and above living with relatives declined from 75 to 62 percent between 1986 and 1996. Looking at different age groups (Table 11.2), one can see that the changes occurred in most age groups except for the group aged 80 years and above.

What caused such a significant change? Costa (1997) finds that in the United States rising incomes were the most important factor enabling the elderly to live alone prior to 1940, but income no longer played as large a role in the later period. During the period examined in this study household

---

[4] In Chapter 7 of this book, the living arrangement choice of the elderly is also classified into three categories, but that chapter mainly focuses on the difference in economic well-being between the elderly who coreside with a spouse and those who coreside with adult children, while we try to explore why the elderly do or do not coreside with their adult children.

Table 11.2. *Living arrangements of the urban elderly by age group, 1988, 1995, and 2002 (% of age group)*

	Age groups					
	60–64	65–69	70–74	75–79	≥80	All elderly
1988						
Live alone	32.29	36.54	24.82	15.83	6.31	28.22
Coreside	67.71	63.46	75.18	84.17	93.69	71.78
1995						
Live alone	43.54	47.21	42.24	20.38	6.33	40.45
Coreside	56.46	52.79	57.76	79.62	93.67	59.55
2002						
Live alone	39.46	42.9	46.34	30.88	8.48	38.79
Coreside	60.54	57.1	53.66	69.12	91.52	61.21

income levels in China increased markedly. For example, Table 11.3 (last column) indicates that real per capita income in the urban sector increased by 6.7 and 6.6 percent per annum for the 1988–1995 and 1995–2002 periods, respectively. The increase in per elderly pension income was even more dramatic. Between 1988 and 1995 the elderly's pension income increased by 12 percent per annum, and between 1995 and 2002 by 10 percent per annum. In both periods pension income per elderly moved much faster than the per capita income increase. Note that the proportion of elderly with a pension increased from 58 percent in 1988, to 74 percent in 1995, and 81 percent in 2002 (see Table 11.3). This may be the main reason why on average pension income for the elderly increased much faster than per capita income.

Further investigation indicates that real per capita income and pension income are higher for those who live alone than for those who coreside in all three survey years. This, perhaps, is because there are often children who do not earn income in coresiding households. With regard to pension income, it seems to suggest that elderly without a pension income are more likely to coreside with children or other relatives than those with a pension income, resulting in a lower average pension income. What is interesting is that growth of real per capita income is faster for the elderly living alone than for those who coreside, whereas growth of real pension income for the two groups is almost the same. This again may relate to the fact that pension income is calculated for older individuals, while per capita income accounts for nonelderly members of households.

Another factor that may have affected elderly living arrangements is housing reform. Before the economic reform initiated in the late 1970s and early

Table 11.3. *Total income and pension income of the urban elderly, 1988, 1995, and 2002*

	Live alone		Coreside		All elderly	
	Mean	SD	Mean	SD	Mean	SD
Real per capita income (yuan)						
1988	1,104	564	897	397	955	460
1995	1,760	722	1,334	828	1,507	814
2002	2,957	1,451	1,973	1,118	2,355	1,346
Average annual growth 1988–1995 (%)	6.9		5.8		6.7	
Average annual growth 1995–2002 (%)	7.7		5.7		6.6	
Real pension per elderly person (yuan)						
1988	697	532	466	545	531	551
1995	1,398	924	1,010	973	1,167	973
2002	2,669	1,724	1,979	1,739	2,246	1,765
Average annual growth 1988–1995 (%)	10.5		11.7		11.9	
Average annual growth 1995–2002 (%)	9.7		10.1		9.8	

Note: Pension income is a component of total income. Income is in constant 1986 prices and deflated using the official urban consumer price index compiled by the National Bureau of Statistics.

1980s, housing in urban areas was owned by the state and assigned to state-sector workers at highly subsidized rents. This situation began to change around the mid-1980s as the state gradually increased rents. In the early 1990s the state began to allow households to purchase the public housing they were renting, and this process accelerated beginning in the mid-1990s. At the same time, private real estate development also gathered momentum, and the private rental market was growing quickly.

The introduction of housing reform has generated an increase in both housing ownership and housing availability (Table 11.4). In 1988 per capita living area in urban China was 15 square meters. In 2002 this had increased to almost 20 square meters. The elderly living alone occupy larger areas than those who coreside.[5] Housing ownership changed the most. In 1988 only 22 percent of households with at least one elderly member owned a house or flat. By 2002 this ratio had increased to 81 percent, an annual increase of 10 percent. The change is similar for those who live alone and those who coreside.

Whether the elderly choose to live with relatives or alone may be influenced by whether they have a place of their own to live. In urban China most

---

[5] Considering that coresidency provides an advantage of sharing public areas in a house, the difference between the living areas may not represent better living conditions.

Table 11.4. *Living area and housing ownership of the urban elderly,*
1988, 1995, and 2002

	Live alone		Coreside		All elderly	
	Mean	SD	Mean	SD	Mean	SD
Per capita living area (m^2)						
1988	19.93	12.50	12.70	7.47	14.69	9.68
1995	23.36	10.17	14.76	11.50	18.24	11.76
2002	26.32	11.71	15.62	7.64	19.77	10.77
Housing ownership (%)						
1988	0.24		0.21		0.22	
1995	0.37		0.38		0.38	
2002	0.80		0.82		0.81	
Elderly own/rent in their name (%)						
1988	0.62		0.24		0.35	
1995	0.57		0.43		0.48	
2002	0.62		0.51		0.56	

of the housing (rental or owner occupied) was distributed within work units up until the mid-1990s. Therefore, from which household member's work unit the household received the housing should be an important determinant of whether the elderly member is living alone or not. This information is not available, however, for the 1988 data. In the 1995 survey the information is available only for those renting houses from the government, which is above 60 percent of the total sample. In the 2002 survey the information is available for households either renting or in housing purchased from the government, which accounts for 77 percent of the total sample. For households in each of the survey years without such information, it is assumed the housing is obtained under the name of the household head. The proportion of the elderly population who rented or owned housing under their own name increased from 35 percent in 1988 to 56 percent in 2002. This may be related to the fast increase in the private rental and real estate market. The increase mainly occurred among elderly who coresided.

Table 11.5 shows that in regard to individual characteristics the average age and gender distribution of the elderly sample did not change much, while the proportion with college degrees and above more than doubled. In addition, the proportion of the elderly who received pension income increased from 58 percent in 1988 to 81 percent in 2002, while the proportion who worked increased between 1988 and 1995, and then declined somewhat

Table 11.5. *Individual characteristics of the urban elderly, 1988, 1995, and 2002*

Mean age (years)	Live alone		Coreside		Total	
	Mean	SD	Mean	SD	Mean	SD
1988	65.97	5.11	68.67	7.56	67.91	7.06
1995	65.44	4.55	67.94	7.57	66.93	6.63
2002	67.06	5.11	68.66	7.41	68.04	6.66
Males (%)						
1988	0.57		0.44		0.48	
1995	0.59		0.49		0.53	
2002	0.54		0.48		0.50	
With college degree and above (%)						
1988	0.09		0.07		0.07	
1995	0.14		0.13		0.13	
2002	0.15		0.16		0.16	
With pension income (%)						
1988	0.73		0.52		0.58	
1995	0.85		0.67		0.74	
2002	0.89		0.76		0.81	
Working (%)						
1988	0.13		0.08		0.10	
1995	0.25		0.22		0.23	
2002	0.20		0.16		0.17	

between 1995 and 2002. Compared to those who live alone, it is found that the elderly who coreside are slightly older than those who live alone, with less chance of having a pension and less likely to work.

III. Model Specification and Methodology

The living arrangements of the elderly are often joint decisions between the elderly and their adult children. Unfortunately, from the data used in this study, only the variables that affect the elderly's decision making can be observed. Thus, following Costa (1997), the elderly's decision is modeled based on their children's decision. Consider $U_i = U_i(P, S, X)$ as utility from living alone and $U_d(P, S, X)$ as utility when the elderly coreside, where P is privacy (assuming to be a normal good), S is services received, and X is a vector of other consumption goods. The elderly choose to live alone if $U_i \geqq U_d$. Living alone increases P but reduces S.

Ideally, an empirical specification to explain elderly living arrangements should include variables that capture the elderly's income, housing, health condition, and number of adult children and these children's income. Most of the surveys, however, do not include information on the health condition or the number of adult children and their income, except for the 2002 survey where health condition variables are available. Keeping in mind data limitations, the reduced-form specification of the elderly's living arrangements may be written as

$$\Pr(L_i = 1 \,|\, X) = \Phi_i(X'\beta + \varepsilon), \quad (L = 0, 1) \tag{1}$$

where $\Phi(\cdot)$ is a standard normal cumulative distribution function, X is a vector of observable characteristics that contribute to the choice of living arrangements, and ε is a standard normal error term.

Independent living is costly, thus elderly with higher incomes will be better able to afford to live alone relative to the low-income elderly. The relationship between income and the elderly's living arrangements, however, may be endogenous. This endogeneity issue could arise because the elderly could adjust their employment decision in order to achieve their preferred living arrangement. If they prefer to live alone, the elderly may decide to work longer and, hence, earn higher income, as living alone is more costly than shared living arrangements. To handle this issue, pension income is used rather than total per capita income to control for the impact of income on living arrangements. The length of one's working life has little impact on individuals' pension income within the current Chinese pension system. Thus, pension income may not be closely related to whether elderly choose to work longer or not and, hence, may be exogenous.

The health condition of the elderly determines the amount of services they require. Less healthy elderly need assistance for many everyday activities, and the services are cheaper to acquire in an extended family living arrangement. Given that individuals' health conditions, and, hence, requirements for services are related to age, age and its squared term are used to capture this effect. The 2002 survey has a direct measure of self-assessed health condition, and this variable is added to test the extent to which missing a direct subjective measure of health may bias the results.

Individuals' preferences for being independent may be related to education level. More educated people may be more likely to value independence. Therefore, a dummy variable is included to indicate whether the elderly individual does or does not hold a college or higher degree. In addition, as mentioned earlier, elderly with their own housing may be less likely to be constrained from living alone. A dummy variable indicating whether housing is rented or purchased by the elderly is used to capture this effect.

Variables indicating gender and location of residence are also included. While gender may capture some of the effect of the need for more care (elderly males are more likely to require care than elderly females, for example), the regional effect may capture the differences in housing availability and in the social norms among different regions.

Equation (1) is estimated using a probit model first for each of the three survey data sets separately. These estimations allow us to investigate the determinants of the elderly's living arrangements as well as the changes in the impact of the determinants by comparing the change in the marginal effects over time. The change in living arrangements is then decomposed to identify the extent to which each determinant contributes to the change in living arrangements over time. We follow Doiron and Riddell (1994) and decompose the difference in the probability of living with relatives for a representative individual elderly between 1988 and 1995, and between 1988 and 2002. The difference in the probabilities of coresidence between any of the two years can be written as

$$\Phi_t\big(\tilde{X}_t^k \hat{\beta}_t^k\big) - \Phi_{t+n}\big(\tilde{X}_{t+n}^k \hat{\beta}_{t+n}^k\big) \simeq \frac{\partial \Phi(\varphi)}{\partial \varphi}\big(\tilde{X}_t^k \hat{\beta}_t^k - \tilde{X}_{t+n}^k \hat{\beta}_{t+n}^k\big), \quad (2)$$

where subscript t and $t + n$ indicate the year of the survey, k is the number of variables included in the probit estimation, and

$$\tilde{X}_t^k = \bar{X}_t^k \left[\frac{\Phi^{-1}(\tilde{\Pr})}{\bar{X}_t \hat{\beta}_t} \right].$$

The first term on the right-hand side of equation (2) is the normal probability density function evaluated at the point φ (the point around which the linearization is performed, $\varphi = (N_t \bar{X}_t^k \hat{\beta}_t^k + N_{t+n} \bar{X}_{t+n}^k \hat{\beta}_{t+n}^k)/(N_t + N_{t+n})$, while the second term is a linear function of characteristics and coefficients. The decomposition allows us to identify whether reduction in coresidency over time is due to income, housing reform, or change in social norms.

IV. Determinants of Living Arrangements of the Elderly

Equation (1) is estimated using a probit model for each survey year separately and the results are reported in Table 11.6. Table 11.6 presents the marginal effects for each independent variable on the probability of coresidence. It is observed that the effect of age on the probability of coresidency is negative, but the relationship is nonlinear for all three years. Figure 11.1 shows the predicted probability of coresidence by age, keeping all other variables fixed at the mean. It indicates that, at every age group, the probability

Table 11.6. *Results from probit regression of elderly coresidency living arrangements (urban)*

	1988	1995	2002
Age	−0.126***	−0.228***	−0.238***
	(0.029)	(0.041)	(0.038)
Age squared	0.001***	0.002***	0.002***
	(0.000)	(0.000)	(0.000)
Log(pension) (yuan)	−0.014***	−0.023***	−0.022***
	(0.003)	(0.004)	(0.004)
Dummy for males	0.158***	0.017	0.035
	(0.023)	(0.026)	(0.025)
Dummy for college and above	−0.051	−0.051	−0.097***
	(0.039)	(0.031)	(0.033)
Dummy for renting/owning house	−0.396***	−0.055**	−0.036
	(0.025)	(0.025)	(0.025)
Shanxi	0.110***	−0.232***	−0.272***
	(0.031)	(0.050)	(0.057)
Liaoning	0.069*	−0.065	−0.034
	(0.036)	(0.049)	(0.056)
Jiangsu	0.027	−0.201***	−0.262***
	(0.033)	(0.045)	(0.052)
Anhui	0.083**	−0.099*	−0.154**
	(0.033)	(0.052)	(0.063)
Henan	0.157***	−0.124**	−0.191***
	(0.025)	(0.049)	(0.053)
Hubei	0.063*	−0.032	−0.019
	(0.033)	(0.049)	(0.059)
Guangdong	0.199***	0.147***	0.231***
	(0.021)	(0.044)	(0.047)
Sichuan		−0.240***	−0.095*
		(0.048)	(0.055)
Yunnan	0.152***	−0.099*	−0.209***
	(0.027)	(0.059)	(0.057)
Gansu	0.163***	−0.006	−0.079
	(0.026)	(0.055)	(0.064)
Number of observations	2452	2408	2382
Pseudo R^2	0.18	0.10	0.10
Actual probability	0.718	0.596	0.612
Predicted probability	0.766	0.626	0.639

Notes:

1. Marginal effects are presented; for continuous variables they are evaluated at the mean, while for dummy variables they are evaluated at discrete changes from 0 to 1.
2. Standard deviations are in parentheses.
3. *, **, and *** indicate significant at 10, 5, and 1 percent levels.

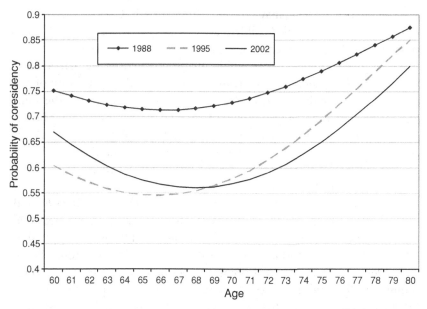

Figure 11.1 Impact of Age on the Probability of Coresidency in Urban China, 1988, 1995, and 2002.

of coresidence is higher for the 1988 data than for the later data. In addition, the slope is much steeper in 1995 and 2002 than in 1988. This may imply two possible changes. First, there has been a preference change among the elderly: that is, in the 1990s the elderly became more inclined to live alone than they had been in the 1980s. Second, while the preference of the elderly did not change, the increase in housing availability in the 1990s and early 2000s allowed the elderly to realize their preferences. We prefer the second explanation: that is, even if elders had similar preferences in 1988 as their counterparts in 1995 and 2002, they were constrained by housing availability. Once such a constraint is eliminated, the real preferences of the elderly are more likely to be revealed.

The negative and nonlinear relationship between age and coresidency shows that younger elders are less likely to live alone. As individuals age, the probability of coresidency is reduced. This negative relationship, however, reverses when the elderly reach around 67–70 years of age. From then on, each additional year of age increases the probability of coresidency by 0.1 to 0.2 percent. At the age of 74–76, the probability of coresidence exceeds that at the age of 60 and continues to increase. Intuitively, this suggests that at a younger age children of elders who are not married, or married but have not had a child of their own, may still live with the elderly. Cai, Giles, and Meng (2006) found that married children are less likely to live with parents, and married children with a child of their own are even less likely to live with parents. As elders age, the probability that their children are married and have children of their own increases, and, hence, the probability of the elderly living with their children decreases. This trend lasts only to the point at which elders can still take care of themselves. At ages 67–70 their health condition may deteriorate, and they begin to trade off privacy for services provided by their children or other relatives by living with them.

The effect of pension income on the probability of coresidency is also negative and statistically significant, suggesting that as the elderly get richer, they tend to choose to live alone. The effect, again, is stronger for the 1995 and 2002 surveys than for the 1988 survey. As the pension income is measured in log terms, the marginal effects here indicate that at the mean log pension income, every 10 percent increase in real pension reduces the probability of coresidency by 0.14 percentage points in 1988, and 0.23 and 0.22 percentage points in 1995 and 2002, respectively. Using the mean probabilities, the elasticities can be calculated as $\frac{\partial \Pr}{\partial \log(pension)} \times \frac{1}{\Pr}$. The calculated elasticities are -0.018, -0.037, and -0.034 for the three years, respectively. These effects are very small.

Note that during the 1988–1995 period, the annual real pension increase was around 12 percent, while over the 1988–2002 period the annual pension increase was 11 percent (Table 11.3). Based on the elasticities and the annual changes in real pension income, the impact of pension increases on the change in the probabilities of coresidency can be calculated (Table 11.7). From 1988 to 1995, this effect results in a 0.22 percent increase in the probability of coresidency per annum using the elasticity of 1988 and a 0.44 percent increase in the probability per annum using the elasticity of 1995. Thus, over the seven-year period the impact of the increase in pension income on reduction in the probability of coresidency was 1.5 to 3.1 percentage points, which accounted for 12 to 25 percent of the total decline in coresidency. Similar calculations can be conducted for the 1988–2002 period, which result in a 0.20 percent and 0.37 percent increase per annum in the probability of coresidency using 1988 and 2002 elasticities, respectively. These annual impacts can be translated into a 2.8 to 5.2 percentage point change in the probability of coresidency over the 14-year period.

Relative to other studies, the effect of pension income on living arrangements in urban China is very low. For example, Costa (1997) estimates an elasticity of -0.77 for elderly veterans in America who retired in 1910. In another study, Costa (1999) finds that for older unmarried women over the

Table 11.7. *Impact of increase in pension income on coresidency (urban)*

	1988	1995	2002	1988–1995	1988–2002
Marginal effect	−0.014	−0.023	−0.022		
Mean probability of coresidency	0.778	0.622	0.647		
Elasticity	−0.018	−0.037	−0.034		
Annual change in pension				0.120	0.110
Annual change in probability (1988 elasticity)				−0.216	−0.198
Reduction in coresidency due to pension, 1988–1995				−1.512	−2.772
Annual change in probability (1995 or 2000 elasticity)				−0.444	−0.374
Reduction in coresidency due to pension, 1988–1995				−3.108	−5.236

1940–1950 period, the elasticity of a government pension on coresidency was around −0.17 to −0.23 for some states and −0.05 for other states, depending on the different policies implemented. Mutchler and Burr (1991) use the Survey of Income and Program Participation 1984 wave for the United States to study the living arrangements of unmarried individuals aged 55 and above and find a marginal effect of the log prior year's income on coresidency as a head of household to be −0.172. With the mean probability of 0.168, the estimated elasticity at the mean log income should be −2.8.

In general, males are more likely to live with relatives than their female counterparts. The effect, however, is not precisely estimated. Controlling for pension income, those with above a college education are more likely to live alone, but the effect is not statistically significant in the 1988 and 1995 surveys.

One of the most interesting effects is housing entitlement. The elderly living in a house that is rented or purchased under their own name were more likely to live alone in 1988 and 1995. The effect is very strong in 1988, when housing was in short supply. Those elderly with a house or flat distributed by his or her work unit (rented or owner occupied) were around 40 percent more likely to live alone than those who did not obtain a house from their work unit. The effect is reduced to 6 percent in 1995, but is still significant. In 2002 when housing availability was abundant, the effect became insignificant.

Table 11.8. *Decomposition of the change in probability of coresidency (urban)*

	Difference between 1988 and 1995		Difference between 1988 and 2002	
	Gap	Percentage of gap	Gap	Percentage of gap
Total difference	−0.127	100.00	−0.134	100.00
Age	−1.900	−1,496.72	−2.812	−2,121.13
Pension	−0.055	−43.09	−0.056	−41.96
Gender	−0.074	−57.95	−0.069	−52.19
Education	−0.004	−2.82	−0.005	−3.87
Housing	0.126	98.96	0.124	93.66
Region	−0.202	−159.46	−0.241	−181.62
Unexplained (constant)	1.982	1,561.08	2.926	2,207.13
	1,988	1,995	1,988	2,002
Predicted probability	0.766	0.638	0.766	0.633

As mentioned above, the model specified here omits the health condition of the elderly due to data availability, which may bias the results. To test the extent to which omitting a health variable biases the results, equation (1) is also estimated including a health indicator for the 2002 survey, in which such data are available. The results show that including the health indicator does not change the estimated results for the other variables.[6]

The results from the probit estimation are then used to decompose the difference in the probability of coresidency between 1988 and 1995, and between 1988 and 2002. Elderly living arrangements have changed very little since 1995, and, hence, it is not meaningful to decompose the difference. The results of the decomposition following equation (2) are reported in Table 11.8. Note that to make the decomposition consistent, Sichuan province is excluded from the 1995 and 2002 data as the 1988 survey did not include this province. The decomposition methodology followed does not decompose the difference in actual probabilities but that in predicted probabilities.

The results comparing both 1995 with 1988 and 2002 with 1988 seem to suggest that the effect of age contributes the most to the reduction in coresidency over time. Considering that over time the average age and its distribution did not change much (Table 11.5), the main component of the contribution is due to the change in the effect of age on coresidency. As shown in Figure 11.1, in both 1995 and 2002 elderly aged less than 70

---

[6] The results are available upon request from the authors.

were considerably less likely to coreside than their counterparts in 1988. This effect dominated the positive effect of aging on coresidency at age 70 and above. The significant effect of age on the reduction in coresidency indicates that elders who have the ability to handle day-to-day life value living alone (privacy) more now than they did in 1988, or, alternatively, as mentioned above, their real preference could be revealed better when the housing availability constraint was eliminated.

The other most important factor is the constant term, which measures the unexplained change. Offsetting the age effect, this effect contributes to the increase in the probability of coresidency. Unfortunately, apart from changes in individual preference and the impact of the change in social norms, it is hard to speculate the reasons for such a strong effect. The positive effect of the unexplained portion seems to indicate that the change in social norms does not work in the same direction as the reduction in the elderly's coresidency.

The regional effect also contributes considerably to the reduction. The effect is mainly due to the relationship between the rest of the provinces and the omitted category, Beijing. In 1988 elders in Beijing were more likely to coreside relative to elders in other provinces, whereas in 1995 and 2002 that effect was reversed. This may be related to the housing situation in Beijing, which perhaps improved more than in other regions.

The elderly's housing entitlement contributes to the increase in coresidency in the later period. As mentioned before, since the mid-1990s the housing supply may have ceased to be a constraint on household living arrangements and, hence, contributed to the increase in coresidency.

Surprisingly, the effect of pension income and the change in the impact of pension income on living arrangements play a less significant role in the change in the elderly's living arrangements than expected. If the effects are ranked by importance, income ranks a second last, just ahead of education, which plays no role in explaining the change in the elderly's living arrangements over the periods. The impact of gender plays a slightly larger role than the impact of income.

In summary, the effect of housing availability seems to play the most important role in the reduction of coresidency in urban China. This effect is observed mainly through the age effect, which reflects the difference in realized preferences of living alone between the 1988 and the later-year data and partly through the regional effect. On the other hand, as housing availability increases, the effect of housing entitlement is reduced, and its constraint on living arrangements declines. If the unexplained portion, in part, measures social norm change, the results seem to indicate that the change in social norms is in a direction that increases coresidency.

V. Conclusions

China has prematurely become an aging society at a relatively low income level. In the next 30 to 50 years the increase in the aging population may place a considerable strain on China's underdeveloped social welfare system. To ensure that elders receive sufficient and sustainable care, the extended family may play an important role through the elderly's living arrangements. This chapter found that over the last 14 years, the rate of elders living with their extended family in China declined significantly, and the change mainly occurred in the first half of the 1990s.

It was found that the main contributing factor to this decline seemed to be the increase in housing availability. In the 1980s, when housing was a constraint on individuals' living choices, the level of coresidency revealed from the data might not reflect real preferences. Once the housing constraint was eliminated, the revealed level of living arrangements reflected the real preference. The fact that, after the housing availability constraint was eliminated, the elderly's living arrangements changed very little from 1995 to 2000 strengthens this conclusion.

In addition, changes in social norms did not seem to work in the direction of reducing coresidency. Furthermore, although real pension income increased at around 10 percent per annum during the period studied, it did not seem to play as important a role in reducing coresidency as found in other studies.

These findings are quite comforting in that they confirm that housing reform has benefited elders in urban China by allowing them to choose their preferred living arrangements. In addition, the results seem to confirm that after 20-some years of economic reform that have stressed the role of individuals in the society, Eastern family values regarding financially taking care of elders in the family do not seem to have deteriorated.

Note that because of limitations of the data, it was not possible to study many interesting aspects of the elderly's living arrangements, in particular, the impact of children's characteristics on elders' living arrangements. These may have a certain impact on the conclusions drawn from this study.

Appendix Table 11A.1. *Sample size of each survey (urban)*

	1988	1995	2002
Individual (full sample)	31,827	21,694	20,632
Household (full sample)	9,009	6,931	6,835
Individual (working sample)	2,453	2,408	2,382
Household (working sample)	1,855	1,654	1,574

References

Agree, E. (1993), *Effects of Demographic Change on the Living Arrangements of the Elderly in Brazil: 1960–1980*, Durham, N.C.: Duke University, Ph.D. dissertation.

Andrade, F. C. D. and S. DeVos (2002), "An Analysis of Living Arrangements among Elderly Women in Brazil," unpublished manuscript.

Benjamin, D., L. Brandt, and S. Rozelle (2000), "Aging, Well-Being, and Social Security in Rural North China," *Population and Development Review*, 26(supp.), 89–116.

Borsch-Supan, A., V. Hajivassiliou, L. J. Kotlikoff, and J. N. Morris (1992), "Health, Children, and Elderly Living Arrangements: A Multiperiod-Multinomial Probit Model with Unobserved Heterogeneity and Autocorrelated Errors," in David A. Wise, ed., *Topics in the Economics of Aging*, Chicago: University of Chicago Press.

Cai, F., J. Giles, and X. Meng (2006), "How Well Do Children Insure Parents against Low Retirement Income: An Analysis Using Survey Data from Urban China," *Journal of Public Economics*, 90(12), 2229–2255.

Cai, F. and X. Meng (2003), "Demographic Change, Pension Reform, and the Sustainability of the Pension System," *Comparative Studies*, 10, 179–206 (in Chinese).

Chan, A. and J. DaVanzo (1996), "Ethnic Difference in Parents' Coresidence with Adult Children in Peninsular Malaysia," *Journal of Cross-Cultural Geronotology*, 11(1), 29–59.

Costa, D. L. (1997), "Displacing the Family: Union Army Pensions and Elderly Living Arrangements," *Journal of Political Economy*, 105(6), 1269–1292.

Costa, D. L. (1999), "A House of Her Own: Old Age Assistance and the Living Arrangements of Older Nonmarried Women," *Journal of Public Economics*, 72, 39–59.

Davis-Friedmann, D. (1991), *Long Lives*, 2nd and expanded edition, Stanford: Stanford University Press.

Doiron, D. and W. C. Riddell (1994), "The Impact of Unionization on Male-Female Earnings Differences in Canada," *Journal of Human Resources*, 29(2), 504–534.

Eichen, M. and M. Zhang (1993), "Annex: The 1988 Household Sample Survey – Data Description and Availability," in K. Griffin and R. Zhao, eds., *The Distribution of Income in China*, New York: St. Martin's Press.

Engelhardt, G. V., J. Gruber, and C. D. Perry (2002), "Social Security and Elderly Living Arrangements: Evidence from the Social Security Notch," unpublished manuscript.

Hoerger, T. J., G. A. Picone, and F. A. Sloan (1996), "Public Subsidies, Private Provision of Care and Living Arrangements of the Elderly," *Review of Economics and Statistics*, 78(3), 428–440.

Kan, K., A. Park, and M. Chang (2001), "A Dynamic Model of Elderly Living Arrangements in Taiwan," unpublished manuscript.

Murton, T. (2002), "Pension Reform in China: Funding the Transition," Department of Family and Community Services, Australia, unpublished manuscript.

Mutchler, J. E. and J. A. Burr (1991), "A Longitudinal Analysis of Household and Non-household Living Arrangements in Later Life," *Demography*, 28(3), 375–390.

National Bureau of Statistics (annual), *China Statistical Yearbook*, Beijing: China Statistics Press.

Palloni, A. (2001), "Living Arrangements of Older Persons," *Population Bulletin of the United Nations*, Special Issue, 42/43, 54–110.

Palloni, A. and S. De Vos (2003), "Elderly's Residential Arrangements: A Comparative Analysis," report prepared for the Population Division, United Nations.

Pezzin, L. E. and B. S. Schone (1999), "Intergenerational Household Formation, Female Labor Supply and Informal Caregiving: A Bargaining Approach," *Journal of Human Resources*, 34(3), 475–503.

Raymo, J. and X. Yu (2000), "Income of the Urban Elderly in Post-Reform China: Political Capital, Human Capital and the State," *Social Science Research*, 29, 1–24.

Saunders, P., P. Guo, G. Chen, L. Sun, K. Zhang, and A. Shang (2003), "Indicators of Poverty and Well-Being among the Aged in China: Preliminary Results," Social Policy Research Centre, University of New South Wales, unpublished manuscript.

Saunders, P. and T. M. Smeeding (1998), "How do the Elderly in Taiwan Fare Cross-Nationally? Evidence from the Luxembourg Income Study Project," SPRC Discussion Paper No. 81.

Schwartz, S., S. Danziger, and E. Smolensky (1984), "The Choice of Living Arrangements by the Elderly," in Henry J. Aaron and Gary Burtless, eds., *Retirement and Economic Behavior*, Washington, D.C.: Brookings Institution.

State Council, People's Republic of China (1991), "The State Council Announcement on Continuing Actively and Steadily Implementing Urban Housing Reform," June 7 (in Chinese), http://www.law110.com/law/guowuyuan/.

Ulker, A. (2003), "Household Structure and Consumption Insurance of the Elderly," unpublished manuscript.

Whiteford, P. (2003), "From Enterprise Protection to Social Protection: Social Security Reform in China," *Global Social Policy*, 3(1), 45–77.

World Bank (1997), *China 2020: Old Age Security*, Washington D. C.: World Bank.

Zeng, Y. and Z. Wang (2003), "Dynamics of Family and Elderly Living Arrangements in China: New Lessons Learned from the 2000 Census," *China Review*, 3(2), 95–119.

Zhang, K. D. (2000), *Textbook on Elderly Law*, Beijing: China Encyclopaedia Press (in Chinese).

TWELVE

The Impact of Village-Specific Factors on Household Income in Rural China

Hiroshi Sato

I. Introduction

A. Setting the Agenda

In contrast to other chapters in this book that focus on the influence of individual and household factors on income inequality, this chapter places special emphasis on the impact of community on household income in rural China. The analytical focus is, first, on the significance of physical infrastructure, human capital, and social capital at the community level, and, second, on the role of public management and public policy at the local level. The estimation results of household income using a hierarchical linear model demonstrate that community-level variables have significant effects on household income, and their impact varies according to the type of community. Regarding public policy, the findings of this chapter suggest the importance of institution building to cultivate governing ability for rural cadres, to promote social stability, and to develop mechanisms to meet local needs for public services.

In the context of this chapter, the term "community level" refers to the administrative villages (*xingzhengcun*) that are at the lowest level of the party/governmental hierarchy (hereafter referred to as "village"). In relation to the main theme of the entire volume, this chapter focuses on the factors at the village level for two reasons, as follows.

First, by looking more closely at the influence of village characteristics we will be able to provide a fuller picture of the determinants of income inequality in rural China. As previous research such as that by Narayan and Pritchett (1999) has noted, household income depends on community-level factors in the rural areas of developing countries. Thus, it will be interesting to examine the type of community factors that affect household income in the Chinese context. Instead of using a simple location dummy variable as is the case in most previous studies, we examine community characteristics in some detail because our survey contains information regarding the villages where the sample households are located. In this context, this chapter complements Chapters 3 and 4, which emphasize the critical importance of location on income inequality.

Second, bearing in mind the multilayered and highly decentralized local administrative/fiscal system in China, we believe that the role of government and public policy regarding income inequality should be examined not only at the macrolevel but also at the mesolevel, that is, at the county and subcounty levels (township and village). In fact, townships and villages have assumed an important responsibility for providing local public goods. As a result, large disparities in the provision of local public goods are observed, even among villages in the same county (see Chapter 13 of this volume).[1] We assume that such regional disparity is one of the causes of regional income inequality in rural China.

It may be claimed that the deepening of marketization in rural China throughout the 1990s, for example, the development of rural-urban migration and the privatization of collectively owned rural enterprises, has weakened the influence of village-level factors on households' economic activities. It may also be argued that recent political and economic reforms in rural areas, including the tax reform and the restructuring of the local administrative system, tend to weaken the direct influence over households of the political economy at the village level. We believe, however, that an investigation focusing on the village level remains important for the following reasons. First, the progress of marketization and political and economic reforms has involved great regional disparities. Second, the progress of marketization has not necessarily reduced the importance of formal institutional arrangements in influencing household income, although it has redefined the role of village management. For example, instead of allocating economic resources directly, the village might have become important as a provider of local public goods, which both directly and indirectly influence household income. Third, by shedding light on the village, we will be able to examine the role of informal institutional factors on household income.

---

[1] The institutional cause of large disparities in the village-level political economy is that the administrative village is regarded as a "self-governing community" (*nongcun jiceng zizhi zuzhi*), not a formal governmental apparatus, in spite of its de facto position as a local government.

This chapter is structured as follows. In the remainder of this section, we discuss previous research and the main data sources. Section II presents the analytical framework and the strategy for empirical study. In Section III we estimate household income functions employing village-specific factors. We then elaborate how the characteristics of village management and public policy affect household income. Section IV concludes the chapter.

B. Previous Research

Researchers who have conducted field surveys in rural China have been surprised by the substantial economic disparities among villages within the same county or even in the same township. Consequently, the literature has focused on the importance of mesolevel disparities. For example, based on a village survey in Handan (Hebei), Knight and Li (1997) discussed the "cumulative causation" of microregional economic development, which resulted in economic disparities among villages in the same district. Using data collected in suburban Tianjin, Perkins (2002) demonstrated that large economic variations existed among villages in a township, including wide differences in size, economic structure, and levels of well-being. Sato (2003) provided a typology of market development at the mesolevel, based on a series of village and household surveys in five provinces.[2]

Studies based on the mesolevel surveys can identify unique regional factors that influence income inequality. For example, Perkins (2002) revealed that intervillage economic disparities were linked closely to historical variations in the survey area. It is difficult, however, to generalize about findings derived from village-based surveys. In contrast, quantitative studies using large micro-datasets allow generalization of results. Such studies generally investigate region-specific factors by employing simple regional or geographical dummy variables; as a result, they cannot shed light on the socioeconomic factors that underlie such dummy variables. This chapter attempts to fill out the simple regional dummies by introducing other region-specific characteristics.

C. Data

The main data source for this analysis is the 2002 CHIP survey and the village (administrative village) survey conducted simultaneously with the

---

[2] Many qualitative studies focus on a single village or several villages (see, e.g., Friedman et al. 1991; Huang 1985; Zhongguo Shehui Kexueyuan Jingji Yanjiusuo "Wubao" Diaocha Ketizu 1999).

household survey.[3] A detailed illustration of the household survey appears in Chapter 1 and the Appendix of this volume, thus in this section we provide only a brief description of the village survey. We collected officially recorded statistical data and other village-level information on the 961 villages where the 9,200 sample households are located by circulating a questionnaire to village cadres (see Appendix Table 12A.1 which shows the distribution of the sample villages in the surveyed provinces).[4] As described in the Appendix of this volume, the sample villages of the National Bureau of Statistics(NBS) household survey were selected in each province by the provincial bureau of the NBS. The sample households were then drawn from each sample village (usually 10 households for each village).

For the basic village statistics, we asked the statisticians to provide the officially recorded figures for 2002 and 1998. For the remaining quantitative data that are not officially recorded and for the historical data, we used the figures provided by the village cadres. Qualitative information on the villages' socioeconomic conditions was also provided by the village cadres.

Because of the small number of sample households in each village, caution is required when using different data sets from the village and the household surveys, especially with regard to village-level variables aggregated from household data. As income-related data from the village survey are consistent with the data aggregated from the household survey, it is safe to argue that the income of the sample households can represent that of the sample villages.[5] This does not, however, hold for other variables. Therefore, for village characteristics, we avoid using aggregated variables with the exception of two variables for which no data are available from the village survey: the degree of social stability evaluated by the heads of households and the village's average education level. We believe that the bias is relatively small for the former variable because, in the context of rural China, villagers will share similar views about their village's social conditions. Concerning the latter variable, we introduce a village-level variable that is not the simple aggregation of the household level. It should be noted that, for the requirements

---

[3] The administrative village survey was funded partly by the Japan Society for the Promotion of Science (JSPS) and Hitotsubashi University.

[4] Note that the work sample for empirical study has only 9,104 households because of missing values for village-level variables (e.g., village expenditure in 1998).

[5] The village mean income for 2002 collected from the village questionnaire has a strong correlation with the village mean income aggregated from the household survey ($r = 0.809$, $n = 951$).

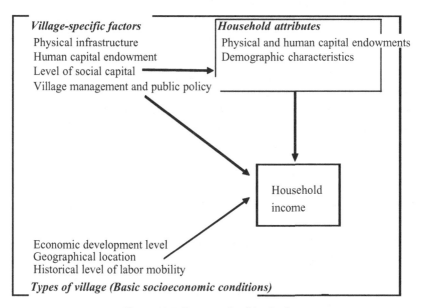

Figure 12.1 Framework of the Study.

of the village-mean centered modeling, several village-level variables aggregated from the household data will also be employed.

II. Framework for the Empirical Study

A. Analytical Framework

Figure 12.1 introduces the analytical framework. Household income, that is, the dependent variable used throughout this chapter, is the log of the per capita annual net income in 2002 (measured in yuan, in 2002 prices) (Table 12.1). The definition of household income employed is consistent with the NBS's official peasant income statistics.[6] We attempt to determine the magnitude and direction of village-specific factors on income inequality by estimating the household income function. As shown in Figure 12.1, we divide the village-specific factors into four categories: physical infrastructure, human capital endowment, level of social capital, and factors relating to village management and public policy at the village level. It is assumed that the effects of village-specific factors vary according to the basic

---

[6] The rental value of housing is not included. See Chapter 1 and the Appendix of this book for detailed discussion of the definition of income.

Table 12.1. *Description and summary statistics of variables used in this chapter*

Variables	Description	Mean (standard deviation)	Data source
Dependent variable			
Per capita income for 2002	The log of per capita annual net income based on NBS definition (yuan, 2002 prices)	7.683 (0.705) [2,755.73 (2,319.16)]	H
Village-level variables			
[a-1: Physical infrastructure] Equipped with electricity before the reform era	Dummy variable for the periods when the village was equipped with electricity	0.640 (0.480)	V
[a-2: Physical infrastructure] Share of irrigated farmland	The logit-transformed share of irrigated farmland in total farmland, 2002	1.789 (4.873) [0.614 (0.362)]	V
[b-1: Human capital] Share of junior high graduates	The share of adult population that has completed junior high school or a higher educational level, 2002	0.621 (0.173)	H
[b-2: Human capital] Village-mean years of education	Average number of years of education of working-age adults (16–65 years old)	7.110 (1.190)	H
[c-1/d-5: Social capital/village management] Social stability	Average of household head's evaluation of the degree of social stability in the village (scale from 1 to 10)	7.552 (1.008)	H
[d-1: Village management] Collective economic entities	Dummy for villages managing collective economic entities in 2002	0.262 (0.440)	V
[d-2: Village management] Inward investment	Dummy for villages having inward investment projects attracted by village cadres until 2002	0.114 (0.318)	V
[d-3: Village management] Irrigation services by the village	Dummy for villages providing irrigation services using collectively owned facilities in 2002	0.263 (0.440)	V
[d-4: Village management] Village budget for public services, 1998	The log of per capita expenditure for public services in 1998 (yuan, 2002 prices)	2.066 (1.612) [29.48 (86.67)]	V
[e-1: External shock] Natural disaster	Dummy for villages suffering natural disaster in 2002	0.514 (0.500)	V

Variables	Description	Mean (standard deviation)	Data source
[e-2] Village-mean farmland	Average area of per capita contracted farmland, 2002 (*mu*)	1.425 (1.512)	H
[e-3] Village-mean fixed assets	Average value of per capita productive fixed assets, 2002 (yuan)	1245.63 (1,699.44)	H
Types of village (Basic socioeconomic conditions)			
[f-1: Level of economic development] Nonagricultural employment share	The logit-transformed share of the labor force in the village that is mainly employed in the nonagricultural sector, 2002 (developed villages = with more than 30 percent share; underdeveloped villages = 30 percent or less share)	−1.027 (6.677) [0.330 (0.221)]	V
[f-2: Geographical location] Nonmountainous villages	Dummy for villages located in nonmountainous area	0.781 (0.414)	V
[f-3: Historical level of labor mobility] Development of out-migration	Dummy for the degree of development of out-migration at the beginning of the 1990s	0.400 (0.490)	V
Household-level variables			
Farmland (in raw score form)	Per capita contracted farmland, 2002 (*mu*)	1.425 (1.856)	H
Village-mean centered farmland	The deviation of the household's farmland from the village-mean		H
Fixed assets	The log of the per capita value of fixed productive assets at the time of purchase, 2002 (yuan, in 2002 prices)	5.708 (2.357) [1,251.50 (3,634.32)]	H
Village-mean centered fixed assets	The deviation of the household's value of fixed assets from the village-mean		H
Education level (in raw score form)	Average years of education of working-age adults, 2002	7.065 (2.023)	H
Village-mean centered education level	The deviation of the household's education level from the village-mean		H

(*continued*)

Table 12.1 (*continued*)

Variables	Description	Mean (standard deviation)	Data source
Party membership	Dummy for households with Communist Party members, 2002	0.211 (0.408)	H
Average age of working-age adults	Average age of working-age adults, 2002	37.670 (7.47)	H
Household size	Total number of household members, 2002	4.141 (1.280)	H
Dependency ratio	Total number of household members divided by the number of household members of working age, 2002	1.416 (0.466)	H
Having income earned outside the village	Dummy for households with income earned outside the village in 2002	0.312 (0.463)	H
Number of observations		9,104	

Notes:
1. H indicates that the data are taken from the household dataset, and V indicates they are from the administrative village dataset
2. Figures in brackets show mean and standard deviation (in parentheses) of the original value of the relevant variable.

socioeconomic conditions of the village. To sort out the differences in the effects of the village-specific factors among the different types of villages, we use measurements of the level of economic development (as measured by the share of village labor employed mainly in the nonagricultural sector), geographical location, and historical level of labor mobility.

As we are interested in the effects of group (village) membership of households on their income, we employ a two-level hierarchical linear model instead of ordinary least squares (OLS). The first (micro-) level is the household level, and the second (macro-) level is the village level.[7] In this model, households are grouped into villages, and village characteristics are assumed to exercise a common influence on all households within the village.

When there exists one household level of characteristics (x) and one village level of characteristics (z) that influence the per capita income (y)

[7] For the methodology of the hierarchical linear model, see Kreft and De Leeuw (1998) and Raudenbush and Bryk (2002).

(in logarithm throughout the chapter), the first (household) level model is written as follows:

$$y_{ij} = \beta_{0j} + \beta_{1j}x_{ij} + \varepsilon_{ij}, \tag{1a}$$

where ε is the micro-error term, subscript i is for the household, and subscript j is for the village. The second (village) level model that includes village characteristics (z) is described as follows:

$$\beta_{0j} = \gamma_{00} + \gamma_{01}z_j + \delta_{0j}, \tag{1b}$$

$$\beta_{1j} = \gamma_{10} + \gamma_{11}z_j + \delta_{1j}, \tag{1c}$$

where subscript j indicates the village, and δ is the macro-error term.

Implicit in this formulation is the assumption that the relationship between household income and household characteristics depends on features of the village. So, for example, the returns to education may differ between villages with higher and lower levels of development.

Substitution provides the following two-level hierarchical linear model:

$$\begin{aligned}
y_{ij} &= \gamma_{00} + \gamma_{01}z_j + \delta_{0j} + (\gamma_{10} + \gamma_{11}z_j + \delta_{1j})x_{ij} + \varepsilon_{ij} \\
&= \gamma_{00} + \gamma_{10}x_{ij} + \gamma_{01}z_j + \gamma_{11}z_jx_{ij} + (\delta_{0j} + \delta_{1j}x_{ij} + \varepsilon_{ij}).
\end{aligned} \tag{2}$$

Equation (2) illustrates that per capita income y is a function of the following components: overall intercept γ_{00} that demonstrates the grand-mean effect; the main effect of village characteristics $z(\gamma_{01})$; the overall slope γ_{10} (the average x–y regression slope across villages) that represents the main effect of household characteristics x; the cross-level interaction of household and village characteristics (γ_{11}); and random effects $(\delta_{0j} + \delta_{1j}x_{ij} + \varepsilon_{ij})$.[8]

Equation (2) can be written as the combination of the fixed part

$$E(y_{ij}) = \gamma_{00} + \gamma_{10}x_{ij} + \gamma_{01}z_j + \gamma_{11}z_jx_{ij}, \tag{3a}$$

and the random part

$$y_{ij} - E(y_{ij}) = \delta_{0j} + \delta_{1j}x_{ij} + \varepsilon_{ij}. \tag{3b}$$

In a hierarchical linear model, the first level variables can be measured either in their original levels (raw score form) or as deviations from the village mean (group mean centered form). We conduct estimations using equations in both raw score form and village-mean centered form. A village-mean centered first level variable $\bar{\bar{x}}_{ij}$ is equal to $\bar{\bar{x}}_{ij} = x_{ij} - \bar{x}_j$, where x_{ij} is

---

[8] As for random effects, δ_{0j} indicates the deviation of each village from the grand mean and δ_{1j} indicates the unique increment to the overall slope associated with village j.

the raw score for household i in village j and $\bar{x}_j$ is the village-mean of the variable for village j.

Both approaches are instructive. If one wants to explain as much variation in the dependent variable as possible, the raw score form is useful. If one is interested in particular village-level effects and cross-level interactions between the village and the household levels, a village-mean centered model with the reintroduction of village-mean variables is appropriate (Kreft and De Leeuw 1998). In the following empirical study, we will first overview the type of household- and village-level characteristics that influence household income using the raw score form, and then examine the second-level effects and cross-level interactions employing the village-mean centered model.

B. Village-Level Variables

As summarized in Table 12.1, we employ the following village-level variables:

[a] *Physical infrastructure:* Previous research emphasized the importance of physical infrastructure for regional economic development and poverty alleviation in developing countries (Antle 1983; Lipton and Ravallion 1995). We concentrate on electricity, a type of small-scale physical infrastructure that is common to almost all villages but introduced at different times historically, as an indicator of the overall level of development of small-scale physical infrastructure. Specifically, we introduce a dummy variable for the periods when the villages were first equipped with electricity: 1 = 1949–1979; 0 = after 1980 [a-1]. We assume that this variable positively correlates with household income.

In addition, as an additional indicator of the level of agricultural infrastructure we employ the logit-transformed share of farmland that is irrigated in 2002 [a-2].[9]

[b] *Village-level human capital:* The literature and other chapters in this volume have confirmed that, along with the marketization, the return to education has increased substantially in rural China (see, e.g., Chapter 4 of this volume; Walder 2002; Zhang, Huang, and Rozelle 2002). We assume that a higher average educational attainment at the village level has a positive effect on household income because it will induce efficient economic interactions among villagers, assisting villagers to exchange useful information and skills.

As the indicator of village-level human capital, we introduce two variables. One is the share of the adult population (over 16 years old) that has

---

[9] Logit-transformed share of farmland R is defined as $R = \ln (r / (1 - r))$, where r is the original figure for the share of irrigated farmland.

completed junior high school or a higher educational level, which is used in the raw score form model [b-1]. The other is the average number of years of education of working-age adults (16–65 years old), which is used in the village-mean centered form model [b-2].

[c] *Village-level social capital:* Generally, social capital is conceptualized as the level of trust, the degree to which common norms are shared, and the density of associational activities among community members (Dasgupta and Serageldin 2000). Narayan and Pritchett (1999), using a village survey in Tanzania, discuss how household income depends greatly on the village-level social capital, specifically the extent and characteristics of the villagers' associational activities. According to their study, the proximate channels through which village social capital influences household income are better public services, greater use of modern technology, more community activity, and greater use of credit.

It would be interesting to examine whether such social factors exhibit positive externalities in rural China. Given the general context of rural China and the framework of this chapter, however, the link between community-level associational activities and household income may not be relevant. This is because such activities are not common in general and because the administrative village is not necessarily a suitable unit of observation for such activities.[10] Instead, we focus on the degree of social stability at the village level as village-specific social capital, considering that social stability can be regarded as the basis for other social factors. Following previous research such as Knack and Keefer (1997), we assume a causal linkage between social stability, higher incentives and lower risks for economic activities, and higher income.

As the proxy of social stability, we asked two attitudinal questions to the head of household. These questions are: "Do you think that there is a good relationship among households belonging to different small village groups (*cunmin xiaozu*)?" and "Do you think that there is a good relationship among households belonging to different family groups?" To measure social stability, we categorized the answers into points ranging from five (strongly agree) to one (strongly disagree), and then summed these numbers to create a scale with a maximum of 10.

Analysis of social capital inevitably encounters the problem of endogeneity, because social stability may be the result rather than the cause of good economic conditions in the village. The justification for introducing this

---

[10] The lineage organization (*zongzu*), that is, the traditional Chinese patrilineal descent, or the natural village (*zirancun*) would be a more suitable unit for analysis, although the administrative village and the natural village sometimes overlap, especially in North China.

variable into the cross-section analysis is that the sociocultural characteristics of villages tend to be stable over time.

[d] *Characteristics of village management:* Activities of the village authority are expected to have both a direct and an indirect influence on household income. While the role of the village in China is rather complicated and multidimensional, we can categorize the role of village management as follows: (1) village as an economic agent, (2) village as a provider of local public goods, and (3) village as a mediator of conflicts within the community.

Since the 1980s one of the unique characteristics of Chinese villages has been their role as an economic agent. First, villages have been owners and operators of rural enterprises and other collective businesses (see, e.g., Chen 1998; Oi 1999). Acting as an economic agent in this manner, the village can directly provide employment opportunities. Many village-level collective economic entities have disappeared under fierce market competition and the wave of privatization of rural industries. Nevertheless, some villages have kept managing collective economic entities. To capture this factor, we compile a dummy variable that indicates whether the village has a collective economic entity (enterprises and other business entities) [d-1].[11] It should be noted that former village-owned enterprises that were privatized in the 1990s are also included because many such enterprises keep informal relationships with the village. Second, villages have recently been inclined to mediate economic opportunities for villagers rather than directly operate collective businesses. To capture the activity of the village in this manner, we employ a dummy variable indicating whether the village cadres have attracted any investment projects from outside the village up to 2002 [d-2].

Concerning the role of the village as the provider of local public goods, we introduce the following two variables. First, as an indicator of production-related public services, we employ a dummy variable indicating whether the village provides irrigation services using collectively owned irrigation facilities [d-3]. Second, as a proxy of the level of local public goods, we employ the log of the per capita expenditure in the administrative village budget [d-4]. This includes expenditures on production-related services, education, public health, and other public services. To avoid the problem of endogeneity and to examine how the initial state of the provision of local public goods influences subsequent economic outcomes, we use the village budget statistics for 1998.

---

[11] The term "economic entity" here refers to *jingji shiti* in Chinese, which means generally an economic unit engaged in business activities.

Village cadres formally and informally act as mediators between villagers with different interests. In this sense the above-mentioned degree of social stability at the village level can also be regarded as an indicator of the governing ability of the village [c-1/d-5].

[e] *Other village-level variables:* In addition to these village-specific variables, we introduce a dummy variable for villages that suffered from a natural disaster in 2002 to control the impact of external shocks on households [e-1]. Also, village-mean variables for farmland [e-2] and productive fixed assets [e-3] are used in the village-mean centered estimations.

[f] *Types of village:* As mentioned above, to control for the different effects of village-level variables in the different types of villages, we classify the sample villages according to the following three criteria.[12]

First, as the proxy of the overall level of economic development, we introduce the logit-transformed share of nonagricultural employment in 2002 [f-1]. Nonagricultural employment share is defined as the share of the total labor force in the village that is mainly employed in the nonagricultural sector.[13] Using this measurement, we also group the villages into underdeveloped villages and developed villages. Underdeveloped villages are villages with a lower nonagricultural employment share (less than the median, that is, 30 percent or less). Developed villages have a higher share (more than 30 percent). Second, regarding the geographical location, we introduce a dummy variable for nonmountainous villages [f-2]. Third, to capture the historical level of labor mobility, we employ a dummy variable for the villages where approximately more than 10 percent of the labor force worked outside their home township for more than one month at the beginning of the 1990s [f-3].

C. Household-Level Variables

For the household-level model, two sets of explanatory variables are used (Table 12.1). First, for cross-referencing, we introduce a set of basic household attributes following the regression estimates in Chapter 4 of this volume (see Tables 4.1 and 4.3): contracted farmland, productive fixed

---

[12] Regarding the typology of villages, we refer to the historical study by Huang. In order to examine village-state relations in North China in the twentieth century, he classified 33 Mantetsu-surveyed villages according to the level of commercialization and labor mobility (see appendix to Huang 1985).

[13] As official village-level documents no longer have reported statistics on employment structure, the figures are based on estimations by village cadres. Logit transformation is made in the same way as that for the share of irrigated farmland.

assets, education level of working-age adults, Communist Party membership, average age of working-age adults, household size, and dependency
ratio (ratio of total household members to working-age adults). Second, we
introduce a set of village-mean centered variables for contracted farmland,
productive fixed assets, and education level of working-age adults employed
for village-mean centered equations.

For our empirical study, in addition to the above-mentioned household
attributes, we need to control the degree to which each household is independent from the village-level political economy. For this purpose, we introduce
a dummy variable indicating whether or not the household had any income
earned outside the village.

III. Empirical Results

In this section we first confirm the magnitude of the intervillage disparity
in household income, and second, we describe the basic findings of the
household income function using the hierarchical linear model.

A. The Magnitude of Village-Level Factors

To confirm the magnitude of the overall effect of village-specific factors
on household income, we first estimate the following intercept-only model
(the one-way ANOVA with random effects) that contains only the dependent
variable (y_{ij}), and no explanatory variables:[14]

$$y_{ij} = \gamma_{00} + \delta_{0j} + \varepsilon_{ij}, \tag{4}$$

The fixed effect γ_{00} demonstrates the average of village mean income (in
logarithm). Two random effects δ_{0j} and ε_{ij} indicate the variance components at the village level (intervillage variance) and household level (intravillage variance), respectively. We can thus decompose the total variation in
household income into variations between and within villages.

Table 12.2 reports the estimation results. The intraclass correlation, that is,
the contribution ratio of intervillage variance to total variance, demonstrates
that about 42 percent of the total variance of per capita income is explained
by the intervillage variance. As is shown in the latter half of the table, the
contribution ratio of intervillage variance is larger for mountainous villages
and developed villages, which suggests that the magnitude of intervillage

---

[14] This is the combined model of the household-level model $y_{ij} = \beta_{0j} + \varepsilon_{ij}$ and the
village-level model $\beta_{0j} = \gamma_{00} + \delta_{0j}$.

Table 12.2. *Magnitude of the intervillage disparity in rural household income, 2002*

Dependent variable: Log of per capita income in 2002		Variance components
1. Whole villages	[$N = 9,104$, 956 villages]	
Intervillage variance		0.208
Intravillage variance		0.289
Intraclass correlation		0.42
(Contribution ratio of intervillage variance to total variance)		
2. Intraclass correlation by the basic socioeconomic conditions of villages		
A. Level of economic development measured by the nonagricultural employment share		
Underdeveloped villages	[$N = 4,469$, 486 villages]	0.30
Developed villages	[$N = 4,635$, 470 villages]	0.49
B. Geographical location		
Mountainous villages	[$N = 1,995$, 201 villages]	0.44
Nonmountainous villages	[$N = 7,109$, 755 villages]	0.38

Note: Intraclass correlation is calculated as intervillage variance / (intervillage variance + intravillage variance).

disparity does not simply decrease along with the level of regional economic development.

B. Overview of the Estimation Results

Table 12.3 summarizes the results of the two-level hierarchical linear models for household income, employing the village- and household-level explanatory variables listed in Table 12.1. The first column of the table is the baseline estimation using the village-mean centered form, which includes village-mean centered household-level variables on the endowments of physical/human capital and other household-level variables, village-mean variables for physical/human capital, and indicators of the basic socioeconomic conditions of the village. This specification is used as the baseline to confirm

Table 12.3. *Estimation of the determinants of household income, 2002*

Dependent variable: Log of per capita income in 2002	(1) Baseline (Village-mean centered form)	(2) Full specification (Village-mean centered form)	(3) Full specification (Raw score form)
Village level			
Equipped with electricity before the reform era		0.089*** (0.025)	0.090*** (0.026)
Share of irrigated farmland		0.055 (0.039)	0.003 (0.003)
Share of junior high school graduates			0.160** (0.074)
Social stability		0.029*** (0.010)	0.031*** (0.011)
Collective economic entities		0.062** (0.026)	0.083*** (0.026)
Irrigation service by the village		0.073*** (0.026)	0.076*** (0.026)
Inward investment		0.024 (0.033)	0.024 (0.033)
Village budget for public services, 1998		0.024*** (0.008)	0.029*** (0.008)
Natural disaster		−0.075*** (0.022)	−0.074*** (0.023)
Village-mean years of education	0.072*** (0.011)	0.059*** (0.010)	
Village-mean farmland	0.036*** (0.009)	0.041*** (0.009)	
Village-mean fixed assets	0.000*** (0.000)	0.000*** (0.000)	
Nonagricultural employment share	0.041*** (0.008)	0.342*** (0.060)	0.039*** (0.008)
Nonmountainous area	0.225*** (0.032)	0.135*** (0.034)	0.158*** (0.035)
Development of out-migration	−0.111*** (0.024)	−0.113*** (0.023)	−0.109*** (0.023)
Household level			
Farmland			0.076*** (0.007)
Farmland squared			−0.001*** (0.0003)
Fixed assets			0.012*** (0.003)
Education level			0.011 (0.013)

Dependent variable: Log of per capita income in 2002	(1) Baseline (Village-mean centered form)	(2) Full specification (Village-mean centered form)	(3) Full specification (Raw score form)
Education level squared			0.002**
			(0.0009)
Village-mean centered education level	0.038***	0.034***	
	(0.004)	(0.004)	
Village-mean centered farmland	0.057***	0.057***	
	(0.005)	(0.005)	
Village-mean centered fixed assets	0.000***	0.000***	
	(0.000)	(0.000)	
Average age of working-age adults	0.018***	0.017***	0.017***
	(0.006)	(0.006)	(0.006)
Average age of working-age adults squared	−0.0002***	−0.0002***	−0.0002***
	(0.000)	(0.000)	(0.000)
Party membership	0.133***	0.132***	0.132***
	(0.014)	(0.014)	(0.014)
Household size	−0.227***	−0.227***	−0.229***
	(0.024)	(0.024)	(0.024)
Household size squared	0.013***	0.013***	0.013***
	(0.002)	(0.002)	(0.002)
Dependency ratio	−0.104***	−0.104***	−0.099***
	(0.013)	(0.013)	(0.013)
Having income earned outside the village	0.126***	0.128***	0.131***
	(0.014)	(0.014)	(0.014)
Constant	7.290***	6.974***	7.170***
	(0.157)	(0.176)	(0.170)
Random-effects parameters			
Village-level variance	0.077	0.070	0.073
	(0.005)	(0.005)	(0.005)
Household-level variance	0.253	0.253	0.252
	(0.004)	(0.004)	(0.004)
Deviance	14,838.67	14,818.48	14,800.23
Number of observations	9,104	9,104	9,104
Number of villages	956	956	956

Notes:

1. All the equations are fitted with fixed slopes for the first-level variables.

2. Standard errors are provided in parentheses. The symbols *, **, and *** denote statistical significance at the 10 percent, 5 percent, and 1 percent levels, respectively.

3. Province dummies are included in all of the equations, but are not reported here. About half of the province dummies are statistically significant, which illustrates the significance of the location factor.

the effects of household-level factors and to elaborate the effects of village-specific factors in the different types of villages. The second column is the full specification using the village-mean centered form, which adds all the village-specific variables to the baseline specification. The third column is the full specification using the raw score form.[15]

Before examining the effects of village-specific factors, it will be convenient to confirm whether the findings on household-level variables are consistent with other chapters of this volume. As mentioned above, we refer to the income function using OLS in Chapter 4 of this volume (see Table 4.3). Table 12.3 demonstrates that the results of the baseline estimation and the full specification using the raw score form equation are basically consistent with Chapter 4.[16]

We now turn to the full specification to determine the effects of village-specific factors. The results from the village-mean centered form and from the raw score form are basically the same and suggest the following facts.

First, village-level physical infrastructure and human capital endowment result in positive externalities on household income. Households living in villages equipped with electricity before the reform era enjoyed approximately 9 percent higher income in 2002. Variables for the education level of the village are positive and statistically significant both in the raw score and in the village-mean centered equation. In the village-mean centered equation, it is revealed that adding one year of education to a village's average educational standard raises the villagers' income by approximately 6 percent.

Second, the degree of social stability, proxy of village social capital, has positive and statistically significant effects on household income. If the measure of stable social relationships rises by one point, the villagers' income rises by around 3 percent. As mentioned above, the result can also be understood as implying the significance of the village cadres' ability to promote good social relationships within the village.

Third, estimation results for the variables relating to village management, on the whole, suggest that public management and public policy at the village level play a significant role in income inequality. All other factors being equal, having a village-level collective economic entity raises the villagers' income by 6–8 percent. Both of the full specification equations demonstrate

---

[15] All the equations are fitted with fixed slopes for household-level variables. This is because our trials to fit random slopes for household-level variables show that the variances of the slopes are not significant and because addition of random slopes will make the fixed part of the parameters more unstable.

[16] Though it is not reported in the table, we also conducted OLS estimation with robust standard error for clustering at the village level and confirmed that the results are consistent with the hierarchical linear equations.

that a larger village expenditure on public services in the past has brought an increase in the villagers' current income. Also, the share of irrigated land in the total arable and permanent cropland and providing collective irrigation management through the village's use of collectively owned facilities have a positive and significant effect on household income. Contrary to these factors, the presence in a village of investment projects attracted by village cadres reveals no statistically significant effect, though the sign is, as expected, positive.

Fourth, basic socioeconomic conditions of the village also significantly correlate with household income. The results show that a higher nonagricultural employment share at the village level is accompanied by higher income. Full specification equations reveal that, given all other factors are equal, being part of nonmountainous villages raises household income by approximately 14–16 percent. The negative and significant coefficient on the historical level of labor mobility suggests that the propensity for outmigration is higher in lower income villages.

C. Role of Village Management and Public Policy

Our next step is to investigate further the role of public management and public policy at the village level. Here we focus on three variables that represent different aspects of village management: (1) a dummy for a collective economic entity representing the village's role as an economic agent; (2) the size of the village budget for public services, which indicates the role of the village as a provider of local public goods; and (3) the degree of social stability, which is regarded as a proxy of village cadres' governing ability. These three variables have positive, significant coefficients in our regressions (Table 12.3). We would like to explore further whether the impact of public management differs among different types of villages. We therefore compare the estimation results obtained by running regressions separately for different village types. In addition, we examine the cross-level interactions between village-level variables and household returns to education.

Table 12.4 reports the estimation results by type of village. Several points are noteworthy. First, the significance of village management is, on the whole, greater in the villages with a lower historical level of labor mobility. Two of the three relevant variables become insignificant in the case of villages that had a high propensity for out-migration at the beginning of the 1990s.

Second, the coefficient on collective economic entities becomes insignificant in underdeveloped villages and mountainous villages, while it is positive and significant in developed villages and nonmountainous villages. One explanation for this finding is that, after the deepening of marketization

Table 12.4. *Effects of village management by the village types, 2002*

| Types of villages | Village-specific variables added to the baseline equation | | |
	Collective economic entities	Village budget for public services, 1998	Social stability
Level of economic development			
Underdeveloped villages	0.049	0.011	0.037**
[$N = 4,469$, 486 villages]			
Developed villages	0.145***	0.059***	0.029*
[$N = 4,635$, 470 villages]			
Geographical location			
Mountainous villages	−0.070	−0.015	0.047*
[$N = 1,995$, 201 villages]			
Nonmountainous villages	0.125***	0.039***	0.031***
[$N = 7,109$, 755 villages]			
Historical level of labor mobility			
Villages of low mobility	0.123***	0.037***	0.053***
[$N = 5,461$, 588 villages]			
Villages of high mobility	0.060	0.032**	0.007
[$N = 3,643$, 368 villages]			

Notes:
1. Estimations are based on the baseline equation in the village-mean centered form (the first column of Table 12.3), and the relevant village-specific variables are added in the equations.
2. The symbols *, **, and *** denote statistical significance at the 10 percent, 5 percent, and 1 percent levels, respectively.

in the 1990s, only competitive village-level collective economic entities in developed nonmountainous regions were economically viable and provided villagers with lucrative opportunities. In other words, most collective economic entities in underdeveloped and mountainous villages had difficulty providing villagers with earning opportunities. Note that former village-owned enterprises that were privatized are included and treated as collective economic entities. Consequently, these results indicate that collective rural industrialization in the early reform era still plays a role in income determination, even after the wave of privatization in the 1990s.

Third, the effect of public expenditure is also insignificant in underdeveloped and mountainous villages. This finding implies that public goods provision at the mesolevel tends to be inefficient in underdeveloped and mountainous villages. This could arise because of the lack of economies of scale in public goods provision caused by the limited financial ability and geographical conditions, or because of the low governing ability at the village level and the lack of provision of complementary public goods by upper levels of government. This finding suggests that it is necessary to improve intergovernmental fiscal transfers to underdeveloped, mountainous regions and, at the same time, to provide an effective mechanism to meet local needs for the delivery of public goods.

Fourth, contrary to the above-mentioned aspects of village management, the coefficient on social stability is larger in underdeveloped and mountainous villages. This suggests that the role of informal institutional factors is more important when the overall level of economic development and marketization is low and the formal institutional infrastructure is underdeveloped. The policy implication of this result is that not only the physical infrastructure but also the development of the institutional infrastructure that promotes social stability may be essential for income growth and poverty alleviation in the underdeveloped regions.

Last, we cannot draw a simple picture of the relationship between the role of village management and the level of economic development or marketization. We cannot simply assume that the overall impact of village management on household income declines along with marketization. The impact of village management on household income appears to be related more to the historical level of labor mobility. Further research is required to elaborate the changing role of public management and public policy at the mesolevel, taking into consideration various other village-level factors and cross-level interactions of village, township, county, and upper administrations.

Let us now turn our attention to the cross-level interaction effects between village management and household income. Here we focus on the influence of the characteristics of village management on the average rate of return to education at the household level. The estimation results are revealed in Tables 12.5a and b, which show a positive and significant interaction effect. It is suggested that a larger village expenditure for public services in the past has brought about a higher rate of return to education (Table 12.5a). By conducting estimates by the types of village, we have determined a larger and more significant interaction effect in nonmountainous villages (Table 12.5b). This finding supports the relevance of the aforementioned larger impact of public expenditure on household income in developed nonmountainous regions.

IV. Concluding Remarks

The major findings of this chapter and their implications are summarized as follows. First, we have confirmed that village-specific factors significantly influence household income determination. This finding is consistent with previous research and suggests that not only the macrolevel institutional

Table 12.5a. *Cross-level interaction effect of village management and rate of return to education*

Coefficient	Collective economic entities	Village budget for public services, 1998	Social stability
Village-level variables on village management	0.098*** (0.026)	0.036*** (0.008)	0.035*** (0.011)
Village-mean centered education level	0.035*** (0.008)	0.031*** (0.008)	0.033 (0.025)
Interaction term of education with village-level variable on village management	0.010 (0.007)	0.004* (0.002)	0.001 (0.003)

Table 12.5b. *Village budget for public services and rate of return to education: By geographical location*

Coefficient	Mountainous villages	Nonmountainous villages
Village budget for public services, 1998	−0.015 (0.023)	0.039*** (0.008)
Village-mean centered education level	0.048*** (0.008)	0.019*** (0.007)
Interaction term of education level with village budget for public services	0.002 (0.005)	0.006*** (0.002)

Notes:

1. Estimations are based on the baseline equation in the village-mean centered form (the first column of Table 12.3), and the relevant variables are added in the equations.
2. The symbols *, **, and *** denote statistical significance at the 10 percent, 5 percent, and 1 percent levels, respectively.

and policy environment and microlevel factors but also mesolevel factors should be considered when we investigate income inequality in rural China. Second, not only the endowments of physical and human capital at the village level but also the community's social capital have a significant effect on household income. It should be noted that social capital's impact is stronger in underdeveloped, mountainous regions. Third, estimation results for the variables relating to village management, on the whole, suggest that many aspects of the role of the village – as economic agent, provider of local public goods, and promoter of social stability – have a significant effect on household income. It is noteworthy that public goods provision at the mesolevel tends to be inefficient in underdeveloped mountainous regions. This finding reveals a serious problem in rural China, that is, the large regional disparity in the effectiveness of public policy caused by the difference between delivery and financing of local public goods, by the lack of an effective mechanism of intergovernmental fiscal transfers, and by the limited governing ability at the local level.

The findings here hold certain implications for incomes and public policy in rural China. First, not only the construction of physical infrastructure but also the development of an institutional infrastructure that promotes social stability is relevant for income growth in underdeveloped regions. Second, the delivery of public services remains ineffective in underdeveloped regions, which suggests that it is necessary to improve intergovernmental fiscal transfers to underdeveloped regions and, at the same time, provide an effective mechanism to capture local needs.

We conclude by stating a concern over possible unfavorable policy outcomes of certain recent rural reforms, including the taxation reform. Although the decrease in the peasants' tax burden has an equalizing impact in the short run, if it is not accompanied by a substantial increase in intergovernmental fiscal transfers and by improved efficiency of delivery of public services, the result may be a reduction of basic public services, and unequal effects in the long run. The village survey provides evidence of such unfavorable consequences. For example, of the 634 villages where the taxation reform was launched in 2002, 304 villages reported that the total amount of funds available for the villages' education needs, which are obtained from the villages' own funds and upper administration, decreased following the reform. Moreover, there was a statistically significant association between income levels and changes in funding for education. Poor villages were more likely to report that they had suffered a reduction in funding for education.[17] Further research is needed on the relationship between income inequality and mesolevel public policy.[18]

---

[17] The percentages of villages that reported a reduction of such funding were: 34 percent of high-income villages (more than 3,500 yuan per capita net annual income), 47 percent of upper-middle-income villages (2,500–3,500 yuan), 51 percent of lower-middle-income villages (1,500–2,500 yuan), and 54 percent of low-income villages (less than 1,500 yuan). Several previous studies have already reported similar findings. See, e.g., Qi et al. (2003); Zhu et al. (2003).

[18] Several other issues also must be deferred to further studies. For example, it would be interesting to employ a microgrowth framework to examine the determinants of income growth at the village level. For relevant previous literature, see Ravallion and Jalan (1996).

Appendix Table 12A.1. *Distribution of sample villages by province, 2002 datasets*

Province	Number of sample administrative villages	Province	Number of sample administrative villages
Beijing	16	Hunan	45
Hebei	37	Guangdong	53
Shanxi	40	Guangxi	40
Liaoning	45	Chongqing	20
Jilin	48	Sichuan	50
Jiangsu	44	Guizhou	40
Zhejiang	53	Yunnan	26
Anhui	44	Shaanxi	37
Jiangxi	43	Gansu	32
Shandong	63	Xinjiang	80
Henan	53		
Hubei	52	Total	961

References

Antle, J. (1983), "Infrastructure and Aggregate Agricultural Productivity: International Perspective," *Economic Development and Cultural Change*, 31(3), 609–619.

Chen, W. (1998), "The Political Economy of Rural Industrialization in China: Village Conglomerates in Shandong Province," *Modern China*, 24(1), 73–96.

Dasgupta, P. and I. Serageldin, eds. (2000), *Social Capital: A Multifaceted Perspective*, Washington D. C.: World Bank.

Friedman, E., P. G. Pickowicz, M. Selden, with K. A. Johnson (1991), *Chinese Village, Socialist State*, New Haven: Yale University Press.

Huang, P. (1985), *The Peasant Economy and Social Change in North China*, Stanford: Stanford University Press.

Knack, S. and P. Keefer (1997), "Does Social Capital Have an Economic Payoff? A Cross-Country Investigation," *Quarterly Journal of Economics*, 112(4), 1251–1288.

Knight, J. and S. Li (1997), "Cumulative Causation and Inequality among Villages in China," *Oxford Development Studies*, 25(2), 149–172.

Kreft, I. and J. De Leeuw (1998), *Introducing Multilevel Modeling*, Thousand Oaks, CA: Sage Publications.

Lipton, M. and M. Ravallion (1995), "Poverty and Policy," in Jere Behrman and T. N. Srinivasan, eds., *Handbook of Development Economics*, vol. 3, New York: Elsevier Science.

Narayan, D. and L. Pritchett (1999), "Cents and Sociability: Household Income and Social Capital in Rural Tanzania," *Economic Development and Cultural Change*, 47(4), 871–897.

Oi, J. (1999), *Rural China Takes Off: Institutional Foundations of Economic Reform*, Berkeley: University of California Press.

Perkins, T. (2002), *Village, Market, and Well-Being in a Rural Chinese Township*, London: Routledge.

Qi, H., W. Zhao, and J. Yuan (2003), "Shuifei Gaige Cunji Caiwu ji Gonggongpin Rongzi: Yixiang Shizheng Yanjiu," *Zhongguo Nongcun Jingji*, no. 7, 10–17.

Raudenbush, S. and A. S. Bryk (2002), *Hierarchical Linear Models: Applications and Data Analysis Methods*, Thousand Oaks, CA: Sage Publications.

Ravallion, M. and J. Jalan (1996), "Growth Divergence Due to Spatial Externalities," *Economic Letters*, 53(2), 227–232.

Sato, H. (2003), *The Growth of Market Relations in Post-Reform Rural China: A Micro-Analysis of Peasants, Migrants, and Peasant Entrepreneurs*, London: Routledge Curzon.

Walder, A. (2002), "Income Determination and Market Opportunity in Rural China, 1978–1996," *Journal of Comparative Economics*, 30(2), 354–375.

Zhang, L., J. Huang, and S. Rozelle (2002), "Employment, Emerging Labor Markets, and the Role of Education in Rural China," *China Economic Review*, 13(2–3), 313–328.

Zhongguo Shehui Kexueyuan Jingji Yanjiusuo "Wubao" Diaocha Ketizu (1999), *Zhongguo Cunzhuang Jingji*, Beijing: Zhongguo Caizheng Jingji Chubanshe.

Zhu, S., H. Zhang, and H. Yan (2003), "Nongcun Shuifei Gaige Shidian he Xiangcun Guanli Tizhi Gaige Genzong Yanjiu Baogao," Research Paper Series of the Research Center for Rural Economy, Ministry of Agriculture.

THIRTEEN

The Redistributive Impact of Taxation in Rural China, 1995–2002

An Evaluation of Rural Taxation Reform at the Turn of the Century

Hiroshi Sato, Li Shi, and Yue Ximing

I. Introduction

A. Setting the Agenda

"The agricultural tax has become history" (*People's Daily*, December 31, 2005). The Chinese government announced abolition of agricultural taxes on January 1, 2006.[1] This was a goal of the "rural tax and fee reform" (hereafter referred to as rural taxation reform) initiated in the late 1990s and an important turning point in rural public policy in China. This chapter examines the redistributive impact of rural taxation using the 1995 and 2002 CHIP surveys and the administrative village survey of 2002.[2] The analytical focus is on changes in tax regressivity between 1995 and 2002.

An empirical study of the redistributive impact of rural taxation is important not only because ad hoc collection of taxes and levies – so-called arbitrary charges, fines, and levies (*luan shoufei, luan fakuan, luan tanpai*) – has been one of the hottest issues in rural public policy throughout the 1990s, but also because a critical aspect of the Chinese local politico-economic system, that is, the multilayered and decentralized local administrative/fiscal system, is embodied in the issue. So far, however, few empirical studies, with some exceptions such as Khan and Riskin (Chapter 3 in this volume) and

---

[1] "Agricultural taxes" is used as the general term for state taxation on agriculture such as the agricultural tax (*nongye shui*), the special agricultural tax (*nongye techan shui*), and the livestock tax (*muye shui*).

[2] See Chapter 1 and the Appendix of this volume for a detailed illustration of the household survey. For a description of the village survey, see Chapter 12 of this volume. The village survey was partly funded by the Japan Society for the Promotion of Science (JSPS) and Hitotsubashi University.

Tao, Liu, and Zhang (2003), have used nationally representative microdata to examine the redistributive outcomes of rural taxation.[3]

The structure of this chapter is as follows. In the latter half of this section, the background of the topic is discussed. Section II summarizes the process of rural taxation reform. Section III presents the definitions of taxes and levies to be employed in the study and introduces measurements of the redistributive impact of taxation. Section IV reports the changes in the amount and rate of taxation between 1995 and 2002 and then draws national and regional pictures of the redistributive impact of rural taxation. Section V concludes the chapter. Note that "rural taxation" is used here to refer to both formal state taxation and various kinds of levies and fees collected at the local level. Detailed definitions of the taxes, levies, and fees mentioned in this chapter are provided in Section III.

B. A Decentralized Fiscal System and Its Consequences

China's local administrative/fiscal system can be characterized as a multilayered and decentralized system (Wong et al. 2003). Interregional disparities in the revenue-raising abilities of local governments at all administrative levels, namely the provincial, subprovincial (city/prefecture, *shi/diqu*), county (*xian/xianjishi*), and township (*xiang/zhen*) levels, are large. Despite the large interregional disparities in local revenue, the provision of most basic public services, such as education, public health, and infrastructure, has been assigned to local governments. For example, from the mid-1980s to the late 1990s, in rural areas most of the fiscal burden of basic education fell on township and administrative village authorities. Such a decentralized system of public service delivery has not been accompanied by an effective mechanism of intergovernmental fiscal transfer, especially at the subprovincial and county levels. Three consequences derive from this malfunction of the local fiscal system: first, strong interhousehold/interregional regressivity in rural taxation; second, huge interregional disparities in the quality of small-scale infrastructure and public services; and third, strong characteristics of underinstitutionalized rural taxation. This chapter focuses on the first consequence, regressive taxation in rural areas.[4]

Based on the 1995 household dataset, Table 13.1 reports the average rate of taxation by income quartile and decile in 1995. Although the average

---

[3] Tao et al. (2003) have used panel data for rural households compiled from the Fixed Observation Points of the Rural Economy of the Ministry of Agriculture.

[4] Other issues will be investigated in our ongoing research.

Table 13.1. *Average rate of taxation by income group, 1995*

Income group	State taxation[a] (%)	Local levies and fees (local quasi tax in the narrow sense) (%)	Total tax burden (%)
Bottom 10%	3.5	10.3	13.7
Bottom 25%	2.9	7.3	10.2
2nd quartile	2.1	4.9	7.0
3rd quartile	1.8	4.1	5.8
Top 25%	1.3	2.2	3.5
Top 10%	1.1	1.7	2.8
Total	1.7	3.7	5.4
Number of observations (households) = 7, 668[b]			

Notes:

[a] See Table 13.4 for definitions of state taxation and local quasi tax narrowly defined. The average rate of taxation is calculated as (sum of taxes, levies, and fees) / (before-tax household income) × 100.

[b] Eighteen of the 19 provinces covered by the 1995 CHIP survey are used in the calculation. Guizhou is not included because data for taxes and levies are missing. For a description of provinces covered in this chapter, see Appendix Table 13A.1.

rate of taxation for all households was not particularly high at 5.4 percent of before-tax income, the burden fell very heavily on lower-income households. It should be noted that tax regressivity was stronger for local levies and fees (*fei*) collected at the township/administrative village level than it was for formal state taxation (*shui*). Local levies and fees were highly regressive because most of them were poll taxes imposed on a per capita (household) basis or a per arable land basis. Formal state taxation was also regressive due to the unique characteristics of the agricultural tax (*nongye shui*) that was universal in rural areas. As described in Sections III and IV, the agricultural tax is only partly sensitive to agricultural income and is not sensitive to nonagricultural income. As a result, the tax burden has been heavier for lower-income groups (regions) that depend heavily on agriculture.

Typically the consequences outlined above have been expressed in situations at the village level, the lowest stratum of the administrative hierarchy. No formal public budget has existed at the administrative village level because it has been regarded as a self-governing community, not a formal governmental apparatus. The administrative village, however, has been acting as a de facto governmental apparatus. Throughout the 1990s, administrative village funds for public services were collected mainly through the administrative village levy (*cun tiliu*) that had a legal basis in the agricultural law of 1993. The levy for rural education (*nongcun jiaoyu jizi*) introduced in the 1990s was also legal. In addition to these items, many of the villages in lower-income regions have depended on various other levies, fees, fines, and compulsory investments/donations that are of dubious legality. By contrast, villages with their own revenue sources have collected little money from villagers. Moreover, it should be noted that administrative villages have had the responsibility for collecting levies, fees, fines, and compulsory investments/ donations imposed by the township government and various government departments at the county level. Conflicts between village cadres and villagers over taxation have been considered to be the main causes of political instability in rural areas (Bernstein and Lü 2003).

II. Overview of Rural Taxation Reform in the 1990s

A. A Brief Chronology

Current rural taxation reform dates back to the beginning of the 1990s. The focus of the policy was to set a limit on the peasants' tax burden (less than 5 percent of the per capita annual net income of the previous year). However, the impact of the policy was limited, and the overburden of the peasants' taxes and levies remained a crucial problem in rural China. At the end of the 1990s, the Party and the central government began to adopt a more comprehensive approach aimed at reducing the peasants' tax burden. As is summarized in Table 13.2, the reform process after the end of the 1990s can be divided into two phases: *phase-1* substitution of local levies with formal taxation (*feigaishui*), and *phase-2* gradual abolition of agricultural taxes.[5]

Phase-1. In 2000 Anhui province was designated as the national model area (*shidian*) of the reform (Zhonggong Zhongyang and Guowuyuan 2000). In March 2002 the Party and the central government expanded coverage of the reform. Most of the provinces (and equivalent administrative units) had launched the reform by the end of 2002.

---

[5] In our discussion of the process of the reform, we draw on the following references: "Caijing" Bianjibu (2003); Chen (2003); Guowuyuan Nongcun Shuifei Gaige Gongzuo-xiaozu Bangongshi (2002); Guo (2003); He and Sun (2000); Ma (2002); Teng (2003); Zhejiang Sheng Caizhengting Ketizu (2003); Electronic Archive of the Ministry of Agriculture (*Zhongguo Nongye Xinxiwang*) (http://www.agri.gov.cn/zcfg/); *People's Daily* (*Renmin Ribao*) and *Economic Daily* (*Jingji Ribao*), various issues.

Table 13.2. *Structure of taxation reform*

Reform policy	Phase-1 (2000–2003) Substitution of local levies with formal taxation	Phase-2 (2004–) Gradual abolition of agricultural taxes
Agricultural taxes	To raise rate of taxation to cover the decline in fiscal revenue of local governments caused by the abolition of local levies (maximum tax rate: 7%) To employ an additional levy on agricultural taxes as a substitute for the administrative village levy (maximum rate: 20% of agricultural tax/special agricultural tax) To abolish the slaughter tax and other related fees	To abolish the agricultural tax, special agricultural tax (excluding taxation on tobacco), and livestock tax
Administrative village levy	To be replaced by an additional levy on agricultural taxes	To be abolished
Township levy	To be abolished	
Levy for rural education	To be abolished	
Other levies and fees	To be abolished	
Compulsory unpaid labor	To be abolished	
"One issue, one discussion" levy	To be employed as a substitute for unpaid labor and other local levies, to be collected based on democratic discussion by villagers	

Source: See text.

The basic policy arrangement in the phase-1 reform is summarized as "three abolitions, two adjustments, and one reform" (*sange quxiao, liangge tiaozheng, yige gaige*). The term "three abolitions" refers to the termination of the township levy (*xiangzhen tongchou*), the levy for rural education, and other levies, fees, and compulsory investments/donations collected directly from peasants by local governments. The term "two adjustments" refers to changes to the agricultural tax and the special agricultural tax (*nongye techan shui*). The "one reform" indicates reform of the collection and usage of the administrative village levy. In addition, it was announced that the slaughter tax (*tuzai shui*) would be terminated. Compulsory unpaid labor (*yiwugong laodong jileigong*), which is imposed by local governments as an in-kind local levy, was to be abolished gradually.

Adjustment of the agricultural tax had two components. The first component was the upward adjustment of the actual tax rate from approximately 2.5 percent to a maximum rate of 7 percent, intended to compensate for the expected decline in the fiscal revenue of local, mainly township, governments caused by the reform.[6] The second component was the introduction of an additional levy of agricultural tax and special agricultural tax (*liang-shui fujia*) as a substitute for levies and fees at the administrative village level (hereafter referred to as the "additional levy on agricultural taxes"). The standard rate of the additional levy on agricultural taxes was 20 percent of the amount of the agricultural taxes.

Phase-2. The reform policy has accelerated sharply since 2004. It shows that the Chinese leadership began to change the urban-biased institutional arrangements inherited from the planned economy era. The leadership is stressing that "unified institutional and policy arrangements for urban and rural development" (*tongchou chengxiang*) are critical to sustaining economic development and social stability, not only at the rural level, but also at the national level (see, for example, the decision of the Third Plenum of the Sixteenth CPC Central Committee, *People's Daily*, October 22, 2003). The Party "Document Number One" (*yihao wenjian*), which was released at the beginning of 2004, declared that the agricultural tax rate should be lowered immediately and abolished gradually (Zhonggong Zhongyang and Guowuyuan 2004). In March 2004 the State Council announced it would abolish agricultural taxes gradually within the next five years, excluding the special agricultural taxes on tobacco and a few other products. Eight provinces that had abolished agricultural taxes in 2004, including Heilongjiang and Jilin, were chosen as the national model provinces for the reform. By September 2005, 28 provinces had abolished agricultural taxes. Many counties in three other provinces (Hebei, Shandong, Yunnan) also stopped collecting agricultural taxes in 2005. On December 29, 2005, the

---

[6] The newly defined taxation formula for the agricultural tax (T) is as follows: $T = A \times Y \times p \times r$. A denotes taxable acreage (*jishui mianji*), based on the acreage of cultivated land fixed in the second round of the household responsibility contract in the 1990s. Y denotes the normal yield (*changnian chanliang*) per unit land of agricultural products, based on average yields over the five years before 1998, p denotes the taxable price of agricultural products (*jishui jiage*), based on a mix of the market price and the government's protected price, and r denotes the tax rate.

Standing Committee of the National People's Congress voted that agricultural taxes should be abolished on January 1, 2006. The abolition of agricultural taxes was thus completed before the original target date.

The 2002 CHIP survey illustrates the situation in the phase-1 reform. As reported in Appendix Table 13A.1, of the 122 counties surveyed, 84 counties, or approximately 70 percent of the sample counties, were categorized as counties where the phase-1 reform had already been launched in 2002 (hereafter referred to as post-reform counties). Another 38 counties had not yet started the phase-1 reform (hereafter referred to as pre-reform counties). Although data limitations do not allow us directly to describe the redistributive impact of the abolition of agricultural taxes, we are still able to investigate to what degree rural taxation influenced income inequality during the 1990s and for what reason the reform was launched. We can also extend our discussion to phase-2 and derive implications for rural public policy in the "post–agricultural tax era" (*hou nongyeshui shidai*).

B. Regional Variation

During the phase-1 reform, considering the complexity of the issue, the Party and the central government took a gradual and rather decentralized approach to rural taxation reform. As a result, considerable regional variations can be seen in the implementation of the reform program. The coverage of reform within particular provinces depended greatly on the policy of the provincial authorities. The unit of policy implementation was the county, and the rate of agricultural taxes was set at the county level. A region (a province or county) in good financial condition could lower the tax rate, whereas lower-income regions, or purely agricultural regions, where local governments rely heavily on agricultural taxes, insisted on setting the maximum rate.

This raises the question of what factors affected the provincial governments' decisions regarding the counties in which taxation reform was to be launched. We assume two background factors influenced policy choice: first, the need for reform, and second, the relative ease of reform. Although the two factors overlap, the following working hypothesis can be established.

The need for reform in the counties is indicated by the average rate of taxation. The heavier the peasants' tax burden, the greater the need for reform. Another factor representing the need for reform is the fiscal structure of local governments. The smaller the size of fiscal expenditure for rural public services, the greater the need for reform because more taxation for fewer service deliveries is a potential source of sociopolitical instability.

This factor controls the average rate of taxation and the level of regional income.

Concerning the relative ease of reform, we take two factors into consideration. One is the revenue-raising ability of each administrative village. Provincial governments will be more confident about conducting reform in a certain county if the administrative villages belonging to that county have the ability to raise funds using methods other than the collection of levies directly from villagers. County officials and village cadres will be able to accept the reform policy more readily when their village budgets can be expanded by the ability to raise funds. The other factor representing the ease of reform is the level of regional income. With other variables remaining the same, a higher regional income makes it easier to conduct reform because local governments in higher-income regions have the potential to exploit new revenue sources.

To test this working hypothesis, a village-based probit estimation was conducted using the administrative village survey and official fiscal statistics at the county level. The dependent variable was the status of reform at the end of 2002, that is, whether the sample villages are post-reform villages (= 1) or pre-reform villages (= 0). Of the 961 administrative villages surveyed, 676 were post-reform villages and 285 were pre-reform villages. With regard to the need for reform, three explanatory variables were employed, all measured in yuan: (a) the log of the per capita amount of local levies and fees, excluding unpaid labor; (b) the log of the per capita amount of a county's budgetary fiscal expenditure for rural public services; and (c) the log of the per capita amount of village expenditure on public services and infrastructure. With regard to the relative ease of reform, we used (d) the log of the per capita amount of revenue from the villages' own revenue sources and (e) the log of the per capita annual household net income averaged at the county level, both measured in yuan. In addition to these variables, a dummy variable for nationally designated poor counties (*pinkunxian*) was employed to control policy factors specific to such counties. The reference year was 1998 for all explanatory variables.

Table 13.3 reports the estimation outcomes, indicating that the above working hypothesis is consistent with the evidence and that both the need for, and the relative ease of, reform underlay the policy choice. The reforms were more likely to be launched where the need for reform was higher, that is, where the level of the tax burden was heavier, but where the amount of public service provision was small compared with the level of the tax burden. Further, assuming the same degree of need for reform, the potential of local governments to absorb the negative impact of reform in their budgets

Table 13.3. *Determinants of reform status (village-based probit estimation)*

	(1) Need for reform	(2) Need for, and relative ease of, reform
Log of the per capita amount of narrowly defined local quasi tax, 1998 (yuan, per capita)	0.292*** (5.90)	0.304*** (6.08)
Log of a county's budgetary fiscal expenditures for rural public services, 1998 (yuan, per capita)	−1.417*** (11.18)	−1.456*** (11.27)
Log of the per capita amount of village expenditure on public services and infrastructure, 1998 (yuan, per capita)	−0.070* (1.85)	−0.092** (2.31)
Log of the revenue from a village's own revenue source, 1998 (yuan, per capita)		0.063* (1.86)
Log of regional income, 1998 (per capita annual net income averaged at the county level, yuan)	0.674*** (4.58)	0.594*** (3.88)
Designated poor county at the national level (dummy)	0.495*** (3.27)	0.491*** (3.24)
Constant	0.832 (0.75)	1.535 (1.31)
Observations	781	781
Pseudo R^2	0.229	0.232

Note: The dependent variable represents the status of the taxation reform, where 1 = post-reform villages, 0 = pre-reform villages. The absolute values of the z statistics are provided in parentheses. The symbols *, **, and *** denote statistical significance at the 10 percent, 5 percent, and 1 percent levels, respectively.

Source: County budget statistics are compiled from Caizhengbu Yusuansi (1999).

appeared to be important when launching reform. In addition, the presence of a poverty alleviation program sponsored by the national level proved to affect the policy choice.

III. Definitions of Taxes and Measurements of the Redistributive Impact of Taxation

A. Definitions of Taxes and Levies

Table 13.4 summarizes the definitions of taxes, levies, and fees employed in this chapter. Two categories, state taxation and local quasi tax, are employed.

Table 13.4. *Definitions of taxes and quasi taxes in this study*

Categories of taxes and quasi taxes	1995	2002 Pre-reform area	Post-reform area
1. State taxation on primary industry (agricultural taxes, slaughter tax, etc.)	*	*	*
2. State taxation on secondary and tertiary industries	*	*	*
3. Total of state taxation (1 + 2)	*	*	*
4. Additional levy on agricultural taxes	–	–	*
5. Village levy, township levy, levy for rural education, "one issue, one discussion" levy, and other levies	*	*	*
6. Local quasi tax in the narrow sense (4 + 5)	*	*	*
7. Unpaid labor	NA	*	*
8. Local quasi tax in the broader sense (6 + 7)	NA	*	*

Note: *denotes the fact that data are available for the specific year or area. NA denotes the fact that the relevant data are not available. – denotes the fact that the tax or quasi tax was not applicable for the specific year or area. Fines are not included.

(a) State Taxation

State taxation is classified into two subcategories: taxation on primary industries and taxation on secondary/tertiary industries.[7] The first category includes the agricultural tax, special agricultural tax, livestock tax, and slaughter tax. The second category includes taxation on manufacturing, construction, commerce, and other service industries.

(b) Local Quasi Tax

We use the term local quasi tax as a general term for various local levies, fees, and compulsory investments/donations imposed at the township and administrative village levels. In addition, the term encompasses various fees collected by the county government through township/village officials. Note that in the following empirical analyses, any additional levy on agricultural

---

[7] Note that state taxation here refers to formal taxes collected by either the central government or local governments. The agricultural taxes are categorized under "local taxes" (*difangshui*), rather than "national taxes" (*guoshui*), as the funds collected belong to local governments under the current tax-sharing system.

taxes belongs in the category of local levies rather than the state taxation category because they are employed as substitutes for the administrative village levy. As the characteristics of the local quasi tax vary greatly, it is convenient to classify it into the following two subcategories.

(b-1) The local quasi tax narrowly defined: the additional levy on agricultural taxes, the village levy, the township levy, the levy for rural education, the "one issue, one discussion levy" (*yishi yiyi chouzi*) (a new levy at the administrative village level, the amount of which will be set by the villagers on the basis of democratic discussion), and other levies, fees, and compulsory investments/donations.

(b-2) The local quasi tax broadly defined: the narrowly defined local quasi tax plus unpaid labor. Unpaid labor (*UPL*) is calculated as follows:

$$UPL = (w \times LD) + C, \tag{1}$$

where w denotes wages per day for temporary labor in each administrative village in which the sample households lived, as calculated from the administrative village survey, LD denotes annual labor days of unpaid labor, and C denotes the total amount of cash paid by households as a substitute for unpaid labor (*yiqian daigong*). As will be discussed below, unpaid labor has a strong impact on the peasants' tax burden.[8] Note that the narrowly defined local quasi tax is used in the comparison of 1995 and 2002 because data on unpaid labor are not available from the 1995 CHIP survey.

B. Measurements of the Redistributive Impact and Regressivity

The basic method of evaluating the total redistributive impact of taxation is to compare the inequality of before-tax income with after-tax income. The total redistributive effect of taxation can be measured as the change in the inequality index, for example, the Gini coefficient, caused by the taxation. The change in inequality can be measured in both absolute and relative terms.

A classical measurement of the change in inequality in absolute terms is the Musgrave and Thin measure (*MT*) (Musgrave and Thin 1948):

$$MT = G - G^*, \tag{2}$$

where G and G^* are the before-tax income and after-tax income Gini coefficients, respectively. A positive (negative) MT indicates a progressive (regressive) taxation and a positive (negative) redistributive impact of taxation

---

[8] Fines for violations of family planning and other policies are not included because their redistributive impact is on average not large.

(Musgrave and Thin 1948). In relative terms, the redistributive impact can be measured by a redistribution coefficient. The redistribution coefficient (R) is measured as follows:

$$R = MT/G^* 100(\%). \tag{3}$$

A disadvantage of MT is that it does not reveal changes in the ranking of individuals or households by income after taxation. When MT equals zero, there are two possibilities: either everyone is paying the same tax rate, or the richest and the poorest sections of society have exchanged their rankings because of a very high tax rate for the former. In the latter case, although there is a highly progressive taxation system, it is not reflected in MT.[9] However, this weakness may not be critical in our analysis because of the obvious regressivity of taxation in rural China. A regressive tax would not change the ranking of individuals in terms of the distribution of after-tax income.

Another popular measurement is the Kakwani index of tax progressivity. The Kakwani index P is defined as

$$P = C - G, \tag{4}$$

where C is the concentration index of taxes and G is the Gini coefficient of the before-tax income (Kakwani 1977). A positive value of P implies progressive taxation and a positive redistributive impact on income inequality, and vice versa.

MT can be rewritten as follows, using the Kakwani index (World Bank 2003):

$$MT = P[t/(1 - t)], \tag{5}$$

where t is the average rate of taxation as a proportion of before-tax income. Then, after-tax income inequality is

$$G^* = G - P[t/(1 - t)]. \tag{6}$$

That is, after-tax income inequality (G^*) is a function of the average rate of taxation (t), the Kakwani index (P), and the before-tax income inequality (G). When taxation is regressive (when P has a negative value), the smaller the average rate of taxation, the more equitable is the after-tax income

[9] For instance, the before-tax income of two persons, A and B, is 100 and 50, respectively. If A pays 75 for income tax and B pays nothing, the after-tax income for A and B is 25 and 50, respectively, and the Gini coefficient is the same for before-tax income. In this case, MT is 0, from which it is concluded that the tax is neutral. However, in reality, a highly progressive taxation system exists. We will elaborate on the measurement of tax regressivity in forthcoming papers.

distribution. In other words, the smaller the absolute value of *t*, the smaller will be the after-tax income inequality.

IV. The Redistributive Impact of Rural Taxation Reform, 1995–2002

A. The Amount and Rate of Taxation

In this section we evaluate the redistributive impact of the rural taxation reform using the 1995 and 2002 CHIP datasets. In the following empirical examination, the sample counties are divided into post-reform counties and pre-reform counties. To ensure comparability between 1995 and 2002, Guizhou, Guangxi, and Xinjiang are not included. This is because all 1995 tax-related data are missing for Guizhou, and Guangxi and Xinjiang are not covered in the 1995 survey. A total of 78 counties fall into the category of post-reform counties, where taxation reform has been launched in the whole area. The post-reform counties are distributed over 18 provinces. A total of 23 counties in which reform has not been launched are categorized as pre-reform counties. Pre-reform counties are distributed over six provinces. (For the distribution of post- and pre-reform counties, see the Appendix Table 13A.1). Changes in the amount and rate of taxation between 1995 and 2002 are summarized in Table 13.5a.

For rural China as a whole, the peasants' total burden, the sum of state taxation and the narrowly defined local quasi tax, declined from 1995 to 2002 in terms of both the absolute value of taxes and levies and the rate of taxation. (All the figures relating to taxation in 2002 are deflated to 1995 prices using the consumer price index for rural households at the provincial level.) Observing the aggregate scene, the major policy target of the taxation reform, which was a reduction in the average rate of taxation, was accomplished.

A large decline in the average rate of taxation is found in the post-reform counties (Table 13.5b). The average rate of taxation declined from 6.0 percent in 1995 to 3.4 percent in 2002. Two trends – the increase of state taxation and the decrease of local quasi taxes – lie behind this change. The average rate of narrowly defined local quasi tax decreased from 3.7 percent in 1995 to 1.0 percent in 2002. If the additional 0.4 percent levy for agricultural taxes is excluded, the average rate has dropped to 0.6 percent. The policy framework of "replacing local levies with formal taxation" was accomplished. However, the average rate of the unpaid labor tax was the same as that of the narrowly defined local quasi tax, excluding the additional levy on agricultural taxes. Unpaid labor remained significant even after the reform.

Table 13.5a. *Changes in the amount and rate of taxation, 1995–2002, whole area*

	1995		2002	
	Per capita amount (yuan)	Rate (%)	Per capita amount (yuan)	Rate (%)
1. State taxation on primary industry	24.5	1.5	43.2	1.7
2. State taxation (total)	28.1	1.7	47.4	1.8
3. Local quasi tax narrowly defined	60.9	3.7	23.4	0.9
4. Subtotal (2 + 3)	89.0	5.4	79.0	3.1
5. Unpaid labor	U	U	16.5	0.7
6. Total burden (4 + 5)	U	U	95.6	3.8
Number of sample counties (households)	106 (7,668)		103 (8,000)	

Table 13.5b. *Post-reform counties*

	1995		2002	
	Per capita amount (yuan)	Rate (%)	Per capita amount (yuan)	Rate (%)
1. State taxation on primary industry	26.2	1.6	49.2	2.0
2. State taxation (total)	29.3	1.8	51.6	2.1
3. Local quasi tax narrowly defined	69.6	4.2	24.0	1.0
4. Subtotal (2 + 3)	98.9	6.0	83.7	3.4
5. Unpaid labor	U	U	15.1	0.6
6. Total burden (4 + 5)	U	U	98.8	4.0
Number of sample counties (households)	78 (6,113)		78 (6,210)	

In contrast to post-reform counties, the absolute level of the peasants' total burden in the pre-reform counties rose by about 10 percent between 1995 and 2002 (Table 13.5c). The decline in the rate of taxation in the pre-reform area is more a product of income growth than of changes in the level of taxation.

Table 13.5c. *Pre-reform counties*

	1995		2002	
	Per capita amount (yuan)	Rate (%)	Per capita amount (yuan)	Rate (%)
1. State taxation on primary industry	17.6	1.0	22.4	0.8
2. State taxation (total)	24.3	1.4	32.9	1.1
3. Local quasi tax narrowly defined	26.3	1.6	16.3	0.6
4. Total burden (2 + 3)	50.6	3.0	56.0	1.9
5. Unpaid labor	U	U	23.3	0.8
6. Total burden (4 + 5)	U	U	85.4	2.7
Number of sample counties (households)	23 (1,246)		23 (1,620)	

Notes:

1. Rate of taxation is calculated as (sum of taxes, levies, and fees / the sum of before-tax household income) × 100. All the figures relating to taxation in 2002 are deflated to 1995 prices using the consumer price index for rural households (*nongcun jumin xiaofei jiage zhishu*) at the provincial level.

2. Guizhou, Guangxi, and Xinjiang are not included. This is because all tax-related data for 1995 are missing for Guizhou and because Guangxi and Xinjiang are not covered in the 1995 survey. The whole area of 2002 includes two counties (170 households) that contain both pre- and post-reform villages. The whole area of 1995 includes counties that are not covered in the 2002 survey because of changes in administrative units and other changes.

3. Figures for the total burden in 2002 (line 4) are larger than the sum of state taxation and narrowly defined local quasi tax because small portions of the burden cannot be categorized properly into state taxation or local quasi tax.

4. U indicates that the relevant data are not available for 1995. NA indicates that the relevant tax item is not applicable for 1995.

When comparing post- and pre-reform counties as discussed above, the level of taxation in 1995 was higher in the areas that carried out the reforms by 2002 than it was in the areas where reform had not yet taken place by 2002. Notably, this pattern did not change by 2002 after the reform was implemented in some counties (Tables 13.5b and 13.5c).

B. Changes in the Redistributive Impact

The rural taxation reform affected the distribution as well as the average rate of taxation. Of particular interest here is whether the reform changed the regressivity of rural taxation. Table 13.6a, which focuses on the post-reform

Table 13.6a. *Redistributive effect of taxation in post-reform counties, 1995–2002, total burden (state taxation plus local quasi tax narrowly defined)*

		1995	2002
Gini coefficient for before-tax income (initial income)	G	0.357	0.336
Gini coefficient for after-tax income (redistribution income)	G^*	0.373	0.345
Musgrave and Thin measure	$MT\,(G - G^*)$	−0.016	−0.009
Redistribution coefficient (%)	$MT/G*100$	−4.5	−2.6
Kakwani index	$P\,(C - G)$	−0.217	−0.226
Concentration index of taxes	C	0.140	0.110
Average rate of taxation of the bottom income decile group (%)	t1	10.1	8.3
Average rate of taxation of the top income decile group (%)	t10	3.4	1.8

counties, summarizes the changes in regressivity and the redistributive impact of taxation between 1995 and 2002. The following points can be made.

First, concerning the total redistributive impact of taxation, the disequalizing effect has decreased over the period, although a disequalizing redistributive impact remains. As seen in Table 13.6a, the Musgrave and Thin measure of the total burden has decreased from −0.016 to −0.009, and the redistribution coefficient has declined from −4.5 percent to −2.6 percent. This is the outcome of two different trends shown in Tables 13.6b and 13.6c, namely, the alleviation of the unfavorable redistributive impact in the local quasi tax (reflected in the change in the redistributive coefficient from −3.3 percent to −0.8 percent) and the worsening of the negative impact in state taxation (reflected in the change in the redistributive coefficient from −0.9 percent to –1.6 percent).[10]

Second, in spite of some alleviation of the unfavorable redistributive impact of taxation as shown in Table 13.6a, the regressivity of taxation itself increased between 1995 and 2002. For the total tax burden, the concentration index changed from 0.140 to 0.110, and the Kakwani index changed from −0.217 to −0.226. Both these changes indicate a worsening of regressivity.

---

[10] This outcome does not change significantly when the sum of taxes and levies minus the sum of public transfers (cash or in-kind incomes from villages, townships, and upper governments) is used as in Chapter 3. Measurements of the redistributive impact for the net peasant burden are as follows. The redistribution coefficient was −4.3 percent in 1995 and −2.5 percent in 2002. The Kakwani index was −0.218 in 1995 and −0.226 in 2002.

Table 13.6b. *Total state taxation*

		1995	2002
Gini coefficient of before-tax income	G	0.357	0.336
Gini coefficient of after-tax income	G^*	0.360	0.341
Musgrave and Thin measure	$MT(G - G^*)$	−0.003	−0.005
Redistribution coefficient (%)	MT/G^*100	−0.9	−1.6
Kakwani index	$P(C - G)$	−0.170	−0.238
Concentration index of taxes	C	0.187	0.098
Average rate of taxation of the bottom income decile group (%)	t1	2.3	5.4
Average rate of taxation of the top income decile group (%)	t10	1.3	1.0

Table 13.6c. *Local quasi tax narrowly defined*

		1995	2002
Gini coefficient of before-tax income	G	0.357	0.336
Gini coefficient of after-tax income	G^*	0.369	0.339
Musgrave and Thin measure	$MT(G - G^*)$	−0.012	−0.003
Redistribution coefficient (%)	MT/G^*100	−3.3	−0.8
Kakwani index	$P(C - G)$	−0.237	−0.265
Concentration index of taxes	C	0.120	0.071
Average rate of taxation of the bottom income decile group (%)	t1	7.9	2.3
Average rate of taxation of the top income decile group (%)	t10	2.1	0.4

Note: All figures are based on Table 13.5.

Therefore, the favorable change in the total redistributive impact of taxation between 1995 and 2002 shown in Table 13.6a was the combined result of a reduction in the average rate of taxation and a more equal before-tax income distribution. Hence, the redistributive impact of the rural taxation reform was mixed.

C. A Comparison of Post- and Pre-Reform Counties

Table 13.7 shows the comparisons of the redistributive effects of taxation in post-reform and pre-reform areas in 2002. The broader definition including unpaid labor is used for local quasi tax. The table reveals that taxes were less regressive in post-reform counties than in pre-reform counties, but

Table 13.7. *Comparison of the redistributive effect of taxation in post- and pre-reform counties, 2002 (state taxation plus local quasi tax broadly defined, including unpaid labor)*

	Post-reform counties	Pre-reform counties	Whole area
Gini coefficient of before-tax income (initial income)	0.335	0.384	0.355
Total burden (state taxation plus local quasi tax broadly defined)			
Gini coefficient of after-tax income (redistribution income)	0.345	0.393	0.365
Redistribution coefficient (%)	−2.9	−2.2	−2.7
Kakwani index	−0.217	−0.294	−0.238
Local quasi tax broadly defined			
Gini coefficient of after-tax income	0.339	0.392	0.360
Redistribution coefficient (%)	−1.2	−1.9	−1.3
Kakwani index	−0.233	−0.507	−0.282
Unpaid labor			
Gini coefficient of after-tax income	0.336	0.389	0.357
Redistribution coefficient (%)	−0.4	−1.3	−0.6
Kakwani index	−0.193	−0.604	−0.327

Note: All figures are based on Table 13.5.

this was offset by a higher average rate of taxation. Consequently, the overall redistributive impact of taxes was more unfavorable in post-reform counties than in pre-reform counties. It is notable that unpaid labor was an important source of tax regressivity in pre-reform counties. Although unpaid labor has not attracted much attention in previous studies, we suggest that it is highly significant because local governments in low-income regions tend to depend greatly on unpaid labor to finance infrastructure construction. Thus, the abolition of unpaid labor is an important component of the taxation reform.

D. Tax and the Income of Primary Industry

So far, the relationship between total income and taxation has been examined. Another interesting issue is the degree to which the taxation of primary industry is sensitive to primary industry income. Table 13.8 reports the outcome for the post-reform counties.

First, in 1995 tax regressivity in the case of income from primary industry is even higher than it was in the case of total income (see Tables 13.6 and 13.8). This finding reveals that the agricultural tax formula before the reform did not adequately reflect differences in agricultural productivity or the structure

Table 13.8. *Redistributive impact of primary industry taxes on agricultural income in post-reform counties, 1995–2002*

		1995	2002
Gini coefficient for before-tax agricultural income	G	0.386	0.430
Gini coefficient for after-tax agricultural income	G^*	0.391	0.438
Musgrave and Thin measure	$MT(G - G^*)$	−0.006	−0.008
Redistribution coefficient (%)	$MT/G*100$	−1.5	−2.0
Kakwani index	$P(C - G)$	−0.219	−0.194
Concentration index of taxes	C	0.167	0.236
Average rate of taxation of the bottom income decile group (%)	t1	11.3	18.9
Average rate of taxation of the top income decile group (%)	t10	1.4	2.4

Note: All figures are based on Table 13.5.

of agricultural production. As a result, the agricultural tax rate was lower for regions/households with higher agricultural profitability.

Second, the degree of regressivity measured by the Kakwani index declined between 1995 and 2002, in contrast to the case of total income in relation to total state taxation. The decrease in tax regressivity in 2002 suggests that the newly defined agricultural tax formula reflects agricultural profitability more adequately than did the old formula.

E. Interregional and Intraregional Regressivity

Regressivity in taxation can be separated into interregional regressivity and intraregional regressivity. One way to separate these two types of regressivity is to estimate the income elasticity of taxation with respect to both household and regional average incomes. Taxation is progressive when the income elasticity of taxes is greater than one and regressive when the elasticity is less than one. Negative elasticity indicates stronger regressivity.

Table 13.9 reports the ordinary least squares (OLS) estimation of intraregional and interregional income elasticity in the post-reform counties. The dependent variables are the log of the per capita amount of total state taxation and the narrowly defined local quasi tax. The independent variables are the log of the per capita before-tax household income, which is used to capture intraregional regressivity, and the log of the per capita before-tax income averaged at the county level, which is used to capture interregional regressivity.

Table 13.9. *Intraregional and interregional income elasticity of taxation in post-reform counties, 1995–2002*

	1995		2002	
	Total state taxation	Local quasi tax narrowly defined	Total state taxation	Local quasi tax narrowly defined
Log of household income (per capita before-tax income)	0.264** (6.98)	0.370** (8.62)	0.157** (4.26)	0.126** (4.04)
Log of regional income (per capita before-tax income, averaged at the county level)	0.220** (3.56)	−0.234** (−3.34)	−0.350** (−3.90)	−0.451** (−5.93)
Log of per capita land-holding (*mu*)	0.342** (7.44)	0.557** (10.71)	0.659** (15.30)	0.592** (16.22)
Observations	6,113	6,113	6,209	6,209
Adj-R^2	0.211	0.261	0.215	0.189

Note: Dependent variables are the logs of the per capita amount of state taxation and narrowly defined local quasi tax. The province dummies and the constant are not reported. Absolute values of t statistics are provided in parentheses. Symbols * and ** denote statistical significance at the 5 percent and the 1 percent levels, respectively.

Two points can be made from Table 13.9. First, both interregional and intraregional regressivities increased after the reform, as income elasticity declined between 1995 and 2002, and in both years it was less than one. Second, interregional regressivity was greater than intraregional regressivity for both state taxation and local quasi tax. Notably, between 1995 and 2002, the increase in the interregional regressivity of state taxation was remarkable. This finding reflects a basic problem of the taxation reform, which was that the rates of agricultural taxes were decided at the county level, and the variables used for calculating the taxes were subject to political manipulation. It is likely that officials of poor counties with small public budgets had strong incentives to set higher tax rates.

F. Regional Variation in the Changes in Tax Regressivity

So far, we have provided a general picture of the redistributive impact of rural taxation reform. Given the huge regional imbalance in local public finance and the decentralized manner of taxation reform, it is useful to examine the regional variation in the redistributive impact of this reform.

Table 13.10 reports the redistributive impact of the reform at the provincial level, focusing on provinces in which all counties have undergone reform.

Table 13.10. *Redistributive impact of taxation in post-reform provinces, 1995–2002*

Province	Gini coefficient for before-tax income		Redistribution coefficient for state taxation on primary industry (%)		Redistribution coefficient for total amount of state taxation (%)		Redistribution coefficient for local quasi tax narrowly defined (%)		Redistribution coefficient for total burden (total state taxation plus local quasi tax narrowly defined) (%)	
	1995	2002	1995	2002	1995	2002	1995	2002	1995	2002
Hebei	0.316	0.298	−0.2	−2.1	−0.04	−1.6	−2.9	−1.2	−3.0	−3.1
Jilin	0.343	0.302	−2.5	−3.1	−2.7	−3.1	−7.1	−1.2	−10.3	−4.7
Jiangsu	0.312	0.306	−0.4	−1.3	−0.4	−1.4	−3.0	−0.4	−3.4	−2.2
Anhui	0.216	0.266	−1.6	−2.1	−1.5	−1.7	−3.3	−0.7	−4.9	−2.5
Jiangxi	0.236	0.282	0.3	−1.1	1.2	−1.1	0.1	−0.7	1.1	−1.7
Shandong	0.453	0.340	−1.0	−1.9	−1.1	−1.9	−7.4	−1.3	−8.9	−3.3
Henan	0.245	0.267	−1.0	−3.0	−0.8	−3.0	−3.4	−0.9	−4.3	−4.2
Hubei	0.281	0.287	−2.8	−1.4	−2.9	−1.4	−10.4	−1.4	−14.3	−2.8
Hunan	0.256	0.317	−0.8	−1.0	−0.6	−1.0	0.6	−0.6	−0.2	−1.5
Shaanxi	0.270	0.304	−0.2	−2.8	−0.1	−2.8	−1.0	−1.4	−1.3	−4.7
Gansu	0.314	0.339	−1.1	−0.5	−1.2	−0.6	0.1	−0.4	−1.1	−1.2

Table 13.11. *Changes in the average rate of taxation in selected post-reform provinces, 1995–2002 (%)*

	Hebei		Hunan		Shaanxi		Jiangxi	
	1995	2002	1995	2002	1995	2002	1995	2002
Total burden								
Bottom 10 percent income decile group	10.4	11.7	3.4	4.3	5.4	13.5	4.6	4.7
Top 10 percent income decile group	4.4	2.0	6.9	2.4	6.3	2.0	8.8	1.8
Total average	4.2	2.9	6.6	3.5	5.6	4.3	5.4	3.0
Local quasi tax narrowly defined								
Bottom 10 percent income decile group	9.6	3.5	1.6	1.2	2.7	3.2	3.2	1.3
Top 10 percent income decile group	3.1	0.2	5.1	0.6	3.2	0.6	5.0	0.6
Total average	3.5	0.7	4.5	1.1	3.1	1.2	3.4	1.0

Changes in the redistributive impact of taxation varied considerably. Five of the 11 post-reform provinces covered in the study – Hebei, Jiangxi, Hunan, Shaanxi, and Gansu – experienced unfavorable changes in the redistributive impact between 1995 and 2002, whereas six other provinces – Jilin, Jiangsu, Anhui, Shandong, Henan, and Hubei – had favorable changes during the same period.

Table 13.11 shows the changes in the average rate of taxation by income decile groups between 1995 and 2002, focusing on four provinces that experienced unfavorable changes in the redistributive impact of taxation. The table confirms that the total taxation burden increased for the bottom 10 percent income decile group between 1995 and 2002 in all four provinces. Ironically, given its aims, the reform disadvantaged lower-income groups and regions in these provinces.

In conclusion, the decentralized manner of taxation reform has resulted in considerable regional disparity in the redistributive impact of taxation reform. The focus on decreasing the average rate of taxation has resulted in neglect of the unfavorable redistributive impact of taxation reform at the local level.

V. Conclusion

This chapter has evaluated the redistributive impacts of rural taxation. Its main findings can be summarized as follows. First, the major policy target of rural taxation reform – reducing the average rate of taxes and levies – was accomplished between 1995 and 2002, with favorable redistributive results (see also Chapter 3 of this volume). When the aggregate scene is observed, the disequalizing redistributive impact of taxation declined between 1995 and 2002. Second, despite these positive results from the aggregate perspective, the favorable impact of the reform was severely limited because overall rural taxation remained disequalizing after the reform and regressivity in taxation itself, measured by the Kakwani index and the income elasticity of taxation, increased between 1995 and 2002. The favorable change in the redistributive impact between these years did not occur as a result of a decrease in the degree of regressivity of the tax itself, but because the average rate of taxation and before-tax income inequality declined. Moreover, when the regional picture is observed, the overall redistributive impact of taxation worsened in several provinces following the reform.

These empirical findings reflect that, under the decentralized fiscal/administrative system, a public policy launched by the central government can bring about considerable regional disparity in its outcomes. In the case of the rural taxation reform, confining policy attention to the average rate of taxation (or the per capita tax burden), the only operational and monitorable policy target for the central government, has not achieved a favorable impact at the local level. In this context the abolition of the agricultural taxes is a natural and necessary extension of the reform policy. We should not, however, be overly optimistic about the policy outcomes of the reform. If the abolition of the agricultural tax is not accompanied by a fiscal transfer to local governments and other fiscal policy adjustments, deterioration in public service delivery could occur. As is discussed in Chapter 12 of this volume, our empirical study provides evidence for such unfavorable consequences. Tao, Liu, and Zhang (2003) also argue that the decrease in the peasants' tax burden has not been accompanied by a systematic policy framework for public service provision at the local level. Although the abolition of agricultural taxes and quasi taxes will have an equalizing impact for rural income inequality in the short run, if it brings about a cutback of basic public services, it may harm regional economic growth and have disequalizing effects in the long run.[11] Moreover, if the township- and village-level governmental apparatuses are not financed adequately, they will continue to collect money from peasants informally and rural taxation may be driven underground once again.

As the next step, empirical studies should focus on the flow of local public finance following the reform and investigate the degree to which the reform has influenced the delivery of local public goods. Moreover, this question

---

[11] In a forthcoming paper we conduct a simulation of the redistributive impact of the abolition of agricultural taxes.

should be examined from the standpoint of long-term institution building in rural areas. That is, we should investigate the relationship between tax policy and other complementary reform policies, such as the restructuring of local administrative systems, the promotion of "village democracy," and the introduction of social security programs for the rural population.

Appendix Table 13A.1. *Distribution of sample villages and counties by status of taxation reform, 2002 dataset*

| | | Number of counties | | |
Reform status	Province	Pre-reform	Post-reform	Total
C	Beijing	1	1	2
A	Hebei	0	5	5
C	Shanxi	5	1	6
C	Liaoning	5	1	6
A	Jilin	0	6	6
B	Jiangsu	0	5	5
B	Zhejiang	4	2	6
A	Anhui	0	5	5
A	Jiangxi	0	6	6
A	Shandong	1	6	7
A	Henan	0	7	7
A	Hubei	0	6	6
A	Hunan	0	5	5
B	Guangdong	4	3	7
C	Guangxi	5	0	5
A	Chongqing	0	2	2
A	Sichuan	0	6	6
A	Guizhou	0	6	6
C	Yunnan	5	0	5
A	Shaanxi	0	6	6
A	Gansu	0	5	5
C	Xinjiang	8	0	8
	Total	38	84	122

Note: The first column ("Reform status") indicates the status of the rural taxation reform in 2002. A and B denote post-reform provinces. Status A provinces have implemented the reform in all or most of the counties after receiving subsidies from the central budget. Status B provinces have implemented the reform in all or most of the counties without receiving subsidies from the central budget. Status C denotes pre-reform provinces, that is, provinces where the reform has been implemented only in part of the counties with or without subsidies from the central budget. Provinces not included in the sampling frame are Tianjin (status C), Inner Mongolia (status A), Heilongjiang (status A), Shanghai (status B), Fujian (status C), Hainan (status C), Ningxia (status A), Qinghai (status A), and Tibet (not included in the scheme of the rural taxation reform). Based on the administrative village survey, three counties contain both pre-reform and post-reform villages. They are Xiaoshan county in Zhejiang (official administrative unit code: 330121), Licheng district in Shandong (370112), and Akesu county in Xinjiang (652901). As the reform status of each village is consistent with the other information in the administrative village questionnaire, we placed the three counties in the pre-reform category.

References

Bernstein, T. and X. Lü (2003), *Taxation without Representation in Contemporary Rural China*, Cambridge: Cambridge University Press.

"Caijing" Bianjibu, ed. (2003), *Zhuanxing Zhongguo*, Beijing: Shehui Kexue Chubanshe.

Caizhengbu Yusuansi, ed. (1999), *1998 Nian Quanguo Di Shi Xian Caizheng Tongji Ziliao*, Beijing: Zhongguo Caizheng Jingji Chubanshe.

Chen, X. (2003), *Zhongguo Xianxiang yu Nongmin Zengshou Wenti Yanjiu*, Taiyuan: Shanxi Jingji Chubanshe.

Guo, F. (2003), *Nongcun Shuifu yu Nongmin Fudan*, Beijing: Jingji Ribao Chubanshe.

Guowuyuan Nongcun Shuifei Gaige Gongzuoxiaozu Bangongshi, ed. (2002), *Nongcun Shuifei Gaige Zhishi Wenda*, Beijing: Dangjian Duwu Chubanshe.

He, K. and S. Li, eds. (2000), *Zhongguo Nongcun Shuifei Gaige Chutan*, Beijing: Zhongguo Zhigong Chubanshe.

Kakwani, N. C. (1977), "Measurement of Tax Progressivity: An International Comparison," *Economic Journal*, 87(345), 71–80.

Ma, X., ed. (2002), *Woguo Nongcun Shuifei Gaige Yanjiu*, Beijing: Zhongguo Jihua Chubanshe.

Musgrave, R. A. and T. Thin (1948), "Income Tax Progression, 1929–48," *Journal of Political Economy*, 56(6), 498–514.

Tao, R., M. Liu, and Q. Zhang (2003), "Nongmin Fudan yu Caizheng Tizhi Gaige," Working Paper Series, China Center for Economic Research at Peking University.

Teng, X. (2003), *Nongcun Shuifei Gaige yu Difang Caizheng Tizhi Jianshe*, Beijing: Jingji Kexue Chubanshe.

Wong, C. (Huang, P.) et al. (2003), *Zhongguo: Guojia Fazhan yu Difang Caizheng*, Beijing: Zhongxin Chubanshe (Chinese version of World Bank, *National Development and Subnational Finance*, Washington, D.C.: World Bank, 2002).

World Bank (2003), "Quantitative Techniques for Health Equity Analysis – Technical Note No. 17," www.worldbank.org/poverty/health/wbact/health_eq_tn17.pdf.

Zhejiang Sheng Caizhengting Ketizu (2003), "Zhejiang Sheng Nongcun Shuifei Gaige de Shijian yu Tansuo," *Zhongguo Nongcun Jingji*, no. 7, 30–34.

Zhonggong Zhongyang and Guowuyuan (2000), "Guanyu Jinxing Nongcun Shuifei Gaige Shidian Gongzuo de Tongzhi," Agricultural Information Network (*Zhongguo Nongye Xinxiwang*), Ministry of Agriculture, http://www.agri.gov.cn/zcfg/.

Zhonggong Zhongyang and Guowuyuan (2004), "Zhonggong Zhongyang Guowuyuan guanyu Cujin Nongmin Zengjia Shouru Ruogan Zhengce de Yijian (2004 Nian Yihao Wenjian)," *People's Daily* [*Renmin Ribao*], February 8.

Appendix

The 1995 and 2002 Household Surveys: Sampling Methods and Data Description

Li Shi, Luo Chuliang, Wei Zhong, and Yue Ximing

Following the successful completion of the first two Chinese household income (CHIP) surveys for 1988 and 1995, a new survey project team, composed of researchers from the Institute of Economics of the Chinese Academy of Social Sciences (CASS) together with associated Chinese and international scholars, and with the assistance of the National Bureau of Statistics (NBS), conducted a third survey in the spring of 2003 for the reference year 2002. The aim of the third survey was to examine the dynamic changes in income distribution in China that had taken place since 1988 and 1995.

Project teams from the 1988 and 1995 surveys published their analyses and research results in two volumes, Griffin and Zhao (1993) and Riskin, Zhao, and Li (2001). The first of these volumes contains an appendix describing the sampling method and data description for the 1988 survey, but the second volume lacks such an appendix for the 1995 survey. In view of this, and since most of the chapters in this volume use data from both the 1995 and 2002 surveys, this appendix describes both the 1995 and 2002 samples.

The CHIP surveys are closely related to the NBS household surveys, so we first give a brief explanation of how the NBS household survey samples were selected. We then describe the sampling method and data for the 1995 and 2002 surveys.

I. Sampling Methodology in the NBS Surveys

As in the 1988 survey, the rural and urban samples in the 1995 and 2002 were drawn from the large sample used by the NBS in its annual household survey. The NBS adopts slightly different sampling procedures for its rural and urban surveys. Its sampling method for the urban surveys can be described as follows. The respondent households are selected using a two-stage stratified systematic random sampling scheme. In the first stage cities and county towns are selected; in the second stage households within the selected cities and county towns are chosen.

The procedure to select cities and county towns is designed as follows. First, all cities and county towns are classified into five categories on the basis of their population size. The categories are extremely large cities, large cities, medium-sized cities, small cities, and county towns. Second, the cities and towns in each category are grouped into the six geographical regions (Northeast, North, East, Center, Northwest, and Southwest). In each region the cities and county towns of each category are arranged according to the average wages of their staff and workers with urban *hukou* (registration). Third, the number of individuals who are staff and workers in the cities is added up, and the sample cities or counties are selected using an interval of one million staff and workers.

At the second stage, the households are selected in each sample city by a multiphase sampling scheme. In the extra-large and large cities, the procedure is a three-phase sampling method. First, the sample subdistricts in each city or county town are selected; second, the sample resident committees (*jumin weiyuan hui*) are selected from the sample subdistricts; third, the sample households are selected from the sample resident committees. In the medium-sized and small cities and counties, the procedure is a two-stage sampling method. First, the sample resident committees are selected; second, the sample households are selected from the sample resident committees. Unfortunately, the NBS does not document how the subdistricts, resident committees, and households are selected. It is believed that a random selection method is more or less adopted.

The above sampling method yields about 35,000 households selected for the NBS annual household survey in 1995 and 45,000 in 2002. These samples represent total urban populations of approximately 350 million and 450 million in the two years, respectively.

The households selected for the urban surveys keep accounts of their daily income and expenditures for three successive years and are interviewed by the enumerators every month. By a rotation sampling scheme, one-third of the old sample households are replaced by new sample households every year.

The NBS rural household surveys follow a slightly different procedure from the urban surveys. The sampling procedure consists of two steps. First, sample villages are selected directly in each province, and second, households are drawn from each sample village. Generally, 10 households are selected from each village. In the years 1995–2002, the rural sample included about 67,000–68,000 households.

Since 2000 the NBS has changed the sampling procedure for its rural household survey in a manner that maintains the representativeness of the sample at the provincial level and above, but is no longer representative at the county level. Under the old procedure, village selection was the responsibility of county bureaus, and each county paid attention to the representativeness of the villages selected within its boundaries. Under the new procedure, provincial bureaus are responsible for drawing the village samples, and they do so on the basis of achieving representativeness at the provincial level. Thus one cannot expect that the villages selected since the year 2000 are representative at the county level.

In order to ensure the accuracy of the survey data, the NBS designed two kinds of accounts for the respondent households, the cash account and the account on goods in kind. Nearly 10,000 assistant enumerators help the households keep reliable accounts and check and tabulate the data. To overcome problems with declining quality due to aging of the sample and to respondent households becoming tired of completing the survey, the NBS has implemented a rotation sampling rule, with the cycle of the complete rotation being five years.

II. Sampling Procedure and Instruments in the 1995 and 2002 CHIP Surveys

A. The 1995 Survey

The 1995 survey adopted different sampling procedures and different instruments from the 1988 survey. Due to increased survey costs and budget limitations, the size of the sample was reduced from 20,000 households in the 1988 survey to 15,000 households in the 1995 survey. The number of provinces in the rural survey was reduced from 28 to 19, while the number of provinces in the urban survey was increased from 10 to 11 (by including Sichuan).

For the rural survey, the 19 provinces were selected with the condition that they should constitute a representative sample of the economic characteristics in rural China's various regions. It was thought that Beijing represented well the three large metropolitan cities (the other two being Shanghai and Tianjin) at that time; Liaoning, Jiangsu, Zhejiang, Shandong, and Guangdong represented the coastal region; Hebei, Shanxi, Jilin, Anhui, Jiangxi, Henan, Hubei, and Hunan represented the central region; and Sichuan, Guizhou, Yunnan, Shaanxi, and Gansu represented the western region. Following the same principle, the 1995 urban survey chose Beijing to represent the three large metropolitan cities, Liaoning, Jiangsu, and

Table A.1. *Distribution of households in 1995 rural and urban surveys, by province*

Province	Rural			Urban		
	Number of counties	Number of households	Number of individuals	Number of cities	Number of households	Number of individuals
Total	102	7,998	34,719	69	6,934	21,696
Beijing	1	100	363	1	500	1,528
Hebei	5	498	2,177			
Shanxi	6	300	1,288	7	650	2,109
Liaoning	5	300	1,186	5	700	2,212
Jilin	5	300	1,191			
Jiangsu	5	500	1,965	9	800	2,450
Zhejiang	5	400	1,575			
Anhui	5	450	1,970	6	500	1,527
Jiangxi	5	350	1,728			
Shandong	7	700	2,879			
Henan	6	700	3,138	8	600	1,939
Hubei	6	402	1,764	7	742	2,310
Hunan	4	500	2,102			
Guangdong	7	500	2,460	8	546	1,821
Sichuan	8	798	3,145	7	848	2,486
Guizhou	5	300	1,465			
Yunnan	5	300	1,452	9	648	2,010
Shaanxi	6	300	1,376			
Gansu	6	300	1,495	3	400	1,304

Guangdong to represent the coastal areas; Anhui, Henan, and Hubei the central region; Sichuan and Yunnan the southwestern region; and Shanxi and Gansu the northwestern region.

The 1995 rural survey covers 7,998 households and 34,719 individuals, and the 1995 urban survey covers 6,934 households and 21,696 individuals. The rural sample of households was selected from 19 provinces and 102 counties, and the urban sample from 11 provinces and 69 cities. For the distributions of the household and individual samples by province in both the rural and urban areas, see Table A.1.

In the rural survey, the total number of households sampled was distributed among the 19 provinces in a manner roughly consistent with their populations. The provincial statistical bureaus were given autonomy to decide the number of counties, but had to meet the condition that the number of surveyed households in each selected county should number no less than 50. The provincial statistical bureaus were also instructed to select counties and villages on the basis of their income levels.

The methods for drawing cities and households for the 1995 urban survey are similar to those for the 1988 urban survey and are described by Eichen and Zhang (1993).

The questionnaires were designed by the members of the project team. Most questions in the questionnaires for the 1988 survey reappeared in the 1995 survey, while some new questions were added. In the urban questionnaire, income questions were posed with the objective of deriving household disposable income; the households were therefore asked questions regarding income in kind and the market value of housing subsidies, as well as imputed rent of privately owned housing. In the rural questionnaire, the respondents were asked the present values of private housing in order to derive their imputed values by adopting a discount rate. Both the rural and urban questionnaires have fairly comprehensive questions about household consumption and its components, as well as questions on household physical and financial assets. The questionnaires for both the 1988 and 1995 surveys are available in the appendix to Zhao, Li, and Riskin (1999).

Table A.1 presents the sample distribution of cities, households, and individuals among the provinces where the survey was conducted. One can see that the sample size increases with the size of the provincial population, but not exactly in proportion. Table A.2 provides the gender ratios for individuals in the sample by province. The rural survey has more males than females, the latter being 95.6 percent of the former, which is consistent with the data from the national census as well as other large surveys. For instance, according to materials published by the NBS, the ratio of females as a percentage of males in rural areas was 95.7 percent in 1995 (Research Institute of All China Women's Federation and Department of Social, Science and Technology Statistics, NBS, 1998, p. 17). For the urban sample, the ratio of females to males is relatively high in the 1995 survey compared to data from other sources.[1] This sampling bias is largely due to a considerably higher female ratio in Jiangsu and Yunnan, but the reason is unknown.

Tables A.3a and A.3b give the distribution of households by household size in the 1995 rural and urban surveys. The tables indicate that households with three to five members account for over 80 percent of the rural household sample, and households with four members account for over one-third of the sample. In the urban sample households with three members are dominant and account for 57 percent of all urban households. Since the NBS data do

---

[1] Females as a percentage of males in cities was 98.8 percent in 1995 (Research Institute of All China Women's Federation and Department of Social, Science and Technology Statistics, NBS, 1998, p. 17).

Table A.2. *Gender distribution of individuals in 1995 survey, by province*

	Rural			Urban		
Province	Male	Female	Female as percentage of male	Male	Female	Female as percentage of male
Total	17,764	16,975	95.6	10,141	10,407	102.6
Beijing	182	201	110.4	761	767	100.8
Hebei	1,097	1,080	98.5			
Shanxi	667	621	93.1	1,068	1,041	97.5
Liaoning	604	582	96.4	1,091	1,121	102.7
Jilin	601	590	98.2			
Jiangsu	1,001	964	96.3	1,181	1,269	107.5
Zhejiang	824	751	91.1			
Anhui	994	976	98.2	763	764	100.1
Jiangxi	886	842	95.0			
Shandong	1,452	1,427	98.3			
Henan	1,610	1,528	94.9	961	978	101.8
Hubei	923	841	91.1	1,149	1,161	101.0
Hunan	1,110	992	89.4			
Guangdong	1,253	1,207	96.3	917	904	98.6
Sichuan	1,576	1,569	99.6	1,237	1,249	101.0
Guizhou	771	694	90.0			
Yunnan	733	719	98.1	972	1,038	106.8
Shaanxi	702	674	96.0			
Gansu	778	717	92.2	662	642	97.0

not provide parallel information, comparison between our survey and the NBS survey in this regard is not possible. Another indicator for household size frequently used by the NBS survey, however, is the average number of household members, which in 1995 was 4.48 in its rural sample and 3.23 in its urban sample. The corresponding numbers in our surveys are 4.34 and 3.13.

Tables A.4a and A.4b and Figure A.1 show the distribution of individuals among different age groups in the 1995 surveys. The presence of differences in the age distribution of individuals in the rural and urban samples is not surprising. One of the major differences is that the rural sample is younger. For example, individuals aged 10 and below constitute 15.4 percent, and those aged over 60 constitute 6.5 percent of the rural sample, while the corresponding figures for the urban sample are 10.4 percent and 9.8 percent, respectively.

Statistics on educational attainment appear in Tables A.5a and A.5b. As expected, few individuals – less than 1 percent – have received a college education in the rural sample. A large proportion of the rural sample has an

Table A.3a. *Distribution of households in 1995 rural survey, by household size and province (%)*

Province	\multicolumn{8}{c}{Household size}
	1	2	3	4	5	6	7 & over	All
Total	0.3	4.6	19.5	35.9	23.9	10.4	5.4	100.0
Beijing	0.0	3.0	39.0	37.0	14.0	7.0	0.0	100.0
Hebei	0.6	7.0	12.7	39.6	25.3	9.0	5.8	100.0
Shanxi	1.0	5.7	13.3	42.3	24.7	9.3	3.7	100.0
Liaoning	0.0	7.7	25.3	41.7	17.0	6.3	2.0	100.0
Jilin	0.3	5.3	29.0	37.7	20.3	6.0	1.4	100.0
Jiangsu	0.2	9.0	32.2	30.8	17.8	6.6	3.4	100.0
Zhejiang	0.3	8.3	26.3	38.8	19.0	6.5	3.0	100.0
Anhui	0.4	4.7	16.4	33.6	31.1	8.9	3.9	100.0
Jiangxi	0.0	0.3	10.0	32.6	28.6	16.9	11.6	100.0
Shandong	0.3	5.0	24.1	39.2	21.6	6.4	3.4	100.0
Henan	0.3	2.3	14.3	39.3	27.1	11.1	5.6	100.0
Hubei	0.0	4.5	17.2	36.6	26.1	11.0	4.7	100.0
Hunan	0.6	3.8	17.8	43.0	24.2	8.6	2.0	100.0
Guangdong	0.0	3.4	10.0	27.6	30.8	19.0	9.2	100.0
Sichuan	0.4	5.4	36.0	31.6	15.9	7.9	2.9	100.0
Guizhou	0.7	4.0	10.7	23.0	32.7	15.3	13.7	100.0
Yunnan	0.3	0.0	11.3	36.7	25.7	15.3	10.6	100.0
Shaanxi	0.3	3.0	11.3	38.3	26.0	14.3	6.7	100.0
Gansu	0.3	1.0	6.0	35.7	25.7	19.3	12.0	100.0

Note: Distribution of household size is calculated based on the number of households rather than of individuals.

Table A.3b. *Distribution of households in 1995 urban survey, by household size and province (%)*

Province	\multicolumn{8}{c}{Household size}
	1	2	3	4	5	6	7 & over	All
Total	0.8	17.4	57.3	18.6	4.7	1.1	0.1	100.0
Beijing	0.0	17.0	65.0	13.8	3.8	0.4	0.0	100.0
Shanxi	0.6	16.9	50.9	22.5	7.2	1.7	0.2	100.0
Liaoning	0.3	13.7	62.3	17.7	5.4	0.6	0.0	100.0
Jiangsu	1.9	21.0	53.8	17.1	5.3	0.6	0.4	100.0
Anhui	0.6	19.2	60.0	15.6	3.8	0.6	0.2	100.0
Henan	0.7	18.0	48.7	24.8	5.8	2.0	0.0	100.0
Hubei	0.3	15.5	62.5	16.9	4.0	0.8	0.0	100.0
Guangdong	0.2	12.9	52.7	24.3	6.8	2.4	0.7	100.0
Sichuan	1.7	23.8	57.9	13.7	2.2	0.7	0.0	100.0
Yunnan	0.9	15.1	61.4	18.7	3.1	0.8	0.0	100.0
Gansu	0.5	14.3	55.0	22.3	5.3	2.5	0.3	100.0

Note: Distribution of household size is calculated based on the number of households rather than of individuals.

Table A.4a. *Distribution of individuals in 1995 rural survey, by age group and province (%)*

Province	\multicolumn{9}{c}{Age group}								
	0–5	6–10	11–20	21–30	31–40	41–50	51–60	61–70	>70	All
Total	5.4	10.0	21.4	17.5	14.7	16.4	8.2	3.7	2.8	100.0
Beijing	2.1	5.7	20.9	14.6	17.5	20.1	11.5	2.6	5.0	100.0
Hebei	4.8	10.7	21.1	16.6	12.0	18.2	11.4	3.0	2.1	100.0
Shanxi	3.8	9.5	22.5	17.2	15.7	16.7	8.6	3.3	2.6	100.0
Liaoning	2.7	6.7	22.1	16.7	15.7	19.6	8.6	4.7	3.2	100.0
Jilin	5.0	10.4	21.2	16.2	18.8	17.1	5.9	3.7	1.8	100.0
Jiangsu	4.4	7.3	18.2	18.3	14.9	19.6	10.6	3.2	3.6	100.0
Zhejiang	4.2	5.7	19.7	17.5	15.4	19.6	9.9	4.4	3.6	100.0
Anhui	7.4	10.8	21.7	19.4	12.9	13.6	8.1	4.2	2.0	100.0
Jiangxi	4.9	10.4	26.0	16.8	15.2	13.9	5.5	3.9	3.5	100.0
Shandong	3.9	9.7	19.8	17.7	14.3	19.1	9.5	3.5	2.4	100.0
Henan	5.2	12.5	22.9	16.0	14.4	16.4	6.6	3.5	2.5	100.0
Hubei	6.5	12.1	21.9	15.0	17.3	15.3	6.7	2.1	3.1	100.0
Hunan	6.2	11.5	21.1	17.9	16.7	13.9	6.5	4.0	2.3	100.0
Guangdong	5.5	9.4	24.9	15.8	12.5	16.0	8.5	3.5	3.8	100.0
Sichuan	4.7	7.9	18.2	21.4	13.7	18.5	8.6	4.3	2.7	100.0
Guizhou	7.9	11.3	25.9	15.0	13.0	12.6	7.4	4.4	2.4	100.0
Yunnan	6.7	10.5	20.1	19.2	15.3	11.6	7.7	5.0	3.8	100.0
Shaanxi	6.8	11.5	21.5	17.4	14.8	15.8	6.5	3.6	2.2	100.0
Gansu	8.1	11.7	18.7	20.1	15.1	12.9	7.5	3.7	2.3	100.0

Table A.4b. *Distribution of individuals in 1995 urban survey, by age group and province (%)*

Province	\multicolumn{9}{c}{Age group}								
	0–5	6–10	11–20	21–30	31–40	41–50	51–60	61–70	>70	All
Total	4.1	6.3	15.3	12.7	19.9	19.8	12.1	7.3	2.5	100.0
Beijing	1.5	4.3	16.2	10.5	15.8	23.7	16.0	9.3	2.7	100.0
Shanxi	7.6	7.9	13.8	18.0	19.1	13.0	11.7	6.6	2.3	100.0
Liaoning	3.5	5.6	15.9	11.5	21.9	21.1	10.8	7.3	2.4	100.0
Jiangsu	3.1	5.7	14.7	11.2	19.0	21.0	12.3	9.1	3.9	100.0
Anhui	4.8	6.6	14.5	11.0	21.6	17.4	13.4	8.6	2.1	100.0
Henan	4.5	8.2	13.7	14.5	19.4	15.2	13.1	9.0	2.5	100.0
Hubei	3.1	5.7	18.0	10.9	19.5	24.0	10.1	6.6	2.1	100.0
Guangdong	3.7	5.5	16.4	12.9	18.6	21.7	11.8	7.2	2.2	100.0
Sichuan	3.4	6.1	14.0	11.6	20.8	23.8	11.3	6.1	2.9	100.0
Yunnan	4.3	7.4	16.4	11.1	23.0	20.6	11.1	3.8	2.3	100.0
Gansu	7.1	5.8	14.0	18.0	18.9	14.3	12.6	7.7	1.6	100.0

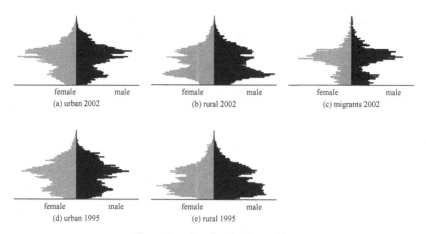

Figure A.1 Age-Gender Pyramids.

Table A.5a. *Educational attainment of individuals aged over 15 in 1995 rural survey, by province (%)*

Province	College and above	Junior college	Professional school	Higher middle school	Lower middle school	>3 years primary school	1–3 years primary school	Illiterate	All
Total	0.2	0.5	1.7	9.2	39.0	28.0	6.1	15.3	100.0
Beijing	0.0	2.5	14.0	19.7	42.2	12.7	1.0	7.9	100.0
Hebei	0.1	0.4	1.3	13.2	41.2	24.8	3.1	16.0	100.0
Shanxi	0.0	0.3	1.3	10.7	45.5	23.9	8.4	9.9	100.0
Liaoning	0.4	1.0	1.7	6.9	46.4	31.8	3.5	8.3	100.0
Jilin	0.3	0.7	2.1	8.4	41.9	34.5	2.3	9.8	100.0
Jiangsu	0.3	0.5	2.3	9.7	38.2	25.0	5.7	18.4	100.0
Zhejiang	0.2	0.4	0.9	7.5	45.4	26.9	7.4	11.3	100.0
Anhui	0.1	0.2	0.6	7.2	34.9	27.8	7.2	21.9	100.0
Jiangxi	0.0	0.6	1.0	6.7	33.8	36.2	8.7	13.1	100.0
Shandong	0.3	1.1	3.0	11.8	42.4	22.1	5.7	13.6	100.0
Henan	0.1	0.4	1.2	10.2	48.9	23.9	3.1	12.2	100.0
Hubei	0.1	0.4	1.7	10.3	37.8	31.4	5.8	12.5	100.0
Hunan	0.2	0.3	0.7	9.9	33.1	35.8	9.2	10.9	100.0
Guangdong	0.1	0.5	2.9	12.1	39.9	27.5	6.5	10.5	100.0
Sichuan	0.5	0.4	1.1	5.1	37.5	34.2	5.8	15.4	100.0
Guizhou	0.1	0.2	0.9	3.4	26.6	24.8	11.6	32.3	100.0
Yunnan	0.3	0.2	0.7	3.8	28.8	36.4	9.7	20.1	100.0
Shaanxi	0.2	0.3	1.5	14.6	42.4	20.1	5.8	15.1	100.0
Gansu	0.5	1.2	1.7	9.6	26.5	23.1	4.0	33.4	100.0

Note: 122 observations have missing values for education.

Table A.5b. *Educational attainment of individuals aged over 15 in 1995 urban survey, by province (%)*

Province	College and above	Junior college	Professional school	Higher middle school	Lower middle school	Primary school	Less than primary school	All
Total	7.3	12.3	15.2	23.3	29.0	9.0	4.0	100.0
Beijing	11.9	16.2	17.3	19.6	26.5	5.5	3.0	100.0
Shanxi	7.7	11.4	15.9	23.1	28.2	9.7	4.0	100.0
Liaoning	5.7	16.5	10.9	19.7	36.7	7.8	2.8	100.0
Jiangsu	6.1	10.5	13.6	24.3	32.9	7.9	4.7	100.0
Anhui	6.0	10.0	14.3	23.1	34.0	8.6	3.9	100.0
Henan	6.8	10.2	13.5	26.0	28.5	9.4	5.6	100.0
Hubei	8.7	13.7	17.5	26.5	23.5	7.0	3.1	100.0
Guangdong	6.4	11.4	12.7	26.7	24.7	13.4	4.7	100.0
Sichuan	7.4	12.9	17.0	20.6	28.6	9.8	3.6	100.0
Yunnan	6.7	11.7	20.7	19.7	27.1	10.6	3.5	100.0
Gansu	7.7	9.4	12.8	27.8	26.5	9.6	6.2	100.0

educational attainment of lower middle school or below. In contrast, the average educational level of the urban sample is much higher, with nearly 20 percent having a college education or above, and only 4 percent with less than a primary school education.

B. The 2002 Survey

The size of the rural household sample in the 2002 survey increased to 9,200 because of the addition of two new provinces, Guangxi and Xinjiang, to the survey. The main purpose of including Guangxi and Xinjiang was to allow further investigation of ethnic minority issues. Also, Chongqing separated from Sichuan after 1995. Consequently, the number of provinces in the rural survey increased to 22. Due to Chongqing's separation, the number of provinces in the urban survey increased to 12. The sample size of the urban household survey for 2002 remains the same as in the 1995 survey. In addition to the survey of urban households (with urban residence or *hukou*), 2000 rural-urban migrant households were also surveyed. To maintain comparability, in provinces that were covered in both 1995 and 2002, the 2002 survey selected almost the same cities and counties as in 1995. Table A.6 shows the distributions of the household and individual samples by province in both rural and urban areas.

The questionnaires employed in the 2002 survey were based on the 1995 questionnaires. Most of the questions in the questionnaires for the 1995

Table A.6. *Distribution of households in 2002 rural and urban surveys, by province*

Province	Rural			Urban		
	Number of counties	Number of households	Number of individuals	Number of cities	Number of households	Number of individuals
Total	120	9,200	37,969	70	6,835	20,632
Beijing	2	160	563	1	484	1,456
Hebei	5	370	1,513			
Shanxi	6	400	1,622	7	640	1,937
Liaoning	6	450	1,583	5	697	2,111
Jilin	5	480	1,763			
Jiangsu	5	440	1,594	9	729	2,163
Zhejiang	6	520	1,932			
Anhui	5	440	1,837	6	493	1,476
Jiangxi	6	430	1,927			
Shandong	7	630	2,343			
Henan	6	530	2,219	8	680	2,086
Hubei	6	520	2,093	7	673	2,063
Hunan	5	450	1,848			
Guangdong	7	530	2,483	8	544	1,763
Guangxi	5	400	2,025			
Chongqing	2	200	677	2	279	832
Sichuan	6	500	1,832	6	585	1,703
Guizhou	6	400	1,825			
Yunnan	5	260	1,199	8	636	1,848
Shaanxi	6	370	1,641			
Gansu	5	320	1,449	3	395	1,194
Xinjiang	8	400	2,001			

survey reappeared in the new survey, and some new questions were added in response to new developments in income and consumption structure and in labor market conditions. So as to be consistent with the 1995 questionnaires, the new questionnaires similarly contain questions about income designed with the objective of deriving household disposable income according to international standards, and the sampled households were asked questions regarding income in kind and the market value of housing subsidies as well as the imputed rent of privately owned housing. In addition, both the rural and urban questionnaires have fairly comprehensive questions on household consumption and its components, as well as on household financial and physical assets.

The gender ratio of individuals is unchanged between the 1995 and 2002 urban surveys, with the number of females remaining slightly larger than

Table A.7. *Gender distribution of individuals in 2002 survey, by province*

	Rural			Urban		
Province	Male	Female	Female as percentage of male	Male	Female	Female as percentage of male
Total	19,750	18,219	92.2	10,141	10,407	102.6
Beijing	289	274	94.8	720	727	101.0
Hebei	774	739	95.5			
Shanxi	850	772	90.8	961	966	100.5
Liaoning	815	768	94.2	1,041	1,069	102.7
Jilin	886	877	99.0			
Jiangsu	813	781	96.1	1,066	1,086	101.9
Zhejiang	981	951	96.9			
Anhui	958	879	91.8	712	754	105.9
Jiangxi	1,035	892	86.2			
Shandong	1,219	1,124	92.2			
Henan	1,135	1,084	95.5	1,019	1,058	103.8
Hubei	1,083	1,010	93.3	1,034	1,026	99.2
Hunan	949	899	94.7			
Guangdong	1,287	1,196	92.9	850	907	106.7
Guangxi	1,118	907	81.1			
Chongqing	351	326	92.9	397	430	108.3
Sichuan	956	876	91.6	835	861	103.1
Guizhou	990	835	84.3			
Yunnan	591	608	102.9	909	929	102.2
Shaanxi	855	786	91.9			
Gansu	752	697	92.7	597	594	99.5
Xinjiang	1,063	938	88.2			

that of males. In the 2002 rural survey, however, the ratio of females decreases (see Table A.7). It is unclear whether this decrease is due to actual change in the rural population over this period, reflecting the frequently reported decline in the gender ratio due to missing baby girls in rural areas, or simply due to sampling in the 2002 survey.

Tables A.8a and A.8b show the distributions of households by household size in the rural and urban surveys. Compared to the 1995 surveys (Tables A.3a and A.3b), the average size of the household in the 2002 rural sample has declined, as reflected in the increased share of households with two-to-three members and the decreased share of households with five or more members. This same direction of change in household size appears in the urban sample, but the magnitude of the change is less than that in the rural sample.

Table A.8a. *Distribution of households in 2002 rural survey, by household size and province (%)*

Province	1	2	3	4	5	6	7 & over	All
				Household size				
Total	0.3	7.9	23.9	33.5	21.3	8.7	4.3	100.0
Beijing	0.6	12.5	40.0	32.5	10.0	4.4	0.0	100.0
Hebei	0.5	13.0	14.3	35.1	25.9	8.9	2.2	100.0
Shanxi	0.8	9.3	16.5	41.5	24.3	5.5	2.3	100.0
Liaoning	0.7	15.8	34.4	32.4	13.8	2.7	0.2	100.0
Jilin	0.2	11.0	36.0	32.1	15.4	5.0	0.2	100.0
Jiangsu	0.7	13.6	38.0	26.8	13.4	6.6	0.9	100.0
Zhejiang	0.6	10.6	32.9	35.6	14.6	4.8	1.0	100.0
Anhui	0.2	4.8	24.3	37.3	20.7	8.0	4.8	100.0
Jiangxi	0.0	3.7	15.8	37.2	26.3	9.5	7.4	100.0
Shandong	0.2	10.3	34.8	33.0	17.1	3.3	1.3	100.0
Henan	0.2	5.8	21.7	36.4	22.1	11.1	2.6	100.0
Hubei	0.2	8.5	24.4	35.2	21.2	8.5	2.1	100.0
Hunan	0.4	6.2	16.7	44.4	24.0	7.6	0.7	100.0
Guangdong	0.0	3.2	11.1	33.6	28.3	16.4	7.4	100.0
Guangxi	0.3	5.8	9.8	22.0	27.0	15.3	19.8	100.0
Chongqing	1.0	14.0	47.5	22.5	13.0	2.0	0.0	100.0
Sichuan	0.2	8.4	40.6	31.4	15.4	3.0	1.0	100.0
Guizhou	0.0	5.3	15.8	29.5	28.8	11.8	8.8	100.0
Yunnan	0.4	2.3	13.1	35.8	25.0	16.5	6.9	100.0
Shaanxi	0.3	3.0	15.9	35.9	28.4	12.4	4.1	100.0
Gansu	0.0	3.4	14.4	36.9	25.0	14.1	6.3	100.0
Xinjiang	0.8	4.5	11.0	23.8	27.3	17.0	15.6	100.0

Note: Distribution of household size is calculated based on the number of households rather than of individuals.

Does the 2002 survey reveal aging of individuals in the sample? The statistics in Tables A.9a and A.9b provide a positive answer to this question. In the rural sample the share of individuals aged 10 or below decreases from 15.4 percent in 1995 to 9.8 percent in 2002, while the share of individuals aged over 50 increases from 14.7 percent to 19.2 percent. Similar changes take place in the urban sample.

Educational attainment of individuals in 2002 appears in Tables A.10a and A.10b, and these numbers can be compared to those for 1995 in Tables A.5a and A.5b. For the rural sample one can observe a striking decline in the illiteracy rate of nearly 7 percentage points between the two surveys. Concurrently, more individuals completed middle school, especially lower middle

Table A.8b. *Distribution of households in 2002 urban survey, by household size and province (%)*

Province	\multicolumn{8}{c}{Household size}							
	1	2	3	4	5	6	7 & over	All
Total	1.1	19.7	61.6	12.6	4.4	0.6	0.1	100.0
Beijing	0.4	13.8	74.4	8.1	2.7	0.4	0.2	100.0
Shanxi	1.4	20.5	59.1	13.3	4.8	0.8	0.2	100.0
Liaoning	0.1	18.7	65.0	11.6	3.7	0.7	0.1	100.0
Jiangsu	2.2	25.4	55.1	9.9	6.0	1.1	0.3	100.0
Anhui	0.4	19.1	65.5	11.4	3.4	0.0	0.2	100.0
Henan	1.8	22.1	53.2	15.0	6.9	0.7	0.3	100.0
Hubei	0.1	16.5	64.6	14.6	3.7	0.4	0.0	100.0
Guangdong	0.2	11.4	61.4	20.0	5.9	0.7	0.4	100.0
Chongqing	1.4	19.7	63.8	10.0	4.3	0.7	0.0	100.0
Sichuan	1.4	24.8	59.0	11.3	3.4	0.2	0.0	100.0
Yunnan	2.0	23.3	60.7	10.5	3.0	0.5	0.0	100.0
Gansu	1.0	17.5	63.5	14.4	3.3	0.3	0.0	100.0

Note: Distribution of household size is calculated based on the number of households rather than of individuals.

Table A.9a. *Distribution of individuals in 2002 rural survey, by age group and province (%)*

Province	\multicolumn{10}{c}{Age group}									
	0–5	6–10	11–20	21–30	31–40	41–50	51–60	61–70	>70	All
Total	3.9	5.9	22.6	15.6	16.7	16.1	11.9	4.5	2.8	100.0
Beijing	2.1	3.9	19.9	11.7	15.5	22.0	17.1	5.3	2.5	100.0
Hebei	2.7	4.1	25.4	13.4	13.2	20.0	13.5	5.9	1.8	100.0
Shanxi	3.2	7.6	25.0	13.3	17.8	18.2	9.7	3.1	2.1	100.0
Liaoning	2.7	4.4	16.3	16.7	12.9	21.9	17.3	5.1	2.8	100.0
Jilin	3.8	4.7	19.7	13.6	22.5	17.2	10.9	4.5	3.1	100.0
Jiangsu	2.6	4.6	17.0	15.6	16.6	19.2	15.9	5.3	3.3	100.0
Zhejiang	3.1	5.4	16.8	14.6	16.3	19.7	14.3	6.8	3.1	100.0
Anhui	4.2	6.6	21.9	19.2	18.3	12.9	12.1	2.3	2.4	100.0
Jiangxi	6.2	5.3	22.6	19.4	14.5	16.1	9.4	4.1	2.4	100.0
Shandong	3.4	4.4	20.2	14.7	18.2	16.3	15.5	4.5	2.9	100.0
Henan	3.2	5.0	26.0	15.0	17.0	16.3	11.2	3.5	2.8	100.0
Hubei	2.4	4.8	26.4	12.3	18.4	18.2	10.6	4.2	2.7	100.0
Hunan	4.3	5.3	25.6	12.7	20.6	14.1	10.5	3.7	3.4	100.0
Guangdong	3.6	6.5	24.7	17.4	13.1	16.1	11.0	4.1	3.5	100.0
Guangxi	4.5	6.4	29.0	19.2	11.5	12.6	9.8	4.4	2.5	100.0
Chongqing	2.2	4.6	15.2	13.6	20.7	17.6	16.8	5.9	3.4	100.0
Sichuan	4.1	5.8	14.8	17.5	19.7	16.3	13.4	5.9	2.6	100.0
Guizhou	5.6	8.9	25.0	14.5	15.8	12.1	10.2	5.3	2.6	100.0
Yunnan	5.8	7.5	20.2	16.4	19.2	13.4	7.9	5.2	4.3	100.0
Shaanxi	3.7	7.2	23.8	14.7	17.4	14.3	12.2	3.6	3.0	100.0
Gansu	4.7	8.0	22.1	14.1	20.5	13.5	9.8	4.6	2.6	100.0
Xinjiang	5.2	8.0	29.4	18.0	12.6	11.2	9.6	4.0	1.8	100.0

Table A.9b. *Distribution of individuals in 2002 urban survey, by age group and province (%)*

Province	0–5	6–10	11–20	21–30	31–40	41–50	51–60	61–70	>70	All
					Age group					
Total	2.9	4.4	13.9	10.6	19.8	23.4	14.3	7.3	3.5	100.0
Beijing	0.9	2.4	13.3	13.0	11.6	27.9	22.2	6.2	2.4	100.0
Shanxi	2.9	5.8	14.0	10.8	23.3	22.0	11.7	7.1	2.4	100.0
Liaoning	2.0	3.3	12.6	12.6	17.2	24.7	17.3	6.3	4.2	100.0
Jiangsu	2.7	3.7	11.3	10.6	17.9	20.4	17.8	9.6	6.0	100.0
Anhui	2.5	4.6	15.4	8.3	22.5	23.9	13.2	6.4	3.1	100.0
Henan	3.8	4.4	13.7	10.9	22.1	18.3	11.6	11.1	4.1	100.0
Hubei	3.1	5.1	14.2	11.4	22.3	22.8	13.1	5.7	2.3	100.0
Guangdong	3.2	5.9	15.2	10.6	18.5	26.4	13.4	4.4	2.4	100.0
Chongqing	3.1	2.6	14.7	11.2	15.9	28.4	14.5	5.4	4.3	100.0
Sichuan	2.7	5.2	14.3	7.4	18.9	27.4	12.4	7.8	3.8	100.0
Yunnan	3.6	4.5	15.3	8.2	23.7	22.2	11.5	7.5	3.4	100.0
Gansu	4.0	4.8	13.8	12.7	20.4	20.7	13.4	7.2	3.0	100.0

Table A.10a. *Educational attainment of individuals aged over 15 in 2002 rural survey, by province (%)*

Province	College and above	Junior college	Professional school	Higher middle school	Lower middle school	>3 years of primary school	1–3 years primary school	Illiterate	All
Total	0.6	1.2	3.8	11.6	45.0	22.1	7.3	8.5	100.0
Beijing	1.0	3.8	16.9	15.6	42.7	9.6	4.6	5.8	100.0
Hebei	0.4	1.2	4.2	15.7	52.6	15.8	5.5	4.6	100.0
Shanxi	0.3	0.7	3.2	13.8	57.7	17.3	3.6	3.4	100.0
Liaoning	1.4	1.0	4.0	10.1	51.8	24.3	3.5	3.9	100.0
Jilin	0.7	1.3	2.5	9.7	52.6	21.3	4.8	7.1	100.0
Jiangsu	0.8	2.1	4.2	14.2	43.9	16.7	12.0	6.0	100.0
Zhejiang	1.3	1.7	4.2	11.6	42.6	20.5	11.6	6.6	100.0
Anhui	0.8	1.0	3.4	7.6	46.9	17.2	11.1	12.0	100.0
Jiangxi	0.3	0.5	2.0	7.9	42.4	27.6	11.4	8.0	100.0
Shandong	0.6	1.9	4.8	16.5	44.5	18.8	4.0	8.7	100.0
Henan	0.5	1.1	4.2	15.1	50.7	14.6	4.9	9.0	100.0
Hubei	0.6	1.3	2.7	12.7	44.9	21.2	8.0	8.7	100.0
Hunan	0.6	0.8	2.5	12.4	44.4	26.1	7.5	5.8	100.0
Guangdong	0.7	1.4	8.1	15.4	44.2	18.4	5.9	5.9	100.0
Guangxi	0.1	1.0	3.6	8.5	45.8	28.8	6.7	5.5	100.0
Chongqing	0.7	0.7	2.8	8.5	37.3	30.2	10.9	9.0	100.0
Sichuan	0.7	0.7	2.5	9.2	42.2	27.6	9.3	7.9	100.0
Guizhou	0.2	0.4	1.7	6.2	30.7	29.2	11.8	19.7	100.0
Yunnan	0.1	0.2	2.0	5.8	31.6	37.5	6.6	16.1	100.0
Shaanxi	0.9	1.4	4.6	11.7	52.2	15.8	3.9	9.6	100.0
Gansu	0.3	1.2	2.5	14.4	37.8	20.5	6.1	17.3	100.0
Xinjiang	0.6	0.8	2.4	9.0	39.4	30.7	6.9	10.2	100.0

Table A.10b. *Educational attainment of individuals in 2002 urban survey, by province (%)*

Province	College and above	Junior college	Professional school	Higher middle school	Lower middle school	Primary school	Less than primary school	All
Total	8.7	16.7	11.3	27.2	26.7	6.9	2.5	100.0
Beijing	13.8	20.0	14.0	27.0	22.5	2.0	0.7	100.0
Shanxi	9.7	17.8	10.5	27.5	26.5	6.3	1.7	100.0
Liaoning	8.5	15.8	11.3	24.6	33.4	4.4	1.9	100.0
Jiangsu	6.7	14.4	10.0	25.8	31.3	8.5	3.3	100.0
Anhui	7.6	15.5	10.7	27.9	28.8	6.7	2.8	100.0
Henan	6.4	17.7	9.9	30.0	25.0	7.7	3.3	100.0
Hubei	11.0	20.3	13.1	27.7	20.2	5.3	2.4	100.0
Guangdong	6.8	15.7	11.9	35.2	20.7	7.9	1.8	100.0
Chongqing	11.8	16.4	8.5	28.2	26.3	5.8	3.1	100.0
Sichuan	6.3	12.9	9.9	25.5	31.7	10.6	3.0	100.0
Yunnan	9.1	15.8	15.6	19.2	26.7	10.4	3.2	100.0
Gansu	8.6	19.1	8.9	30.1	24.7	6.4	2.3	100.0

Note: 25 observations have missing values for education.

Table A.11. *Distribution of households and individuals in 2002 rural-urban migrant survey, by gender, household size, and province*

Province	Sample size		Gender		Household size					
	Household	Individual	Male	Female	1	2	3	4	5	6
Total	2,005	5,327	2,786	2,532	213	667	781	290	47	7
Beijing	100	267	139	128	1	49	37	8	5	0
Shanxi	151	316	178	136	66	29	36	16	4	0
Liaoning	201	552	276	274	2	78	95	21	5	0
Jiangsu	201	510	262	247	32	54	94	18	2	1
Anhui	200	547	292	255	11	69	86	30	4	0
Henan	201	521	274	245	31	63	68	35	4	0
Hubei	201	619	322	295	4	45	91	54	6	1
Guangdong	200	554	291	263	6	82	78	22	10	2
Chongqing	100	268	131	137	0	46	42	11	0	1
Sichuan	150	398	212	186	9	59	57	25	0	0
Yunnan	150	406	211	195	19	43	55	30	2	1
Gansu	150	369	198	171	32	50	42	20	5	1

Note: Distribution of household size is calculated based on the number of households rather than of individuals.

school, compared to 1995. In the urban sample, as expected, more urban residents had achieved a college education, as higher education expanded rapidly during this period.

C. The Rural-Urban Migrant Household Survey

One of the unique features of the 2002 survey is the inclusion of 2,000 rural-urban migrant households. These households were selected from all the provinces, but not from all the cities, in the urban survey. As rural-urban migrants are concentrated in large cities, all the provincial capital cities, plus one or two middle-sized cities in each of the provinces, were selected for the migrant survey. The principle for the sample distribution among the provinces was that 200 households were chosen in the provinces of the coastal and central regions, and 150 households in the provinces of the western regions. Within each province, 100 migrant households were in the capital city and 50 households in another city or cities.

Within cities, because of sampling frame limitations, rural-urban migrant households were selected from resident committees. In other words, migrant workers living in construction sites and factories were not included in the sampling selection. Consequently, most of the migrants selected had families with them. So as to make the sample more representative, the number of households selected from each resident committee was 20 or less. Table A.11 gives information on the composition of the migrant sample.

References

Eichen, M. and M. Zhang (1993), "Annex: The 1988 Household Sample Survey – Data Description and Availability," in K. Griffin and R. Zhao, eds., *The Distribution of Income in China*, New York: St. Martin's Press.

Griffin, K. and R. Zhao, eds. (1993), *The Distribution of Income in China*, New York: St. Martin's Press.

Research Institute of the All China Women's Federation and Department of Social, Science and Technology Statistics, National Bureau of Statistics (1998), *Gender Statistics in China, 1990–1995* (in Chinese), Beijing: China Statistics Press.

Riskin, C., R. Zhao, and S. Li, eds. (2001), *China's Retreat from Equality: Income Distribution and Economic Transition*, Armonk, NY: M.E. Sharpe.

Zhao, R., S. Li, and C. Riskin (1999), *Further Studies on Income Distribution in China* (in Chinese), Beijing: China Finance and Economics Publishing House.

Index

age, 97, 108. *See also* elderly
  aging population of China, 284
  coresidency and, 277, 279, 282,
    283
  gender income gap and, 250
  of household members, 92
  income and, 98, 100
  wages and, 230
agricultural tax, 314, 318, 321, 322, 324,
    329, 330, 331. *See also* rural taxation
    and tax reform
  elimination of, 139, 312, 315, 316, 317,
    318, 334
Anhui province, 77
Appleton, S., 225

Beijing,
  elderly in, 283
  housing availability in, 283
  ranking in Human Development
    Index, 9
Benjamin, D., 269
Brandt, L., 269
Burr, J. A., 281

Cai, F., 280
central region
  income inequality in, 49, 51
  urban-rural income gap in, 53
Chen, S., 62
children, 26, 193. *See also* elderly, living
    arrangements of

Chinese Household Income Project. *See*
    CHIP surveys
CHIP surveys, 11–13, 40, 119
  household income surveys, 89, 119
  migrant income and, 74, 80
  migrant sample of, 4
  on per capita income, 92
  poverty trends and, 147
  rural sample of, 40
  urban sample of, 40, 78
  wage survey and, 221
Communist Party, 2, 89
  gender income ratios and, 252
  membership in, and income, 91, 92,
    94, 97, 100, 104, 107, 109, 113
  wage income and, 229
coresidency
  age and, 277, 279, 282, 283
  changing social norms and, 187, 268,
    284
  housing availability and, 284
  pensions and, 272, 280
  probability of, 277, 282, 283, 284
  reduction in, 284
Costa, D. L., 271, 275, 280
Cultural Revolution, 185

danwei (work unit), 5, 6, 8, 128, 209, 225,
    231, 244, 274, 281
Davies, J., 135
Davis-Friedmann, D., 269
definitions, 37–40

355